Lecture Notes in Computer Scie

T0250860

Commenced Publication in 1973
Founding and Former Series Editors:
Gerhard Goos, Juris Hartmanis, and Jan van Leeuwen

Editorial Board

Cristina Baroglio   Piero A. Bonatti
Jan Małuszyński   Massimo Marchiori
Axel Polleres   Sebastian Schaffert (Eds.)

Reasoning Web

4th International Summer School 2008
Venice, Italy, September 7-11, 2008
Tutorial Lectures

 Springer

Volume Editors

Cristina Baroglio
Università degli Studi di Torino, Italy
E-mail: baroglio@di.unito.it

Piero A. Bonatti
Università di Napoli Federico II, Italy
E-mail: bonatti@na.infn.it

Jan Małuszyński
Linköping University, Sweden
E-mail: janma@ida.liu.se

Massimo Marchiori
University of Venice, Mestre - Venice, Italy
E-mail: massimo@math.unipd.it

Axel Polleres
National University of Ireland, Galway
E-mail: axel.polleres@deri.org

Sebastian Schaffert
Salzburg Research Forschungsgesellschaft, Austria
E-mail: sebastian.schaffert@salzburgresearch.at

Library of Congress Control Number: 2008933847

CR Subject Classification (1998): H.4, H.3, I.2.4, C.2, H.5.3, K.4

LNCS Sublibrary: SL 3 – Information Systems and Application, incl. Internet/Web and HCI

ISSN   0302-9743
ISBN-10   3-540-85656-0 Springer Berlin Heidelberg New York
ISBN-13   978-3-540-85656-6 Springer Berlin Heidelberg New York

Springer is a part of Springer Science+Business Media

springer.com

© Springer-Verlag Berlin Heidelberg 2008
Printed in Germany

Typesetting: Camera-ready by author, data conversion by Scientific Publishing Services, Chennai, India
Printed on acid-free paper   SPIN: 12513673   06/3180   5 4 3 2 1 0

Preface

The Reasoning Web summer school series is a well-established event, attracting experts from academia and industry as well as PhD students interested in foundational and applicational aspects of the Semantic Web. This volume contains the lecture notes of the fourth summer school, which took place in Venice, Italy, in September 2008. This year, the school focussed on a number of important application domains, in which semantic web techniques have proved to be particularly effective or promising in tackling problems.

The first three chapters provide introductory material to:

- languages, formalisms, and standards adopted to encode semantic information;
- "soft" extensions that might be useful in contexts such as multimedia or social network applications;
- controlled natural language techniques to bring ontology authoring closer to end users.

The remaining chapters cover major application areas such as social networks, semantic multimedia indexing and retrieval, bioinformatics, and semantic web services.

The presentations highlighted which techniques are already being successfully applied for purposes such as improving the performance of information retrieval algorithms, enabling the interoperation of heterogeneous agents, modelling user's profiles and social relations, and standardizing and improving the accuracy of very large and dynamic scientific databases.

Furthermore, the lectures pointed out which aspects are still waiting for a solution, and the possible role that semantic techniques may play, especially those reasoning methods that have not yet been exploited to their full potential. We hope that the school's material will inspire further exciting research in these areas.

We are grateful to all the lecturers and their co-authors for their excellent contributions, to the Reasoning Web School Board, and Norbert Eisinger in particular, who helped in several critical phases, and to the organizations that supported this event: the University of Padua, the MOST project, and the Network of Excellence REWERSE.

September 2008

Cristina Baroglio
Piero A. Bonatti
Jan Małuszyński
Massimo Marchiori
Axel Polleres
Sebastian Schaffert

Organization

Program Committee

Cristina Baroglio, University of Torino
Piero A. Bonatti, University of Napoli Federico II   (Chair)
Jan Małuszyński, Linköping University
Axel Polleres, Digital Enterprise Research Institute (DERI)
Sebastian Schaffert, Salzburg Research

Local Organization

Massimo Marchiori, University of Padova

Sponsoring Institutions

MOST project
http://www.most-project.eu

Università di Padova
http://www.unipd.it

REWERSE
http://rewerse.net

Table of Contents

Rules and Ontologies for the Semantic Web[*]

Thomas Eiter[1], Giovambattista Ianni[2],
Thomas Krennwallner[1], and Axel Polleres[3]

[1] Institut für Informationssysteme, Technische Universität Wien
Favoritenstraße 9-11, A-1040 Vienna, Austria
{eiter,tkren}@kr.tuwien.ac.at
[2] Department of Mathematics, Universitá della Calabria, Rende, Italy
ianni@mat.unical.it
[3] Digital Enterprise Research Institute, National University of Ireland, Galway
{firstname.lastname}@deri.org

Abstract. Rules and ontologies play a key role in the layered architecture of the Semantic Web, as they are used to ascribe meaning to, and to reason about, data on the Web. While the Ontology Layer of the Semantic Web is quite developed, and the Web Ontology Language (OWL) is a W3C recommendation since a couple of years already, the rules layer is far less developed and an active area of research; a number of initiatives and proposals have been made so far, but no standard as been released yet. Many implementations of rule engines are around which deal with Semantic Web data in one or another way. This article gives a comprehensive, although not exhaustive, overview of such systems, describes their supported languages, and sets them in relation with theoretical approaches for combining rules and ontologies as foreseen in the Semantic Web architecture. In the course of this, we identify desired properties and common features of rule languages and evaluate existing systems against their support. Furthermore, we review technical problems underlying the integration of rules and ontologies, and classify representative proposals for theoretical integration approaches into different categories.

1 Introduction

The issue of having rules on top or aside ontologies written in OWL is an important milestone on the World Wide Web Consortium's (W3C) agenda for completing the Semantic Web architecture. Despite arising theoretical issues, due to the complementary nature of existing ontology and rules languages a plethora of rule based systems have been developed over the last years, driven by the need for rule-based integration of constantly growing Semantic Web data; currently, the W3C is designing of a unifying exchange format – the Rule Interchange Format (RIF) [9] – for the various existing languages. This article aims at giving a snapshot overview of existing languages and systems implementations, of their features and of the theoretical approaches they build upon.

[*] This research has been partially supported by the European FP6 projects inContext (IST-034718) and REWERSE (IST-2003-506779), by the Austrian Science Fund (FWF) projects P17212, P20840, and P20841, and by the Science Foundation Ireland under Grant No. SFI/02/CE1/I131.

C. Baroglio et al. (Eds.): Reasoning Web 2008, LNCS 5224, pp. 1–53, 2008.
© Springer-Verlag Berlin Heidelberg 2008

Given the mature state of the RDF and the OWL standards, the building of a rule language is not just a cheap add-on to the standards created so far. During research on Semantic Web technologies the demand for combined formalisms, which integrate ontology and rule languages, emerged as a consequence to supply advanced reasoning capabilities in this setup. Ontology languages are good for describing knowledge adhering to the Open World Assumption, i.e., the encoded knowledge is considered incomplete and conclusions, which cannot be derived from an ontology, are treated agnostically. But under this assumption, one might not get certain rational conclusions, which are reasonable to infer even under incomplete knowledge. To weaken the conservative stance of the Open World Assumption, rule languages, which are proponents of the Closed World Assumption, have been conceived as partners for ontologies. This assumption maintains, hence the name, a closed view of the world; everything which is not derivable from such kind of knowledge base is assumed to be false. This allows for reasoning in problem domains which have to deal with default knowledge, i.e., knowledge that "usually holds" like "birds typically fly," unless there is evidence to the contrary.

Ontology languages on their own cannot fulfill all the prescribed requirements; rule languages should close at least some of the known obstacles. But such a combination of rules and ontologies, which integrates well with current W3C standards, is not a simple task due to various reasons shown later.

We direct our attention here to rule-based approaches for the Semantic Web, in view of rule systems operating upon RDF data, and ontology languages for the Web, in particular RDF Schema, OWL, and its dialects. This article takes a view on these approaches from the perspective of integrating knowledge gathered from the Semantic Web under several aspects. In particular, we consider modelling features that are needed for practical use cases, and also their mutual relationships. We then discuss several implemented systems and evaluate their support of these features. Finally we give an overview of semantic problems that rise with introducing rules, particularly when they should be combined with expressive ontology languages like OWL. We discuss directions on how these problems might be overcome; furthermore, issues for further research are pointed out.

When we talk about rule-based approaches here, the focus will be on deductive rules languages approaches with a two-valued semantics; probabilistic, fuzzy, dynamic (event-condition-action rules, production rules) approaches, etc., will not be considered. For students interested in these areas, we point to previous editions of the Reasoning Web Summer school and other contributions in the present volume where these topics have been presented in more depth [9,37,88,93].

The remainder of this article is organized as follows. The next section provides some preliminaries, including RDF/RDF Schema and Description Logics as well as OWL. In Section 3, we then turn to rule-based aggregation and integration of Semantic Web data, where – based on practical use cases – we discuss several features that are interesting to compare different available rule systems. After that, we examine in Section 4 several languages and systems with respect to these criteria. The second part of the article addresses then combinations of rules and ontologies using a dedicated approach and semantics. In Section 5, first general issues that come up in combining logic-based rules and ontologies are revisited in more detail; after that, three different generic settings for the combination are considered that allow to group existing approaches into different categories. Example instances of approaches falling into each of these settings are discussed in Section 6. We conclude the article in Section 7 with a short summary and a brief discussion of issues for research.

2   Preliminaries

The Semantic Web architecture [8] defines at its bottom a simple, and at the same time extremely flexible data model, the *Resource Description Framework* (RDF) [48,101]. Based on RDF data, which can be used to annotate Web pages and export data from legacy sources, ontologies and rules represent the two main components in the Semantic Web vision – the heart of the Semantic Web –, which shall enable to integrate and make new inferences from existing data. While there are already standard languages for ontologies recommended by W3C, viz. *RDF Schema* (RDFS) [12] and the *Web Ontology Language* (OWL) [27] (which are becoming increasingly used), there is no standard for a rules language available yet. Many rule languages and systems have been proposed, and they offer varying features to reason over Semantic Web data. To mitigate the situation, the *Rule Interchange Format* (RIF) working group of W3C [9,10] is currently developing a standard exchange format for rules on the Web that takes languages features into account, but is less concerned with a committed semantics. Before we turn our attention to the various rules languages and systems, let us briefly review the basics of RDF, RDFS, and OWL.

In this section, we chose as motivating problem domain a publication scenario, in which we express knowledge about authors and their co-authors, the publications they made, etc. To this end, we start with RDF graphs of the authors of this chapter which encode information like relationships to persons and bibliographic information (see Figure 2–5). We will increase the expressiveness of the represented knowledge by using a description logic ontology given in Example 2. Later on, in Section 3, we will extend the context of our problem domain and look for suitable reviewers of unpublished articles based on given RDF(S) and OWL data using RIF rules.

Along the path of this scenario, we will define the notions used and provide helpful pointers to the interested reader.

2.1   RDF and RDF Schema

The *Resource Description Framework* (RDF) defines the data model for the Semantic Web. Driven by the goal of least possible commitment to a particular data schema, the simplest possible structure for representing information was chosen – labeled, directed graphs. An RDF dataset (that is, a *RDF graph*) can be viewed as a set of the edges of such a graph, commonly represented by *triples* (or *statements*) of the form:

$$\textit{Subject Predicate Object}$$

where

- the edge links *Subject*, which is a *resource* identified by a URI or a *blank node*, to *Object*, which is either another resource, a blank node, a *datatype literal*, or an *XML literal*;
- *Predicate*, in RDF terminology referred to as *property*, is the edge label.

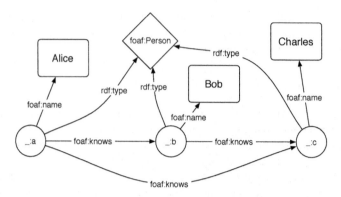

Fig. 1. A simple RDF graph

The next example will clarify the main concepts of RDF.

Example 1. Take a scenario in which three persons named Alice, Bob, and Charles, have certain relationships among each other: Alice knows both Bob and Charles, Bob just knows Charles, and Charles knows nobody. The graphical representation of this simple example showing the relationships between these persons is given in Figure 1. Note that we encode the information using the so called FOAF (friend-of-a-friend) RDF vocabulary [42].

A subgraph of Figure 1 states that "a person called Bob knows a person called Charles." This can be given by several RDF triples:

```
_:b rdf:type foaf:Person, _:b foaf:name "Bob", _:b foaf:knows _:c,
_:c rdf:type foaf:Person, and _:c foaf:name "Charles".
```

For instance, the triple

```
    _:b foaf:name "Bob"
```

expresses that "someone has the name Bob." _:b is a blank node and can be seen as an anonymous identifier. In fact, the name for a blank node is meaningful only in the context of a given RDF graph; conceptually, blank node names can be uniformly substituted inside a RDF graph without changing the meaning of the encoded knowledge. The semantics of blank nodes will be sketched later on.

RDF information can be represented in different formats. One of the most common is the RDF/XML syntax.[1] Our graphical representation above can be given as RDF/XML document:

```
<rdf:RDF xmlns:rdf="http://www.w3.org/1999/02/22-rdf-syntax-ns#"
         xmlns:foaf="http://xmlns.com/foaf/0.1/">
<foaf:Person rdf:nodeID="a">
 <foaf:name>Alice</foaf:name>
 <foaf:knows>
  <foaf:Person rdf:nodeID="b">
   <foaf:name>Bob</foaf:name>
```

---

[1] http://www.w3.org/TR/rdf-syntax-grammar/

```
  <foaf:knows>
   <foaf:Person rdf:nodeID="c">
    <foaf:name>Charles</foaf:name>
   </foaf:Person>
  </foaf:knows>
 </foaf:Person>
</foaf:knows>
<foaf:knows rdf:nodeID="c"/>
</foaf:Person>
</rdf:RDF>
```

Unfortunately, this XML representation is hard to deal with, and, on top of that, the same RDF graph can look very different in distinct RDF/XML documents due to ambiguous variants of this format. From a didactic point of view, the much simpler Turtle[2] representation of our RDF graph is preferable:

```
@prefix rdf: <http://www.w3.org/1999/02/22-rdf-syntax-ns#>.
@prefix foaf: <http://xmlns.com/foaf/0.1/>.
_:a rdf:type foaf:Person .
_:a foaf:name "Alice" .
_:a foaf:knows _:b .
_:a foaf:knows _:c .
_:b rdf:type foaf:Person .
_:b foaf:name "Bob" .
_:b foaf:knows _:c .
_:c rdf:type foaf:Person .
_:c foaf:name "Charles" .
```

The above encoding explicitly states triples carrying the same information as the RDF/XML example before. We will make heavy usage of a Turtle shortcut notation throughout this chapter, like

```
_:a rdf:type foaf:Person ;
    foaf:name "Alice" ;
    foaf:knows _:b ;
    foaf:knows _:c .
```

which is a condensed version of the first four triples stated before.

A constantly growing number of RDF graphs – typically in RDF/XML format – is already accessible on the Web. Other common notations, more or less human readable, are N-Triples,[3] Notation 3,[4] and Turtle. We will adopt Turtle in the following, since it is also a fundamental part of SPARQL, which will be described later on.

Figures 2–5 show some information about the authors of this article extracted from RDF data that are available on the Web. RDF defines a special property rdf:type,[5]

---

[2] http://www.w3.org/TeamSubmission/turtle/

[3] http://www.w3.org/2001/sw/RDFCore/ntriples/

[4] http://www.w3.org/DesignIssues/Notation3.html

[5] Short for the full URI http://www.w3.org/1999/02/22-rdf-syntax-ns#type

```
@prefix rdfs:  <http://www.w3.org/2000/01/rdf-schema#> .
@prefix rdf:   <http://www.w3.org/1999/02/22-rdf-syntax-ns#> .
@prefix foaf:  <http://xmlns.com/foaf/0.1/> .
<http://www.mat.unical.it/~ianni/foaf.rdf> a foaf:PersonalProfileDocument.
<http://www.mat.unical.it/~ianni/foaf.rdf> foaf:maker _:me .
<http://www.mat.unical.it/~ianni/foaf.rdf> foaf:primaryTopic _:me .
_:me a foaf:Person .
_:me foaf:name "Giovambattista Ianni" .
_:me foaf:homepage <http://www.gibbi.com> .
_:me foaf:phone <tel:+39-0984-496430> .
_:me foaf:knows [ a foaf:Person ;
        foaf:name "Axel Polleres" ;
        rdfs:seeAlso <http://www.polleres.net/foaf.rdf>].
_:me foaf:knows [ a foaf:Person ;
        foaf:name "Wolfgang Faber" ;
        rdfs:seeAlso <http://www.kr.tuwien.ac.at/staff/faber/foaf.rdf>].
_:me foaf:knows [ a foaf:Person ;
        foaf:name "Francesco Calimeri" ;
        rdfs:seeAlso <http://www.mat.unical.it/kali/foaf.rdf>].
_:me foaf:knows [ a foaf:Person .
        foaf:name "Roman Schindlauer" .
        rdfs:seeAlso <http://www.kr.tuwien.ac.at/staff/roman/foaf.rdf>].
```

Fig. 2. Giovambattista Ianni's personal FOAF file

```
@prefix rdfs:  <http://www.w3.org/2000/01/rdf-schema#> .
@prefix rdf:   <http://www.w3.org/1999/02/22-rdf-syntax-ns#> .
@prefix foaf:  <http://xmlns.com/foaf/0.1/> .
@prefix owl:   <http://www.w3.org/2002/07/owl#> .
@prefix :      <http://www.postsubmeta.net/> .
:foaf a foaf:PersonalProfileDocument .
:foaf foaf:maker <http://www.postsubmeta.net/foaf#TK> .
:foaf foaf:primaryTopic <http://www.postsubmeta.net/foaf#TK> .
:foaf owl:sameAs <http://www.postsubmeta.net/foaf.rdf> .
<http://www.postsubmeta.net/foaf#TK> a foaf:Person ;
        foaf:name "Thomas Krennwallner" ;
        foaf:homepage <http://www.postsubmeta.net/> ;
        rdfs:seeAlso <http://www.postsubmeta.net/foaf> ;
        owl:sameAs <http://www.postsubmeta.net/foaf.rdf#TK> ;
        foaf:knows [ a foaf:Person ; foaf:name "Roman Schindlauer" ;
                rdfs:seeAlso <http://www.kr.tuwien.ac.at/staff/roman/foaf.rdf> ] ;
        foaf:knows [ a foaf:Person ; foaf:name "Giovambattista Ianni" ;
                rdfs:seeAlso <http://www.gibbi.com/foaf.rdf> ] ;
        foaf:knows [ a foaf:Person ; foaf:name "Axel Polleres" ;
                rdfs:seeAlso <http://www.polleres.net/foaf.rdf> ] ;
        foaf:knows [ a foaf:Person ; foaf:name "Francesco Calimeri" ;
                rdfs:seeAlso <http://www.mat.unical.it/kali/foaf.rdf> ] ;
        foaf:knows [ a foaf:Person ; foaf:name "Wolfgang Faber" ;
                rdfs:seeAlso <http://www.kr.tuwien.ac.at/staff/faber/foaf.rdf> ] ;
        foaf:knows [ a foaf:Person ; foaf:name "Alessandra Martello" ] .
        foaf:knows [ a foaf:Person ; foaf:name "Thomas Eiter" ] .
```

Fig. 3. Thomas Krennwallner's personal FOAF file

abbreviated in Turtle syntax by the "a" letter. It allows the specification of "IS-A" relations, such as, for instance,

```
<http://www.mat.unical.it/~ianni/foaf.rdf> a foaf:PersonalProfileDocument.
```

in Figure 2 links the resource `<http://www.mat.unical.it/~ianni/foaf.rdf>` to the resource `foaf:PersonalProfileDocument` via `rdf:type`.

Qualified names like `foaf:Person` are shortcuts for full URIs like `http://xmlns.com/foaf/0.1/Person`, making usage of *namespace prefixes* from XML, for ease of legibility. For instance, `:me` is a shortcut for `http://www.polleres.net/foaf.rdf#me` in the graph of Figure 4. If we compare this graph with Figure 2, we see that there is no obligation to give identifiers to entities on the Semantic Web: while the graph in Figure 2 uses a blank node to refer to the entities Giovambattista Ianni and Axel Polleres, the graph in Figure 4 assigns a URI to the entity Axel Polleres.

```
@prefix rdfs: <http://www.w3.org/2000/01/rdf-schema#>.
@prefix owl: <http://www.w3.org/2002/07/owl#>.
@prefix foaf: <http://xmlns.com/foaf/0.1/>.
@prefix : <http://www.polleres.net/foaf.rdf#>.
<http://www.polleres.net/foaf.rdf> foaf:maker :me;
                                    foaf:primaryTopic :me.
:me a foaf:Person; foaf:name "Axel Polleres";
 foaf:givenname "Axel"; foaf:surname "Polleres";
 foaf:phone <tel:+35391495723>, <fax:+35391495541>;
 foaf:workplaceHomepage <http://www.deri.ie/> .
 owl:sameAs
  <http://dblp.13s.de/d2r/resource/authors/Axel_Polleres>.
...
:me foaf:knows
   <http://www.harth.org/~andreas/foaf.rdf#ah>.
<http://www.harth.org/~andreas/foaf.rdf#ah>
 a foaf:Person;   foaf:name "Andreas Harth";
 rdfs:seeAlso <http://www.harth.org/~andreas/foaf.rdf>.
<http://www.polleres.net/foaf.rdf#me> foaf:knows _:b1
_:b1 a foaf:Person; foaf:name "John Breslin";
 rdfs:seeAlso <http://www.johnbreslin.com/foaf/foaf.rdf>.
<http://www.polleres.net/foaf.rdf#me> foaf:knows _:b2.
_:b2 a foaf:Person; foaf:name "Giovambattista Ianni";
 rdfs:seeAlso> <http://www.gibbi.com/foaf.rdf> .
...
```

Fig. 4. Axel Polleres' personal FOAF file

```
@prefix xsd:  <http://www.w3.org/2001/XMLSchema#> .
@prefix rdfs: <http://www.w3.org/2000/01/rdf-schema#> .
@prefix foaf: <http://xmlns.com/foaf/0.1/> .
@prefix dcterms: <http://purl.org/dc/terms/> .
@prefix dc:  <http://purl.org/dc/elements/1.1/> .
@prefix swrc: <http://swrc.ontoware.org/ontology#> .
<http://dblp.L3S.de/d2r/resource/authors/Thomas_Eiter>
 a foaf:Agent ;
 foaf:name "Thomas Eiter" .
...
<http://dblp.L3S.de/d2r/resource/publications/conf/foiks/2002>
 a swrc:Proceedings ; a foaf:Document;
 swrc:editor <http://dblp.L3S.de/d2r/resource/authors/Thomas_Eiter>.
...
<http://dblp.L3S.de/d2r/resource/publications/conf/icdt/2005>
 a swrc:Proceedings ; a foaf:Document;
 swrc:editor <http://dblp.L3S.de/d2r/resource/authors/Thomas_Eiter>.
...
<http://dblp.L3S.de/d2r/resource/publications/conf/webi/EiterIST06>
  dc:creator <http://dblp.L3S.de/d2r/resource/authors/Thomas_Eiter>,
      <http://dblp.L3S.de/d2r/resource/authors/Giovambattista_Ianni>,
      <http://dblp.L3S.de/d2r/resource/authors/Hans_Tompits>,
      <http://dblp.L3S.de/d2r/resource/authors/Roman_Schindlauer>;
  a foaf:Document; dcterms:issued "2006"^^xsd:gYear ;
  dcterms:bibliographicCitation
      <http://dblp.uni-trier.de/rec/bibtex/conf/webi/EiterIST06>.
  dcterms:partOf
      <http://dblp.L3S.de/d2r/resource/publications/conf/webi/2006>.
...
<http://dblp.L3S.de/d2r/resource/publications/conf/webi/2006>
 rdfs:label
 "2006 IEEE/WIC/ACM Int.1 Conference on Web Intelligence"^^xsd:string;
 swrc:series <http://dblp.L3S.de/d2r/resource/conferences/webi>.
...
<http://dblp.L3S.de/d2r/resource/authors/Giovambattista_Ianni>
      foaf:name "Giovambattista Ianni" .
<http://dblp.L3S.de/d2r/resource/authors/Hans_Tompits>
      foaf:name "Hans Tompits" .
<http://dblp.L3S.de/d2r/resource/authors/Roman_Schindlauer>
      foaf:name "Roman Schindlauer" .
...
```

Fig. 5. An RDF graph about Thomas Eiter extracted from DBLP

Types supported for RDF property values are URIs, or the two basic types, viz. rdf:Literal and rdf:XMLLiteral. Under the latter, a basic set of XML schema datatypes are supported.

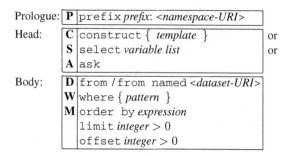

Fig. 6. A schematic overview of SPARQL

SPARQL Query Language for RDF. SPARQL is the W3C standard language for querying RDF data.[6] A query in this language can be roughly divided in two parts: (i) the retrieval part (*body*) and (ii) the result construction part (*head*).

Figure 6 shows a schematic overview of the building blocks that SPARQL queries consist of. We do not go into details of SPARQL here (see [82,76,77] for formal details).

The first part of a SPARQL query (the prologue part **P**) consists of namespace prefix declarations, which are used in the where part in the body to shortcut IRI literals.

The body part of a SPARQL query (**DWM**) offers the following features. An RDF *dataset* (**D**), i.e., the set of source RDF graphs used as input data, is specified using multiple from or from named clauses. Merging multiple RDF sources specified in consecutive from clauses is a crucial feature of SPARQL, which complements the lack of this possibility in plain RDF format. The where part (**W**) allows to match parts of the RDF dataset at hand, by specifying a graph *pattern* possibly involving variables (variable symbols are prefixed with a ? sign). This pattern is given in a Turtle-based syntax, in the simplest case by a list of consecutive triple patterns, i.e., triples containing variables, IRIs, blank nodes, and RDF literals. More involved patterns allow unions of graph patterns, optional matching of parts of a graph, matching of named graphs selected in from named clauses, etc. Finally, variable bindings matching the where pattern in the source graphs can be ordered, but also other solution modifiers (**M**) such as limit and offset are allowed to restrict the number of solutions considered in the result.

In the head portion, SPARQL allows to specify one of four query forms. Each one is associated to a specific result format representing a view over the solutions of the pattern matching mechanism. The three most-used query forms (**CSA**) are construct, select, and ask; the describe query form can be used to get RDF graphs describing resources, but no formal semantics is defined for this operator and the output depends on the used SPARQL implementation, hence we omit a discussion here. The construct query form takes a *template* as parameter, which consists of a list of triple patterns in Turtle syntax, possibly involving variables that carry over bindings from the where part. This operator can be used to translate between different RDF formats. The select query form is used to retrieve the bindings for variables mentioned in the

---

[6] http://www.w3.org/TR/rdf-sparql-query/

graph pattern of the `where` part. The `ask` query form returns true, if there is a binding for the supplied graph pattern, or false otherwise.

An example for a simple SPARQL `select` query is

```
prefix foaf: <http://xmlns.com/foaf/0.1/>
select ?name
from <http://www.mat.unical.it/~ianni/foaf.rdf>
from <http://www.postsubmeta.net/foaf.rdf>
from <http://www.polleres.net/foaf.rdf>
where {
    ?person foaf:knows ?friend .
    ?friend foaf:name ?name .
}
```

which retrieves all `?name`s of `?friend`s known by `?person`s over the combined RDF graphs shown in Figure 2–4.

Usage on the Web. RDF graphs are gaining wide popularity. Driven by efforts such as the Linked Data initiative, [7] RDF datasets are becoming available in several ways, making the current amount of available RDF data substantial. Available datasets can be categorized as:

– *Data exposed directly in RDF format and publicly accessible from the web.*
  This direct way is preferred when advertised data has relatively small size. For instance, a lot of RDF data is available on the Web in personal graphs using the FOAF vocabulary mentioned before. The personal FOAF files of some of the authors are shown in Figures 2–4.[8]
– *Data available as SPARQL endpoint.*
  The SPARQL query language, as shown above, allows to query RDF data using SPARQL endpoints, which are standardized Web Services that answer SPARQL queries by following the SPARQL protocol [18].
    For example, the widely known DBLP online citation index is accessible in two ways: as plain and huge RDF document and via a SPARQL endpoint.[9] By means of the SPARQL endpoint, only the interesting portion of the data is returned to the user, which means that both client and server save time and network bandwidth. DBLP contains a huge amount of information about scientific publications and their authors (see Figure 5 for an example).
– *Data available by means of conversion services, also called wrappers.*
  Converters from popular data formats of heterogeneous provenance such as iCAL (calendar and agenda description format) and RSS (Web feeds) are available, as well as adapters from, e.g., Amazon and eBay Web services.[10] In this context,

---

[7] http://linkeddata.org/

[8] Data accessible from the Web at
http://www.gibbi.com/foaf.rdf, http://www.postsubmeta.net/foaf, and http://www.polleres.net/foaf.rdf, resp.

[9] http://dblp.l3s.de/d2r/

[10] See http://esw.w3.org/topic/ConverterToRdf for a comprehensive list.

W3C's Gleaning Resource Descriptions from Dialects of Languages [19] (GRDDL) working group has the goal to complement the concrete RDF/XML syntax with a mechanism to relate to other XML dialects (especially XHTML or "microformats") [19]. GRDDL focuses on extracting RDF from XML. To this end, the working group recently published a finished Recommendation which specifies how XML documents or XML Schema namespace documents can reference transformations that are then processed by a GRDDL-aware application to extract RDF from the respective source file.

An excerpt of the RDF data available about Thomas Eiter from DBLP is shown in Figure 5. This graph contains information such as the papers Thomas Eiter authored, links to co-authors of these papers, etc. The property dc:creator belongs to the Dublin Core vocabulary [71] and is used to denote the authorship relation. For instance, the statement

```
<http://dblp.L3S.de/d2r/resource/publications/conf/webi/EiterIST06>
    dc:creator <http://dblp.L3S.de/d2r/resource/authors/Thomas_Eiter> .
```

says that the article with URI

```
http://dblp.L3S.de/d2r/resource/publications/conf/webi/EiterIST06
```

was created by the person with URI

```
http://dblp.L3S.de/d2r/resource/authors/Thomas_Eiter
```

Semantics and logical characterization. RDF graphs may contain anonymous, existential nodes, also called "blank" nodes, in order to express incomplete information about the identity of the subject or the object of a statement. An RDF graph can be equally viewed as a first-order formula, where we use a special predicate *triple* to denote statements made in the graph and where blank nodes are viewed as existentially quantified variable. For instance, the graph from Figure 2 corresponds to the following formula:

$$
\begin{aligned}
&\exists me, b1, b2, b3, b4 \\
&(triple(\texttt{foaf.rdf}, \texttt{rdf:type}, \texttt{foaf:PersonalProfileDocument}) \\
&\land triple(\texttt{foaf.rdf}, \texttt{foaf:maker}, me) \\
&\land triple(\texttt{foaf.rdf}, \texttt{foaf:primaryTopic}, me) \\
&\land triple(me, \texttt{rdf:type}, \texttt{foaf:Person}) \\
&\land triple(me, \texttt{foaf:name}, \texttt{"Giovambattista Ianni"}) \\
&\land triple(me, \texttt{foaf:homepage}, \texttt{http://www.gibbi.com}) \\
&\land triple(me, \texttt{foaf:phone}, \texttt{tel:+39-0984-496430}) \\
&\land triple(me, \texttt{foaf:knows}, b1) \land triple(b1, \texttt{rdf:type}, \texttt{foaf:Person}) \\
&\land triple(b1, \texttt{foaf:name}, \texttt{"Axel Polleres"}) \\
&\land triple(b1, \texttt{rdfs:seeAlso}, \texttt{http://www.polleres...}) \\
&\land triple(me, \texttt{foaf:knows}, b2) \land triple(b1, \texttt{rdf:type}, \texttt{foaf:Person}) \\
&\land triple(b2, \texttt{foaf:name}, \texttt{"Wolfgang Faber"}) \\
&\land triple(b2, \texttt{rdfs:seeAlso}, \texttt{http://www.kr.tuwien...}) \\
&\land triple(me, \texttt{foaf:knows}, b3) \land triple(b1, \texttt{rdf:type}, \texttt{foaf:Person}) \\
&\land triple(b3, \texttt{foaf:name}, \texttt{"Francesco Calimeri"}) \\
&\land triple(b3, \texttt{rdfs:seeAlso}, \texttt{http://www.mat.unical...}) \\
&\land triple(me, \texttt{foaf:knows}, b4) \land triple(b1, \texttt{rdf:type}, \texttt{foaf:Person}) \\
&\land triple(b4, \texttt{foaf:name}, \texttt{"Roman Schindlauer"}) \\
&\land triple(b4, \texttt{rdfs:seeAlso}, \texttt{http://www.kr.tuwien...})) .
\end{aligned} \tag{1}
$$

There are different alternative logical representations conceivable for formula (1). For instance, Frame Logic (F-Logic) [56] has often been proposed as an adequate representation for RDF graphs [26,105]. F-Logic extends classical first-order logic by concepts from object-oriented programming like objects and class inheritance, and allows to reason about complex objects, which are built from simpler ones. The name Frame Logic stems from the similarity to frame-based languages, which deal with objects and classes and relationships between themselves. F-Logic has a special representation for the class membership relation (`rdf:type`) denoted as "`:`", or "`#`", and frames are expressed in square brackets denoting slots with "`→`". As a frame logic formula, the graph from Figure 2 would look as follows:

$$\exists me, b1, b2, b3, b4 \; (\texttt{foaf.rdf\#foaf:PersonalProfileDocument}$$
$$\wedge \; \texttt{foaf.rdf[foaf:maker} \rightarrow me]$$
$$\wedge \; \texttt{foaf.rdf[foaf:primaryTopic} \rightarrow me] \tag{2}$$
$$\wedge \; me\texttt{\#foaf:Person} \wedge \cdots) \, .$$

Alternatively, the OWL community tends to favor a representation using unary and binary predicates for RDF properties, where unary predicates are used for the `rdf:type` predicate and binary predicates for all other predicates. In that representation, the graph from Figure 2 would look as follows:

$$\exists me, b1, b2, b3, b4 \; (\texttt{foaf:PersonalProfileDocument(foaf.rdf)}$$
$$\wedge \; \texttt{foaf:maker(foaf.rdf}, me)$$
$$\wedge \; \texttt{foaf:primaryTopic(foaf.rdf}, me) \tag{3}$$
$$\wedge \; \texttt{foaf:Person}(me) \wedge \cdots) \, .$$

The semantics of an RDF graph can be essentially viewed as corresponding to the first-order representation chosen in Figure 4 plus entailment of several axiomatic triples. For instance, the triple X `rdf:type rdf:Property` is an axiom for all X which occur in the predicate position of any other triple. In particular, this also makes, for instance, `rdf:type rdf:type rdf:Property` an axiom.

The semantics of RDF involves some more peculiarities in the handling of XML literals, RDF containers, and lists. We refer the interested reader to [37,48] for more details.

RDF Schema (RDFS). *RDF Schema* (RDFS) is a semantic extension of basic RDF. In a nutshell, by giving special meaning to the properties `rdfs:subClassOf` and `rdfs:subPropertyOf`, to `rdfs:domain` and `rdfs:range`, as well as to several types (like `rdfs:Class`, `rdfs:Resource`, `rdfs:Literal`, `rdfs:Datatype`, etc.), RDFS allows to express simple taxonomies and hierarchies among properties and resources, as well as domain and range restrictions for properties.

The axiomatization of RDFS can to a large extent be approximated by a set of sentences of first-order logic (FOL), as shown in Table 1, plus the axiomatic triples from [48, Sections 3.1 and 4.1].[11] Note that our choice of using a ternary predicate *triple* in favor of a binary representation helped us to avoid higher-order-like rules such as

$$\forall S, P, O \, (P(S, O) \supset \texttt{rdf:type}\,(P, \texttt{rdf:Property}))$$

in this axiomatization. Roughly speaking, a triple t is true in a RDF graph G under RDFS semantics if the theory constructed as the union of

- Axiomatic triples,
- Entailment clauses (as in Table 1), and
- The encoding of G as an existentially quantified conjunction of atoms (as in Figure 1)

---

[11] We use '$\supset$' for material implication to avoid confusion with '$\leftarrow$' as commonly used in logic programming.

Table 1. Semantics of RDFS

$\forall S, P, O\ (triple(S, P, O) \supset triple(S, \texttt{rdf:type}, \texttt{rdfs:Resource}))$

$\forall S, P, O\ (triple(S, P, O) \supset triple(P, \texttt{rdf:type}, \texttt{rdf:Property}))$

$\forall S, P, O\ (triple(S, P, O) \supset triple(O, \texttt{rdf:type}, \texttt{rdfs:Resource}))$

$\forall S, P, O\ (triple(S, P, O) \wedge triple(P, \texttt{rdfs:domain}, C) \supset triple(S, \texttt{rdf:type}, C))$

$\forall S, P, O, C\ (triple(S, P, O) \wedge triple(P, \texttt{rdfs:range}, C) \supset triple(O, \texttt{rdf:type}, C))$

$\forall C\ (triple(C, \texttt{rdf:type}, \texttt{rdfs:Class}) \supset triple(C, \texttt{rdfs:subClassOf}, \texttt{rdfs:Resource}))$

$\forall C_1, C_2, C_3\ (triple(C_1, \texttt{rdfs:subClassOf}, C_2) \wedge$
$\qquad\qquad triple(C_2, \texttt{rdfs:subClassOf}, C_3) \supset triple(C_1, \texttt{rdfs:subClassOf}, C_3))$

$\forall S, C_1, C_2\ (triple(S, \texttt{rdf:type}, C_1) \wedge triple(C_1, \texttt{rdfs:subClassOf}, C_2) \supset triple(S, \texttt{rdf:type}, C_2))$

$\forall S, C\ (triple(S, \texttt{rdf:type}, C) \supset triple(C, \texttt{rdf:type}, \texttt{rdfs:Class}))$

$\forall C\ (triple(C, \texttt{rdf:type}, \texttt{rdfs:Class}) \supset triple(C, \texttt{rdfs:subClassOf}, C))$

$\forall P_1, P_2, P_3\ (triple(P_1, \texttt{rdfs:subPropertyOf}, P_2) \wedge$
$\qquad\qquad triple(P_2, \texttt{rdfs:subPropertyOf}, P_3) \supset triple(P_1, \texttt{rdfs:subPropertyOf}, P_3))$

$\forall S, P_1, P_2, O\ (triple(S, P_1, O) \wedge triple(P_1, \texttt{rdfs:subPropertyOf}, P_2) \supset triple(S, P_2, O))$

$\forall P\ (triple(P, \texttt{rdf:type}, \texttt{rdf:Property}) \supset triple(P, \texttt{rdfs:subPropertyOf}, P))$

---

entails t. Again, we do not elaborate upon peculiarities and additional rules or axioms in the context of RDF containers, XML literals, etc. here. A thorough formalization of RDF(S) semantics can be found in [66].

2.2 Description Logics and the OWL Web Ontology Language

The next layer in the Semantic Web stack serves to formally define domain models as shared conceptualizations, also often called ontologies [46], on top of the RDF/RDFS data model. In order to formally specify such domain models, the W3C has chosen a language which is close to a syntactic variant of an expressive but still decidable Description Logic (DL) [4], namely $\mathcal{SHOIN}(\mathbf{D})$. More precisely, the OWL DL variant coincides with this DL, at the cost of imposing several restrictions on the usage of RDF(S). These restrictions (e.g., disallowing that a resource is used both as a class and an instance) are lifted in OWL Full which combines the description logic flavor of OWL DL and the syntactic freedom of RDF(S). For an in-depth discussion of the peculiarities of OWL Full, we refer the interested reader to the language specification [27] and restrict our observations to OWL DL here.

While RDFS itself may already be viewed as a simple ontology language, OWL adds several features beyond RDFS' simple capabilities to define hierarchies (`rdfs:sub-PropertyOf`, `rdfs:subClassOf`) among properties and classes.

As for properties, OWL allows to specify transitive, symmetric, functional, inverse, and inverse functional properties. The correspondences of respective OWL properties and classes with respective description logics and first-order logic axioms can be found in Table 2. Note that we switch to the binary representation $P(S, O)$ of triples here,

Table 2. Expressing OWL DL Property axioms to DL and FOL

OWL property axioms as RDF triples	DL syntax	FOL short representation
$\langle P$ rdfs:domain $C\rangle$	$\top \sqsubseteq \forall P^-.C$	$\forall x,y.P(x,y) \supset C(x)$
$\langle P$ rdfs:range $C\rangle$	$\top \sqsubseteq \forall P.C$	$\forall x,y.P(x,y) \supset C(y)$
$\langle P$ owl:inverseOf $P_0\rangle$	$P \equiv P_0^-$	$\forall x,y.P(x,y) \equiv P_0(y,x)$
$\langle P$ rdf:type owl:SymmetricProperty$\rangle$	$P \equiv P^-$	$\forall x,y.P(x,y) \equiv P(y,x)$
$\langle P$ rdf:type owl:FunctionalProperty$\rangle$	$\top \sqsubseteq \,\leqslant 1P$	$\forall x,y,z.P(x,y) \wedge P(x,z) \supset y = z$
$\langle P$ rdf:type owl:InverseFunctionalProperty$\rangle$	$\top \sqsubseteq \,\leqslant 1P^-$	$\forall x,y,z.P(x,y) \wedge P(z,y) \supset x = z$
$\langle P$ rdf:type owl:TransitiveProperty$\rangle$	$P^+ \sqsubseteq P$	$\forall x,y,z.P(x,y) \wedge P(y,z) \supset P(x,z)$

Table 3. Mapping of OWL DL Complex Class Descriptions to DL and FOL

OWL complex class descriptions[*]	DL syntax	FOL short representation
owl:Thing	$\top$	$x = x$
owl:Nothing	$\bot$	$\neg x = x$
owl:intersectionOf $(C_1 \ldots C_n)$	$C_1 \sqcap \cdots \sqcap C_n$	$C_1(x) \wedge \cdots \wedge C_n(x)$
owl:unionOf $(C_1 \ldots C_n)$	$C_1 \sqcup \cdots \sqcup C_n$	$C_1(x) \vee \cdots \vee C_n(x)$
owl:complementOf (C)	$\neg C$	$\neg C(x)$
owl:oneOf $(o_1 \ldots o_n)$	$\{o_1, \ldots, o_n\}$	$x = o_1 \vee \cdots \vee x = o_n$
owl:restriction $(P$ owl:someValuesFrom $(C))$	$\exists P.C$	$\exists y.P(x,y) \wedge C(y)$
owl:restriction $(P$ owl:allValuesFrom $(C))$	$\forall P.C$	$\forall y.P(x,y) \supset C(y)$
owl:restriction $(P$ owl:value $(o))$	$\exists P.\{o\}$	$P(x,o)$
owl:restriction $(P$ owl:minCardinality $(n))$	$\geqslant nP$	$\exists y_1 \ldots y_n. \bigwedge_{k=1}^{n} P(x, y_k) \wedge \bigwedge_{i<j} y_j \neq y_j$
owl:restriction $(P$ owl:maxCardinality $(n))$	$\leqslant nP$	$\forall y_1 \ldots y_{n+1}. \bigwedge_{k=1}^{n+1} P(x, y_k) \supset \bigvee_{i<j} y_i = y_j$

[*]For reasons of legibility, we use a variant of the OWL abstract syntax [73] in this table.

since in description logics (and thus in OWL DL), predicate names and resources are assumed to be disjoint.

Moreover, OWL allows the specifications of complex class descriptions to be used in rdfs:subClassOf statements. Complex descriptions may involve class definitions in terms of union or intersection of other classes, as well as restrictions on properties. Table 3 gives an overview of the expressive possibilities of OWL for class descriptions and its semantic correspondences with description logics and first-order logics.[12] Such class descriptions can be related to each other using rdfs:subClassOf, owl:equivalentClass, and owl:disjointWith keywords, which allow us to express description-logic axioms of the form $C_1 \sqsubseteq C_2$, $C_1 \equiv C_2$, and $C_1 \sqcap C_2 \sqsubseteq \bot$, respectively, in OWL.

Finally, OWL allows to express explicit equality or inequality relations between individuals by means of the owl:sameAs and owl:differentFrom properties, e.g., the triples

$\langle$http://www.polleres.net/foaf.rdf#me$\rangle$ owl:sameAs
$\langle$http://dblp.l3s.de/d2r/page/authors/Axel_Polleres$\rangle$.

---

[12] We use a simplified notion for the first-order logic translation here—actually, the translation needs to be applied recursively for any complex DL term. For a formal specification of the correspondence between DL expressions and first-order logic, cf. [4].

and

⟨http://polleres.net/foaf.rdf#me⟩ owl:differentFrom
    ⟨http://www.gibbi.com/foaf.rdf#me⟩.

boil down to

http://www.polleres.net/foaf.rdf#me =
    http://dblp.13s.de/d2r/page/authors/Axel_Polleres
∧ http://polleres.net/foaf.rdf#me ≠
    http://www.gibbi.com/foaf.rdf#me.

For details on the description logics notions used in the Tables 2 and 3, we refer the interested reader to, e.g., [4]. For our purposes, basic understanding of the corresponding definitions in terms of first-order logic will be sufficient. What makes description logics the formalism of choice is the fact that they resemble *decidable fragments* of first-order logic, i.e., queries for entailment of subclass relationships or class membership of a particular individual are effectively computable. At the moment of writing, the next iteration of OWL (version 2) has the status of a member submission at W3C and is further developed by the recently relaunched OWL working group.[13] If accepted in the present form, OWL2 will, based on the decidable description logic $\mathcal{SROIQ}$ [51], support additional features such as acyclic role composition, qualified number restrictions, possibility to declare (for simple roles) symmetry, reflexivity, or disjointness axioms.

Example 2 (Ontologies in Description Logics). We take a simple ontology about publications available online at http://asptut.gibbi.com/sandbox/reviewers.rdf as an example to illustrate some of the conceptualizations therein in their corresponding DL syntax:

$$\exists ex{:}title.\top \sqsubseteq ex{:}Paper \tag{i}$$

$$\exists ex{:}title^{-}.\top \sqsubseteq xsd{:}string \tag{ii}$$

$$ex{:}isAuthorOf^{-} \equiv dc{:}creator \tag{iii}$$

$$ex{:}Publication \equiv ex{:}Paper \sqcap \exists ex{:}publishedIn.\top \tag{iv}$$

$$\top \sqsubseteq\, \leqslant 1\ ex{:}publishedIn^{-} \tag{v}$$

$$ex{:}Senior \equiv foaf{:}Person \sqcap\, \geqslant 10\ ex{:}isAuthorOf \sqcap \tag{vi}$$
$$\exists ex{:}isAuthorOf.ex{:}Publication$$

$$ex{:}Club100 \equiv foaf{:}Person \sqcap\, \geqslant 100\ ex{:}isAuthorOf \tag{vii}$$

This knowledge base expresses the following information: *ex:title* is a datatype property on *ex:Papers* that takes strings as values (axioms (i) and (ii)). Furthermore, the property *ex:isAuthorOf* is the inverse of the property *dc:creator* (axiom (iii)). Next, the ontology defines in (iv) a class *ex:Publication* which consists of all the papers which have been published, and in (v), we state that *ex:publishedIn* to be an inverse functional property (i.e., every paper is published in at most one venue). A *ex:Senior* researcher (vi) is defined as a person who has at least ten papers, some of which are published. Finally, the class *ex:Club100* is defined as the persons having authored more than 100 papers.

---

[13] http://www.w3.org/2007/OWL/wiki/OWL_Working_Group

3   Rule-Based Aggregation and Integration of Semantic Web Data

The main use case we want to address in this article is rule-based aggregation and integration of Semantic data. In other words, we will focus on how it would be possible to reach the goal of combining existing data from the Web, by exploiting rule-based technologies and available Semantic Web rules languages and engines.

To give a condensed introduction into rule-based languages, consider this rule specimen from non-monotonic logic programming: a disjunctive rule is of form

$$a_1 \lor \cdots \lor a_l \leftarrow b_1, \ldots, b_k, not\ b_{k+1}, \ldots, not\ b_m \ , \tag{4}$$

where $l \geq 0$, $m \geq k \geq 0$, and all a_i and b_j are literals, i.e., possibly negated atoms. The disjunction $a_1 \lor \cdots \lor a_l$ is called the head of a rule, while the conjunction $b_1, \ldots, b_k, not\ b_{k+1}, \ldots, not\ b_m$ is the body of a rule. Each expression $not\ b_j$ is a *negation as failure (NAF) literal*, which is true by default, i.e., if we cannot infer that b_i is true. In the usual semantics of such languages, the head of a rule is true if the body is true, i.e., we can infer new knowledge from other knowledge. As an example, $male(X) \lor female(X) \leftarrow person(X)$ and $author(X) \leftarrow isAuthorOf(X, Y)$, $not\ unpublished(Y)$ are valid rules. For a more detailed explanation of the syntax and the semantics of rule-based languages see, e.g., [13,37].

3.1   Common Formats for Rule Interchange on the Web

Since all available rule languages use fairly differing syntaxes, we will illustrate rules using a simplified version of the *Rule Interchange Format Basic Logic Dialect* (RIF-BLD) presentation syntax [10]. RIF-BLD is basically a syntactic variant of Horn rules, which most available rule systems can process. RIF allows frames as in F-Logic notation and the use of URIs as object identifiers,[14] where URIs are enclosed in angle brackets as in Turtle. Likewise, (typed) literals as in Turtle notation are allowed, i.e., for instance we write the RDF triple

```
<http://dblp.L3S.de/d2r/resource/publications/conf/webi/EiterIST06>
   dcterms:issued "2006"^^xsd:gYear.
```

from Figure 5 as a RIF frame

```
<http://dblp.L3S.de/d2r/resource/publications/conf/webi/EiterIST06>[
   dcterms:issued -> "2006"^^xsd:gYear]
```

RIF uses the Prolog style ": –" for separating rule head (consequent) and body (antecedent). We start our illustration with a simple example use case for rule based integration.

Example 3 (Reviewer Selection). Let us assume that we have FOAF and DBLP information about the authors of the present article available as given above. Based on that information, we want to find more information about which are suitable reviewers for this article, and on persons, which, having conflicts of interests, can not be instead

---

[14] Strictly speaking, RIF allows IRIs (International Resource Identifier) [32]. IRIs are a generalization of URIs, allowing for example Kanji, Chinese, Arabic or Hebrew characters.

elected as reviewers. In order to do so, we want to use an available Semantic Web rules engine which we wish to feed with information shown next:[15]

- The namespace declarations:

```
Prefix(xsd http://www.w3.org/2001/XMLSchema#)
Prefix(rdfs http://www.w3.org/2000/01/rdf-schema#)
Prefix(owl http://www.w3.org/2002/07/owl#)
Prefix(foaf http://xmlns.com/foaf/0.1/)
Prefix(ex http://www.example.org/)
```

- The set of conflicting reviewers, that is, either persons having the same names as individuals the authors know personally, according to their FOAF files:

```
Forall ?P ?A ?P1 ?N
( ?P#ex:ConflictingReviewer :- And(
     <http://dblp.l3s.de/d2r/page/publications/conf/rweb/EiterIKP08>
        [dc:creator -> ?A]
     ?A[foaf:knows -> ?P1]
     ?P1[foaf:name -> ?N]                                                    (5)
     ?P[foaf:name -> ?N]
     ?P#foaf:Person
     )
 )
```

- or, persons having the same names as people that, according to DBLP, co-authored papers with the authors of the paper in question.

```
Forall ?P ?A ?Pub ?P1 ?N
( ?P#ex:ConflictingReviewer :- And(
     <http://dblp.l3s.de/d2r/page/publications/conf/rweb/EiterIKP08>
        [dc:creator -> ?A]
     ?Pub[dc:creator -> ?A]
     ?Pub[dc:creator -> ?P1]                                                 (6)
     ?P1[ foaf:name -> ?N]
     ?P[ foaf:name -> ?N]
     ?P#foaf:Person
     )
 )
```

- People with the same names as people who have published in the same conferences or journals as the authors are, instead, possible reviewers.

```
Forall ?P ?A ?Pub ?ConfOrJournal ?P1 ?N
( ?P#ex:CandidateReviewer :- And(
     <http://dblp.l3s.de/d2r/page/publications/conf/rweb/EiterIKP08>
        [dc:creator -> ?A]
     ?Pub[dc:creator -> ?A]
     ?Pub[dcterms:partOf  -> ?ConfOrJournal]
     ?Pub1[dcterms:partOf -> ?ConfOrJournal]                                 (7)
     ?Pub1[dc:creator -> ?P1]
     ?P1[ foaf:name -> ?N]
     ?P[ foaf:name -> ?N]
     ?P#foaf:Person
     )
 )
```

In principle, any rule system which (i) provides access to RDF data, such as Figures 2–5, via import facilities, and (ii) uses the Frame style RDF representation analog to (2) would be capable of processing the rules (5)–(7) and computing conflicting reviewers.

---

[15] We will assume the URI of the present work is
   http://dblp.l3s.de/d2r/page/publications/conf/rweb/EiterIKP08

We could easily transform these rules to the alternative RDF representation styles in (1) or in (3) above for other rules systems which support them. We will show these representations later on, when discussing concrete rules systems and their supported syntaxes.

In the following, we will discuss the different features which are (or, should be) present in available rules systems. Small illustrating examples extending the basic reviewer selection scenario from above will be exploited. We will focus on the following aspects:

- RDF data import
- RDF schema support
- OWL support
- Modules, context, and named graphs
- Blank nodes and function symbols
- Built-in predicates and functions
- Defaults and negation as failure
- Advanced features including unstratified negation, constraints, and disjunction

3.2 RDF Data Import

The first and most basic feature for processing Semantic Web data, which we have already mentioned in the previous section, is an import or access facility for RDF data from one or more RDF graphs (or RDF data extracted by a GRDDL [19] transformation from an HTML or XML source). Many available rules systems provide such import facilities, either

- By import directives or mapping definitions, external to the rules language, to access RDF graphs accessible on the Web; or
- By special built-in predicates as part of the rule language to import RDF graphs.

As a special case, we expect that many future rules systems for the Semantic Web will – as opposed to direct import of whole RDF graphs – allow access to RDF stores via a SPARQL [18,82] endpoint, i.e., providing import directives or built-predicates to dispatch SPARQL queries. More details on how different existing rules systems support this feature are given in Section 4 below.

3.3 RDF Schema Support

The next feature which we would expect from a reasonable rules language/system operating on Semantic Web data is obviously that ontological statements from RDF Schema are taken into account.

Let us have a closer look at the rules above, and assume that we execute them just on the "raw" RDF data available on the Web. Without taking additional RDFS inferences into account, we would not be able to find out that Thomas Eiter is a conflicting reviewer, since for `http://dblp.L3S.de/d2r/resource/authors/ Thomas_Eiter` only the membership in the class `foaf:Agent` is known in the data in Figure 5, but all the rules above have membership in the class `foaf:Person` in its prerequisites for inferring that somebody is a conflicting reviewer.

Fortunately, we have – in our own knowledge base – some knowledge which relates the DC [71], SWRC [94], and FOAF [42] ontologies referred to in Figure 5. As we have seen above, RDFS supports taxonomies on classes and properties as well as domain and range restrictions on properties. Let us assume that our own knowledge base contains the following statements relating SWRC and FOAF:

```
foaf:maker rdfs:subPropertyOf dc:creator .
swrc:editor rdfs:domain foaf:Document .
swrc:editor rdfs:range foaf:Person .
swrc:Person rdfs:subClassOf foaf:Person .
```
(8)

From this and the rules in Table 1, we can conclude that Thomas is indeed a conflicting reviewer. From the DBLP data we can conclude truth of the body condition in rule (6) for binding the variable `?Pub` to `http://dblp.l3s.de/d2r/page/publications/conf/rweb/EiterIKP08`, all the variables `?A`, `?P1`, and `?P` to `http://dblp.L3S.de/d2r/resource/authors/Thomas_Eiter`, and the variable `?N` to `"Thomas Eiter"`. These bindings make all atoms of the condition except the last one – `?P#foaf:Person` – true. However, the inference of the necessary RDF statement

```
<http://dblp.L3S.de/d2r/resource/authors/Thomas_Eiter> a foaf:Person .
```

follows from the RDF statement

```
<http://dblp.L3S.de/d2r/resource/publications/conf/foiks/2002>
    swrc:editor <http://dblp.L3S.de/d2r/resource/authors/Thomas_Eiter>.
```

plus the third statement of (8) and the fifth RDFS inference rule in Table 1. In fact, we can write this and all other RDFS inference rules from Table 1 similarly in RIF syntax:

```
Forall ?S ?P ?O ?C ( ?O#?C :- And( ?S[ ?P -> ?O] ?P[ rdfs:range -> ?C] )) (9)
```

So, basically for any rule engine that is capable of processing rules (5)–(7), we can equally encode all the RDFS inference rules analogous to (9), and we would be able to compute all conflicting reviewers when taking in addition the RDFS inferences into account.

3.4 OWL Support

Note that we did a little shortcut in the previous example by making in the third statement of (8) explicit that the *swrc:editor* had `foaf:Person` in its range, adding a respective RDFS statement. However, in fact the SWRC ontology is specified in OWL and states this in a different way. Among others, the SWRC ontology contains the following statements, which is not expressible in RDFS alone:

$$swrc{:}Proceedings \sqsubseteq \forall swrc{:}editor.swrc{:}Person;$$

this particular axiom can still be translated into a rule:

```
Forall ?P ?Proc( ?P#swrc:Person :- And( ?Proc#swrc:Proceedings
                          ?Proc[ swrc:editor -> ?P] ) ).
```
(10)

From above rule, we can still derive that `http://dblp.L3S.de/d2r/resource/` `authors/Thomas_Eiter` is a `foaf:Person`, namely by

```
<http://dblp.L3S.de/d2r/resource/publications/conf/foiks/2002>
    a swrc:Proceedings ;
    swrc:editor <http://dblp.L3S.de/d2r/resource/authors/Thomas_Eiter>.
```

plus the last statement of (8) and the respective RDFS inference rule. So, by translating to rules the OWL axioms from the SWRC ontology and all other involved ontologies, i.e., the DC ontology and the FOAF ontology, then adding the resulting rulebase to imported data, we could still compute all conflicting reviewers within a rules engine. Faithful preservation of semantics when translating OWL to rules is however a known problem. A premier fragment of OWL which can be translated into rules quite since (since it has a one-to-one correspondence with Horn rules), is described e.g. in [96] or [21, Section 9.3].

Unfortunately, not all OWL axioms can be translated to rules. To illustrate this, let us have a look into the axioms in the Reviewer ontology from above: it is not difficult to translate the rules (i)–(ii) in Example 2 to rules similar to (10), looking at the equivalent FOL representation for OWL statements in Tables 2 and 3. The remaining three rules are equivalences; each equivalence $A \equiv B$ can be "decomposed" into two axioms $A \sqsubseteq B$ and $B \sqsupseteq A$, which are then translated to rules. As for the axiom (iv), this is easy for the $\sqsubseteq$-axiom:

```
Forall ?P ?X ( ?P#ex:Publication :- And( ?P#Paper
                                          ?P[ ex:pulishedIn -> ?X] ) )
```
(11)

However, for the $\sqsupseteq$-axiom we end up with a rule which is not Horn:

```
Forall ?P ( And( ?P#ex:Paper Exists ?X( ?P[ ex:pulishedIn -> ?X] ) )
            :- ?P#Publication )
```
(12)

In fact, rule (12) is not admissible in RIF-BLD syntax. Likewise the axioms (v) and (vi) from Example 2 are not translatable to rules. However, we can easily imagine situations in which we would need inferences both in OWL and also over rules in order to aggregate Semantic Web data for our reviewer selection scenario.

Suppose we have collected a list of experts from the Semantic Web or Knowledge Representation areas all of which have over a hundred publications which are possibly candidates to review the paper at hand, i.e., we know that they are all members of the $ex\mathord{:}Club100$[16] defined above which we could state in an RDF graph as follows:

```
<http://dblp.l3s.de/d2r/page/authors/Stefan_Decker> a ex:Club100.
<http://dblp.l3s.de/d2r/page/authors/Dieter_Fensel> a ex:Club100.
<http://dblp.l3s.de/d2r/page/authors/Georg_Gottlob> a ex:Club100.
<http://dblp.l3s.de/d2r/page/authors/Ian_Horrocks> a ex:Club100.
<http://dblp.l3s.de/d2r/page/authors/Michael_Gelfond> a ex:Club100.
<http://dblp.l3s.de/d2r/page/authors/Michael_Kifer> a ex:Club100.
<http://dblp.l3s.de/d2r/page/authors/Vladimir_Lifschitz> a ex:Club100.
```
(13)

We want to find candidate reviewers from this list and the remaining information from DBLP based on the following additional rules. Firstly, we want to add that those documents having a *dcterms:bibliographicCitation* count as publications:

```
Forall ?X ?C ( ?X#ex:Publication :- And(
                ?X#foaf:Document
                ?X[ dcterms:bibliographicCitation -> ?C ] ) )
```
(14)

---

[16] Although this may not necessarily reflect current and actual content of DBLP, we assume the set of authors given has more than 100 certified publications each.

Secondly, we want to state that any senior researcher, i.e., any member of the class *ex:Senior*, is a candidate reviewer:

```
Forall ?P ( ?P#ex:CandidateReviewer :- ?P#ex:Senior )
```
(15)

Note that the above rule can be stated just as well as part of our ontology using the DL axiom *ex:CandidateReviewer* $\sqsubseteq$ *ex:Senior*. Regarding (15), obviously, without OWL reasoning support in our Semantic Web Rules engine we cannot come to the conclusion that our designated *ex:Club100* members from (13) are indeed candidate reviewers. An OWL reasoner, like Pellet [92] or Racer [47], that supports the inference of such a rule engine would allow to infer class membership of, e.g., `http://dblp.l3s.de/d2r/page/authors/Vladimir_Lifschitz` in the *ex:Senior* class and thus making him a *ex:CandidateReviewer* by the following rationale:

1. Each of Vladimir's publications in DBLP would by rule (14) trigger class membership of the respective publication in the class *ex:Publication*.
2. By Vladimir being member of the *ex:Club100* class and the ontology axioms (vii) from Example 2 we know that Vladimir has more than 100 fillers for the property *ex:isAuthorOf*, and thus obviously is also an author of more than 10 papers.
3. Now, class membership for Vladimir in the *ex:Senior* class is established by rule (vi) from Example 2.
4. Finally, rule (15) establishes that Vladimir is indeed a candidate Reviewer.

This inference chain needs both rules and ontological inferences from the OWL ontology.

In the next rule (16), we want to state that for each *ex:Publication* $?X$, which according to our knowledge base is *dcterms:partOf* another entry $?Y$, we can also assert that $?X$ was *ex:publishedIn* $?Y$:

```
Forall ?X ?Y ?P ( ?X[ex:publishedIn -> ?Y] :- And (
                  ?X#ex:Publication ?X[dc:partOf -> ?Y] ) )
```
(16)

Like (15), the above rule can be expressed using DL axioms as part of an ontology, but is far less legible than the simple rule above.

As we already discussed, not all OWL axioms are expressible in Horn rules; on the other hand, also not all rules, even not all Horn rules, are expressible in OWL. Take, for instance, the next rule, which is a variant of the uncle rule in [52]:

```
Forall ?A ?E ( ?A[ex:editedBy -> ?E] :- Exists ?C ( And (
                  ?A[dc:partOf -> ?C] ?C[swrc:editor -> ?E] ) ) )
```
(17)

This rule simply states that every article $?A$ has an editor $?E$, if $?E$ is the editor of $?A$'s collection $?C$. This property is not expressible in OWL alone. One formalism that is capable of expressing it is SWRL, which adds a form of rules to OWL and will be described in section 4.1; this already shows the increase in expressivity obtained by combining rules and ontologies. See also the discussion in [67].

We note at this point that in the general case, a combination of such rules and ontologies poses several problems, such as defining the right semantics or ensuring decidability, in particular for rule systems that allow to take OWL reasoning into account. This is discussed in more detail in Section 5.

3.5   Modules, Context, and Named Graphs

As mentioned in Section 3.2, a flexible rules system should enable access to one or more RDF graphs. However, we did not yet discuss facilities to refer to data coming from different RDF graphs within rules or across several rules. For instance, we could simplify rule (14) from above. Instead of stating that the documents having a *dcterms:bibliographicCitation* count as publications, we could simply say that *all documents listed at DBLP* count as publications. Given that an RDF graph containing all documents listed at DBLP is accessible at the URL http://dblp.l3s.de/d2r/all/ Publications, we could reformulate the rule (14) for extracting *ex:Publication*s as follows:

```
Forall ?X ( ?X#ex:Publication :-
            ?X#foaf:Document @ <http://dblp.l3s.de/d2r/all/Publications> )
```
(18)

Here, we used the '@' symbol to denote the *module* [55,91], or the *context* [78] to which a particular statement belongs. This module mechanism is not (yet) part of the standard RIF syntax; we borrowed this syntax from systems like $\mathcal{F}$lora-2 [55] or Triple [91] for the moment. Often a context is associated with the physical URL where a certain statement can be found, but there are also more general definitions of named RDF Graphs [17], where the graph name or context does not necessarily corresponds to a Web-accessible URL. Note that named graphs are also present in SPARQL via the GRAPH keyword.

3.6   Blank Nodes and Function Symbols

As mentioned in Section 2.1, blank nodes are used in RDF to denote unknown nodes, akin to existential variables in first-order logic. If we want to write rules that create new statements including such blank nodes we run into similar problems as in rule (12), since a rule creating blank nodes boils down to a rule with existential variables in the head. In fact, rule (12) could be viewed as a rule creating a new blank node $\_:X_{?P}$ for each binding for $?P$. Although hardly any rule system supports existentials in rule heads, rule systems which support function symbols can typically work around this by creating new identifiers using a Skolem function (see [13, Section 4.1.5] for details about Skolemization). That is, each existential variable X in the head of a Horn rule can be replaced by a term $f_X(Y_1, \ldots, Y_n)$ using a new function symbol f_X whose parameters are all variables Y_i that have an unbound occurrence inside the scope of the existential variable. For example, the Skolemized version of rule (12) is

```
Forall ?P ( And( ?P#ex:Paper ?P[ ex:publishedIn -> f_X(?P)] )
            :- ?P#Publication )
```
(19)

Here f_X is a fresh function symbol, not occurring elsewhere in the rule set to be processed, and P is its single parameter.

The RIF BLD syntax – and most existing rule systems – do not allow conjunctions but only atomic formulas in the rule head, but following the transformations defined by Lloyd and Topor [62] we can equivalently rewrite rule (19) to two Horn rules as follows:

```
Forall ?P ( ?P#ex:Paper :- ?P#Publication )
Forall ?P ( ?P[ ex:pulishedIn -> f_X(?P)] :- ?P#Publication )
```
(20)

Rule systems supporting complex terms with function symbols (such as for instance all Prolog systems), can use this method to emulate rules such as (12). However, function symbols also cause problems with respect to decidability and termination; many existing rule systems therefore simply disallow them. There exists however a substantial effort for including and implementing function symbols in rule languages under a fully declarative framework, such as the Answer Set semantics [11,15,90].

3.7   Built-in Predicates and Functions

Many rule systems and languages support a range of built-in functions and predicates for string manipulations, arithmetics and alike, up to flexible APIs for adding procedural attachments to rules which allow to implement and invoke arbitrary external functions from rules. By "built-in" functions and predicates we mean here functions and predicates with a fixed, semantics, that is "built in" in the rules system.

An example for a kind of standard list of functions and predicates is provided by the XQuery/XPath Functions and Operators [65] by W3C, which encompass – besides standard arithmetics – a number of useful manipulations for XML and Web data manipulation.

A built-in predicate could for instance be used to extract a substring from a URI. The following variant of rule (18) checks – instead of the data source of a triple – directly its Document URI to determine whether an article corresponds to one listed at DBLP:

```
Forall ?X ?A ( ?X#ex:Publication :- And(
    ?X#foaf:Document
    ?X[ dc:creator-> ?A ]
    fn:startsWith(?X,"http://dblp.l3s.de/d2r/") ) )
```
$$(21)$$

Another example, now for a built-in function, (see [80]) is the mapping from vCard/RDF (`http://www.w3.org/TR/vcard-rdf`) to FOAF. Here we want to combine from vCard the given name and the family name to a `foaf:name` by string concatenation using a built-in function directly in the rule head:

```
Forall ?X ?N ?F ?G ( ?X[ foaf:name -> fn:concat(?F," ",?G) ] :-
    And( ?X [vCard:N -> ?N]
        ?N[ vCard:Given-> ?G ]
        ?N[ vCard:Family-> ?F ] ) )
```
$$(22)$$

Some rules languages do not support built-in functions but only predicates. Note that built-in functions can be "emulated" by respective built-in predicates. For instance, if a rule system doesn't offer the XPath function `fn:concat` directly, but a ternary built-in predicate $CONCAT(X, Y, Z)$ having fixed interpretation such that $CONCAT(x, y, z)$ is true whenever z is the concatenation of strings x and y. Using this, we can emulate rule (22) as follows:

```
Forall ?X ?N ?F ?G ?F1 ?F2 ( ?X[ foaf:name -> ?F2 ] :-
    And( ?X [vCard:N -> ?N]
        ?N[ vCard:Given-> ?G ]
        ?N[ vCard:Family-> ?F ]
        CONCAT(?F," ",?F1)
        CONCAT(?F1,?G,?F2) )
```
$$(23)$$

Furthermore, many rules systems restrict the use of variables in built-in predicates and functions in the sense that variables occurring in built-ins must be *bound*, i.e., they must occur also in some non-built-in body atom. This is similar to the notion of variable safety [98] in Datalog rules.

We note here that some subtle issues arise with introducing built-ins in Semantic Web rules languages. For instance, it is not entirely clear whether a string-function like fn:startsWith in (21) can be applied to an IRI bound to the variable $?A$. That is, it is debatable what it means to convert IRIs – which are actually only a syntactic (and atomic) representation of a constant (an RDF resource in this case), but have no "syntactic" meaning by themselves – to a string. This and other issues which are handled differently in existing rule-based approaches are currently under discussion in the RIF working group.

3.8 Defaults and Negation as Failure

A common extension in many rules languages is negation in rule bodies. For instance, after having established who are conflicting reviewers in rules (5)–(7), one may want to extend rule (15) by stating that candidate reviewers are exactly those senior researchers *not* in conflict:

```
Forall ?P ( ?P#ex:CandidateReviewer :-
            And( ?P#ex:Senior Not( ?P#ex:ConflictingReviewer) ) )
```
(24)

Note that, when integrating data from open sources such as the Web, we have to take care about what "*not* in conflict" means here. Particularly, most rules systems that support rules like (24), would read *Not* there as nonmonotonic or weak negation, or negation as failure. That means, the rule would fire for any $?P$ for whom we could prove that $?P$ is a senior researcher, but we cannot prove that $?P$ is a conflicting reviewer. These rules are called *nonmonotonic*, since additional information might lead to retraction of a previously made inference, e.g., if we add new RDF statements stating that a senior researcher has published papers with one of the authors.

This is different from classical logic, which always behaves monotonically. If we try to formulate rule (24) as an OWL DL axiom, we could write:

$$ex{:}Senior \sqcap \neg ex{:}ConflictingReviewer \sqsubseteq ex{:}CandidateReviewer$$

or in a rule:

```
Forall ?P ( ?P#ex:CandidateReviewer :-
            And( ?P#ex:Senior Neg( ?P#ex:ConflictingReviewer) ) )
```
(25)

However, such a rule would only fire for individuals $?P$ about which we have *explicit* knowledge that they are not conflicting reviewers, which is also sometimes called *strong negation*. Such explicit knowledge about negated facts is typically not available on the Web and, as opposed to rule (25), rule (24) rather expresses a default assumption stating that "unless we know that $?P$ is a conflicting reviewer, we assume that $?P$ is a possible candidate."

3.9 Advanced features: Unstratified Negation, Constraints, and Disjunction

Rules involving negation, as those shown in the previous section, are particularly tricky for rules systems if such negation occurs in recursive rules, i.e., if negative rules depend on each other. Imagine we add the following rule, that states that if some candidate reviewer was not chosen, she is an available reviewer.

```
Forall ?P ( ?P#ex:AvailableReviewer :-
          And( ?P#ex:CandidateReviewer Not( ?P#ex:AssignedReviewer )))
```
(26)

Likewise, one could state it the other way around, i.e., if some candidate reviewer was not available, she is an chosen reviewer.

```
Forall ?P ( ?P#ex:AssignedReviewer :-
          And( ?P#ex:CandidateReviewer Not( ?P#ex:AvailableReviewer )))
```
(27)

Many rules systems, in particular Prolog-based systems have difficulties with rules that involve cyclic (or unstratified, see [13, Section 5.3.1]) negation; for any candidate reviewer, it is not clear which of the two rules should fire: without further discrimination, both rules should fire, but upon firing one, the other should be blocked.

Sections 5.3.2–5.3.5 of [13] illustrate several possible semantics for such unstratified rule sets, including the stable model semantics (now more widely known as answer set semantics) [43] and the well-founded semantics [100]:

- Given a candidate reviewer x who is a *ex:CandidateReviewer*, the stable model semantics would allow for two possible stable models (*answer sets*). In one of them, the fact $x\#ex:AssignedReviewer$ holds, but not $x\#ex:AvailableReviewer$, in the other stable model it is the other way round.
- The well-founded semantics, which is a 3-valued semantics, would take an agnostic view here, with only a single model, but assigning *unknown* as a third truth value to both $x\#ex:AssignedReviewer$ and $x\#ex:AvailableReviewer$.

There are rule systems supporting either of these semantics; we refer to Section 4 below.

We remark here that the multiple-model view of the stable model semantics, as a opposed to a canonical model semantics, can be profitably used for declarative problem solving when multiple solutions exist. The idea is that a problem is represented by a non-monotonic logic program such that its stable models correspond to the solutions of the problem, which then can be computed using a logic programming engine; this paradigm is often referred to as *Answer Set Programming* (ASP). For example, consider in our scenario the problem "give me all possible sets of reviewer assignments." A rule set including both rules (26) and (27) would have exactly these sets as answers (i.e., stable models) under the stable model semantics.

Constraints. Constraints are special rules that have an empty head, and lead to the inference of a contradiction if their body is true. In the multi-model approach of the stable model semantics, constraints are customary to filter out unwanted models which correspond to "wrong" assignments with respect to candidate solutions.

For instance, if we add the constraint

```
Forall ?P1 ?P2 ( :- And( ?P1#ex:AssignedReviewer ?P2#ex:AssignedReviewer
          ?P1 != ?P2 ) )
```
(28)

to the rules (26) and (27), all assignments where two or more reviewers are assigned would be excluded from possible answers. The following rule and constraint guarantee that at least one reviewer is assigned:

```
Forall ?P ( someoneAssigned :- ?P#ex:AssignedReviewer )
:- Not( someoneAssigned )
```
(29)

In combination, the rules (26)–(29) guarantee that exactly one candidate reviewer is assigned. Constraints are supported by several rules systems for the stable model semantics.

Disjunctive Rules. One useful extension are disjunctive rules, i.e., rules which do not only permit atomic formulas in the head but also a disjunction of atoms. Disjunction enables us to write (26) and (27) more concisely in just one rule, which reads very natural:

```
Forall ?P ( Or( ?P#ex:AssignedReviewer
               ?P#ex:AvailableReviewer ) :- ?P#ex:CandidateReviewer )
```
(30)

This disjunction has the following semantics: for each $?P\#ex{:}CandidateReviewer$, either $?P\#ex{:}AssignedReviewer$ is made true or $?P\#ex{:}AvailableReviewer$; this is different from classical logic, according to which we would just know that at least one of the two is true.

Although we used a "RIF style" syntax here, both negation as failure as well as disjunction in rule heads is beyond the current version of RIF BLD. For more details and examples on Answer Set Programming as well as particular rules systems, see [6,13,36].

4   Languages and Systems

In this section, we present languages and tools for reasoning with RDF data. This kind of data will be classified in two categories: RDF(S) and OWL, which have been defined in Section 2.

One important use case for combining rules and ontologies is ontology alignment, or in general data integration from different data sources. In OWL ontologies, you can import additional ontologies using *owl:import* statements, but this feature can be seen as splitting ontologies into partitions rather than integrating ontologies from different sources. RDF(S) has no built-in support for integrating other RDF data; this task is outsourced to SPARQL [82]: to merge different RDF data sources, one can specify every RDF graph in a `from` clause of a SPARQL query. Typically, rule systems can easily reference data from multiple sources and provide even more expressive reasoning support than SPARQL alone.

Several languages and systems exist which support accessing and querying RDF data and allow to combine data sources under several aspects. In the following, we will look into this in more detail and outline the features of prominent languages and systems. We classify the languages into four categories (SWRL, RDF Stores, Logic Programming, and Hybrid Combinations), which should make their flavour more visible. Please note that we can only describe a fragment of available tools, hence the next sections display an inherent incomplete list of rule systems with ontology support.

4.1   SWRL – OWL Reasoners with Rules Support

The *Semantic Web Rules Language* (SWRL) is an ontology language that integrates OWL with a rule layer [52] built on top of it. SWRL's goal of enhancing description logics with rules is aimed at overcoming some known expressive limitation in ontology languages, which can be easily fixed by adding rules to the ontology. The addition of rules is also the main cause why reasoning in SWRL is in general undecidable, but decidable fragments are known, like DL-safe rules [70]. This language is a non-hybrid coupling approach of rules and ontologies; see also Section 5 for fundamental issues of amalgamating rules and ontology reasoning.

SWRL supports a rich set of built-ins inspired by XQuery and XPath2 functions [65]. Since SWRL is an extension of the OWL ontology language, it is restricted to unary and binary DL-predicates. Furthermore, it does not support nonmonotonic inference. Also, combining OWL data from outside ontologies is only possible through *owl:import* constructs.

A SWRL ontology is composed of ordinary OWL axioms and SWRL rules. The rules constitute of antecedents and consequents, which both consist of lists of atoms. Atoms may be OWL class expressions, property definitions, or built-ins.

Usually, SWRL rules are part of an OWL ontology encoded in XML or in abstract syntax. The next example might serve as an illustration for the SWRL abstract syntax, which is just a different way for representing rule (17):

```
Implies( Antecedent( dc:partOf(I-variable(A) I-variable(C))
                     swrc:editor(I-variable(C) I-variable(E)) )
         Consequent( ex:editedBy(I-variable(A) I-variable(E))) )
```

DL reasoners now increasingly support SWRL. For instance, state of the art engines like KAON2[17] and Pellet [92] facilitate the DL-safe fragment of SWRL, while Racer-Pro [47] supports a SWRL-like syntax with a slightly different semantics (for instance, closed world reasoning is supported in RacerPro's variant of SWRL).

4.2 RDF Stores with Rules Support

RDF stores (or triple stores) are frameworks for managing, accessing, and processing RDF data. These kind of systems do not employ standardized languages. Instead, they provide their own proprietary rules implementations. These implementations are not as expressive as SWRL, in favor of manageable computational properties.

In the following, we will briefly show three of the most common proponents of this category and address different aspects on how rules are managed. One of such aspects, mentioned quite often, is the handling of forward- and backward-chaining rules. For instance, the well-known RETE algorithm is the backbone of many forward-chaining systems. Depth-first backtracking traversal of rule sets based on SLD-Resolution [61] is the most widely known representative of backward-chaining algorithms for rule processing, deployed in most Prolog systems.

For a more in-depth explanation of the differences between forward- and backward-chaining, we refer the interested reader to [13].

In the following, we will show how to write some of the rules modelling conflict of interest for reviewers from Example 3 in systems with rule support.

Jena. The Jena[18] Semantic Web framework comes with both forward- and backward-chaining rule support, where the former implementation uses the RETE algorithm, and the latter a standard logic programming style engine. Both engines can be tied together and run in a hybrid mode where rules to be processed in a forward-chaining fashion are syntactically distinguished from those to be processed by backward-chaining.

---

[17] http://kaon2.semanticweb.org/
[18] http://jena.sourceforge.net/

As an example for a rule expressed in Jena's forward-chaining syntax, we show next the translation of rule (5). Recall that this rule expresses that a conflicting reviewer is a person which knows an author of this paper:

```
[ conflict1:
  (http://dblp.13s.de/d2r/page/publications/conf/rweb/EiterIKP08 dc:creator ?A),
  (?A foaf:knows ?P1), (?P1 foaf:name ?N), (?P foaf:name ?N),
  (?P rdf:type foaf:Person)
  ->
  (?P rdf:type ex:ConflictingReviewer) ]
```

In this example, *conflict1* is simply a name for the rule, and the atoms in the antecedent of a rule might be either triple patterns of the form (*Subject Predicate Object*) or built-ins of the form *builtin(Subject Predicate Object)*. The terms in subject, predicate, or object position could be RDF terms in the style of [82] or variables prefixed with a "?" symbol.

Similarly, the above rule could be executed using the backward chaining inference engine. In this reasoning mode, the same rule is just written with the consequent first:

```
[ conflict1back: (?P rdf:type ex:ConflictingReviewer)  <-
  (http://dblp.13s.de/d2r/page/publications/conf/rweb/EiterIKP08 dc:creator ?A),
  (?A foaf:knows ?P1), (?P1 foaf:name ?N), (?P foaf:name ?N),
  (?P rdf:type foaf:Person) ]
```

Jena comes with support for custom rules, i.e., rules which are used to define a semantics using the predefined RDF(S) or OWL semantics.

Sesame/OWLIM. The Sesame[19] project maintains a reasoning and storage framework for querying and persistently storing RDF data. By means of the OWLIM[20] forward-chaining engine, Sesame can be turned into a reasoning platform which supports the ontology languages RDFS, as well as the non-standard OWL fragments OWL DLP [45], and OWL-Horst [96]. OWL DLP is a fragment of OWL DL expressible entirely in function-free Horn rules. The OWL fragment defined by Herman ter Horst (thus sometimes referred to as OWL-Horst) adds more, yet incomplete, support for the fragment of OWL Full translatable to rules.[21]

To give a glimpse on how OWLIM rules look like, we render rule (6) from Section 3, which expresses that a conflicting reviewer is a person who co-authored a paper with an author of the article in question:

```
Id: conflict2
<http://dblp.13s.de/d2r/page/publications/conf/rweb/EiterIKP08> <dc:creator> A
Pub <dc:creator> A
Pub <dc:creator> P1
P1 <foaf:name> N
P <foaf:name> N
P <rdf:type> <foaf:Person>
-------------------------
?P#ex:ConflictingReviewer
```

---

[19] http://www.openrdf.org/

[20] http://www.ontotext.com/owlim/

[21] Different other rule-expressible fragments of OWL exist in the literature, e.g., (i) the *intentional OWL* fragment defined in Jos de Bruijn's thesis [21, Section 9.3] which does a rigid analysis of ter Horst's work and tries to fix some of the problems therein, (ii) the OWL⁻ fragment [25] which is a slight extension of OWL DLP, or (iii) OWLPrime [104] discussed below.

Moreover, OWLIM supports constraints on the variable bindings in each triple, i.e., the user can filter certain matches. Another feature are custom rule-sets (*Axioms*), which allows users of this system to define their own semantics and control the complexity of reasoning.

Oracle 11*g*. The Oracle 11*g* RDF database[22] provides full RDF(S) support and comes with a reasoning engine for a subset of OWL DL, more specifically, OWLPrime [104]. It includes support for forward-chaining rules and extends its SQL dialect with new constructs for querying RDF inside of Oracle's relational DBMS, i.e., it features a rule system built entirely on top of the existing Oracle DBMS infrastructure. Like Jena and Sesame/OWLIM, Oracle 11*g* facilitates adding inference rules on top of the built-in rules for implementing user-defined semantics based on RDF.

For instance, our rule (17) can be defined as new element in the rulebase store of the RDF database:

```
INSERT INTO mdsys.semr_user_rulebase VALUES ('editedby_rule',
 '(?x <http://purl.org/dc/elements/1.1/partOf> ?y)
 (?y <http://swrc.ontoware.org/ontology#editor> ?z)',
NULL, '(?x <http://www.example.org/editedBy> ?z)', null);
```

Getting the extension of the *ex:editedBy* predicate can be done using the following extended SQL query:

```
SELECT s,o FROM table(SEM_MATCH('(?s <http://www.example.org/editedBy> ?o)',
         SEM_MODELS('OWLTST'),
         SEM_RULEBASES('OWLPRIME','USER_RULEBASE'),  null, null ));
```

which retrieves all *ex:editedBy*-related pairs using OWLPrime plus our user-rulebase as entailment regime.

4.3   Logic Programming Engines with RDF Support

Logic programming has a long tradition in rule-based knowledge representation. Here programs are composed of sets of rules in the form of (4). Inferencing with rules is in logic programming is mostly performed using reasoning engines such as backward-chaining Prolog systems. Other systems implementing logic programming paradigms such as Answer Set Programming[6,36] often rely on a forward-chaining Datalog engine underneath.

Among systems following the logic programming spirit, we next present such representatives which at least have support for importing RDF data (from possibly different locations), and thus allow to partially address our use cases outlined above.

Prolog Systems with RDF libraries. SWI-Prolog[23] is a Prolog engine with many features. It can import RDF using the Semantic Web Library [103] for SWI-Prolog and reason about this data using Prolog-style backward chaining. RDFS and query support works by using standard Prolog rules. For example, the fifth axiom in our RDFS axiomatization (see Table 1) can be specified as

```
triple(O, rdf:type, C) :- rdf(S, P, O), rdf(P, rdfs:range, C).
```

---

[22] http://www.oracle.com/technology/tech/semantic_technologies/
[23] http://www.swi-prolog.org/

As any common Prolog system, SWI Prolog only supports stratified negation as failure, denoted in Prolog by '\+'.

Rule (24) could (assuming all the relevant data is in the graph data.rdf) be expressed in SWI-Prolog as follows.

```
triple(P, rdf:type, ex:CandidateReviewer) :-
                    rdf(P, rdf:type, ex:Senior),
                    \+ (rdf( P, rdf:type, ex:ConflictingReviewer)).
?- rdf_assert(S,P,O), triple(S,P,O).
```

ℱLORA-2. The ℱLORA-2 system is an F-Logic reasoner with built-in support for RDF(S).[24] Negation as failure is supported under well-founded semantics. ℱLORA-2 is implemented on top of the XSB Prolog engine.[25] Reconsidering the fifth axiom in our RDFS axiomatization (Table 1), it can be specified as

```
?O[rdf:type -> ?C] :- ?S[?P -> ?O], ?P[rdfs:range -> ?C].
```

which is very close to RIF's presentation syntax. Note that also the KAON2 system mentioned above has limited support for F-Logic.

cwm. Finally, an example for a rule-based RDF engine in spirit of logic programming is cwm.[26] It is built for *Notation3* (N3),[27] which is an RDF notation enhanced with support for modelling formulae and rules. An example is our rule (7), which can be expressed in N3 as

```
@forAll P, A, P1, N .
{ <http://dblp.l3s.de/d2r/page/publications/conf/rweb/EiterIKP08> dc:creator A .
  Pub dc:creator A .
  Pub dcterms:partOf ConfOrJournal .
  Pub1 dcterms:partOf ConfOrJournal .
  Pub1 dc:creator P1 .
  P1 foaf:name N .
  P foaf:name N .
  P rdf:type foaf:Person .
  } log:implies { P rdf:type ex:ConflictingReviewer } .
```

N3 is based on a proprietary forward-chaining engine implemented in Python. It also supports also a rich set of built-ins. Interestingly, N3/cwm also support for stratified negation as failure with the log:notIncludes directive. Rule (24) could (assuming all the relevant data is in the graph data.rdf) be expressed in N3 as follows.

```
@forAll :P.
{ <data.rdf>.log:semantics.log:conclusion
          log:notIncludes { :P a ex:ConflictingReviewer };
          log:includes    { :P a ex:Senior.  } }
     log:implies {:P a ex:CandidateReviewer}.
```

4.4   Systems for Hybrid Combinations

In anticipation of Section 6, we show here systems which apply some of the more complex approaches to combine rules and ontologies introduced there. These systems

---

[24] http://flora.sourceforge.net/
[25] http://xsb.sourceforge.net/
[26] http://www.w3.org/2000/10/swap/doc/cwm.html
[27] http://www.w3.org/DesignIssues/Notation3

are typically very expressive, and combine full DL reasoning with some form of logic programming.

Hybrid Rules. HD-rules,[28] which realizes *Hybrid rules under well founded semantics* as defined in [31,30]. The system is implemented using XSB[29] and a DL reasoner of choice capable of handling the DIG format.

dl-Programs. The software prototype NLP-DL[30] implements dl-programs as described in [35,40,41], under stable model and well-founded semantics, by integrating the ASP reasoner DLV [58] and RACER [47]. An example is given in the next section, and further details will be shown in Section 6.1.

HEX-programs. HEX-programs, proposed in [38,39], are an extension of nonmonotonic logic programs under the answer set semantics [43] with support for higher-order and external atoms. External atoms are a very generic form of built-ins. They generalize the semantics of dl-programs by providing a special notion of *external atom* which enables access to DL reasoners and, above that, ensures the possibility of integrating generic external software modules.

dlvhex[31] is an implementation of a large fragment of HEX-programs. It has been used for a variety of applications such as ontology merging, bio-ontologies, e-government, web querying, and policy management.

HEX-programs combine many approaches into a single extensible language for RDF and DL reasoning, among others. Remarkably, external atoms allow a bidirectional data flow between external sources and HEX-programs, i.e., inferences can be fed as input to the outside data source.

An example for RDF support is the rdf external atom of dlvhex, which is of the form $\&rdf[U](S, P, O)$. Through such an atom, RDF triples (S, P, O) from URL U can be accessed:

```
triple(S,P,O) :- &rdf[<http://...>](S,P,O).
triple(S,"rdf:type","ex:ConflictingReviewer") :-
    triple("http://dblp.l3s.de/d2r/page/publications/conf/rweb/EiterIKP08",
           "dc:creator:, A),
    triple(Pub, "dc:creator", A), triple(Pub, "dc:creator", P1),
    triple(P1, "foaf:name", N), triple(P, "foaf:name", N),
    triple(P, "rdf:type", "foaf:Person").
```

By the notion of DL external atoms, HEX-programs are able to query external description logics reasoners; the dlvhex system is able to accommodate dl-atoms in the style of Section 6.1, which give a more concise syntax:

```
publishedIn(X,Y) :- DL[ex:Publication](X), DL[dc:partOf](X,Y).
```

Table 4 summarizes features of the previously introduced rules languages. As we focus here on Semantic Web rule languages, it is no wonder that almost all support RDF(S), and those systems, which do not have support for this language, have OWL

---

[28] http://www.ida.liu.se/hswrl/

[29] http://xsb.sourceforge.net/

[30] http://www.kr.tuwien.ac.at/research/systems/semweblp/

[31] http://www.kr.tuwien.ac.at/research/systems/dlvhex/

Table 4. Overview of rule systems features

System (Language)	RDF(S)	OWL	Modules	Functions	Built-ins	HO	Constraints	NAF	V
cwm (N3)	+	−	−	−	+	−	−	+	−
dlvhex (HEX)	+	+	−	−	+	+	+	+	+
$\mathcal{F}$LORA-2 (F-Logic)	+	−	+	+	+	+	−	+	−
HD-rules (Hybrid rules)	−	+	−	+	−	−	−	+	−
Jena (Jena Rules)	+	+	−	−	+	−	−	−	−
KAON2 (SWRL)	+	+	−	−	+	−	−	−	+
NLP-DL (dl-programs)	−	+	−	−	−	−	+	+	−
Oracle 11g (OWLPrime)	+	+~	−	−	+	−	−	−	−
OWLIM (OWL Horst)	+	+~	−	−	−	−	−	−	−
Pellet (SWRL)	+	+	−	−	−	−	−	−	−
RacerPro (SWRL)	+	+	−	−	+	−	−	−	−
SWI-Prolog (RDF(S))	+	−	+	+	+	−	−	+	−

Legenda: HO = Higher Order predicates, + = yes, − = no, +~ = yes, with some proviso

support instead. The OWL column shows then which systems promote the description logics part of OWL, i.e., OWL Lite and OWL DL; we did not consider OWL Full systems. The next column reveals tools with module support, which can be found in $\mathcal{F}$LORA-2 and SWI-Prolog. Similarly, function symbols are only present in those two systems and HD-rules, since they are based on Prolog engines. In contrast, built-in predicates or functions are not available in OWLIM and Pellet. Typically, all built-in-aware systems provide an API, which allows the system users to specify their own built-ins, but only dlvhex provides a declarative semantics for this feature. Higher-order predicates (HO), that is the possibility of making a variable quantify over predicate names, are only supported in two systems, whereas dlvhex and NLP-DL are the only engines with constraint rules. As shown in Table 4, support for (unstratified) negation as failure (NAF) is typical for descendants of logic programming systems and hybrid combination approaches. Our last category, disjunctive rules, are only present in dlvhex and KAON2 due to their heritage of disjunctive Datalog.

5   Combining Rules with Ontologies

Whereas we focused on practical features and implemented systems so far, in this section we examine the general issues that come up when combining logic-programming based (nonmonotonic) rules and (monotonic) ontology languages from a more theoretical perspective. After discussing the semantic discrepancies which are the source of difficulties when integrating logic programs with FOL – namely the Description Logics fragment corresponding to OWL DL – we classify the integration approaches in three categories. Eventually, we will present some representative approaches for each category in more detail.

5.1   The Issue of Combining Rules with Description Logics

The combination and extension of terminological concepts defined in a DL theory by means of rules is nowadays acknowledged as an important tool enriching knowledge representation capabilities of traditional ontology languages such as OWL. As a prototypical example, one cannot define the role *uncleOf*, given the roles *brotherOf* and *fatherOf* in OWL DL (see e.g. [52]). OWL DL does not feature a role composition construct or, more generally, a mechanism for defining axiomatic rules. Such aspects are covered by extensions of OWL DL: for instance OWL2, based on $\mathcal{SROIQ}$, adds the possibility of constructing roles by composition, while SWRL adds the possibility to declare arbitrary Horn clauses, which however leads to undecidability of crucial reasoning tasks such as subsumption in OWL. More troubles arise when rules governed by nonmonotonic semantics should be introduced in a monotonic context, like a description logic knowledge base [22].

As well-known, the core of logic programming, i.e., definite positive programs (positive Datalog programs), has a direct correspondence with the Horn subset of classical FOL. To wit, a rule of the form

$$a_1 \vee \cdots \vee a_l \leftarrow b_1, \ldots, b_k, not\, b_{k+1}, \ldots, not\, b_m, \tag{31}$$

which is definite (i.e., when $l = 1$) and *not*-free (i.e., when $m = k$) can be read as a first-order sentence

$$(\forall)\, b_1 \wedge \ldots \wedge b_k \supset a_1 \tag{32}$$

where $(\forall)$ denotes the universal quantification of all variables. This subset of FOL allows for a sound and complete decision procedure for entailment of ground atomic formulae.

Several attempts to embrace such definite rules within a homogeneous (which can be classified as *non-hybrid coupling*) semantic framework based on classical first-order semantics have been made; most noticeable is SWRL, which is submitted to the W3C (see Section 4.1 and [52]). SWRL embeds rules and terminological knowledge bases under the same first-order semantics, but is restricted to (monotonic) Horn rules. This approach has a smooth and homogeneous semantics, but still suffers from undecidability problems; this can be addressed by introducing appropriate syntactic restrictions to the rules, such as *DL-safety* [70]. DL-safe Horn rules can be combined with Description Logics still retaining decidability.

Among non-hybrid approaches, also DLP [45] is noticeable. DLP, in contrast to SWRL, restricts the syntax of the supported OWL DL fragment to those axioms expressible in Horn rules, while allowing arbitrary Horn rules to be added while still staying within the Horn fragment.

As opposed to these non-hybrid approaches we will now mainly concentrate on the possibility of combining nonmonotonic rule sets under traditional logic programming semantics with a (monotonic) Description Logics knowledge base, which we refer to as the so-called *hybrid approaches*.

While equivalence theorems between Horn Clausal Logic and function-free positive Datalog under minimal model semantics are well known traditional results, the latter diverts crucially as soon as nonmonotonic constructs are introduced. Hybrid approaches have thus to take the great semantic and philosophical differences among the two worlds into account.

We will in the following denote a *hybrid knowledge base* $\mathcal{KB} = \langle T, P \rangle$ as the combination of:

– A first-order theory T (the *classical component*), expressed in a FO language with signature Σ_T; and
– A logic program P (the *rules component*), formulated with a signature Σ_P.

The combined signature of $\mathcal{KB}$ is $\Sigma_{\mathcal{KB}} = \Sigma_T \cup \Sigma_P$. Predicates in Σ_T (resp. Σ_P) are termed *classical (resp. rule) predicates*.

5.2 Logic Programming Versus First-Order Logic

We summarize next some of the crucial differences among logic programming (into which ASP [43] and Frame Logic under nonmonotonic semantics [56] fall), and Classical Logic (into which OWL DL and, in general, Description Logics, fall).

Closed vs. Open World Assumption and single vs. multiple models. A logic program is seen as a description of a single world, over which knowledge is complete. Incomplete knowledge about a proposition is simply resolved by turning it into falsity. Indeed, logic programming embraces Reiter's *Closed World Assumption* (CWA) [83]: If a theory T does not logically entail a ground atom A, then conclude $\neg A$.

On the other hand, a set of FOL sentences (or DL axioms) is intended as a description of possible worlds (interpretation), in which all the sentences must hold. Conclusions about propositions which cannot be proven to be true in all the possible worlds are kept open. Under *Open World Assumption* (OWA) incomplete information is treated agnostically (i.e., under a theory T it might be that neither $T \models A$ nor $T \not\models A$ holds for a proposition A).

The OWA is often reasonable in the Semantic Web context. However, taking the agnostic stance of OWA may be not helpful for drawing rational conclusions under incomplete information. Indeed, one can see the Web as a set of knowledge sources. A locally scoped closed world assumption might be preferred when, for instance, one has complete knowledge over a given source. In such cases a mix of CWA and OWA may be appropriate, cf. [20,79].

It is worth noting that the issue of OWA vs. CWA is strictly related, but not equivalent, to the multiple models approach taken in FOL versus the single model approach taken in logic programming. Indeed, Answer Set Programming is a representative of a logic programming paradigm where the closed world assumption is combined with the possibility to control the modelling of multiple worlds. Also, there are fragments of first-order which can be seen as the description of a single, canonical model (e.g., Horn logic or DL-Lite [16]).

Negation as failure vs. classical negation. *Negation as failure (NAF)* is the traditional operator for inferring negative knowledge from incomplete information, and is peculiar of logic programming. The behavior of NAF compared the classical negation is noticeably different. For instance, consider the logic program

$$P: \quad person(X) \leftarrow author(X).$$
$$nonAuthor(X) \leftarrow not\ author(X).$$
$$person(joe\_doe).$$

From P, we can conclude the fact $nonAuthor(joe\_doe)$. Now consider the first-order counterpart of P:

$$\mathcal{T}: \quad \forall X.\,(Author(X) \supset Person(X)) \wedge$$
$$\forall X.\,(\neg Author(X) \supset NonAuthor(X)) \wedge$$
$$Person(joe\_doe).$$

From $\mathcal{T}$, we cannot conclude $NonAuthor(joe\_doe)$.

Strong negation vs. classical negation. Several logic programming formalisms feature the possibility to avoid negation as failure and use the so-called *strong negation*. For instance, the seminal paper about Answer Set Programming [43] introduces a language comprising both negation as failure and strong negation. Strong negation is often seen as a "surrogate" of classic negation, but it must not be mispelled as equivalent to the latter, due to some crucial semantic differences.

For instance, given the logic program

$$P: person(X) \leftarrow author(X).$$
$$-person(joe\_doe).$$

where "$-$" is used for denoting strong negation, we cannot $-auther(joe\_doe)$ from P; on the other hand, from the corresponding first-order theory:

$$\mathcal{T}: \forall X.\,(Author(X) \supset Person(X)) \wedge$$
$$\neg Person(joe\_doe).$$

we can conclude $\neg Author(joe\_doe)$ from $\mathcal{T}$.

This discrepancy can be traced to the different setting in which the two types of negation live: strong negation can be seen as negation under OWA but in a single model setting. In a single model (in the sense of logic programming) knowledge about strongly negated atoms might be incomplete. For instance, it might be that in a stable model M neither an atomic proposition A nor its strong negation $-A$ is known (i.e., evaluates to true).

On the other hand, classical negation inherits its behavior from a scenario where the OWA is obtained by quantifying the truth of possible answers over multiple interpretations. The uncertainty of an assertion A is given by the fact that there might be interpretations in which A holds, and others in which A is false. In a single first-order interpretation, classical negation is interpreted under a complete knowledge assumption, and thus either A or $\neg A$ evaluates to true.

However, like in the example above, FOL semantics allows to determine that there is no interpretation in which $Author(joe\_doe)$ can hold, hence we can infer that $\mathcal{T} \models \neg Author(joe\_doe)$, while the same conclusion does not hold using strong negation in a logic programming setting. Note that adding to P the rule

$$-author(X) \leftarrow -person(X).$$

is in general not enough to enforce a similar behavior, since logic programming lacks the *tertium non datur* property for strong negation; to enforce it, a rule $-p(X) \vee p(X) \leftarrow$ for every predicate p would need to be added.

Treatment of equality. Logic programming formalisms, including ASP, typically employ a Unique Name Assumption (UNA), i.e., different ground terms denote different objects, and do not support real equality reasoning, i.e., the possibility to infer knowledge about (in)equality of names. This does not comply necessarily with the view in classical logic, and thus with RDF and OWL, where no such assumption is made. While equality "$=$" and inequality "$\neq$" predicates are allowed in rule bodies, they represent syntactic equality and (default) negation thereof only. This shall not be confused with OWL's `owl:sameAs` and `owl:differentFrom` directives. Following up the example from Section 2.2, consider the following rule base:

$knowsOtherPeople(X) \leftarrow knows(X, Y), X \neq Y;$
$knows(\text{``}\mathtt{http://polleres.net/foaf.rdf\#me}\text{''},$
        $\text{``}\mathtt{http://www.polleres.net/foaf.rdf\#me}\text{''}).$

Under standard ASP semantics, "$\neq$" amounts to "$not =$". Hence,

$knowsOtherPeople(\text{``}\mathtt{http://polleres.net/foaf.rdf\#me}\text{''})$

would be entailed, while the same would not hold in similarly modelled OWL knowledge bases. Enabling reasoning with equality has usually a very high computational cost. Indeed, common DL reasoners like FACT++ [97] or RACER [47] also do not support full equality reasoning and nominals.

Existential quantification. The inability of expressing existence of individuals in logic programming is also matter of semantic discrepancy. Consider the theory

$$\mathcal{T} : \forall X \exists Y. (Person(X) \supset hasNationality(X, Y))$$

which, in DL Syntax, is equivalent to $Person \sqsubseteq \exists hasNationality$. This can be rendered as an equi-satisfiable Horn clause, by skolemizing the Y in the head (see above):

$$\mathcal{T} : \forall X. (Person(X) \supset hasNationality(X, f_Y(X)))$$

This clause can be rendered as a rule in logic programming, but not in standard Datalog, where function symbols are not allowed. However, most implemented systems can not actually evaluate a logic program equivalent to the clause above, since corresponding models are infinite. Elimination of functions symbols from logic programs or their evaluation in a decidable setting is indeed matter of continuous research (see, e.g., [11,7,90] and references therein).

Decidability. Finally, the probably largest obstacle towards combining the description logics world of OWL and the logic-programming world stems from the fact that these two worlds face undecidability issues from two completely different angles.

Indeed, decidability of logic programming (and in particular of its answer set programming dialects) follows from the fact that it is based on function-free Horn logic

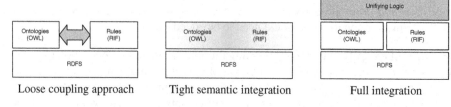

Fig. 7. Different combination categories for rules and ontologies

where ground entailment can be determined by checking finite subsets of the Herbrand base, i.e., decidability and termination of evaluation strategies is guaranteed by the finiteness of the domain. However, this is not so for description logics. Decidability of reasoning tasks such as satisfiability, class subsumption, or class membership in description logics is often strictly dependent on the combination of constructs which are allowed in the terminological language, living in a infinite domain.

For description logics, it is often possible to prove decidability of reasoning by means of the so called *tree-model property*. This property expresses that a DL knowledge base has a model iff it has a (possibly infinite) tree shaped model whose branching factor is bounded by the size of the knowledge base [4], such that the model gets, loosely speaking, repetitive after a finite number of steps. It is worth noting, however, that the DL $\mathcal{SHOIN}$ has not the tree-model property, and also not the finite-model property [53].

Unfortunately, it is difficult to combine two decidable fragments coming from the two worlds. As shown already in [59], the naive combination of even a very simple DL with an arbitrary Horn logic program is undecidable. Levy & Rousset [59] highlighted recursion and *unsafety* of rules as culprits for undecidability, and suggested *role-safety* as a remedy: at least one of variables X, Y in a role atom $R(X, Y)$ in a rule r must occur in a rule predicate in r that does not occur in any rule head of the program. As we will see later, most of the hybrid approaches indeed provide a notion of safety as a key tool for ensuring decidability.

5.3   Taxonomy of Hybrid Approaches

We can group hybrid rule formalisms into three main categories:

- Loose coupling (strict semantic separation);
- Tight integration; and
- Full integration.

We summarize next the peculiarities of the three categories. The reader can find further interesting material and discussion in [3,22,72,88].

Loose coupling. Languages that are classified under the loose coupling category are denoted by a high level of semantic separation between P and $\mathcal{T}$.

Roughly speaking, the rule base P and the first-order theory $\mathcal{T}$ are treated as separate and independent components. An interface mechanism is then defined that allows the exchange of knowledge between the two sides. The particular design of the interfacing mechanism (*safe interfacing*) guarantees decidability of the combined knowledge base, although the flow of knowledge between the two sides is restricted, and in some cases, unidirectional (e.g., the rules component can import data from the classical component, but not vice versa). In important note is that loose coupling approaches are better suited for practical implementation on top of existing reasoners for the two sides.

As representatives of loose coupling frameworks, we mention nonmonotonic dl-programs [35,40], defeasible logic coupled with description logic bases [102], and probabilistic dl-programs [63].

Tight semantic integration. With respect to loose coupling approaches, formalisms categorized under the tight semantic integration scenario tend to integrate FOL statements with the logic program to a larger extent, while keeping the vocabularies of the first-order predicates and the logic programming predicates distinct.

In general, a tightly integrated language is built on the notion of an integrated model which satisfies both the rules part P and the first-order part T of the knowledge base. Such a model can be often seen as $M = (M_o, M_l)$, that is, it is composed of two separate models M_o and M_l that share the same domain. M_o should satisfy the first-order theory, while M_l should satisfy the corresponding program. Depending on the semantics of the language at hand, there are different ways to define "agreement" of M_o and M_l on the overall knowledge base, thus defining a "safe interaction" method between the two worlds; see, e.g., [22] for more discussion. Representative of this category are CARIN [59], r-hybrid KBs, r^+-hybrid KBs, and $\mathcal{DL}+log$ [85,86,87,89].

Full integration. Full integration approaches are mostly distinct by the absence of separation between the two vocabularies at hand: the two universes are treated to a large extent in a homogeneous way; this, however, does not exclude to ascribe a certain intended role to a particular predicate (to be a rule predicate, or a classical predicate), which has to be done by proper axiomatization within the formalism.

Representative examples are Hybrid MKNF knowledge bases [69], first-order Autoepistemic Logic [23] and Open Answer Set Programs [49]. Terminological Default Logic [5], and Description Logics of Minimal Knowledge [29] can be viewed as related precursors.

In their work on g-hybrid knowledge bases [50], Heymans et al. show that actually tight integration approaches, such as r-hybrid KBs [86] from above, can partially be embedded into the above-mentioned Open Answer Set Programs. Likewise, in [24] de Bruijn et al. show that a non-classical logic can embrace several tight-coupling approaches by an elegant embedding into Quantified Equilibrium Logic [74,75]. These two proposed approaches can be seen as frameworks unifying classical logic with disjunctive logic programs under *open* answer set programming in a common logical framework and thus may – despite keeping up the separation between classical and rules predicates – be viewed among the full integration approaches.

6   Sample Combination Approaches

In this section, we briefly review some concrete approaches for combining rules and ontologies that were mentioned in the previous section, one representative for each of the general kinds of integration, viz. non-monotonic dl-programs as an example for loose coupling, [33,34], $\mathcal{DL}+log$ [89], as an example for tight coupling, and Hybrid MKNF knowledge bases [69] as an example for full integration. After that, we compare these approaches in Section 6.4 with respect to several criteria.

6.1   Loose Coupling: Non-monotonic dl-Programs

dl-programs extend (function-free) answer set programs with *queries to DL knowledge bases* through dl-*atoms* [35,40], which may be tuned to allow to query a DL knowledge base in different ways. How the DL knowledge base and the logic program are matched is under control of the knowledge designer.

The actual implementation combines a DL engine and an ASP solver, whose interaction is clearly separated. The two sides can transfer knowledge bidirectionally through dl-atoms, which serves as an interface. The basic idea of dl-atoms is to provide a means for posing queries to the DL base $\mathcal{T}$ from the program P, by exploiting the native query facilities of the DL engine. In the course of this, also knowledge can flow from P to $\mathcal{T}$.

More in detail, a query Q can be a concept/role instance $C(X)/R(X,Y)$, or a subsumption $C \sqsubseteq D$. When submitting a query, a dl-atom allows to modify the extensional part (ABox) of $\mathcal{T}$, by adding positive ($\uplus$) or negative ($\cup\!\!\!-$) assertions that are computed by the logic program P.[32] The dl-atom evaluates to true iff the modified $\mathcal{T}$ proves Q.

For example, the dl-atom $DL[Wine]("ChiantiClassico")$ asks whether it holds that $\mathcal{T} \models Wine("ChiantiClassico")$; a dl-atom with a variable, $DL[Wine](X)$ evaluated to true for all the known individual x such that $\mathcal{T} \models Wine(x)$ holds.

The atom $DL[RedWine \uplus my\_red; Wine](X)$ adds all assertions $RedWine(c)$ to $\mathcal{T}$, such that $my\_red(c)$ holds in the logic program P, while $DL[RedWine \cup\!\!\!- my\_white; hasColor](X, "Red")$ adds all assertions $\neg RedWine(c)$ to $\mathcal{T}$ such that $my\_white(c)$ holds in P. In both cases, the resulting theory $\mathcal{T}'$ is used for the query entailment test.

More formally, a *dl-program* [35,40] is a pair $(\mathcal{T}, P)$ where P consists of rules of the form (31) where $l = 1$ and based on a function-free first order language, each a_i is a classical literal and each b_j is either a classical literal or a dl-atom; an extension allowing arbitrary $l \geq 0$ (and thus also disjunctive rules) has been considered in [37].

Answer sets of a dl-program $(\mathcal{T}, P)$ are defined via grounding all the rules in P with a set of constants C, where C contains the constants in P and additional constants from $\mathcal{T}$; by default, these additional constants are all the constants in $\mathcal{T}$, but they may also be designated (see [35]). A *model* is a consistent set of classical ground literals M built from the predicates in P and the constants in C. A ground dl-atom $DL[\langle Add\rangle; Q](\mathbf{c})$ is true in M, iff $\mathcal{T} \cup \langle Add\rangle^M \models Q(\mathbf{c})$. Note that $\langle Add\rangle^M$ is dependent on M; this enables a knowledge flow from P to $\mathcal{T}$.

A model M is called a *strong answer set* of $(\mathcal{T}, P)$, if it is the least model of sP^M, which is akin to the famous Gelfond-Lifschitz reduct P^M of an ordinary logic program with respect to M [43]. It generalizes P^M by handling dl-atoms, which are treated like ordinary atoms. That is, sP^M contains all rules obtained from the grounding of P by

---

[32] Other modifications have been conceived, which we for simplicity disregard here. They lead to non-monotonic dl-atoms, i.e., queries to $\mathcal{T}'$ that can have non-monotonic behavior, which require special treatment.

- Removing all rule instances r of form (31) such that for some b_j, where $j \in \{k + 1, \ldots, m\}$, it holds that b_j is true in M (which for a classical literal b_j means $b_j \in M$), and
- Removing all negation-as-failure literals $not\ b_j$ from the remaining rules.

In case of a dl-program with arbitrary rule heads ($l \geq 0$), in the above definition by "the least model" is replaced "a minimal model."

dl-programs are decidable, provided that evaluating dl-atoms over $\mathcal{T}$ is decidable; in particular, they are NEXP-complete for $\mathcal{T} \in \mathcal{SHIF}(\mathbf{D})$ and $\mathrm{P}^{\mathrm{NEXP}}$-complete for $\mathcal{T} \in \mathcal{SHOIN}(\mathbf{D})$ [35,40].

As an example dl-program, consider a scenario where a computer network is encoded in an OWL DL knowledge base $\mathcal{T}''$, through the concept *Node* and the role *wiredTo*. Imagine now that some new node x must be added to $\mathcal{T}''$, and it must be decided to which existing node x should be connected to. When choosing new connections, nodes belonging to the concept *HighTrafficNode* should be avoided. High traffic nodes could be restricted in a way such that, e.g., $HighTrafficNode \sqsubseteq \geqslant k\ wired$, for some threshold value k. Thus connecting new nodes might trigger new high traffic nodes. This kind of interplay between the two sides of knowledge can be modelled with the following program:

$$connect(X, Y) \leftarrow newNode(X), DL[Node](Y), not\ overloaded(Y).$$

$$overloaded(X) \leftarrow DL[wired \uplus connect; HighTrafficNode](X).$$

The usage of dl-programs facilitates several advanced reasoning tasks: appropriate encodings allow to emulate CWA and *Extended CWA (ECWA)* [44] on top of a DL knowledge base. Similarly, dl-programs can incorporate Poole's-style [81] and a restricted fragment of Reiter's Default Logic [84] over DL bases. We show next how to emulate default reasoning and ECWA in dl-programs. The reader may refer to [35] for an extensive description of applications of dl-programs.

Default Reasoning. Reconsider the candidate reviewer selection scenario in Section 3.8, and suppose we have the following small knowledge base:

$$\mathcal{T} = \{\ \neg ex{:}ConflictingReviewer \sqsubseteq ex{:}CandidateReviewer,$$
$$ex{:}Senior(joe),\ ex{:}Senior(bob),\ ex{:}ConflictingReviewer(bob)\ \}.$$

The rule that a senior author is a candidate reviewer by default (unless a conflict is apparent), can be mimicked by the following dl-program:

$r_1 : cand\_rev(P) \leftarrow DL[ex{:}Senior](P), not\ conflict(P);$

$r_2 : \quad conflict(P) \leftarrow DL[ex{:}CandidateReviewer \uplus cand\_rev; ex{:}ConflictingReviewer](P).$

Roughly speaking, r_1 encodes the fact that a senior author should be considered as a canidate reviewer, unless a conflict can be proven. Under Answer Set Semantics, r_2 effects maximal application of r_1 over $\mathcal{T}$. The single answer set M will thus be as follows:

$$\{\ cand\_rev(joe),\ conflict(bob)\ \}.$$

Minimal Models and ECWA. If one considers a DL base with disjunctive information, such as:

$$\mathcal{T} = \{\; Publication(p1), \quad Publication \equiv Journal\_Pub \sqcup Conference\_Pub \;\}$$

one can consider the goal of maximizing negative information (thus, minimizing positive knowledge) without raising inconsistency. The program shown next singles out "minimal" models, in the setting of Extended CWA (ECWA):

$$\overline{j\_pub}(X) \;\leftarrow\; not\; j\_pub(X).$$
$$\overline{c\_pub}(X) \;\leftarrow\; not\; c\_pub(X).$$
$$j\_pub(X) \;\leftarrow\; DL[Journal\_Pub \uplus \overline{j\_pub}, Conference\_Pub \uplus \overline{c\_pub}; Journal\_Pub](X).$$
$$c\_pub(X) \;\leftarrow\; DL[Journal\_Pub \uplus \overline{j\_pub}, Conference\_Pub \uplus \overline{c\_pub}; Conference\_Pub](X).$$

In simple terms, the first two rules effect CWA on the concepts of journal and conference publication. The last two rules maximally propagate inferred negative information to $\mathcal{T}$. The answer sets, corresponding to minimal models, of the above program are:

$$M_1 = \{j\_pub(p1), \overline{c\_pub}(p1)\},$$
$$M_2 = \{c\_pub(p1), \overline{j\_pub}(p1)\}.$$

The same encoding structure can be extended to select those concept to be kept "fixed" as in the general ECWA setting.

In [35], also *weak answer sets* have been introduced, which are defined like strong answer sets with the only difference that in building the reduct, besides the *not*-literals, also dl-atoms b_j that are not under *not* are "evaluated" for rule and literal elimination. However, in contrast to strong answer sets, weak answer sets are not guaranteed to be minimal, in the sense that a weak answer set may contain some other weak answer set properly; intituively, they are less "grounded" than strong answer sets. Furthermore, dl-programs have been recently extended to support also (union of) conjunctive queries over the DL base [33,34].

6.2   Tight Integration: $\mathcal{DL}+log$

$\mathcal{DL}+log$ [89] is the latest in a chain of extensions of the DL $\mathcal{ALC}$ with rules such as $\mathcal{AL}$-*log*, r- and r$^+$-hybrid knowledge bases. The key semantic choices of $\mathcal{DL}+log$ can be summarized as follows:

(a) A distinction between rule-predicates and classical predicates.

(b) a fixed, countably infinite domain, whose elements e can be accessed in all interpretations with distinguished constant c_e in a one-to-one correspondence; this is called the *Standard Names Assumption* (note that this implies the UNA, and that interpretations are isomorphic to Herbrand interpretations in absence of function symbols).

(c) Models (called *NM-models*) of $\mathcal{KB} = \langle \mathcal{T}, P \rangle$ are of form $\mathcal{I} \cup M$, where $\mathcal{I}$ is a model of the classical predicates, M of the rules-predicates, after deletion of classical atoms satisfied by $\mathcal{I}$ in P.

(d) The language has no strong negation, and weak negation is limited to rules-predicates, but classical predicates can appear in rules heads; function symbols are not considered.

(e) To ensure decidability, *weak (DL-)safety* is used: each variable X in a rule r must occur in some positive body atom of r, and this atom must have a rule predicate if X occurs in an atom with classical predicate in the head of r.

Note that weak safety allows to access unnamed individuals in classical atoms. For instance, take $\mathcal{KB} = \langle \mathcal{T}, P \rangle$, where $\mathcal{T} = \{author \sqsubseteq \exists isAuthorOf, author(turing)\}$ and P consists of the weakly DL-safe rule:

$$scientist(X) \leftarrow isAuthorOf(X, Y), not\ likes(X, astrology);$$

Here *isAuthorOf* is a classical predicate and *scientist* and *likes* are rule predicates. The variable Y, which does not occur in any atom with a rule predicate, can access also unknown individuals. We have $\mathcal{KB} = \langle \mathcal{T}, P \rangle \models_{NM} scientist(turing)$ as intuitively expected, although Y can not be instantiated and might vary from interpretation to interpretation. The same rule expressed as a dl-program would look like

$$scientist(X) \leftarrow DL[isAuthorOf](X, Y), not\ likes(X, astrology)$$

which does not entail *scientist(turing)*. However, the remodeled dl-program

$$scientist(X) \leftarrow DL[\exists isAuthorOf](X), not\ likes(X, astrology);$$

yields the expected answer; using the extended syntax proposed in [33,34] (allowing also conjunctive queries), this dl-atoms can be expressed as $DL[father(X, Y)](X)$.

The stable model (or answer set) semantics of $\mathcal{DL}+log$ is conceived in a 2-step reduction.

- In the first step, an interpretation $\mathcal{I}$ of the classical predicates is taken. Then P is grounded and "reduced" with respect to $\mathcal{I}$, by "evaluating" and eliminating classical atoms from rules (that is, classical atoms satisfied in $\mathcal{I}$ and appearing in bodies are eliminated, classical atoms not satisfied in $\mathcal{I}$ and appearing in heads are eliminated, rules which have falsified body and/or true head are eliminated). The resulting ground program $P_{\mathcal{I}}$ contains no classical predicates.
- In the second step, we define M as a stable model of $P_{\mathcal{I}}$ as usual.

The $\mathcal{DL}+log$ formalism is decidable, if containment between union of conjunctive queries is decidable in $\mathcal{T}$.

For an example, consider the following $\mathcal{KB} = \langle \mathcal{T}, P \rangle$:

$$\mathcal{T} = \{\ Multilingual \sqsubseteq \neg Monolingual;$$
$$Multilingual \sqcup Monolingual \sqsubseteq Author;$$
$$Author \sqsubseteq \exists isAuthorOf;\ Author(joey)\ \}$$
$$P = \{novelist(X) \lor scientist(X) \leftarrow writer(X);$$
$$Monolingual(X) \leftarrow novelist(X);$$
$$Multilingual(X) \leftarrow scientist(X);$$
$$writer(joey);$$
$$scientist(X) \leftarrow writer(X), isAuthorOf(X, Y), not\ likes(X, astrology)\}$$

(33)

Given a consistent interpretation $\mathcal{I}_1$, s.t. the set of classical atoms $\{Author(joey), Multilingual(joey)\}$ holds in $\mathcal{I}_1$, we have

$$P_{\mathcal{I}_1} = \{\ novelist(joey) \vee scientist(joey) \leftarrow writer(joey);$$
$$\leftarrow novelist(joey);$$
$$writer(joey);$$
$$scientist(joey) \leftarrow writer(joey), not\ likes(joey, astrology)\}$$

The interpretation $M_1 = \{writer(joey), scientist(joey)\}$ is a stable model, while $M_2 = \{writer(joey), novelist(joey)\}$ is not a stable model. Indeed, we have

$$P_{\mathcal{I}}{}^{M_1} = \{\ novelist(joey) \vee scientist(joey) \leftarrow writer(joey);$$
$$\leftarrow novelist(joey);$$
$$writer(joey);$$
$$scientist(joey) \leftarrow writer(joey)\}$$

which has as single minimal model M_1. Since $P_{\mathcal{I}}{}^{M_2} = P_{\mathcal{I}}{}^{M_1}$, M_2 is not a stable model.

If we take $\mathcal{I}_2$, where *joey* belongs to *Monolingual* and *Author*, we get

$$P_{\mathcal{I}_2} = \{\ novelist(joey) \vee scientist(joey) \leftarrow writer(joey);$$
$$\leftarrow scientist(joey);$$
$$writer(joey);$$
$$scientist(joey) \leftarrow writer(joey), not\ likes(joey, astrology)\}$$

We cannot find any stable model, since in any such M, $likes(joey, astrology)$ must be false, otherwise $scientist(joey)$ would be true, in contradiction with the constraint $\leftarrow scientist(joey)$.

6.3 Full Integration: Hybrid MKNF Knowledge Bases

Building on Lifschitz's bimodal *Logic of Minimal Knowledge and Negation as Failure (MKNF)* [60], hybrid MKNF knowledge bases [68,69] aim at a seamless integration of classic and nonmonotonic semantics beyond tight integration approaches. The formalism uses two modal operators: $\mathbf{K}\phi$, which intuitively should mean that ϕ is necessarily known, and $\mathbf{not}\phi$, which intuitively means that ϕ is not true, i.e., there is some scenario in which ϕ is false.

In hybrid MKNF KBs, the rules in P have the form

$$\mathbf{K}h_1 \vee \cdots \vee \mathbf{K}h_l \leftarrow \mathbf{K}b_1, \ldots \mathbf{K}b_m, \mathbf{not}\ b_{m+1}, \ldots, \mathbf{not}\ b_n$$

where all h_i and b_j are function-free first-order atoms; they are seen as MKNF formulas

$$(\forall)\mathbf{K}b_1 \wedge \cdots \wedge \mathbf{K}b_m \wedge \mathbf{not}\ b_{m+1}, \wedge \cdots \wedge \mathbf{not}\ b_n \supset \mathbf{K}h_1 \vee \cdots \vee \mathbf{K}h_l.$$

The first-order part $\mathcal{T}$ is converted to the formula $\mathbf{K} \bigwedge_{\phi \in \mathcal{T}} \phi$, assuming that $\mathcal{T}$ is finite. As in other formalisms, no function symbols are allowed.

The semantics of the hybrid MKNF KB $\mathcal{KB} = \langle \mathcal{T}, P \rangle$ is then defined in terms of the semantics of the conjunction of these MKNF formulas, which we denote by MKNF($\mathcal{KB}$). As in $\mathcal{DL}+log$, a fixed, countably infinite domain and the Standard Names Assumption is used, but in addition Herbrand interpretations are explicitly assumed.

In the tradition of Kripke-style semantics for modal logics, models are sets of interpretations $\mathcal{M}$ rather than single interpretations $\mathcal{I}$. Intuitively, a model $\mathcal{M}$ represents a group of interpretations or "possible worlds" $\mathcal{I}$ in which a given formula is true. The operator $\mathbf{K}\phi$ can be seen as the logical necessity operator under modal logic $S5$ axiomatization; in Kripke-semantic terms, this means that given a model $\mathcal{M}$, each world $\mathcal{I}$ can access each world $\mathcal{I}'$ in $\mathcal{M}$ (including itself); thus, a formula $\mathbf{K}\phi$ evaluates to true at a world $\mathcal{I}$, if ϕ evaluates to true at each world $\mathcal{I}'$ in $\mathcal{M}$. Similarly, $\mathbf{not}\ \phi$ evaluates to false at $\mathcal{I}$ if ϕ evaluates to false at some $\mathcal{I}'$ in $\mathcal{M}$. Atoms, propositional combinations of formulas, and quantifiers are evaluated at $\mathcal{I}$ as usual in first-order logic.

A model $\mathcal{M}$ is now an *MKNF model* of $\mathcal{KB} = \langle \mathcal{T}, P \rangle$, if the formula $\mathrm{MKNF}(\mathcal{KB})$ evaluates to true at each world of $\mathcal{M}$, and it is not possible to increase $\mathcal{M}$ to some $\mathcal{M}' \supset \mathcal{M}$ such that $\mathrm{MKNF}(\mathcal{KB})$ evaluates to true at some world of $\mathcal{M}'$, if $\mathbf{K}$ would be evaluated with respect to $\mathcal{M}'$ but $\mathbf{not}$ with respect to $\mathcal{M}$. Intuitively, $\mathcal{M}$ is "maximal" and embodies the Minimal Knowledge Principle in the sense that the more interpretations (possible worlds) a model contains, the less certain knowledge is associated with it. Note that for a modal-free formula ϕ, the formula $\mathbf{K}\phi$ is equivalent to ϕ, as the only maximal model $\mathcal{M}$ such that $\mathcal{M} \models \mathbf{K}\phi$ coincides with the set of all the first-order interpretations $\mathcal{I}$ such that $\mathcal{I} \models \phi$. On the other hand, the $\mathbf{not}$ operator implements negation as failure and can be read as "there is the possibility that ϕ is false."

Although in hybrid MKNF KBs there is no distinction between classical and rules predicates for defining the semantics, this issue becomes relevant for ensuring decidability of reasoning. To this end, DL-safety of the rules in P is adopted, where predicates that appear in $\mathcal{T}$ are considered as DL-predicates, and all other ones (occurring only in P) as non-DL-predicates. Furthermore, on the first-order side $\mathcal{T}$ is restricted to a decidable DL.

Hybrid MKNF KBs can be seen as a generalization of CARIN [59], $\mathcal{AL}$-log [28], and DL-safe rules [70]. They extend, like dl-programs, and $\mathcal{DL}$+log, logic programs and description logic faithfully in the sense that the consequences of hybrid KBs $(\emptyset, P)$ and $(\mathcal{T}, \emptyset)$ reflect consequences of stable model semantics and first-order semantics, respectively (where for dl-programs, only consequences given by queries make sense).

For an example, consider the following extension of the hybrid KB (33). The ontology part is extended to

$$\mathcal{T} = \{\ Multilingual \sqsubseteq \neg Monolingual;$$
$$Multilingual \sqcup Monolingual \sqsubseteq Author;$$
$$Author \sqsubseteq \exists isAuthorOf;\ \ Author(joey);\ \ Lefthanded \sqsubseteq Author\ \}$$

where the last axiom introduces a class of authors using their left hand to write. To the rules part, we add that the rule that authors write with their right hand if they are not left-handed, and this is the default. This leads to the following program part P:

$$P = \{\mathbf{K}novelist(X) \vee \mathbf{K}scientist(X) \leftarrow \mathbf{K}writer(X);$$
$$\mathbf{K}Monolingual(X) \leftarrow \mathbf{K}novelist(X);$$
$$\mathbf{K}Multilingual(X) \leftarrow \mathbf{K}scientist(X);$$
$$\mathbf{K}scientist(X) \leftarrow \mathbf{K}writer(X), \mathbf{K}isAuthorOf(X,Y), \mathbf{not}\,likes(X, astrology);$$
$$\mathbf{K}writer(joey);$$
$$\mathbf{K}Righthanded(X) \leftarrow \mathbf{K}Author(X), \mathbf{not}\ Lefthanded(X)\ \}$$

Note that compared to $\mathcal{DL}+log$ (in which the new rule cannot be formulated), it is now possible to use negation as failure over first-order predicates such as *Lefthanded*. As the authors of [69] describe, in some sense "closed world glasses" can be put on classical predicates, allowing to state exceptions.

By treating DL concepts and roles as objective knowledge (i.e., without the **K** operator), and the rule predicates as modal, it is possible to port a $\mathcal{DL}+log$ knowledge base into an equi-satisfiable generalized hybrid MKNF KB. For more details, see [68].

6.4   Assessment

Some noticeable features of the semantics of dl-programs, $\mathcal{DL}+log$, and hybrid MKNF knowledge bases are summarized Table 5, following a similar assessment in [22]. For the sake of comparison, we have added also SWRL there as a prominent non-hybrid approach. The first row identifies which formalisms have different vocabularies for classical and rule predicates names, respectively. Note that this feature is not distinctive of loose coupling approaches, although it can be seen as an indication of the level of coupling between classic and logic programming semantics.

The second group of features identifies which choice is taken regarding the domain of discourse for the logic programming part P of a knowledge base. The choice varies between taking a single arbitrary domain, such as for SWRL, or adopting a combined, yet overlapping, signature (such as for hybrid MKNF and dl-programs). Such a signature usually defines two distinct domains of discourse and their interaction. In this latter setting, it can be chosen whether to take the Herbrand Universe as domain for P.

As it can be seen in the second group of features, dl-programs, $\mathcal{DL}+log$, and hybrid MKNF KBs have unique names in the Herbrand universe of the rules part. In fact,

Table 5. Comparison table for some hybrid approaches

	dl-programs	$\mathcal{DL}+log$	hybrid MKNF	SWRL
Distinguish classical and rule predicates	+	+	–	–
Domain of Discourse for P				
Herbrand Universe of P	–	+∼	+	–
Combined Signature	+	+∼	+	–
Arbitrary domains	–	–	–	+
Uniqueness of Names				
unique names in HU of P	+	+	+	–
Special equality predicate	+∼	+∼	+	+
No uniqueness	–	–	–	+
Knowledge Interaction: from First-Order Theories to Rules				
Per single model	–	+	–	+
Entailment	+	–	+	–
Knowledge Interaction: from Rules to First-Order Theories				
Per single model	–	+	+	+
Entailment	+	–	–	–
Decidability	+∼	+∼	+∼	–

Legenda: + = yes, – = no, +∼ = yes, with some proviso

$\mathcal{DL}$+*log* and hybrid MKNF KBs fulfill the UNA in the whole knowledge base, which is implied by the Standard Names Assumptions they adopt. Note, however, that $\mathcal{DL}$+*log* is not committed to Herbrand interpretations of constants in the rules part.

Although under UNA, it is possible to identify different names using a special equality predicate such as $\approx$ in hybrid MKNFs. The same is in principle possible for both $\mathcal{DL}$+*log* and dl-programs, which are extensible with axioms defining an appropriate congruence relation. This has actually been theoretically introduced and implemented for dl-programs [35,40], which feature the possibility of simulating a congruence relation or defining a customized behavior for equality. Note that dl-programs tolerate non-uniqueness of names on the classical logic side of the knowledge base signature. SWRL has native features for reasoning with non-uniqueness of names, which is the default setting.

Regarding the interaction from the ontology (first-order theory) to the rules, we distinguish whether the truth of literal with "classical" predicate in a rule depends for model construction on a single model of the first-order part of the hybrid KB, or on entailment from multiple models. Here, "model" is understood in the wider sense of first-order logics interpretation/hybrid model; for hybrid MKNF, it is a first-order interpretation in a MKNF model (which is a set of first-order interpretations). $\mathcal{DL}$+*log* and SWRL work on a single model basis, while dl-programs and hybrid MKNF employ inference from multiple models; in dl-programs, information from the first-order theory is imported to rules only if a query is proven from the (possibly constrained) set of models of the first-order part. Similarly, the operators **K** and **not** in hybrid MKNFs imply a quantification over multiple first-order models before knowledge can be considered true/false within a rule.

For the reverse direction (from the rules to the first-order part), single-model interaction is understood in the sense that each model $\mathcal{I}$ of the rules part P *constrains* the models of the first order part $\mathcal{T}$ such that only models will be considered in which all classical predicates have a larger extent than in $\mathcal{I}$. Entailment based interaction, instead, simply adds positive conclusions about the classical predicates that can be drawn from the model of the logic program to the first-order part. Note that this may make a difference, if we can have elements in interpretations that can not be accessed via some ground term. Here, only dl-programs are conceived according to the second principle, through the special dl-atom device, which adds conclusions about classical predicates to the ontology.

As a last yet important parameter, we consider decidability. Both dl-programs and hybrid MKNF KBs are decidable, provided that satisfiability checking for the underlying description logic base is decidable, and the rules part is DL-safe (for dl-programs, DL-safety is implicitly ensured). Compared to MKNF, the $\mathcal{DL}$+*log* formalism asks only for *weak* DL-safety, but in turn containment between union of conjunctive queries must be decidable in the underlying first-order theory $\mathcal{T}$.

6.5 Further Aspects

There are many interesting aspects that we can not cover here. Probabilistic and fuzzy hybrid systems under stable model semantics for the rules have been investigated under both the loose coupling and tight coupling approach; see [14,63,64]. An extension of RDF(S) with stable models has been proposed in [2].

Besides stable models semantics, the research community also paid attention to hybrid knowledge bases with well-founded semantics on the rules side: for example, a well-founded semantics for dl-programs [41] and for hybrid MKNF knowledge bases [57] has been defined, while *hybrid rules* under well-founded semantics [31] follow the approach of the $\mathcal{DL}+log$ family.

A rich line of research has investigated the possibility of emulating first-order semantics by mapping first-order theories into equivalent logic programs. A noticeable translation from $\mathcal{SHIQ}$ to positive disjunctive Datalog (which has an exponential blow up in the worst case) was given in [54]. A correspondence between open logic programming and $\mathcal{ALCN}$ has been shown in [99]. Other attempts to map description logics into answer set semantics are [95] and [1]. A decidable fragment of ASP extended with function symbols that is rich enough to capture $\mathcal{ALC}$ has been recently described [90].

7 Conclusion

Advanced reasoning frameworks for future Semantic Web applications need to deal with both rules and ontologies in an integrated manner, which is currently not supported well and an active area of research. In this article, we have considered a number of rule-based formalisms to work on top of or aside ontology bases. They work at different levels of integration, ranging from a low level, at which the integration is ad hoc, to a high level, where a genuine semantics is given to a combination of rules and ontologies.

In the course of this, we have developed a number of criteria and discriminating features, which we then used to profile the various formalisms and systems. As for implemented systems, we have briefly addressed the languages they support, and we related them to foundational approaches to combining rules and ontologies. Furthermore, we have also discussed selected approaches at the high level that are on the forefront of research, whose impact for future developments remains to be seen.

Looking at the tool support that is currently available, we found that many – and quite diverse – systems and languages exist, and that there is no easy way to change from one system to another in general; this means that once the user gets stuck when modeling her application with a specific system, then she has to port the whole rule base to another system; this is however not always feasible for any arbitrary target system. In this regard, the RIF standardization effort of the W3C is not only useful to promote rule languages, but also to give more freedom to the users in choosing the "right" system for their application. The Semantic Web as such is a good application playground for pushing the frontiers in the implementations and for providing solid and scalable implementation of rule/ontology languages.

When we looked at the issue of combining rules and ontologies into a unifying framework, we found that this is not easy given the quite different features underlying logic programs and ontologies, since the latter are mainly based on classical logic while the former are not. Recent proposals are a step forward but the issue is not resolved yet (as it seems), and more research efforts will be necessary. After the successful ontology initiative of the W3C which resulted in the OWL standard, it is to be hoped that the RIF effort will converge to a useful standard as well, even though this is far less clear given the many facets of rules and views what rules are.

Current and future research centers around the following questions.

Semantics for rules plus ontologies. While a number of proposals for a semantics of rules combined with ontologies have been made, it is not clear whether these proposals are already sufficient and will show satisfactory behavior in relevant cases. What is missing at this point are case studies and large(r) scale examples beyond the toy examples which have been considered in the seminal papers that introduced the approaches. This, in turn, may also provide guidance in the development of a "gold standard" for rules plus ontologies.

Semantic and computational properties. Related with these, we need to know more about the semantic and computational properties of the various approaches for rules and ontologies, and also how they relate to each other. Studies on how knowledge bases in the one formalism can be transformed into knowledge bases in the other formalism are useful in this regard, as well as to understand what scenarios can be expressed in a formalism (and which not). Related to this is the issue of computational complexity, which gives us however a somewhat coarser view than the expressiveness of a formalism in terms of (sets of) models that it can represent. Current complexity studies provide us with basic results, but more refined ones and studies of expressiveness issues are missing.

Efficient implementations, algorithms. Of most reasoning engines, especially at the high level of integration, only simple prototypes or even no implementations are available. Implementations, however, are barely needed in order to experiment with a formalism not only to measure performance, but also to understand and analyze its behavior. Doing this on paper is cumbersome (and tedious). Guided by the results of complexity studies, efficient implementations have to be developed, and the great challenge of scalability has to be met. This, however, might require to modify the semantics or to develop suitable approximation methods to facilitate reasoning with manageable resources.

Beyond logic rules. The current integration efforts aim at logic rules, be it in the reading of rules as logical clauses, or in the style of (non-monotonic) rules as in logic programming. In fact, there are many more kinds of rules out there which we need to integrate with ontologies as well; for example, production rules as available in traditional expert systems engines, that are based on an operational semantics; business rules, which are used in the context of business policies and whose semantics is not always clear; etc.

Knowledge combination/integration beyond rules and ontologies. Connected to the previous issue, knowledge integration beyond a simple pair of a rules and an ontology part is an issue. Both the rules and the ontology part need not be homogeneous, but composed of parts itself that have difference semantics; furthermore, knowledge bases of a different kind than rules (e.g., descriptions of temporal processes like work flows or protocols in a temporal logic, or action theories) may need to be integrated. This calls for a logic framework in which knowledge modules, having different native semantics, can be put together under a meaningful semantics, ideally in a plug and play manner – realizing this vision is a challenging goal.

References

1. Alsaç, G., Baral, C.: Reasoning in description logics using declarative logic programming. Technical report, CS Dept, Arizona State University (2001)
2. Analyti, A., Antoniou, G., Damásio, C.V., Wagner, G.: Stable Model Theory for Extended RDF Ontologies. In: Gil, Y., Motta, E., Benjamins, V.R., Musen, M.A. (eds.) ISWC 2005. LNCS, vol. 3729, pp. 21–36. Springer, Heidelberg (2005)
3. Antoniou, G., Damásio, C.V., Grosof, B., Horrocks, I., Kifer, M., Maluszynski, J., Patel-Schneider, P.F.: Combining Rules and Ontologies: A survey. Technical Report IST506779/Linköping/I3-D3/D/PU/a1, Linköping University, IST-2004-506779 REWERSE Deliverable I3-D3. (February 2005), http://rewerse.net/publications/
4. Baader, F., Calvanese, D., McGuinness, D.L., Nardi, D., Patel-Schneider, P.F. (eds.): The Description Logic Handbook: Theory, Implementation, and Applications, 2nd edn. Cambridge University Press, Cambridge (2007)
5. Baader, F., Hollunder, B.: Embedding defaults into terminological representation systems. J. Automated Reasoning 14, 149–180 (1995)
6. Baral, C.: Knowledge Representation, Reasoning and Declarative Problem Solving. Cambridge University Press, Cambridge (2002)
7. Baselice, S., Bonatti, P.A., Criscuolo, G.: On finitely recursive programs. In: Dahl, V., Niemelä, I. (eds.) ICLP 2007. LNCS, vol. 4670, pp. 89–103. Springer, Heidelberg (2007)
8. T. Berners-Lee. Web for Real People, April 2005. Keynote Speech at the 14th World Wide Web Conference WWW2005, http://www.w3.org/2005/Talks/0511-keynote-tbl/.
9. Boley, H., Kifer, M., Pătrânjan, P.-L., Polleres, A.: Rule interchange on the web. In: Antoniou, G., Aßmann, U., Baroglio, C., Decker, S., Henze, N., Patranjan, P.-L., Tolksdorf, R. (eds.) Reasoning Web. LNCS, vol. 4636, pp. 269–309. Springer, Heidelberg (2007)
10. Boley, H., Kifer, M. (eds.): RIF Basic Logic Dialect, W3C Working Draft (October2007), http://www.w3.org/TR/2007/WD-rif-bld-20071030
11. Bonatti, P.A.: Reasoning with infinite stable models. Artificial Intelligence 156(1), 75–111 (2004)
12. Brickley, D., Guha, R. (eds.): RDF vocabulary description language 1.0: RDF Schema, W3C Recommendation (February 2004), http://www.w3.org/TR/rdf-schema/
13. Bry, F., Eisinger, N., Eiter, T., Furche, T., Gottlob, G., Ley, C., Linse, B., Pichler, R., Wei, F.: Foundations of rule-based query answering. In: Antoniou, G., Aßmann, U., Baroglio, C., Decker, S., Henze, N., Patranjan, P.-L., Tolksdorf, R. (eds.) Reasoning Web. LNCS, vol. 4636, pp. 1–153. Springer, Heidelberg (2007)
14. Calì, A., Lukasiewicz, T.: Tightly integrated probabilistic description logic programs for the semantic web. In: Dahl, V., Niemelä, I. (eds.) ICLP 2007. LNCS, vol. 4670, pp. 428–429. Springer, Heidelberg (2007)
15. F. Calimeri, S. Cozza, G. Ianni, N. Leone. DLV-Complex homepage, since 2008, http://www.mat.unical.it/dlv-complex
16. Calvanese, D., Giacomo, G.D., Lembo, D., Lenzerini, M., Rosati, R.: Embedding defaults into terminological representation systems. J. Automated Reasoning 39, 385–429 (2007)
17. Carroll, J., Bizer, C., Hayes, P., Stickler, P.: Named graphs. Journal of Web Semantics 3(4) (2005)
18. Clark, K.G., Feigenbaum, L., Torres, E.: SPARQL Protocol for RDF, W3C Proposed Recommendation (November 2007), http://www.w3.org/TR/2007/PR-rdf-sparql-protocol-20071112/

19. Connolly, D. (ed.): Gleaning Resource Descriptions from Dialects of Languages (GRDDL) (September 2007)
20. Damásio, C.V., Analyti, A., Antoniou, G., Wagner, G.: Supporting open and closed world reasoning on the web. In: Alferes, J.J., Bailey, J., May, W., Schwertel, U. (eds.) PPSWR 2006. LNCS, vol. 4187, pp. 149–163. Springer, Heidelberg (2006)
21. de Bruijn, J.: Semantic Web Language Layering with Ontologies, Rules, and Meta-Modeling. PhD thesis, Faculty of Mathematics, Computer Science and Physics of the University of Innsbruck, Innsbruck, Austria (2008)
22. de Bruijn, J., Eiter, T., Polleres, A., Tompits, H.: On representational issues about combinations of classical theories with nonmonotonic rules. In: Lang, J., Lin, F., Wang, J. (eds.) KSEM 2006. LNCS (LNAI), vol. 4092, pp. 1–22. Springer, Heidelberg (2006)
23. de Bruijn, J., Eiter, T., Polleres, A., Tompits, H.: Embedding non-ground logic programs into autoepistemic logic for knowledge base combination. In: Veloso, M. (ed.) Proceedings 20th International Joint Conference on Artificial Intelligence (IJCAI 2007), pp. 304–309. AAAI Press, Menlo Park (2007)
24. de Bruijn, J., Pearce, D., Polleres, A., Valverde, A.: A logic for hybrid rules. In: Proceedings Second International Conference on Rules and Rule Markup Languages for the Semantic Web (RuleML 2006), IEEE, Los Alamitos (2006),
    http://2006.ruleml.org/online-proceedings/rule-integ.pdf
25. de Bruijn, J., Polleres, A., Lara, R., Fensel, D.: OWL⁻. Final draft d20.1v0.2, WSML (2005)
26. J. de Bruijn (ed.). RIF RDF and OWL Compatibility, W3C Working Draft (October 2007),
    http://www.w3.org/TR/2007/WD-rif-bld-20071030
27. Dean, M., Schreiber, G., Bechhofer, S., van Harmelen, F., Hendler, J., Horrocks, I., McGuinness, D.L., Patel-Schneider, P.F., Stein, L.A.: OWL Web Ontology Language Reference, W3C Recommendation (February 2004)
28. Donini, F.M., Lenzerini, M., Nardi, D., Schaerf, A.: $\mathcal{AL}$-log: Integrating Datalog and Description Logics. Journal of Intelligent Information Systems 10(3), 227–252 (1998)
29. Donini, F.M., Nardi, D., Rosati, R.: Description logics of minimal knowledge and negation as failure. ACM Trans. Comput. Log. 3(2), 177–225 (2002)
30. Drabent, W., Henriksson, J., Maluszynski, J.: HD-Rules: a hybrid system interfacing prolog with dl-reasoners. In: 2nd International Workshop on Applications of Logic Programming to the Web, Semantic Web and Semantic Web Services. ALPSWS 2007 (2007)
31. Drabent, W., Maluszynski, J.: Well-founded semantics for hybrid rules. In: Marchiori, M., Pan, J.Z., Marie, C. (eds.) RR 2007. LNCS, vol. 4524, pp. 1–15. Springer, Heidelberg (2007)
32. Duerst, M., Suignard, M.: Internationalized Resource Identifiers (IRIs). RFC 3987 (Proposed Standard) (January 2005)
33. Eiter, T., Ianni, G., Krennwallner, T., Schindlauer, R.: Exploiting conjunctive queries in description logic programs. In: Proceedings of the 2007 International Workshop on Description Logics (DL 2007), pp. 259–266 (2007)
34. Eiter, T., Ianni, G., Krennwallner, T., Schindlauer, R.: Exploiting conjunctive queries in description logic programs. Technical Report INFSYS RR-1843-08-02, Institut für Informationssysteme, Technische Universität Wien, A-1040 Vienna, Austria, Extended version of the DL 2007/ISAIM 2008 abstract (March 2008)
35. Eiter, T., Ianni, G., Lukasiewicz, T., Schindlauer, R., Tompits, H.: Combining Answer Set Programming with Description Logics for the Semantic Web. Technical Report INFSYS RR-1843-07-04, Institut für Informationssysteme, TU Wien (2007) (to appear in Artificial Intelligence)
36. T. Eiter, G. Ianni, A. Polleres, and R. Schindlauer. Answer set programming for the semantic web, (June 2006), http://asptut.gibbi.com/

37. Eiter, T., Ianni, G., Polleres, A., Schindlauer, R., Tompits, H.: Reasoning with rules and ontologies. In: Barahona, P., Bry, F., Franconi, E., Henze, N., Sattler, U. (eds.) Reasoning Web 2006. LNCS, vol. 4126, pp. 93–127. Springer, Heidelberg (2006)
38. Eiter, T., Ianni, G., Schindlauer, R., Tompits, H.: A Uniform Integration of Higher-Order Reasoning and External Evaluations in Answer Set Programming. In: Kaelbling, L.P., Saffiotti, A. (eds.) In: Proceedings of the 19th International Joint Conference on Artificial Intelligence (IJCAI 2005), Professional Book Center, pp. 90–96 (2005)
39. Eiter, T., Ianni, G., Schindlauer, R., Tompits, H.: Effective Integration of Declarative Rules with External Evaluations for Semantic Web Reasoning. In: Sure, Y., Domingue, J. (eds.) ESWC 2006. LNCS, vol. 4011, pp. 273–287. Springer, Heidelberg (2006)
40. Eiter, T., Lukasiewicz, T., Schindlauer, R., Tompits, H.: Combining answer set programming with description logics for the Semantic Web. In: Proceedings KR 2004, pp. 141–151 (2004)
41. Eiter, T., Lukasiewicz, T., Schindlauer, R., Tompits, H.: Well-Founded Semantics for Description Logic Programs in the Semantic Web. In: Antoniou, G., Boley, H. (eds.) RuleML 2004. LNCS, vol. 3323, pp. 81–97. Springer, Heidelberg (2004)
42. The Friend of a Friend (FOAF) Project, http://www.foaf-project.org/
43. Gelfond, M., Lifschitz, V.: Classical Negation in Logic Programs and Disjunctive Databases. New Generation Computing 9, 365–385 (1991)
44. Gelfond, M., Przymusinska, H., Przymusinski, T.C.: The Extended Closed World Assumption and its Relationship to Parallel Circumscription. In: Proceedings Fifth ACM Symposium on Principles of Database Systems (PODS 1986), pp. 133–139 (1986)
45. Grosof, B.N., Horrocks, I., Volz, R., Decker, S.: Description logic programs: Combining logic programs with description logics. In: Proceedings WWW 2003, pp. 48–57 (2003)
46. Gruber, T.R.: A Translation Approach to Portable Ontology Specifications. Knowledge Acquisition 5, 199–220 (1993)
47. Haarslev, V., Möller, R.: RACER System Description. In: Goré, R.P., Leitsch, A., Nipkow, T. (eds.) IJCAR 2001. LNCS (LNAI), vol. 2083, pp. 701–705. Springer, Heidelberg (2001)
48. Hayes, P.: RDF semantics, http://www.w3.org/TR/rdf-mt/
49. Heymans, S., Nieuwenborgh, D.V., Vermeir, D.: Open answer set programming for the semantic web. J. Applied Logic 5(1), 144–169 (2007)
50. Heymans, S., Predoiu, L., Feier, C., der Bruijn, J., van Nieuwenborgh, D.: G-hybrid knowledge bases. In: Etalle, S., Truszczyński, M. (eds.) ICLP 2006. LNCS, vol. 4079, pp. 39–54. Springer, Heidelberg (2006)
51. Horrocks, I., Kutz, O., Sattler, U.: The even more irresistible SROIQ. In: Proceedings of the 10th International Conference of Knowledge Representation and Reasoning (KR 2006), pp. 57–67 (2006)
52. Horrocks, I., Patel-Schneider, P.F., Boley, H., Tabet, S., Grosof, B., Dean, M.: SWRL: A Semantic Web Rule Language Combining OWL and RuleML, W3C Member, May (2004), http://www.w3.org/Submission/SWRL/
53. Horrocks, I., Sattler, U., Tobies, S.: Practical Reasoning for Very Expressive Description Logics. Logic Journal of the IGPL 8(3), 239–264 (2000)
54. Hustadt, U., Motik, B., Sattler, U.: Reasoning in description logics by a reduction to disjunctive datalog. J. Autom. Reasoning 39(3), 351–384 (2007)
55. Kifer, M.: Nonmonotonic reasoning in FLORA-2. In: Baral, C., Greco, G., Leone, N., Terracina, G. (eds.) LPNMR 2005. LNCS (LNAI), vol. 3662, pp. 1–12. Springer, Heidelberg (2005)
56. Kifer, M., Lausen, G., Wu, J.: Logical foundations of object-oriented and frame-based languages. Journal of the ACM 42(4), 741–843 (1995)

57. Knorr, M., Alferes, J.J., Hitzler, P.: A well-founded semantics for hybrid mknf knowledge bases. In: Proceedings of the 2007 International Workshop on Description Logics (DL 2007), pp. 347–354 (2007)
58. Leone, N., Pfeifer, G., Faber, W., Eiter, T., Gottlob, G., Perri, S., Scarcello, F.: The dlv system for knowledge representation and reasoning. ACM Trans. Comput. Log. 7(3), 499–562 (2006)
59. Levy, A.Y., Rousset, M.-C.: Combining Horn Rules and Description Logics in CARIN. Artificial Intelligence 104(1-2), 165–209 (1998)
60. Lifschitz, V.: Nonmonotonic databases and epistemic queries. In: Proceedings IJCAI 1991, pp. 381–386 (1991)
61. Lloyd, J.W.: Foundations of logic programming, 2nd edn. Springer, New York (1987)
62. Lloyd, J.W., Topor, R.W.: Making prolog more expressive. Journal of Logic Programming 1(3), 225–240 (1984)
63. Lukasiewicz, T.: Probabilistic description logic programs. Int. J. Approx. Reasoning 45(2), 288–307 (2007)
64. Lukasiewicz, T., Straccia, U.: Description logic programs under probabilistic uncertainty and fuzzy vagueness. In: Symbolic and Quantitative Approaches to Reasoning with Uncertainty, 9th European Conference, ECSQARU, pp. 187–198 (2007)
65. Malhotra, A., Melton, J., Walsh, N. (eds.): XQuery 1.0 and XPath 2.0 Functions and Operators, W3C Recommendation (January 2007),
    `http://www.w3.org/TR/xpath-functions/`
66. Marin, D.: A formalization of RDF. Technical Report TR/DCC-2006-8, TR Dept. Computer Science, Universidad de Chile (2006)
67. Motik, B., Horrocks, I., Rosati, R., Sattler, U.: Can OWL and logic programming live together happily ever after? In: Cruz, I., Decker, S., Allemang, D., Preist, C., Schwabe, D., Mika, P., Uschold, M., Aroyo, L.M. (eds.) ISWC 2006. LNCS, vol. 4273, pp. 501–514. Springer, Heidelberg (2006)
68. B. Motik and R. Rosati. Closing semantic web ontologies. Technical report, University of Manchester, March 2007, `http://web.comlab.ox.ac.uk/oucl/work/boris.motik/publications/mr06closing-report.pdf`
69. Motik, B., Rosati, R.: A faithful integration of description logics with logic programming. In: IJCAI 2007, Proceedings of the 20th International Joint Conference on Artificial Intelligence, pp. 477–482 (2007)
70. Motik, B., Sattler, U., Studer, R.: Query Answering for OWL-DL with Rules. Journal of Web Semantics: Science, Services and Agents on the World Wide Web 3(1), 41–60 (2005)
71. Nilsson, M., Powell, A., Johnston, P., Naeve, A.: Expressing dublin core metadata using the resource description framework (rdf), DCMI Recommendation (January 2008)
72. Pan, J.Z., Franconi, E., Tessaris, S., Stamou, G., Tzouvaras, V., Serafini, L., Horrocks, I.R., Glimm, B.: Specification of Coordination of Rule and Ontology Languages. Project Deliverable D2.5.1, KnowledgeWeb NoE (June 2004)
73. Patel-Schneider, P.F., Hayes, P., Horrocks, I.: OWL Web Ontology Language Semantics and Abstract Syntax, W3C Recommendation (February 2004)
74. Pearce, D.: Equilibrium logic. Ann. Math. Artif. Intell. 47(1-2), 3–41 (2006)
75. Pearce, D., Valverde, A.: Quantfied equilibrium logic. Technical report, Universidad Rey Juan Carlos (2006)
76. Pérez, J., Arenas, M., Gutierrez, C.: Semantics and complexity of sparql. In: Cruz, I., Decker, S., Allemang, D., Preist, C., Schwabe, D., Mika, P., Uschold, M., Aroyo, L.M. (eds.) ISWC 2006. LNCS, vol. 4273, pp. 30–43. Springer, Heidelberg (2006)
77. Polleres, A.: From SPARQL to rules (and back). In: Proceedings of the 16th World Wide Web Conference (WWW 2007), Banff, Canada (May 2007)

78. Polleres, A., Feier, C., Harth, A.: Rules with contextually scoped negation. In: Sure, Y., Domingue, J. (eds.) ESWC 2006. LNCS, vol. 4011. Springer, Heidelberg (2006)
79. Polleres, A., Feier, C., Harth, A.: Rules with contextually scoped negation. In: Sure, Y., Domingue, J. (eds.) ESWC 2006. LNCS, vol. 4011, pp. 332–347. Springer, Heidelberg (2006)
80. Polleres, A., Scharffe, F., Schindlauer, R.: SPARQL++ for mapping between RDF vocabularies. In: Meersman, R., Tari, Z. (eds.) OTM 2007, Part I. LNCS, vol. 4803, pp. 878–896. Springer, Heidelberg (2007)
81. Poole, D.: A Logical Framework for Default Reasoning. Artificial Intelligence 36, 27–47 (1988)
82. Prud'hommeaux, E., Seaborne, A. (eds.): SPARQL Query Language for RDF, W3C Recommendation (January 2007),
    http://www.w3.org/TR/2008/REC-rdf-sparql-query-20080115/
83. Reiter, R.: On Closed-World Databases. In: Gallaire, H., Minker, J. (eds.) Logic and Data Bases, pp. 55–76. Plenum Press, New York (1978)
84. Reiter, R.: A logic for default reasoning. Artificial Intelligence 13, 81–132 (1980)
85. Rosati, R.: Towards Expressive KR Systems Integrating Datalog and Description Logics: Preliminary Report. In: Proceedings of the 1999 International Workshop on Description Logics (DL 1999), pp. 160–164 (1999)
86. Rosati, R.: On the Decidability and Complexity of Integrating Ontologies and Rules. Journal of Web Semantics 3(1), 61–73 (2005)
87. Rosati, R.: Semantic and computational advantages of the safe integration of ontologies and rules. In: Fages, F., Soliman, S. (eds.) PPSWR 2005. LNCS, vol. 3703, pp. 50–64. Springer, Heidelberg (2005)
88. Rosati, R.: Integrating Ontologies and Rules: Semantic and Computational Issues. In: Barahona, P., Bry, F., Franconi, E., Henze, N., Sattler, U. (eds.) Reasoning Web 2006. LNCS, vol. 4126, pp. 128–151. Springer, Heidelberg (2006)
89. Rosati, R.: Tight Integration of Description Logics and Disjunctive Datalog. In: Proceedings of the Tenth International Conference on Principles of Knowledge Representation and Reasoning (KR 2006), pp. 68–78. AAAI Press, Menlo Park (2006)
90. Simkus, M., Eiter, T.: FDNC: Decidable non-monotonic disjunctive logic programs with function symbols. In: Logic for Programming, Artificial Intelligence, and Reasoning, 14th International Conference, LPAR, pp. 514–530, Full paper Tech.Rep.INFSYS RR-1843-08-01, TU Vienna. (2007),
    http://www.kr.tuwien.ac.at/research/reports/rr0801.pdf
91. Sintek, M., Decker, S.: TRIPLE - A Query, Inference, and Transformation Language for the Semantic Web. In: Horrocks, I., Hendler, J. (eds.) ISWC 2002. LNCS, vol. 2342, pp. 364–378. Springer, Heidelberg (2002)
92. Sirin, E., Parsia, B., Cuenca Grau, B., Kalyanpur, A., Katz, Y.: Pellet: A practical OWL-DL reasoner. Technical Report 68, UMIACS, University of Maryland (2005)
93. Straccia, U.: Reasoning about Uncertainty. In: Reasoning Web, Fourth International Summer School 2008, Tutorial Lectures. LNCS, vol. 5224. Springer, Heidelberg (2008)
94. Sure, Y., Bloehdorn, S., Haase, P., Hartmann, J., Oberle, D.: The SWRC ontology - semantic web for research communities. In: Bento, C., Cardoso, A., Dias, G. (eds.) EPIA 2005. LNCS (LNAI), vol. 3808, pp. 218–231. Springer, Heidelberg (2005)
95. Swift, T.: Deduction in ontologies via ASP. In: Lifschitz, V., Niemelä, I. (eds.) LPNMR 2004. LNCS (LNAI), vol. 2923, pp. 275–288. Springer, Heidelberg (2003)
96. ter Horst, H.J.: Completeness, decidability and complexity of entailment for rdf schema and a semantic extension involving the owl vocabulary. Journal of Web Semantics 3(2) (July 2005)

97. Tsarkov, D., Horrocks, I.: Fact++ Description Logic Reasoner: System Description. In: Furbach, U., Shankar, N. (eds.) IJCAR 2006. LNCS (LNAI), vol. 4130. Springer, Heidelberg (2006)

98. Ullman, J.D.: Principles of Database & Knowledge Base Systems. Comp. Science Press (1989)

99. Van Belleghem, K., Denecker, M., De Schreye, D.: A strong correspondence between description logics and open logic programming. In: Proceedings ICLP 1997, pp. 346–360 (1997)

100. Van Gelder, A., Ross, K.A., Schlipf, J.S.: The Well-Founded Semantics for General Logic Programs. Journal of the ACM 38(3), 620–650 (1991)

101. W3C. The Resource Description Framework, http://www.w3.org/RDF/

102. Wang, K., Billington, D., Blee, J., Antoniou, G.: Combining Description Logic and Defeasible Logic for the Semantic Web. In: Antoniou, G., Boley, H. (eds.) RuleML 2004. LNCS, vol. 3323, pp. 170–181. Springer, Heidelberg (2004)

103. Wielemaker, J., Schreiber, G., Wielinga, B.: Prolog-based infrastructure for RDF: Scalability and performance. In: Fensel, D., Sycara, K.P., Mylopoulos, J. (eds.) ISWC 2003. LNCS, vol. 2870, pp. 644–658. Springer, Heidelberg (2003)

104. Wu, Z., Eadon, G., Das, S., Chong, E.I., Kolovski, V., Annamalai, M., Srinivasan, J.: Implementing and Inference Engine for RDFS/OWL Constructs and User-Defined Rules in Oracle. In: Proccedings of ICDE 2008, IEEE Computer Society Press, Los Alamitos (to appear, 2008)

105. Yang, G., Kifer, M.: Reasoning about anonymous resources and meta statements on the semantic web. In: Spaccapietra, S., March, S., Aberer, K. (eds.) Journal on Data Semantics I. LNCS, vol. 2800, pp. 69–97. Springer, Heidelberg (2003)

Managing Uncertainty and Vagueness in Description Logics, Logic Programs and Description Logic Programs

Umberto Straccia

ISTI-CNR, Via G. Moruzzi 1, I-56124 Pisa, Italy
straccia@isti.cnr.it

Abstract. Managing uncertainty and/or vagueness is starting to play an important role in Semantic Web representation languages. Our aim is to overview basic concepts on representing uncertain and vague knowledge in current Semantic Web ontology and rule languages (and their combination).

1 Introduction

The management of uncertainty and/or vagueness is an important issue whenever the real world information to be represented is of imperfect nature, which likely occurs in Semantic Web tasks. In this work we overview the relevant work in the context of Description Logics [6], Logic Programs [141] and their combination. This work should act as a reference/citation guide to the relevant literature, and, thus, we keep the formal level to a minimum.

2 Uncertainty and Vagueness Basics

There has been a long-lasting misunderstanding in the literature of artificial intelligence and uncertainty modelling, regarding the role of probability/possibility theory and vague/fuzzy theory. A clarifying paper is [63]. We recall here salient notes, which may clarify the role of these theories for the inexpert reader.

A standard example that points out the difference between degrees of uncertainty and degrees of truth is that of a bottle [63]. In terms of binary truth values, a bottle is viewed as full or empty. But if one accounts for the quantity of liquid in the bottle, one may e.g. say that the bottle is "half-full". Under this way of speaking, "full" becomes a fuzzy predicate [287] and the degree of truth of "the bottle is full" reflects the amount of liquid in the bottle. The situation is quite different when expressing our ignorance about whether the bottle is either full or empty (given that we know that only one of the two situations is the true one). Saying that the probability that the bottle is full is 0.5 does not mean that the bottle is half full.

We recall that under *uncertainty theory* fall all those approaches in which statements rather than being either true or false, are true or false to some *probability* or *possibility* (for example, "it will rain tomorrow"). That is, a statement is true or false in any world, but we are "uncertain" about which world to consider as the right one, and thus we

C. Baroglio et al. (Eds.): Reasoning Web 2008, LNCS 5224, pp. 54–103, 2008.

speak about e.g. a probability distribution or a possibility distribution over the worlds. For example, we cannot exactly establish whether it will rain tomorrow or not, due to our *incomplete* knowledge about our world, but we can estimate to which degree this is probable, possible, and necessary.

As for the main differences between probability and possibility theory, the probability of an event is the sum of the probabilities of all worlds that satisfy this event, whereas the possibility of an event is the maximum of the possibilities of all worlds that satisfy the event. Intuitively, the probability of an event aggregates the probabilities of all worlds that satisfy this event, whereas the possibility of an event is simply the possibility of the "most optimistic" world that satisfies the event. Hence, although both probability and possibility theory allow for quantifying degrees of uncertainty, they are conceptually quite different from each other. That is, probability and possibility theory represent different facets of uncertainty.

On the other hand, under *vagueness/fuzziness theory* fall all those approaches in which statements (for example, "the tomato is ripe") are true to some degree, which is taken from a truth space. That is, an interpretation maps a statement to a truth degree, since we are unable to establish whether a statement is completely true or false due to the involvement of vague concepts, such as "ripe", which only have an *imprecise* definition. For example, we cannot exactly say whether a tomato is ripe or not, but rather can only say that the tomato is ripe to some degree. Usually, such statements involve so-called *vague/fuzzy predicates* [287].

Note that all vague/fuzzy statements are truth-functional, that is, the degree of truth of every statement can be calculated from the degrees of truth of its constituents, while uncertain statements cannot be a function of the uncertainties of their constituents [62]. More concretely, in probability theory, only negation is truth-functional (see Eq. 1), while in possibility theory, only disjunction resp. conjunction is truth-functional in possibilities resp. necessities of events (see Eq. 4). Furthermore, mathematical fuzzy logics are based on truly many-valued logical operators, while uncertainty logics are defined on top of standard binary logical operators.

In the following, we illustrate a typical formalization of uncertain statements and vague statements. In the former case, we consider a basic probabilistic/possibilistic logic, while in the latter, we consider a basic many-valued logic.

2.1 Probabilistic Logic

Probabilistic logic has its origin in philosophy and logic. Its roots can be traced back to Boole in 1854 [17]. There is a wide spectrum of formal languages that have been explored in probabilistic logic, ranging from constraints for unconditional and conditional events to rich languages that specify linear inequalities over events (see especially the work by Nilsson [207], Fagin et al. [74], Dubois and Prade et al. [5, 60, 64, 65], Frisch and Haddawy [81], and the first author [154, 157, 161]; see also the survey on sentential probability logic by Hailperin [94]). Recently, nonmonotonic generalizations of probabilistic logic have been developed and explored; see especially [165] for an overview. In this section, for illustrative purposes, we recall only the simple probabilistic logic described in [207].

We first define probabilistic formulas and probabilistic knowledge bases. We assume a set of *basic events* $\Phi = \{p_1, \ldots, p_n\}$ with $n \geqslant 1$. We use $\bot$ and $\top$ to denote *false* and *true*, respectively. We define *events* by induction as follows. Every element of $\Phi \cup \{\bot, \top\}$ is an event. If ϕ and ψ are events, then also $\neg\phi$, $(\phi \wedge \psi)$, $(\phi \vee \psi)$, and $(\phi \rightarrow \psi)$ are events. We use $(\phi \leftrightarrow \psi)$ as a shortcut for $(\phi \rightarrow \psi) \wedge (\psi \rightarrow \phi)$. We adopt the usual conventions to eliminate parentheses. A *probabilistic formula* is an expression of the form $\phi \geqslant l$, where ϕ is an event, and l is a real number from the unit interval $[0, 1]$. Informally, $\phi \geqslant l$ says that ϕ is true with a probability of at least l. For example, $rain\_tomorrow \geqslant 0.7$ may express that it will rain tomorrow with a probability of at least 0.7. Notice also that $\neg\phi \geqslant 1 - u$ encodes that ϕ is true with a probability of at most u. Also, we use $\phi = l$ as a shortcut for having both $\phi \geqslant l$ and $\neg\phi \geqslant 1 - l$. A *probabilistic knowledge base KB* is a finite set of probabilistic formulas.

We next define worlds and probabilistic interpretations. A *world I* associates with every basic event in Φ a binary truth value. We extend I by induction to all events as usual. We denote by $\mathcal{I}_\Phi$ the (finite) set of all worlds for Φ. A world I *satisfies* an event ϕ, or I is a *model* of ϕ, denoted $I \models \phi$, iff $I(\phi) = \mathbf{true}$. A *probabilistic interpretation Pr* is a probability function on $\mathcal{I}_\Phi$ (that is, a mapping $Pr \colon \mathcal{I}_\Phi \rightarrow [0, 1]$ such that all $Pr(I)$ with $I \in \mathcal{I}_\Phi$ sum up to 1). Intuitively, $Pr(I)$ is the degree to which the world $I \in \mathcal{I}_\Phi$ is probable, that is, the probability function Pr encodes our "uncertainty" about which world is the right one. The *probability* of an event ϕ in Pr, denoted $Pr(\phi)$, is the sum of all $Pr(I)$ such that $I \in \mathcal{I}_\Phi$ and $I \models \phi$. The following equations are an immediate consequence of the above definitions: for all probabilistic interpretations Pr and events ϕ and ψ, the following relationships hold:

$$
\begin{aligned}
Pr(\phi \wedge \psi) &= Pr(\phi) + Pr(\psi) - Pr(\phi \vee \psi) \,; \\
Pr(\phi \wedge \psi) &\leqslant \min(Pr(\phi), Pr(\psi)) \,; \\
Pr(\phi \wedge \psi) &\geqslant \max(0, Pr(\phi) + Pr(\psi) - 1) \,; \\
Pr(\phi \vee \psi) &= Pr(\phi) + Pr(\psi) - Pr(\phi \wedge \psi) \,; \\
Pr(\phi \vee \psi) &\leqslant \min(1, Pr(\phi) + Pr(\psi)) \,; \\
Pr(\phi \vee \psi) &\geqslant \max(Pr(\phi), Pr(\psi)) \,; \\
Pr(\neg\phi) &= 1 - Pr(\phi) \,; \\
Pr(\bot) &= 0 \,; \\
Pr(\top) &= 1 \,.
\end{aligned}
\tag{1}
$$

A probabilistic interpretation Pr *satisfies* a probabilistic formula $\phi \geqslant l$, or Pr is a *model* of $\phi \geqslant l$, denoted $Pr \models \phi \geqslant l$, iff $Pr(\phi) \geqslant l$. We say Pr *satisfies* a probabilistic knowledge base KB, or Pr is a *model* of KB, iff Pr satisfies all $F \in KB$. We say KB is *satisfiable* iff a model of KB exists. A probabilistic formula F is a *logical consequence* of KB, denoted $KB \models F$, iff every model of KB satisfies F. We say $\phi \geqslant l$ is a *tight logical consequence* of KB iff l is the infimum of $Pr(\phi)$ subject to all models Pr of KB. Notice that the latter is equivalent to $l = \sup\{r \mid KB \models \phi \geqslant r\}$.

Note that often also *conditional events* of the form $\phi \mid \psi$ are allowed, which may then be used in *conditional probabilistic formulae* of the form $\phi \mid \psi \geqslant l$, where ϕ and ψ are events. These statements intuitively encode that the conditional probability of ϕ

given ψ is equal or greater than l. For instance, $flies \mid bird \geqslant 0.8$ dictates that at least 80% of birds fly. From a semantics point of view, we define

$$Pr(\phi \mid \psi) = \begin{cases} \frac{Pr(\phi \wedge \psi)}{Pr(\psi)} & \text{if} Pr(\psi) \neq 0 \\ 1 & \text{otherwise} \end{cases} \tag{2}$$

and, thus, $Pr \models \phi \mid \psi \geqslant l$, iff $Pr(\phi \mid \psi) \geqslant l$.

The main decision and optimization problems in probabilistic logic are deciding the satisfiability of probabilistic knowledge bases and logical consequences from probabilistic knowledge bases, as well as computing tight logical consequences from probabilistic knowledge bases, which can be done by deciding the solvability of a system of linear inequalities and by solving a linear optimization problem, respectively. In particular, column generation techniques from operations research have been successfully used to solve large problem instances in probabilistic logic; see especially the work by Jaumard et al. [114] and Hansen et al. [98].

Bayesian Network. We recall here also some basics of *Bayesian Networks* (BN), as they play an important role in many probabilistic logic formalisms in the sense that BNs can be expressed in these logics (see, e.g. [29, 125, 215, 285]).

A Bayesian network is a directed acyclic graph whose nodes represent random variables, and whose arcs encode conditional independencies between the variables. If there is an arc from node b to another node a, b is called a parent of a, and a is a child of b. The set of parent nodes of a node a_i is denoted by $parents(a_i)$. If nodes $b_1, \ldots, b_n$ are parents of a node a, then we have an associated conditional probability table $Pr(a \mid b_1, \ldots, b_n)$. If node a_i has no parents, its local probability distribution is said to be unconditional, otherwise it is conditional. If the value of a node is observed, then the node is said to be an evidence node. It is required that the joint distribution of the node values can be written as the product of the local distributions of each node and its parents: that is,

$$Pr(a_1, \ldots, a_n) = \Pi_{i=1}^n Pr(a_i \mid parents(a_i)) \,.$$

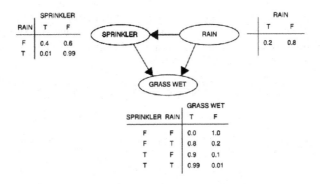

Fig. 1. A Bayesian network

We may also encode a BN in a probabilistic propositional logic using conditional events, as shown in the following example.

Example 2.1. Suppose that there are two events, which could cause grass to be wet: either the sprinkler is on or it's raining. Also, suppose that the rain has a direct effect on the use of the sprinkler (namely that when it rains, the sprinkler is usually not turned on). Then the situation can be modelled with a Bayesian network, as shown in Fig. 1. All three variables (*Rain*, *Sprinkler* and *GrassWet*) have two possible values T (for true) and F (for false). *Rain* has an unconditional probability distribution: $Pr(Rain = T) = 0.2$, while $Pr(Rain = F) = 0.8$. The conditional probability table associated to the node *Sprinkler* provides the conditional probabilities $Pr(Sprinkler = X \mid Rain = Y)$ for any $X, Y \in \{T, F\}$, while the conditional probability table associated to the node *GrassWet* provides the conditional probabilities $Pr(GrassWet = X \mid Sprinkler = Y_1, Rain = Y_2)$ for any $X, Y_i \in \{T, F\}$. The joint probability function is:

$$Pr(GrassWet, Sprinkler, Rain) = Pr(GrassWet \mid Sprinkler, Rain) \qquad (3)$$
$$\cdot Pr(Sprinkler \mid Rain) \cdot Pr(Rain) \,.$$

The model can answer questions like "What is the probability that it is raining, given the grass is wet?" using Eq. 3:

$$Pr(Rain = T \mid GrassWet = T) = \frac{Pr(Rain = T, GrassWet = T)}{Pr(GrassWet = T)}$$
$$= \frac{\sum_{Y \in \{T,F\}} Pr(Rain = T, GrassWet = T, Sprinkler = Y)}{\sum_{Y_1, Y_2 \in \{T,F\}} Pr(GrassWet = T, (Rain = Y_1, Sprinkler = Y_2))}$$
$$= \frac{0.99 \cdot 0.01 \cdot 0.2 + 0.8 \cdot 0.99 \cdot 0.2}{0.99 \cdot 0.01 \cdot 0.2 + 0.9 \cdot 0.4 \cdot 0.8 + 0.8 \cdot 0.99 \cdot 0.2 + 0 \cdot 0.6 \cdot 0.8}$$
$$\approx 0.3577 \,.$$

We may encode the BN in a probabilistic propositional logic using conditional events. Indeed, for every node a, we use a propositional letters $a(T), a(F)$, where the former encodes the event "a is true" and the latter encodes the event "a is false". Of course, we have to consider also $(a(T) \leftrightarrow \neg a(F)) = 1$. If a node a has no parents then we can easily encode its associated probability table with the formula $a(T) = p$. Hence, we have the formula $Rain(T) = 0.2$. If a node has parents, we encode its associated conditional probability table using conditional probability formulae. In particular, we will have the conditional probabilistic formulae

$$(Sprinkler(T) \mid Rain(F)) = 0.4$$
$$(Sprinkler(T) \mid Rain(T)) = 0.01$$

$$(GrassWet(T) \mid Sprinkler(F) \wedge Rain(F)) = 0.0$$
$$(GrassWet(T) \mid Sprinkler(F) \wedge Rain(T)) = 0.8$$
$$(GrassWet(T) \mid Sprinkler(T) \wedge Rain(F)) = 0.9$$
$$(GrassWet(T) \mid Sprinkler(T) \wedge Rain(T)) = 0.0 \,. \qquad \square$$

2.2 Possibilistic Logic

We next recall possibilistic logic; see especially [59]. The main syntactic and semantic differences to probabilistic logic can be summarized as follows. Syntactically, rather than using probabilistic formulas to constrain the probabilities of propositional events, we now use possibilistic formulas to constrain the necessities and possibilities of propositional events. Semantically, rather than having probability distributions on worlds, each of which associates with every event a unique probability, we now have possibility distributions on worlds, each of which associates with every event a unique possibility and a unique necessity. Differently from the probability of an event, which is the sum of the probabilities of all worlds that satisfy that event, the possibility of an event is the maximum of the possibilities of all worlds that satisfy the event. As a consequence, probabilities and possibilities of events behave quite differently from each other (see Eqs. 1 and 4). These fundamental semantic differences between probabilities and possibilities can also be used as the main criteria for using either probabilistic logic or possibilistic logic in a given application involving uncertainty. In addition, possibilistic logic may especially be used for encoding user preferences, since possibility measures can actually be viewed as rankings (on worlds or also objects) along an ordinal scale.

The semantic differences between probabilities and possibilities are also reflected in the computational properties of possibilistic and probabilistic logic, since reasoning in probabilistic logic generally requires to solve linear optimization problems, while reasoning in possibilistic logic does not, and thus can generally be done with less computational effort. Note that although possibility measures can be viewed as sets of upper probability measures [61], and possibility and probability measures can be translated into each other [56], no translations are known between possibilistic and probabilistic knowledge bases as described here.

We first define possibilistic formulas and knowledge bases. *Possibilistic formulas* have the form $\mathsf{P}\,\phi \geqslant l$ or $\mathsf{N}\,\phi \geqslant l$, where ϕ is an event, and l is a real number from $[0,1]$. Informally, such formulas encode to what extent ϕ is *possibly* resp. *necessarily* true. For example, $\mathsf{P}\,rain\_tomorrow \geqslant 0.7$ encodes that it will rain tomorrow is possible to degree 0.7, while $\mathsf{N}\,father \rightarrow man \geqslant 1$ says that a father is necessarily a man. A *possibilistic knowledge base KB* is a finite set of possibilistic formulas.

A *possibilistic interpretation* is a mapping $\pi \colon \mathcal{I}_\Phi \rightarrow [0,1]$. Intuitively, $\pi(I)$ is the degree to which the world I is *possible*. In particular, every world I such that $\pi(I) = 0$ is *impossible*, while every world I such that $\pi(I) = 1$ is *totally possible*. We say π is *normalized* iff $\pi(I) = 1$ for some $I \in \mathcal{I}_\Phi$. Intuitively, this guarantees that there exists at least one world, which could be considered as the real one.

The *possibility* of an event ϕ in a possibilistic interpretation π, denoted $Poss(\phi)$, is then defined by $Poss(\phi) = \max\{\pi(I) \mid I \in \mathcal{I}_\Phi, I \models \phi\}$ (where $\max \emptyset = 0$). Intuitively, the possibility of ϕ is evaluated in the most possible world where ϕ is true. The dual notion to the possibility of an event ϕ is the *necessity* of ϕ, denoted $Nec(\phi)$, which is defined by $Nec(\phi) = 1 - Poss(\neg\phi)$. It reflects the lack of possibility of $\neg\phi$, that is, $Nec(\phi)$ evaluates to what extent ϕ is certainly true. The following properties follows immediately from the above definitions.

For all possibilistic interpretations π and events ϕ and ψ, the following relationships hold:

$$
\begin{aligned}
Poss(\phi \wedge \psi) &\leqslant \min(Poss(\phi), Poss(\psi)); \\
Poss(\phi \vee \psi) &= \max(Poss(\phi), Poss(\psi)); \\
Poss(\neg\phi) &= 1 - Nec(\phi); \\
Poss(\bot) &= 0; \\
Poss(\top) &= 1 \quad \text{(in the normalized case)};
\end{aligned}
$$

$$
\begin{aligned}
Nec(\phi \wedge \psi) &= \min(Nec(\phi), Nec(\psi)); \\
Nec(\phi \vee \psi) &\geqslant \max(Nec(\phi), Nec(\psi)); \\
Nec(\neg\phi) &= 1 - Poss(\phi); \\
Nec(\bot) &= 0 \quad \text{(in the normalized case)}; \\
Nec(\top) &= 1.
\end{aligned}
$$

(4)

A possibilistic interpretation π *satisfies* a possibilistic formula $\mathsf{P}\,\phi \geqslant l$ (resp., $\mathsf{N}\,\phi \geqslant l$), or π is a *model* of $\mathsf{P}\,\phi \geqslant l$ (resp., $\mathsf{N}\,\phi \geqslant l$), denoted $\pi \models \mathsf{P}\,\phi \geqslant l$ (resp., $\pi \models \mathsf{N}\,\phi \geqslant l$), iff $Poss(\phi) \geqslant l$ (resp., $Nec(\phi) \geqslant l$). The notions of satisfiability, logical consequence, and tight logical consequence for possibilistic knowledge bases are then defined as usual (in the same way as in the probabilistic case). We refer the reader to [59,107] for algorithms for possibilistic logic.

2.3 Many-Valued Logics

In the setting of many-valued logics, the convention prescribing that a proposition is either true or false is changed. A more refined range is used for the function that represents the meaning of a proposition. This is usual in natural language when words are modelled by fuzzy sets. For example, the compatibility of "tall" in the phrase "a tall man" with some individual of a given height is often graded: The man can be judged not quite tall, somewhat tall, rather tall, very tall, etc. Changing the usual true/false convention leads to a new concept of proposition, whose compatibility with a given state of facts is a matter of degree and can be measured on an ordered scale S that is no longer $\{0,1\}$, but e.g. the unit interval $[0,1]$. This leads to identifying a "fuzzy proposition" ϕ with a fuzzy set of possible states of affairs; the degree of membership of a state of affairs to this fuzzy set evaluates the degree of fit between the proposition and the state of facts it refers to. This degree of fit is called *degree of truth* of the proposition ϕ in the interpretation $\mathcal{I}$ (state of affairs). Many-valued logics provide compositional calculi of degrees of truth, including degrees between "true" and "false". A sentence is now not true or false only, but may have a truth degree taken from a *truth space* S, usually $[0,1]$ (in that case we speak bout *Mathematical Fuzzy Logic* [95]) or $\{\frac{0}{n}, \frac{1}{n}, \ldots, \frac{n}{n}\}$ for an integer $n \geqslant 1$. Often S may be also a complete lattice or a bilattice [85,79] (often used in logic programming [80]). In the sequel, we assume $S = [0,1]$.

In the many-valued logic that we consider here, *many-valued formulas* have the form $\phi \geqslant l$ or $\phi \leqslant u$, where $l, u \in [0,1]$ [93,95], which encode that the degree of truth of ϕ is *at least* l resp. *at most* u. For example, $ripe\_tomato \geqslant 0.9$ says that we have a rather ripe tomato (the degree of truth of $ripe\_tomato$ is at least 0.9).

Semantically, a *many-valued interpretation* $\mathcal{I}$ maps each basic proposition p_i into $[0, 1]$ and is then extended inductively to all propositions as follows:

$$
\begin{aligned}
\mathcal{I}(\phi \wedge \psi) &= \mathcal{I}(\phi) \otimes \mathcal{I}(\psi)\,; \\
\mathcal{I}(\phi \vee \psi) &= \mathcal{I}(\phi) \oplus \mathcal{I}(\psi)\,; \\
\mathcal{I}(\phi \rightarrow \psi) &= \mathcal{I}(\phi) \Rightarrow \mathcal{I}(\psi)\,; \\
\mathcal{I}(\neg \phi) &= \ominus \mathcal{I}(\phi)\,,
\end{aligned}
\tag{5}
$$

where $\otimes$, $\oplus$, $\Rightarrow$, and $\ominus$ are so-called *combination functions*, namely, *triangular norms* (or *t-norms*), *triangular co-norms* (or *s-norms*), *implication functions*, and *negation functions*, respectively, which extend the classical Boolean conjunction, disjunction, implication, and negation, respectively, to the many-valued case.

Several t-norms, s-norms, implication functions, and negation functions have been given in the literature. An important aspect of such functions is that they satisfy some properties that one expects to hold for the connectives; see Tables 1 and 2. Note that in Table 1, the two properties Tautology and Contradiction follow from Identity, Commutativity, and Monotonicity. Usually, the implication function $\Rightarrow$ is defined as *r-implication*, that is, $a \Rightarrow b = \sup \{c \mid a \otimes c \leqslant b\}$.

Some t-norms, s-norms, implication functions, and negation functions of various fuzzy logics are shown in Table 3 [95]. In fuzzy logic, one usually distinguishes three different logics, namely, Łukasiewicz, Gödel, and Product logic; the popular Zadeh logic is a sublogic of Łukasiewicz logic. Some salient properties of these logics are shown in Table 4. For more properties, see especially [95, 209]. Note also, that a many-valued logic having all properties shown in Table 4, collapses to boolean logic, that is the truth-set can be $\{0, 1\}$ only.

The implication $x \Rightarrow y = \max(1 - x, y)$ is called *Kleene-Dienes implication* in the fuzzy logic literature. Note that we have the following inferences: Let $a \geqslant n$ and $a \Rightarrow b \geqslant m$. Then, under Kleene-Dienes implication, we infer that if $n > 1 - m$ then $b \geqslant m$. Under r-implication relative to a t-norm $\otimes$, we infer that $b \geqslant n \otimes m$.

Note that implication functions and t-norms are also used to define the degree of subsumption between fuzzy sets and the composition of two (binary) fuzzy relations. A *fuzzy set* R over a countable crisp set X is a function $R \colon X \rightarrow [0, 1]$. The *degree of subsumption* between two fuzzy sets A and B, denoted $A \sqsubseteq B$, is defined as $\inf_{x \in X} A(x) \Rightarrow B(x)$, where $\Rightarrow$ is an implication function. Note that if $A(x) \leqslant B(x)$, for all $x \in [0, 1]$, then $A \sqsubseteq B$ evaluates to 1. Of course, $A \sqsubseteq B$ may evaluate to a value $v \in (0, 1)$ as well. A (binary) *fuzzy relation* R over two countable crisp sets X and Y is a function $R \colon X \times Y \rightarrow [0, 1]$. The *inverse* of R is the function $R^{-1} \colon Y \times X \rightarrow [0, 1]$ with membership function $R^{-1}(y, x) = R(x, y)$, for every $x \in X$ and $y \in Y$. The *composition* of two fuzzy relations $R_1 \colon X \times Y \rightarrow [0, 1]$ and $R_2 \colon Y \times Z \rightarrow [0, 1]$ is defined as $(R_1 \circ R_2)(x, z) = \sup_{y \in Y} R_1(x, y) \otimes R_2(y, z)$. A fuzzy relation R is *transitive* iff $R(x, z) \geqslant (R \circ R)(x, z)$.

A many-valued interpretation $\mathcal{I}$ *satisfies* a many-valued formula $\phi \geqslant l$ (resp., $\phi \leqslant u$) or $\mathcal{I}$ is a *model* of $\phi \geqslant l$ (resp., $\phi \leqslant u$), denoted $\mathcal{I} \models \phi \geqslant l$ (resp., $\mathcal{I} \models \phi \leqslant u$), iff $\mathcal{I}(\phi) \geqslant l$ (resp., $\mathcal{I}(\phi) \leqslant u$). The notions of satisfiability, logical consequence, and tight logical consequence for many-valued knowledge bases are then defined in the standard way (in the same way as in the probabilistic case). We refer the reader to [92, 93, 95] for algorithms for many-valued logics.

Table 1. Properties for t-norms and s-norms

Axiom Name	T-norm	S-norm
Tautology / Contradiction	$a \otimes 0 = 0$	$a \oplus 1 = 1$
Identity	$a \otimes 1 = a$	$a \oplus 0 = a$
Commutativity	$a \otimes b = b \otimes a$	$a \oplus b = b \oplus a$
Associativity	$(a \otimes b) \otimes c = a \otimes (b \otimes c)$	$(a \oplus b) \oplus c = a \oplus (b \oplus c)$
Monotonicity	if $b \leqslant c$, then $a \otimes b \leqslant a \otimes c$	if $b \leqslant c$, then $a \oplus b \leqslant a \oplus c$

Table 2. Properties for implication and negation functions

Axiom Name	Implication Function	Negation Function
Tautology / Contradiction	$0 \Rightarrow b = 1,\ a \Rightarrow 1 = 1,\ 1 \Rightarrow 0 = 0$	$\ominus 0 = 1,\ \ominus 1 = 0$
Antitonicity	if $a \leqslant b$, then $a \Rightarrow c \geqslant b \Rightarrow c$	if $a \leqslant b$, then $\ominus a \geqslant \ominus b$
Monotonicity	if $b \leqslant c$, then $a \Rightarrow b \leqslant a \Rightarrow c$	

Table 3. Combination functions of various fuzzy logics

	Łukasiewicz Logic	Gödel Logic	Product Logic	Zadeh Logic
$a \otimes b$	$\max(a + b - 1, 0)$	$\min(a, b)$	$a \cdot b$	$\min(a, b)$
$a \oplus b$	$\min(a + b, 1)$	$\max(a, b)$	$a + b - a \cdot b$	$\max(a, b)$
$a \Rightarrow b$	$\min(1 - a + b, 1)$	$\begin{cases} 1 & \text{if } a \leqslant b \\ b & \text{otherwise} \end{cases}$	$\min(1, b/a)$	$\max(1 - a, b)$
$\ominus a$	$1 - a$	$\begin{cases} 1 & \text{if } a = 0 \\ 0 & \text{otherwise} \end{cases}$	$\begin{cases} 1 & \text{if } a = 0 \\ 0 & \text{otherwise} \end{cases}$	$1 - a$

Table 4. Some additional properties of combination functions of various fuzzy logics

Property	Łukasiewicz Logic	Gödel Logic	Product Logic	Zadeh Logic
$x \otimes \ominus x = 0$	+	+	+	−
$x \oplus \ominus x = 1$	+	−	−	−
$x \otimes x = x$	−	+	−	+
$x \oplus x = x$	−	+	−	+
$\ominus \ominus x = x$	+	−	−	+
$x \Rightarrow y = \ominus x \oplus y$	+	−	−	+
$\ominus (x \Rightarrow y) = x \otimes \ominus y$	+	−	−	+
$\ominus (x \otimes y) = \ominus x \oplus \ominus y$	+	+	+	+
$\ominus (x \oplus y) = \ominus x \otimes \ominus y$	+	+	+	+

3 Managing Imperfect Knowledge in Semantic Web Languages

3.1 The Case of Description Logics

Probabilistic Uncertainty and Description Logics. Although there are several previous approaches to probabilistic description logics without semantic web background, P-$\mathcal{SHOIN}(\mathbf{D})$ [86, 167, 171] (see also [175]) is the most expressive probabilistic description logic, both in terms of the generalized classical description logic and in terms of the supported forms of terminological and assertional probabilistic knowledge. The syntax of the probabilistic description logic P-$\mathcal{SHOIN}(\mathbf{D})$ uses the notion of a conditional constraint from [157] to express probabilistic knowledge in addition to the axioms of $\mathcal{SHOIN}(\mathbf{D})$. Its semantics is based on the notion of lexicographic entailment in probabilistic default reasoning [159, 163], which is a probabilistic generalization of the sophisticated notion of lexicographic entailment by Lehmann [132] in default reasoning from conditional knowledge bases. Due to this semantics, P-$\mathcal{SHOIN}(\mathbf{D})$ allows for expressing both terminological probabilistic knowledge about concepts and roles, and also assertional probabilistic knowledge about instances of concepts and roles. It naturally interprets terminological and assertional probabilistic knowledge as statistical knowledge about concepts and roles and as degrees of belief about instances of concepts and roles, respectively, and allows for deriving both statistical knowledge and degrees of belief. As an important additional feature, it also allows for expressing default knowledge about concepts (as a special case of terminological probabilistic knowledge), which is semantically interpreted as in Lehmann's lexicographic default entailment [132].

Roughly, every probabilistic knowledge base consists of (i) a PTBox, which is a classical (description logic) knowledge base along with probabilistic terminological knowledge, and (ii) a collection of PABoxes, which encode probabilistic assertional knowledge about a certain set of individuals. To this end, we partition the set of individuals $\mathbf{I}$ into the set of *classical individuals* $\mathbf{I}_C$ and the set of *probabilistic individuals* $\mathbf{I}_P$, and we associate with every probabilistic individual a PABox. That is, probabilistic individuals are those individuals in $\mathbf{I}$ for which we explicitly store some probabilistic assertional knowledge in a PABox.

We first define conditional constraints as follows. We assume a finite nonempty set $\mathcal{C}$ of *basic classification concepts* (or *basic c-concepts* for short), which are (not necessarily atomic) concepts in $\mathcal{SHOIN}(\mathbf{D})$ that are free of individuals from $\mathbf{I}_P$. Informally, they are the relevant description logic concepts for defining probabilistic relationships. The set of *classification concepts* (or *c-concepts*) is inductively defined as follows. Every basic c-concept $\phi \in \mathcal{C}$ is a c-concept. If ϕ and ψ are c-concepts, then $\neg\phi$ and $(\phi \sqcap \psi)$ are also c-concepts. We often write $(\phi \sqcup \psi)$ to abbreviate $\neg(\neg\phi \sqcap \neg\psi)$, as usual.

A *conditional constraint* is an expression of the form $(\psi|\phi)[l, u]$, where ϕ and ψ are c-concepts, and l and u are reals from $[0, 1]$. Informally, $(\psi|\phi)[l, u]$ encodes that the probability of ψ given ϕ lies between l and u.

A PTBox, a PABox, and a probabilistic knowledge bases are defined as follows: (i) A *PTBox* $PT = (T, P)$ consists of a classical (description logic) knowledge base T and a finite set of conditional constraints P; (ii) A *PABox* P is a finite set of conditional constraints; and (iii) a *probabilistic knowledge base* $KB = (T, P, (P_o)_{o \in \mathbf{I}_P})$ relative to $\mathbf{I}_P$ consists of a PTBox $PT = (T, P)$ and one PABox P_o for every probabilistic individual $o \in \mathbf{I}_P$. The meaning of a conditional constraint $(\psi|\phi)[l, u]$ depends on whether it belongs to P or to P_o for some probabilistic individual $o \in \mathbf{I}_P$:

- Each $(\psi|\phi)[l, u]$ in P informally encodes that "generally, if an object belongs to ϕ, then it belongs to ψ with a probability in $[l, u]$". For example, $(\exists R.\{o\}|\phi)[l, u]$ in P, where $o \in \mathbf{I}_C$ and $R \in \mathbf{R}_A$, encodes that "generally, if an object belongs to ϕ, then it is related to o by R with a probability in $[l, u]$".

– Each $(\psi|\phi)[l, u]$ in P_o, where $o \in \mathbf{I}_P$, informally encodes that "if o belongs to ϕ, then o belongs to ψ with a probability in $[l, u]$". For example, $(\exists R.\{o'\}|\phi)[l, u]$ in P_o, where $o \in \mathbf{I}_P$, $o' \in \mathbf{I}_C$, and $R \in \mathbf{R}_A$, expresses that "if o belongs to ϕ, then o is related to o' by R with a probability in $[l, u]$".

So, a probabilistic knowledge base $KB = (T, P, (P_o)_{o \in \mathbf{I}_P})$ extends a classical knowledge base T by probabilistic terminological knowledge P and probabilistic assertional knowledge P_o about every $o \in \mathbf{I}_P$. That is, P represents our statistical knowledge about concepts, while every P_o represents our degrees of belief about o.

Observe that the axioms in T and the conditional constraints in every P_o with $o \in \mathbf{I}_P$ are strict (that is, they must always hold), while the conditional constraints in P are defeasible (that is, they may have exceptions and thus do not always have to hold), since $T \cup P$ may not always be satisfiable as a whole in combination with our degrees of belief (and then we ignore some elements of P).

Consequently, a conditional constraint $(\psi|\phi)[1, 1]$ in P encodes "generally, if an object belongs to ϕ, then it also belongs to ψ", while $(\psi|\phi)[1, 1]$ in P_o encodes "if o belongs to ϕ, then o also belongs to ψ". The latter is equivalent to the implication $o : \phi \Rightarrow o : \psi$, while the former is in general not equivalent to $\phi \sqsubseteq \psi$.

Semantics. Now we define the semantics of P-$\mathcal{SHOIN}(\mathbf{D})$. After some preliminaries, we introduce the notions of consistency and lexicographic entailment for probabilistic knowledge bases, which are based on the notions of consistency and lexicographic entailment, respectively, in probabilistic default reasoning [159, 163].

We now define (possible) objects and probabilistic interpretations, which are certain sets of basic c-concepts resp. probability functions on the set of all (possible) objects. We also define the satisfaction of classical knowledge bases and conditional constraints in probabilistic interpretations.

A *(possible) object* o is a set of basic c-concepts $\phi \in \mathcal{C}$ such that $\{i : \phi \,|\, \phi \in o\} \cup \{i : \neg\phi \,|\, \phi \in \mathcal{C} \setminus o\}$ is satisfiable, where i is a new individual. Informally, every object o represents an individual i that is fully specified on $\mathcal{C}$ in the sense that o belongs (resp., does not belong) to every c-concept $\phi \in o$ (resp., $\phi \in \mathcal{C} \setminus o$). We denote by $\mathcal{O}_\mathcal{C}$ the set of all objects relative to $\mathcal{C}$. An object o *satisfies* a classical knowledge base T, or o is a *model* of T, denoted $o \models T$, iff $T \cup \{i : \phi \,|\, \phi \in o\} \cup \{i : \neg\phi \,|\, \phi \in \mathcal{C} \setminus o\}$ is satisfiable, where i is a new individual. An object o *satisfies* a basic c-concept $\phi \in \mathcal{C}$, or o is a *model* of ϕ, denoted $o \models \phi$, iff $\phi \in o$. The satisfaction of c-concepts by objects is inductively extended to all c-concepts, as usual, by (i) $o \models \neg\phi$ iff $o \models \phi$ does not hold, and (ii) $o \models \phi \sqcap \psi$ iff $o \models \phi$ and $o \models \psi$. It is not difficult to verify that a classical knowledge base T is satisfiable iff an object $o \in \mathcal{O}_\mathcal{C}$ exists that satisfies T.

A *probabilistic interpretation* Pr is a probability function on $\mathcal{O}_\mathcal{C}$ (that is, a mapping $Pr : \mathcal{O}_\mathcal{C} \to [0, 1]$ such that all $Pr(o)$ with $o \in \mathcal{O}_\mathcal{C}$ sum up to 1). We say Pr *satisfies* a classical knowledge base T, or Pr is a *model* of T, denoted $Pr \models T$, iff $o \models T$ for every $o \in \mathcal{O}_\mathcal{C}$ such that $Pr(o) > 0$. We define the probability of a c-concept and the satisfaction of conditional constraints in probabilistic interpretations as follows. The *probability* of a c-concept ϕ in a probabilistic interpretation Pr denoted $Pr(\phi)$, is the sum of all $Pr(o)$ such that $o \models \phi$. For c-concepts ϕ and ψ such that $Pr(\phi) > 0$, we write $Pr(\psi|\phi)$ to abbreviate $Pr(\phi \sqcap \psi) / Pr(\phi)$. We say Pr *satisfies* a conditional constraint $(\phi|\psi)[l, u]$, or Pr is a *model* of $(\psi|\phi)[l, u]$, denoted $Pr \models (\psi|\phi)[l, u]$, iff $Pr(\phi) = 0$ or $Pr(\psi|\phi) \in [l, u]$. We say Pr *satisfies* a set of conditional constraints $\mathcal{F}$, or Pr is a *model* of $\mathcal{F}$, denoted $Pr \models \mathcal{F}$, iff $Pr \models F$ for all $F \in \mathcal{F}$. It is not difficult to verify that a classical knowledge base T is satisfiable iff there exists a probabilistic interpretation that satisfies T.

The notion of consistency for PTBoxes and probabilistic knowledge bases is based on the notion of consistency in probabilistic default reasoning [159, 163]. We first give some preparative definitions. A probabilistic interpretation Pr *verifies* a conditional constraint $(\psi|\phi)[l, u]$ iff $Pr(\phi) = 1$ and $Pr(\psi) \in [l, u]$, that is, iff $Pr(\phi) = 1$ and $Pr \models (\psi|\phi)[l, u]$. We say Pr *falsifies* $(\psi|\phi)[l, u]$ iff $Pr(\phi) = 1$ and $Pr \not\models (\psi|\phi)[l, u]$. A set of conditional constraints $\mathcal{F}$ *tolerates* a conditional constraint F under a classical knowledge base T iff $T \cup \mathcal{F}$ has a model that verifies F.

A PTBox $PT = (T, P)$ is *consistent* iff (i) T is satisfiable and (ii) there exists an ordered partition $(P_0, \ldots, P_k)$ of P such that each P_i with $i \in \{0, \ldots, k\}$ is the set of all $F \in P \setminus (P_0 \cup \cdots \cup P_{i-1})$ that are tolerated under T by $P \setminus (P_0 \cup \cdots \cup P_{i-1})$. Informally, condition (ii) means that P has a natural ordered partition into collections of conditional constraints of increasing specificities such that every collection is locally consistent. That is, any inconsistencies can be naturally resolved by preferring more specific pieces of knowledge to less specific ones. For example, the inconsistency between $(\neg \exists HasColor.\{red\} \mid Car)[1, 1]$ and $(\exists HasColor.\{red\} \mid SportsCar)[1, 1]$ when reasoning about sports cars is naturally resolved by preferring the latter to the former. We call the above (unique) ordered partition $(P_0, \ldots, P_k)$ of P the *z-partition* of PT. A probabilistic knowledge base $KB = (T, P, (P_o)_{o \in \mathbf{I}_P})$ is *consistent* iff (i) $PT = (T, P)$ is consistent and (ii) $T \cup P_o$ is satisfiable for every probabilistic individual $o \in \mathbf{I}_P$. Informally, (ii) says that the strict knowledge in T must be compatible with the strict degrees of belief in P_o, for every probabilistic individual o. Observe that (i) involves T and P, while (ii) involves T and P_o, for every probabilistic individual o. This separate treatment of P and the P_o's is due to the fact that P represents probabilistic terminological knowledge, while each P_o represents probabilistic assertional knowledge (about o).

The notion of lexicographic entailment for probabilistic knowledge bases is based on lexicographic entailment in probabilistic default reasoning [159, 163]. In the sequel, let $KB = (T, P, (P_o)_{o \in \mathbf{I}_P})$ be a consistent probabilistic knowledge base. We first define a lexicographic preference relation on probabilistic interpretations, which is then used to define the notion of lexicographic entailment for sets of conditional constraints under PTBoxes. We finally define the notion of lexicographic entailment for deriving statistical knowledge and degrees of belief about probabilistic objects from PTBoxes and probabilistic knowledge bases, respectively.

We use the (unique) z-partition $(P_0, \ldots, P_k)$ of (T, P) to define a lexicographic preference relation on probabilistic interpretations Pr and Pr': We say Pr is *lexicographically preferable* (or *lex-preferable*) to Pr' iff some $i \in \{0, \ldots, k\}$ exists such that $|\{F \in P_i \mid Pr \models F\}| > |\{F \in P_i \mid Pr' \models F\}|$ and $|\{F \in P_j \mid Pr \models F\}| = |\{F \in P_j \mid Pr' \models F\}|$ for all $i < j \leqslant k$. Roughly speaking, this preference relation implements the idea of preferring more specific pieces of knowledge to less specific ones in the case of local inconsistencies. It can thus be used for ignoring the latter when drawing conclusions in the case of local inconsistencies. A model Pr of a classical knowledge base T

and a set of conditional constraints $\mathcal{F}$ is a *lexicographically minimal* (or *lex-minimal*) *model* of $T \cup \mathcal{F}$ iff no model of $T \cup \mathcal{F}$ is lex-preferable to Pr.

We define the notion of lexicographic entailment of conditional constraints from sets of conditional constraints under PTBoxes as follows. A conditional constraint $(\psi|\phi)[l, u]$ is a *lexicographic consequence* (or *lex-consequence*) of a set of conditional constraints $\mathcal{F}$ under a PTBox PT, denoted $\mathcal{F} \|\!\!\sim^{lex} (\psi|\phi)[l, u]$ under PT, iff $Pr(\psi) \in [l, u]$ for every lex-minimal model Pr of $T \cup \mathcal{F} \cup \{(\phi|\top)[1, 1]\}$. We say $(\psi|\phi)[l, u]$ is a *tight lexicographic consequence* (or *tight lex-consequence*) of $\mathcal{F}$ under PT, denoted $\mathcal{F} \|\!\!\sim^{lex}_{tight} (\psi|\phi)[l, u]$ under PT, iff l (resp., u) is the infimum (resp., supremum) of $Pr(\psi)$ subject to all lex-minimal models Pr of $T \cup \mathcal{F} \cup \{(\phi|\top)[1, 1]\}$. Note that $[l, u] = [1, 0]$ (where $[1, 0]$ represents the empty interval) when no such model Pr exists. Furthermore, for inconsistent PTBoxes PT, we define $\mathcal{F} \|\!\!\sim^{lex} (\psi|\phi)[l, u]$ and $\mathcal{F} \|\!\!\sim^{lex}_{tight} (\psi|\phi)[1, 0]$ under PT for all sets of conditional constraints $\mathcal{F}$ and all conditional constraints $(\psi|\phi)[l, u]$.

We now define which statistical knowledge and degrees of belief follow under lexicographic entailment from PTBoxes PT and probabilistic knowledge bases $KB = (T, P, (P_o)_{o \in \mathbf{I}_P})$, respectively. A conditional constraint F is a *lex-consequence* of PT, denoted $PT \|\!\!\sim^{lex} F$, iff $\emptyset \|\!\!\sim^{lex} F$ under PT. We say F is a *tight lex-consequence* of PT, denoted $PT \|\!\!\sim^{lex}_{tight} F$, iff $\emptyset \|\!\!\sim^{lex}_{tight} F$ under PT. A conditional constraint F for a probabilistic individual $o \in \mathbf{I}_P$ is a *lex-consequence* of KB, denoted $KB \|\!\!\sim^{lex} F$, iff $P_o \|\!\!\sim^{lex} F$ under $PT = (T, P)$. We say F is a *tight lex-consequence* of KB, denoted $KB \|\!\!\sim^{lex}_{tight} F$, iff $P_o \|\!\!\sim^{lex}_{tight} F$ under $PT = (T, P)$.

The main reasoning problems in P-$\mathcal{SHOIN}(\mathbf{D})$ are summarized by the following decision and computation problems (where every lower and upper bound in the PTBox $PT = (T, P)$, the probabilistic knowledge base $KB = (T, P, (P_o)_{o \in \mathbf{I}_P})$, and the set of conditional constraints $\mathcal{F}$ is rational):

PTBOX CONSISTENCY (PTCON): Given a PTBox $PT = (T, P)$, decide whether PT is consistent.

PROBABILISTIC KNOWLEDGE BASE CONSISTENCY (PKBCON): Given a probabilistic knowledge base $KB = (T, P, (P_o)_{o \in \mathbf{I}_P})$, decide whether KB is consistent.

TIGHT LEXICOGRAPHIC ENTAILMENT (TLEXENT): Given a PTBox $PT = (T, P)$, a finite set of conditional constraints $\mathcal{F}$, and two c-concepts ϕ and ψ, compute the rational numbers $l, u \in [0, 1]$ such that $\mathcal{F} \|\!\!\sim^{lex}_{tight} (\psi|\phi)[l, u]$ under PT.

Some important special cases of TLEXENT are given as follows: (PCSUB) given a consistent PTBox PT and two c-concepts ϕ and ψ, compute the rational numbers $l, u \in [0, 1]$ such that $PT \|\!\!\sim^{lex}_{tight} (\psi|\phi)[l, u]$; (PCRSUB) given a consistent PTBox PT, a c-concept ϕ, a classical individual $o \in \mathbf{I}_C$, and an abstract role $R \in \mathbf{R}_A$, compute the rational numbers $l, u \in [0, 1]$ such that $PT \|\!\!\sim^{lex}_{tight} (\exists R.\{o\}|\phi)[l, u]$; (PCMEM) given a consistent probabilistic knowledge base KB, a probabilistic individual $o \in \mathbf{I}_P$, and a c-concept ψ, compute $l, u \in [0, 1]$ such that $KB \|\!\!\sim^{lex}_{tight} (\psi|\top)[l, u]$ for o; and (PRMEM) given a consistent probabilistic knowledge base KB, a classical individual $o' \in \mathbf{I}_C$, a probabilistic individual $o \in \mathbf{I}_P$, and an abstract role $R \in \mathbf{R}_A$, compute $l, u \in [0, 1]$ such that $KB \|\!\!\sim^{lex}_{tight} (\exists R.\{o'\}|\top)[l, u]$ for o.

Another important decision problem in P-$\mathcal{SHOIN}$(**D**) is PROBABILISTIC CON-
CEPT SATISFIABILITY (PCSAT): Given a consistent PTBox PT and a c-concept ϕ,
decide whether $PT \not\Vdash^{lex} (\phi|\top)[0,0]$. This problem is reducible to CSAT (classical,
non-probabilistic concept satisfiability), since $(T,P) \not\Vdash^{lex} (\phi|\top)[0,0]$ iff $T \not\models \phi \sqsubseteq \bot$.

There exists an algorithm for deciding whether a PTBox (resp., probabilistic knowledge base) in P-$\mathcal{SHOIN}$(**D**) is consistent, which is based on a reduction to deciding
whether a classical knowledge base in $\mathcal{SHOIN}$(**D**) is satisfiable and to deciding whether
a system of linear constraints is solvable. More specifically, one has to solve a sequence
of solvability problems of systems of linear constraints, whose variables are computed
by deciding classical knowledge base satisfiability in $\mathcal{SHOIN}$(**D**) (see [167] for further details). This shows that the two consistency problems in P-$\mathcal{SHOIN}$(**D**) are both
decidable. Furthermore, there is a similar algorithm for computing tight intervals under
lexicographic entailment in P-$\mathcal{SHOIN}$(**D**), which is based on a reduction to deciding
classical knowledge base satisfiability in $\mathcal{SHOIN}$(**D**) and to solving linear optimization
problems (see [167]). Thus, also lexicographic entailment in P-$\mathcal{SHOIN}$(**D**) is computable. As for the computational complexity, deciding the two consistency problems
in P-$\mathcal{SHOIN}$(**D**) is complete for the complexity class NEXP, while computing tight
intervals under lexicographic entailment in P-$\mathcal{SHOIN}$(**D**) belongs to FP^{NEXP} [167].

Note that if the chosen classical description logic allows for decidable knowledge
base satisfiability, then also the main reasoning tasks in the probabilistic extension are
all decidable. (see [167, 171] for further details).

There are already implementations of its predecessor P-$\mathcal{SHOQ}$(**D**) (see [200]) and of
a probabilistic description logic based on probabilistic default reasoning as in [159, 163].
Recently, the Pronto system [1], claims to have implemented P-$\mathcal{SHOIN}$(**D**).

Example 3.1. Suppose we have the following KB, *KB*, where T contains *Eagle* $\sqsubseteq$
Bird and *Penguin* $\sqsubseteq$ *Bird*, while P contains $(Fly \mid Bird)[0.95, 1]$ and $(Fly \mid$
$Penguin)[0, 0.05]$. Then we can infer the tightest bounds $KB \models (Fly \mid Eagle)[0.95, 1]$
and $KB \models (Fly \mid Penguin)[0, 0.05]$. $\qquad\qquad\square$

Other approaches. Other approaches to probabilistic description logics can be classified
according to the generalized classical description logics, the supported forms of probabilistic knowledge, the underlying probabilistic semantics, and the reasoning techniques.

One of the earliest approaches to probabilistic description logics is due to Heinsohn [99], who presents a probabilistic extension of the description logic $\mathcal{ALC}$, which
allows to represent terminological probabilistic knowledge about concepts and roles,
and which is based on the notion of logical entailment in probabilistic logics, similar
to [5, 81, 157, 207]. Heinsohn [99], however, does not allow for assertional (classical or
probabilistic) knowledge about concept and role instances. The main reasoning problems are deciding the consistency of probabilistic terminological knowledge bases and
computing logically entailed tight probability intervals. Heinsohn proposes a sound and
complete global reasoning technique based on classical reasoning in $\mathcal{ALC}$ and linear
programming, as well as a sound but incomplete local reasoning technique based on the
iterative application of local inference rules.

---

[1] http://clarkparsia.com/weblog/2007/09/27/introducing-pronto/

Another early approach to probabilistic description logics is due to Jaeger [112], who also proposes a probabilistic extension of the description logic $\mathcal{ALC}$, which allows for terminological probabilistic knowledge about concepts and roles, and assertional probabilistic knowledge about concept instances, but does not support assertional probabilistic knowledge about role instances (but he mentions a possible extension in this direction). The entailment of terminological probabilistic knowledge from terminological probabilistic knowledge is based on the notion of logical entailment in probabilistic logic, while the entailment of assertional probabilistic knowledge from terminological and assertional probabilistic knowledge is based on a cross-entropy minimization relative to terminological probabilistic knowledge. The main reasoning problems are terminological probabilistic consistency and inference, which are solved by linear programming, and assertional probabilistic consistency and inference, which are solved by an approximation algorithm.

The recent work by Dürig and Studer [66] presents a further probabilistic extension of $\mathcal{ALC}$, which is based on a model-theoretic semantics as in probabilistic logics, but which only allows for assertional probabilistic knowledge about concept and role instances, and not for terminological probabilistic knowledge. The paper also explores independence assumptions for assertional probabilistic knowledge. The main reasoning problem is deciding the consistency of assertional probabilistic knowledge, but neither an algorithm nor a decidability result is given.

Jaeger's recent work [113] focuses on interpreting probabilistic concept subsumption and probabilistic role quantification through statistical sampling distributions, and develops a probabilistic version of the guarded fragment of first-order logic. The semantics is different from the semantics of all the other probabilistic description logics in this paper, since it is based on probability distributions over the domain, and not on the more commonly used probability distributions over a set of possible worlds. The paper proposes a sound Gentzen-style sequent calculus for the logic, but it neither proves the completeness of this calculus nor decidability in general.

Koller et al.'s work [125] presents the probabilistic description logic P-CLASSIC, which is a probabilistic generalization (of a variant) of the description logic CLASSIC. Similar to Heinsohn's work [99], it allows for encoding terminological probabilistic knowledge about concepts, roles, and attributes (via so-called p-classes), but it does not support assertional (classical or probabilistic) knowledge about instances of concepts and roles. However, in contrast to [99], its probabilistic semantics is based on a reduction to Bayesian networks. The main reasoning problem is to determine the exact probabilities for conditionals between concept expressions in canonical form. This problem is solved by a reduction to inference in Bayesian networks. As an important feature of P-CLASSIC, the above problem can be solved in polynomial time, when the underlying Bayesian network is a polytree. Note that a recent implementation of P-CLASSIC is described in [115].

Closely related work by Yelland [285] proposes a probabilistic extension of a description logic close to $\mathcal{FL}$, whose probabilistic semantics is also based on a reduction to Bayesian networks, and it applies this approach to market analysis. The approach allows for encoding terminological probabilistic knowledge about concepts and roles, but it does not support assertional (classical or probabilistic) knowledge about instances of concepts and roles. Like in Koller et al.'s work [125], the main reasoning problem is to determine the exact probabilities for conditionals between concepts, which is solved by a reduction to inference in Bayesian networks.

Probabilistic Web Ontology Languages. The literature contains several probabilistic generalizations of web ontology languages. Many of these approaches focus especially on combining the web ontology language OWL with probabilistic formalisms based on Bayesian networks.

In particular, da Costa [28], da Costa and Laskey [29], and da Costa et al. [30] suggest a probabilistic generalization of OWL, called PR-OWL, whose probabilistic semantics is based on multi-entity Bayesian networks (MEBNs). The latter are a Bayesian logic that combines first-order logic with Bayesian networks. Roughly speaking, PR-OWL represents knowledge as parameterized fragments of Bayesian networks. Hence, it can encode probability distributions on the interpretations of an associated first-order theory as well as repeated structure.

In [54, 55], Ding et al. propose a probabilistic generalization of OWL, called Bayes-OWL, which is based on standard Bayesian networks. BayesOWL provides a set of rules and procedures for the direct translation of an OWL ontology into a Bayesian network, and it also provides a method for incorporating available probability constraints when constructing the Bayesian network. The generated Bayesian network, which preserves the semantics of the original ontology and which is consistent with all the given probability constraints, supports ontology reasoning, both within and across ontologies, as Bayesian inferences. In [55, 212], Ding et al. also describe an application of the BayesOWL approach in ontology mapping.

In closely related work, Mitra et al. [194] describe an implemented technique, called OMEN, to enhancing existing ontology mappings by using a Bayesian network to represent the influences between potential concept mappings across ontologies. More concretely, OMEN is based on a simple ontology model similar to RDF Schema. It uses a set of meta-rules that capture the influence of the ontology structure and the semantics of ontology relations, and matches nodes that are neighbours of already matched nodes in the two ontologies.

Yang and Calmet [282] present an integration of the web ontology language OWL with Bayesian networks, called OntoBayes. The approach makes use of probability and dependency-annotated OWL to represent uncertain information in Bayesian networks. The work also describes an application in risk analysis for insurance and natural disaster management. Pool and Aikin [214] also provide a method for representing uncertainty in OWL ontologies, while Fukushige [83] proposes a basic framework for representing probabilistic relationships in RDF. Nottelmann and Fuhr [208] present two probabilistic extensions of variants of OWL Lite, along with a mapping to locally stratified probabilistic Datalog.

Another important work is due to Udrea et al. [272], who present a probabilistic generalization of RDF, which allows for representing terminological probabilistic knowledge about classes and assertional probabilistic knowledge about properties of individuals. They provide a technique for assertional probabilistic inference in acyclic probabilistic RDF theories, which is based on the notion of logical entailment in probabilistic logic, coupled with a local probabilistic semantics. They also provide a prototype implementation of their algorithms.

An important application for probabilistic ontologies (and thus probabilistic description logics and ontology languages) is especially information retrieval. In particular, Subrahmanian's group [109, 271] explores the use of probabilistic ontologies in relational databases. They propose to extend relations by associating with every attribute a constrained probabilistic ontology, which describes relationships between terms occurring in the domain of that attribute. An extension of the relational algebra then allows for an increased recall (which is the proportion of documents relevant to a search query in the collection of all returned documents) in information retrieval. In closely related work, Mantay et al. [182] propose a probabilistic least common subsumer operation, which is based on a probabilistic extension of the description logic $\mathcal{ALN}$. They show that applying this approach in information retrieval allows for reducing the amount of retrieved data and thus for avoiding information flood. Another closely related work by Holi and Hyvönen [101, 102] shows how degrees of overlap between concepts can be modelled and computed efficiently using Bayesian networks based on RDF(S) ontologies. Such degrees of overlap indicate how well an individual data item matches the query concept, and can thus be used for measuring the relevance in information retrieval tasks. Finally, Weikum et al. [280] and Thomas and Sheth [268] describe the use of probabilistic ontologies in information retrieval from a more general perspective.

Possibilistic Uncertainty and Description Logics. Similar to probabilistic extensions of description logics, possibilistic extensions of description logics have been developed by Hollunder [107]; Dubois et al. [58] and more recently in [217].

A *possibilistic axiom* is of the form $\mathsf{P}\,\alpha \geq l$ or $\mathsf{N}\,\alpha \geq l$, where α is a classical description logic axiom, and l is a real number from $[0, 1]$. A *possibilistic RBox* (resp., *TBox, ABox*) is a finite set of possibilistic axioms $\mathsf{P}\,\alpha \geq l$ or $\mathsf{N}\,\alpha \geq l$, where α is an RBox (resp., TBox, ABox) axiom. A *possibilistic knowledge base* $KB = (\mathcal{R}, \mathcal{T}, \mathcal{A})$ consists of a possibilistic RBox $\mathcal{R}$, a possibilistic TBox $\mathcal{T}$, and a possibilistic ABox $\mathcal{A}$. The semantics is a straightforward extension from the propositional case to the FOL case.

The main reasoning problems related to possibilistic description logics are deciding whether a possibilistic knowledge base is satisfiable, deciding whether a possibilistic axiom is a logical consequence of a possibilistic knowledge base, and computing the tight lower and upper bounds entailed by a possibilistic knowledge base for the necessity and the possibility of a classical description logic axiom. As shown by Hollunder [107], deciding logical consequences, and thus also deciding satisfiability and computing tight lower and upper bounds can be reduced to deciding logical consequences in classical description logics.

Example 3.2. Suppose that the KB, KB, contains

$$\mathsf{N}(\exists owns.Porsche \sqsubseteq CarFanatic \sqcup RichPerson) \geq 0.8$$
$$\mathsf{P}(RichPerson \sqsubseteq Golfer) \geq 0.7$$
$$\mathsf{N}((tom, 911): owns) \geq 1$$
$$\mathsf{N}(911: Porsche) \geq 1$$
$$\mathsf{N}(tom: \neg CarFanatic) \geq 0.7\,.$$

We are interested to the question whether or not that Tom is a golfer. It can be shown that

$$KB \models \mathsf{P}(tom\colon Golfer) \geqslant 0.7.$$ □

A recent implementation of reasoning in possibilistic description logics using KAON2[2] is reported in [218, 219].

We recall that Liau and Yao [139] report on an application of possibilistic description logics in information retrieval. More concretely, they define a possibilistic generalization of the description logic $\mathcal{ALC}$ and show that it can be used in typical information retrieval problems, such as query relaxation, query restriction, and exemplar-based retrieval. Possibilistic description logics can also be used for handling inconsistencies in ontologies [218, 219]. Another important application of possibilistic description logics is the representation of user preferences in the Semantic Web. For example, the recent work by Hadjali et al. [90] shows that possibilistic logic can be nicely used for encoding user preferences in the context of databases.

Vagueness and Description Logics. There are several extensions of description logics and ontology languages using the theory of fuzzy logic. They can be classified according to (a) the description logic resp. ontology language that they generalize, (b) the allowed fuzzy constructs, (c) the underlying fuzzy logics, and (d) their reasoning algorithms.

In general, fuzzy DLs allow expressions of the form $(a\colon C, n)$, stating that a is an instance of concept C with degree at least n, that is the FOL formula $C(a)$ is true to degree at least n (it is straightforward to map DL expressions into FOL formulae). Similarly, $(C_1 \sqsubseteq C_2, n)$ and $(R_1 \sqsubseteq R_2, n)$ state vague subsumption relationships. Informally, $(C_1 \sqsubseteq C_2, n)$ dictates that the FOL formula $\forall x.C_1(x) \rightarrow C_2(x)$ is always true to degree at least n (note that in mathematical fuzzy logic, the universal quantification $\forall x$ is interpreted as $\inf_x$, and similarly, $\exists x$ is interpreted as $\sup_x$ and, that not always $\neg\forall$ is the same as $\exists\neg$, –this is true only for Zadeh logic and Łukasiewicz logic).

Specifically, fuzzy DLs supports concrete data types such as reals, integers, strings and allows the definition of concepts with explicit representation of fuzzy membership functions. This is implemented by relying on so-called fuzzy data type theory. A *fuzzy data type theory* $\mathbf{D} = (\Delta_{\mathbf{D}}, \cdot_{\mathbf{D}})$ is such that $\cdot_{\mathbf{D}}$ assigns to every n-ary data type predicate d an n-ary fuzzy relation over $\Delta_{\mathbf{D}}$ [176]. For instance, the predicate $\leqslant_{18}$ may be a unary crisp predicate over the natural numbers denoting the set of integers smaller or equal to 18. Concerning non-crisp fuzzy domain predicates, we recall that in fuzzy set theory and practice, there are many functions for specifying fuzzy set membership degrees. However, the trapezoidal (Fig. 2 (a)), the triangular (Fig. 2 (b)), the L-function (left-shoulder function, Fig. 2 (c)), and the R-function (right-shoulder function, Fig. 2 (d)) are simple, but most frequently used to specify membership degrees. These functions are defined over the set of non-negative rationals $\mathbb{Q}^+ \cup \{0\}$ For instance, we may define $Young\colon \mathbb{N} \rightarrow [0, 1]_D$ to be a fuzzy concrete predicate over the natural numbers denoting the degree of youngness of a person's age, as $Young(x) = ls(10, 30)$.

---

[2] http://kaon2.semanticweb.org/

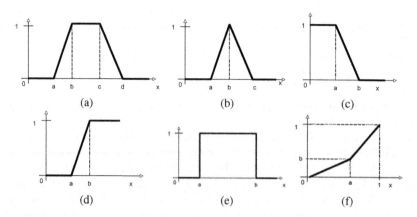

Fig. 2. (a) Trapezoidal function $trz(a, b, c, d)$; (b) Triangular function $tri(a, b, c)$; (c) L-function $ls(a, b)$; (d) R-function $rs(a, b)$; (e) Crisp interval $cr(a, b)$; (f) Linear function $ln(a, b)$

Fuzzy DLs allow fuzzy modifiers, such as *very*, *more_or_less* and *slightly*, which apply to fuzzy sets to change their membership function. Formally, a *modifier* is a function $f_m : [0, 1] \rightarrow [0, 1]$. We will allow modifiers defined in terms of linear hedges (Figure 2 (f)) and triangular functions (Figure 2 (d)). Modifiers have also been considered in [105, 269].

Furthermore, fuzzy DLs extend crisp DLs with some specific constructs, which we define next (see, e.g. [14]). Let $\mathbf{A}$, $\mathbf{R}_A$, $\mathbf{R}_D$, $\mathbf{I}$, I_c and $\mathbf{M}$ be non-empty finite and pairwise disjoint sets of *concepts names* (denoted A), *abstract roles names* (denoted R), *concrete roles names* (denoted T), *abstract individual names* (denoted x, y), *concrete individual names* (denoted v) and *modifiers* (denoted m). Concepts may be seen as unary predicates, while roles may be seen as binary predicates. $\mathbf{R}_A$ also contains a non-empty subset $\mathbf{F}_a$ of *abstract feature names* (denoted r), while $\mathbf{R}_D$ contains a non-empty subset $\mathbf{F}_c$ of *concrete feature names* (denoted t). Features are functional roles. Besides the usual concept forming constructs, a fuzzy DL supports also constructs dealing with concrete data types, that is it has the additional concept constructs:

$$C, D := \forall T.d \mid \exists T.d \mid DR$$
$$d := cr(a, b) \mid ls(a, b) \mid rs(a, b) \mid$$
$$tri(a, b, c) \mid trz(a, b, c, d)$$
$$DR := \geqslant t\ val \mid \leqslant t\ val \mid = t\ val$$

where *val* is an integer, a real or a string depending on the range of the concrete feature t. For instance, the expression $Human \sqcap (\leqslant hasAge\ 18)$ will denote the set of humans, which have an age less or equal than 18, while $Human \sqcap \exists hasAge.ln(10, 30)$ will denote the set of young humans (their age is $L(10, 30)$).

Finally, additional useful concept constructs are:

$$C, D := C \sqcap_G D \mid C \sqcap_{\text{Ł}} D \mid C \sqcup_G D \mid C \sqcup_{\text{Ł}} D \mid$$
$$C \rightarrow D \mid C \rightarrow_G D \mid C \rightarrow_{\text{Ł}} D \mid m(C) \mid$$
$$nC \mid w_1 C_1 + \cdots + w_k C_k \mid C[\geqslant n] \mid C[\leqslant n]$$
$$m := ln(a, b) \mid tri(a, b, c)$$

where $n \in [0,1]_D$, $w_i \in [0,1]_D$, $\sum_{i=1}^{k} w_i = 1$. For instance, the concept $m(C)$ applies the modifier m to the concept C and, thus, e.g. $Human \sqcap \exists hasAge.ln(0.8, 0.3)$ $(ls(10, 30))$ denotes the set of *very* young humans.

A *fuzzy knowledge base* (KB) $KB = (\mathcal{A}, \mathcal{T}, \mathcal{R})$ consists of a fuzzy ABox $\mathcal{A}$, a fuzzy TBox $\mathcal{T}$ and a fuzzy RBox $\mathcal{R}$.

A *fuzzy ABox* $\mathcal{A}$ consists of a finite set of *fuzzy concept* and *fuzzy role assertion axioms* of the form $\langle x : C, \alpha \rangle$ and $\langle (x, y) : R, \alpha \rangle$, where $\alpha \in (0, 1]_D$. Informally, from a semantical point of view, $\langle \tau, \alpha \rangle$ constrains the membership degree of τ to be at least α. Hence, $\langle jim : YoungPerson, 0.2 \rangle$ says that jim is a $YoungPerson$ with degree at least 0.2, while $\langle (jim, tom) : hasFriend, 1 \rangle$, states that jim and tom are friends. If the α is omitted, 1 is assumed.

A *fuzzy TBox* $\mathcal{T}$ is a finite set of *fuzzy General Concept Inclusion axioms* (GCIs) $\langle C \sqsubseteq D, \alpha \rangle$, where $\alpha \in (0, 1]_D$ and C, D are concepts. Informally, $\langle C \sqsubseteq D, \alpha \rangle$ states that all instances of concept C are instances of concept D to degree α, that is, the subsumption degree between C and D is at least α. For instance, $\langle Elephant \sqsubseteq Animal, 1 \rangle$ states that the class of elephants is a subclass of the class of animals. We write $C = D$ as a shorthand of the two axioms $\langle C \sqsubseteq D, 1 \rangle$ and $\langle D \sqsubseteq C, 1 \rangle$. For instance, $Minor = Person \sqcap (\leqslant hasAge\ 18)$ defines a person, whose age is less or equal to 18 ($hasAge$ is a concrete feature), that is a minor. If the truth value α is omitted then the value 1 is assumed.

Fuzzy DLs also allow to write $\sqsubseteq_\Rightarrow$ in order to specify the particular implication function to be used in the semantics of the GCI (General Concept Inclusion Axiom), e.g., Łukasiewicz or Gödel.

A *fuzzy RBox* $\mathcal{R}$ is a finite set of role axioms of the form:

- $(fun\ R)$, stating that a role R is functional, that is R is a feature.
- $(trans\ R)$, stating that a role R is transitive.
- $R_1 \sqsubseteq R_2$, meaning that role R_2 subsumes role R_1.
- $(inv\ R_1\ R_2)$, stating that role R_2 is the inverse of R_1 (and vice versa).

A simple role is a role which is neither transitive nor has a transitive subroles. An important restriction is that functional needs to be simple.

Semantics. The main idea is that concepts and roles are interpreted as fuzzy subsets of an interpretation's domain. Therefore, axioms, rather than being "classical" evaluated (being either true or false), they are "many-valued" evaluated in $[0, 1]_D$.

A *fuzzy interpretation* $\mathcal{I} = (\Delta^{\mathcal{I}}, \cdot^{\mathcal{I}})$ relative to a fuzzy data type theory $\mathbf{D} = (\Delta_{\mathbf{D}}, \cdot_{\mathbf{D}})$ consists of a nonempty set $\Delta^{\mathcal{I}}$ (the *domain*), disjoint from $\Delta_{\mathbf{D}}$, and of a *fuzzy interpretation function* $\cdot^{\mathcal{I}}$ that coincides with $\cdot_{\mathbf{D}}$ on every data value, data type, and fuzzy data type predicate, and it assigns:

- to each abstract concept C a function $C^{\mathcal{I}} : \Delta^{\mathcal{I}} \to [0, 1]$;
- to each abstract role R a function $R^{\mathcal{I}} : \Delta^{\mathcal{I}} \times \Delta^{\mathcal{I}} \to [0, 1]$;
- to each abstract feature r a partial function $r^{\mathcal{I}} : \Delta^{\mathcal{I}} \times \Delta^{\mathcal{I}} \to [0, 1]$ such that for all $x \in \Delta^{\mathcal{I}}$ there is an unique $y \in \Delta^{\mathcal{I}}$ on which $r^{\mathcal{I}}(x, y)$ is defined;
- to each concrete role T a function $R^{\mathcal{I}} : \Delta^{\mathcal{I}} \times \Delta_{\mathbf{D}} \to [0, 1]$;

Table 5. Semantics of the complex fuzzy concepts

$$\perp^{\mathcal{I}}(x) = 0$$
$$\top^{\mathcal{I}}(x) = 1$$
$$(\neg C)^{\mathcal{I}}(x) = \ominus C^{\mathcal{I}}(x)$$
$$(C \sqcap D)^{\mathcal{I}}(x) = C^{\mathcal{I}}(x) \otimes D^{\mathcal{I}}(x)$$
$$(C \sqcap_G D)^{\mathcal{I}}(x) = C^{\mathcal{I}}(x) \otimes_G D^{\mathcal{I}}(x)$$
$$(C \sqcap_{\mathbf{L}} D)^{\mathcal{I}}(x) = C^{\mathcal{I}}(x) \otimes_{\mathbf{L}} D^{\mathcal{I}}(x)$$
$$(C \sqcup D)^{\mathcal{I}}(x) = C^{\mathcal{I}}(x) \oplus D^{\mathcal{I}}(x)$$
$$(C \sqcup_G D)^{\mathcal{I}}(x) = C^{\mathcal{I}}(x) \oplus_G D^{\mathcal{I}}(x)$$
$$(C \sqcup_{\mathbf{L}} D)^{\mathcal{I}}(x) = C^{\mathcal{I}}(x) \oplus_{\mathbf{L}} D^{\mathcal{I}}(x)$$
$$(C \to D)^{\mathcal{I}}(x) = C^{\mathcal{I}}(x) \Rightarrow D^{\mathcal{I}}(x)$$
$$(C \to_G D)^{\mathcal{I}}(x) = C^{\mathcal{I}}(x) \Rightarrow_G D^{\mathcal{I}}(x)$$
$$(= t\ val)^{\mathcal{I}}(x) = \sup_{c \in \Delta_D} t(x, v) \otimes (v = val)$$
$$(C \to_{\mathbf{L}} D)^{\mathcal{I}}(x) = C^{\mathcal{I}}(x) \Rightarrow_L D^{\mathcal{I}}(x)$$

$$(m(C))^{\mathcal{I}}(x) = f_m(C^{\mathcal{I}}(x))$$
$$(\forall R.C)^{\mathcal{I}}(x) = \inf_{y \in \Delta^{\mathcal{I}}} R^{\mathcal{I}}(x, y) \Rightarrow C^{\mathcal{I}}(y)$$
$$(\exists R.C)^{\mathcal{I}}(x) = \sup_{y \in \Delta^{\mathcal{I}}} R^{\mathcal{I}}(x, y) \otimes C^{\mathcal{I}}(y)$$
$$(\forall T.d)^{\mathcal{I}}(x) = \inf_{y \in \Delta_D} T^{\mathcal{I}}(x, v) \Rightarrow d^{\mathcal{I}}(y)$$
$$(\exists T.d)^{\mathcal{I}}(x) = \sup_{y \in \Delta_D} T^{\mathcal{I}}(x, v) \otimes d^{\mathcal{I}}(y)$$
$$(n\ C)^{\mathcal{I}}(x) = n\ C^{\mathcal{I}}(x)$$
$$(w_1 C_1 + \cdots + w_k C_k)^{\mathcal{I}}(x) = w_1 C_1{}^{\mathcal{I}}(x) + \cdots + w_k C_k{}^{\mathcal{I}}(x)$$
$$(C[\geqslant n])^{\mathcal{I}}(x) = \begin{cases} C^{\mathcal{I}}(x), & \text{if } C^{\mathcal{I}}(x) \geqslant n \\ 0, & \text{otherwise} \end{cases}$$
$$(C[\leqslant n])^{\mathcal{I}}(x) = \begin{cases} C^{\mathcal{I}}(x), & \text{if } C^{\mathcal{I}}(x) \leqslant n \\ 0, & \text{otherwise} \end{cases}$$
$$(\geqslant t\ val)^{\mathcal{I}}(x) = \sup_{c \in \Delta_D} t(x, v) \otimes (v \geqslant val)$$
$$(\leqslant t\ val)^{\mathcal{I}}(x) = \sup_{c \in \Delta_D} t(x, v) \otimes (v \leqslant val)$$

Table 6. Semantics of other constructs

$$(x : C)^{\mathcal{I}} = C^{\mathcal{I}}(x^{\mathcal{I}})$$
$$((x, y) : R)^{\mathcal{I}} = R^{\mathcal{I}}(x^{\mathcal{I}}, y^{\mathcal{I}})$$
$$(C \sqsubseteq D)^{\mathcal{I}} = \inf_{x \in \Delta^{\mathcal{I}}} C^{\mathcal{I}}(x) \Rightarrow D^{\mathcal{I}}(x)$$
$$(C \sqsubseteq_G D)^{\mathcal{I}} = \inf_{x \in \Delta^{\mathcal{I}}} C^{\mathcal{I}}(x) \Rightarrow_G D^{\mathcal{I}}(x)$$
$$(C \sqsubseteq_{\mathbf{L}} D)^{\mathcal{I}} = \inf_{x \in \Delta^{\mathcal{I}}} C^{\mathcal{I}}(x) \Rightarrow_{\mathbf{L}} D^{\mathcal{I}}(x)$$

- to each concrete feature t a partial function $t^{\mathcal{I}} : \Delta^{\mathcal{I}} \times \Delta_{\mathbf{D}} \to [0, 1]$ such that for all $x \in \Delta^{\mathcal{I}}$ there is an unique $v \in \Delta_{\mathbf{D}}$ on which $t^{\mathcal{I}}(x, v)$ is defined;
- to each modifier m the modifier function $f_m : [0, 1] \to [0, 1]$;
- to each abstract individual x an element in $\Delta^{\mathcal{I}}$;
- to each concrete individual v an element in $\Delta_{\mathbf{D}}$.

The mapping $\cdot^{\mathcal{I}}$ is extended to roles and complex concepts as specified in Table 5, while the mapping $\cdot^{\mathcal{I}}$ is extended to the other constructs as specified in Table 6.

The notion of *satisfaction* of a fuzzy axiom E by a fuzzy interpretation $\mathcal{I}$, denoted $\mathcal{I} \models E$, is defined as follows:

- $\mathcal{I} \models (\tau, \alpha) \geqslant$ iff $\tau^{\mathcal{I}} \geqslant \alpha$,
- $\mathcal{I} \models (trans\ R)$ iff $\forall_{x, y \in \Delta^{\mathcal{I}}}, R^{\mathcal{I}}(x, y) \geqslant \sup_{z \in \Delta^{\mathcal{I}}} R^{\mathcal{I}}(x, z) \otimes R^{\mathcal{I}}(z, y)$,
- $\mathcal{I} \models R_1 \sqsubseteq R_2$ iff $\forall x, y \in \Delta^{\mathcal{I}}.R_1{}^{\mathcal{I}}(x, y) \leqslant R_2{}^{\mathcal{I}}(x, y)$,
- $\mathcal{I} \models (inv\ R_1\ R_2)$ iff $\forall x, y \in \Delta^{\mathcal{I}}.R_1{}^{\mathcal{I}}(x, y) = R_2{}^{\mathcal{I}}(y, x)$.

We say that concept C is *satisfiable* iff there is an interpretation $\mathcal{I}$ and an individual $x \in \Delta^{\mathcal{I}}$ such that $C^{\mathcal{I}}(x) > 0$.

For a set of axioms $\mathcal{E}$, we say that $\mathcal{I}$ *satisfies* $\mathcal{E}$ iff I satisfies each element in $\mathcal{E}$. We say that $\mathcal{I}$ is a *model* of E (resp. $\mathcal{E}$) iff $\mathcal{I} \models E$ (resp. $\mathcal{I} \models \mathcal{E}$). $\mathcal{I}$ *satisfies* (is a *model* of) a fuzzy KB $KB = (\mathcal{A}, \mathcal{T}, \mathcal{R})$, denoted $\mathcal{I} \models KB$, iff $\mathcal{I}$ is a model of each component $\mathcal{A}, \mathcal{T}$ and $\mathcal{R}$, respectively.

An axiom E is a *logical consequence* of a knowledge base KB, denoted $KB \models E$ iff every model of KB satisfies E.

Given *KB* and a fuzzy axiom τ of the forms $\langle x\colon C, \alpha\rangle$, $\langle (x,y)\colon R, \alpha\rangle$ or $\langle C \sqsubseteq D, \alpha\rangle$, it is of interest to compute τ's best lower degree value bound. The *greatest lower bound* of τ w.r.t. *KB* (denoted $glb(KB, \tau)$) is $glb(KB, \tau) = \sup\{n \mid KB \models (\tau, n)\geqslant\}$, where $\sup \emptyset = 0$. Determining the *glb* is called the *Best Degree Bound* (BDB) problem.

Finally, another similar problem is to compute the *best satisfiability bound* of a concept *C* and amounts to determine $glb(KB, C) = \sup_{\mathcal{I}} \sup_{x\in\Delta^{\mathcal{I}}}\{C^{\mathcal{I}}(x) \mid \mathcal{I} \models KB\}$. Essentially, among all models $\mathcal{I}$ of the KB, we are determining the maximal degree of truth that the concept *C* may have over all individuals $x \in \Delta^{\mathcal{I}}$.

Example 3.3. Assume, that a car seller sells a sedan car. A buyer is looking for a second hand passenger car. Both the buyer as well as the seller have preferences (restrictions). Our aim is to find the best agreement. The preferences are as follows. Concerning the buyer:

1. He does not want to pay more than 26000 euro (buyer reservation value).
2. If there is an alarm system in the car then he is completely satisfied with paying no more than 22300 euro, but he can go up to 22750 euro to a lesser degree of satisfaction.
3. He wants a driver insurance and either a theft insurance or a fire insurance.
4. He wants air conditioning and the external colour should be either black or grey.
5. Preferably the price is no more than 22000 euro, but he can go up to 24000 euro to a lesser degree of satisfaction.
6. The kilometer warranty is preferrably at least 175000, but he may go down to 150000 to a lesser degree of satisfaction.
7. The weights of the preferences 2-6 are, $(0.1, 0.2, 0.1, 0.2, 0.4)$. The higher the value the more important is the preference.

Concerning the seller:

1. He wants to sell no less than 22000 euro (seller reservation value)
2. If there is an navigator pack system in the car then he is completely satisfied with paying no less than 22750 euro, but he can go down to 22500 euro to a lesser degree of satisfaction.
3. Preferably the buyer buys the Insurance Plus package.
4. The kilometer warranty is preferrably at most 100000, but he may go up to 125000 to a lesser degree of satisfaction.
5. The monthly warranty is preferrably at most 60, but he may go up to 72 to a lesser degree of satisfaction.
6. If the colour is black then the car has air conditioning.
7. The weights of the preferences 2-6 are, $(0.3, 0.1, 0.3, 0.1, 0.2)$. The higher the value the more important is the preference.

We have also some background theory about the domain:

1. A sedan is a passenger car.
2. A satellite alarm system is an alarm system.
3. The navigator pack is a satellite alarm system with a GPS system.
4. The Insurance Plus package is a driver insurance together with a theft insurance.
5. The car colours are black or grey.

Now, the background theory can be encoded as:

$$Sedan \sqsubseteq PassengerCar$$
$$SatelliteAlarm \sqsubseteq AlarmSystem$$
$$NavigatorPack = SatelliteAlarm \sqcap GPS\_system$$
$$InsurancePlus = DriverInsurance \sqcap TheftInsurance$$
$$\top \sqsubseteq ExColorBlack \sqcup ExColorGray$$
$$ExColorBlack \sqcap ExColorGray \sqsubseteq \bot$$
$$(fun\ HasAlarmSystem)$$
$$(fun\ HasAirConditioning)$$
$$(fun\ HasExColor)$$
$$(fun\ HasNavigator)$$
$$(fun\ HasMWarranty)$$
$$(fun\ HasPrice)$$
$$(fun\ HasKMWarranty)$$

The buyer's preferences can be encoded as follows:

1. $B = (PassengerCar \sqcap (\leqslant HasPrice\ 26000))$
2. $B_1 = ((\exists HasAlarmSystem.AlarmSystem) \rightarrow (\exists Has\ Price.ls(22300, 22750)))$
3. $B_2 = ((\exists HasInsurance.DriverInsurance) \sqcap ((\exists HasInsurance.TheftInsurance)$
   $\sqcup (\exists HasInsurance.FireInsurance)))$
4. $B_3 = ((\exists HasAirConditioning.Airconditioning) \sqcap (\exists HasExColor.(ExColorBlack$
   $\sqcup ExColorGray)))$
5. $B_4 = (\exists HasPrice.ls(22000, 24000))$
6. $B_5 = (\exists HasKMWarranty.R(15000, 175000))$
7. $Buy = (B \sqcap ((0.1B_1) + (0.2B_2) + (0.1B_3) + (0.2B_4) + (0.4B_5)))$

Please note that the concept Buy collects all the buyer's preferences together in such a way that the higher is the maximal degree of satisfiability of Buy (that is $glb(KB, Buy)$), the more the buyer is satisfied.

The seller's preferences can be encoded as follows:

1. $S = (Sedan \sqcap (\geqslant HasPrice\ 22000))$
2. $S_1 = ((\exists HasNavigator.NavigatorPack) \rightarrow (\exists Has\ Price.rs(22500, 22750))))$
3. $S_2 = (\exists HasInsurance.InsurancePlus)$
4. $S_3 = (\exists HasKMWarranty.rs(100000, 125000))$
5. $S_4 = (\exists HasMWarranty.rs(60, 72))$
6. $S_5 = ((\exists HasExColor.ExColorBlack) \rightarrow (\exists Has\ AirConditioning.AirCondi-$
   $tioning))$
7. $Sell = (S \sqcap ((0.3S_1) + (0.1S_2) + (0.3S_3) + (0.1S_4) + (0.2S_5)))$

Similarly to the buyer case, the concept $Sell$ collects all the seller's preferences together in such a way that the higher is the maximal degree of satisfiability of $Sell$ (that is $glb(KB, Sell)$), the more the seller is satisfied.

Now, it is clear that the best agreement among the buyer and the seller is determined by the maximal degree of satisfiability of the conjunction $Buy \sqcap Sell$, that is we have to determine $glb(KB, Buy \sqcap Sell)$. In particular, we rely on Łukasiewicz conjunction, which guarantees that the solution is Pareto optimal [220]. In particular, we have that

$$glb(KB, Buy \sqcap_{\mathbf{L}} Sell) = 0.7$$
$$HasPrice = 22000.0$$
$$HasKMWarranty = 175000.0$$
$$HasMWarranty = 0.0 \ .$$

So an optimal match (the Pareto optimal degree is 0.7625) would be an agreement with a price of 22500 euro, with 100000 kilometer warranty and a 60 month warranty.   □

The first work about fuzzy DLs is due to Yen [286], who proposes a fuzzy extension of a very restricted sublanguage of $\mathcal{ALC}$, called $\mathcal{FL}^-$ [18, 133]. The work includes fuzzy terminological knowledge, but no fuzzy assertional knowledge, and it is based on Zadeh logic. It already informally talks about the use of fuzzy modifiers and fuzzy concrete domains. Though, the unique reasoning facility, the subsumption test, is a crisp yes/no questioning. Tresp and Molitor [269] consider a more general extension of fuzzy $\mathcal{ALC}$. Like Yen, they also allow for fuzzy terminological knowledge along with a special form of fuzzy modifiers (which are a combination of two linear functions), but no fuzzy assertional knowledge, and they assume Zadeh logic as underlying fuzzy logic. The work also presents a sound and complete reasoning algorithm testing the subsumption relationship using a linear programming oracle.

Another fuzzy extension of $\mathcal{ALC}$ is due to Straccia [243, 245, 251, 256, 265], who allows for both fuzzy terminological and fuzzy assertional knowledge, but not for fuzzy modifiers and fuzzy concrete domains, and again assumes Zadeh logic as underlying fuzzy logic. Straccia [243, 245] also introduces the best truth value bound problem and provides a sound and complete reasoning algorithm based on completion rules. In [244], Straccia reports a four-valued variant of fuzzy $\mathcal{ALC}$. In the same spirit, Hölldobler et al. [103, 104] extend Straccia's fuzzy $\mathcal{ALC}$ with concept modifiers of the form $f_m(x) = x^\beta$, where $\beta > 0$, and present a sound and complete reasoning algorithm (based on completion rules) for the graded subsumption problem.

Straccia's works [247, 255, 261] are essentially as [245], except that now the set of possible truth values is a complete lattice rather than $[0, 1]$.

Sanchez and Tettamanzi [227, 228, 229] consider a fuzzy extension of the description logic $\mathcal{ALCQ}$ (without assertional component) under Zadeh logic, and they start addressing the issue of a fuzzy semantics of quantifiers. Essentially, fuzzy quantifiers allow to state sentences such as $FaithfulCustomer \sqcap (Most)buys.LowCalorie\text{-} Food$ encoding "the set of all individuals that mostly buy low calorie food". An algorithm is presented, which calculates the satisfiability interval for a fuzzy concept.

Hájek [96, 97] considers a fuzzy extension of the description logic $\mathcal{ALC}$ under arbitrary t-norms. He provides in particular algorithms for deciding whether $(C \sqsubseteq D, 1) \geqslant$ is a tautology and whether $(C \sqsubseteq D, 1) \geqslant$ is satisfiable, which are based on a reduction to the propositional BL logic for which a Hilbert-style axiomatization exists [95] (but see also [97] for the complexity of rational Pavelka logic, and see [16] for some complexity results on reasoning in fuzzy description logics).

Straccia [246] provides a translation of fuzzy $\mathcal{ALC}$ (with general concept inclusion axioms) into classical $\mathcal{ALC}$. The translation is modular, and thus expected to be extendable to more expressive fuzzy description logics as well. The main idea is to translate a fuzzy assertion of the form $(a\colon C, n) \geqslant$ into a crisp assertion $a\colon C_n$, with the intended meaning "a is an instance of C to degree at least n". Then, concept inclusion axioms are used to correctly relate the C_n's. For example, $C_{0.7} \sqsubseteq C_{0.6}$ is used to encode that whenever an individual is an instance of C to degree at least 0.7, then it is also an instance of C to degree at least 0.6. The translation is at most quadratic in the size of the fuzzy knowledge base. Note that the translation does not yet work in the presence of fuzzy modifiers and fuzzy concrete domains. Bobillo et al. [12] extend the approach to a variant of fuzzy $\mathcal{SHOIN}$. The idea has further been considered in the works [137, 138], which essentially provide a crisp language in which expressions of, e.g., the form $a\colon \forall R_{0.8}.C_{0.9}$ are allowed, with the intended meaning "if a has an R-successor to degree at least 0.8, then this successor is also an instance of C to degree at least 0.9". The idea has further been extended to a distributed variant of fuzzy description logics in [149]. A mapping to classical DLs under Łukasiewicz semantics has been provided in [15] for the fuzzy DL $\mathcal{ALCHOI}$.

An interesting extension is due to Kang et al. [43], who extends fuzzy description logics by comparison operators, e.g., to state that "Tom is taller than Tim". Another interesting extension is proposed by Dubois et al. [58], who combine fuzzy description logics with possibility theory. Essentially, since $(a\colon C, n) \geqslant$ is Boolean (either an interpretation satisfies it or not), we can build on top of it an uncertainty logic, which is based on possibility theory in [58].

We recall that usually the semantics used for fuzzy description logics is based on Zadeh logic, but where the concept inclusion is crisp, that is, $C \sqsubseteq D$ is viewed as $\forall x.C(x) \leqslant D(x)$. In [106, 269], a calculus for fuzzy $\mathcal{ALC}$ [230] with fuzzy modifiers and simple TBoxes under Zadeh logic is reported. No indication for the BTVB problem is given. Straccia [243, 245] reports a calculus for fuzzy $\mathcal{ALC}$ and simple TBoxes under Zadeh logic and addresses the BTVB problem. How the satisfiability problem and the BTVB problem can be reduced to classical $\mathcal{ALC}$, and thus can be solved by means of tools like FaCT and RACER is shown in [246]. Results providing a tableaux calculus for fuzzy $\mathcal{SHIN}$ under Zadeh logic (but only allowing for a restricted form of concept inclusion axioms, which are called *fuzzy inclusion introductions* and *fuzzy equivalence introductions*), by adapting similar techniques as for the classical counterpart, are shown in [239, 240]. Fuzzy general concept inclusion axioms under Zadeh logic can be managed as described in [242]. Also interesting is the work [283], which provides a tableau for fuzzy $\mathcal{SHI}$ with general concept inclusion axioms. Finally, the reasoning techniques for classical $\mathcal{SHOIN}(\mathbf{D})$ [108] can be extended to [245], as [238, 239, 240, 241] already show.

On the other hand, fuzzy tableaux algorithms under Zadeh semantics do not seem to be suitable to be adapted to other semantics, such as Łukasiewicz logic. Even more problematic is the fact that they are yet unable to deal with fuzzy concrete domains [248], that is the possibility to allow an explicit representation of fuzzy membership functions. Despite these negative results, recently, [248, 249] report a calculus for fuzzy $\mathcal{ALC}(\mathbf{D})$ whenever the connectives, the modifiers, and the fuzzy datatype predicates are representable as bounded mixed integer linear programs (MILPs). For example, Łukasiewicz logic satisfies these conditions as well as the membership functions for fuzzy datatype predicates that we have presented in this paper. Additionally, modifiers should be a combination of linear functions. In that case, the calculus consists of a set of constraint propagation rules and an invocation to an oracle for MILP. The method has been extended to fuzzy $\mathcal{SHIF}(\mathbf{D})$ [262] (the description logic behind OWL Lite) and a reasoner, called *fuzzyDL* [14], has been implemented and is available at Straccia's web page. *FuzzyDL* supports more features, which we do not address here. The use of MILP for reasoning in fuzzy description logics is not surprising as their use for automated deduction in many-valued logics is well-known [92,93]. Bobillo and Straccia [13] provide a calculus for fuzzy $\mathcal{ALC}(\mathbf{D})$ under product semantics.

A very recent problem for fuzzy description logics is the top-k retrieval problem. While in classical semantics, a tuple satisfies or does not satisfy a query, in fuzzy description logics, a tuple may satisfy a query to a degree. Hence, for example, given a conjunctive query over a fuzzy description logic knowledge base, it is of interest to compute only the top-k answers. While in relational databases, this problem is a current research area (see, e.g., [73,110,135]), very few is known for the case of first-order knowledge bases in general (but see [259]) and description logics in particular. The only works that we are aware of are [254, 260, 266], which deal with the problem of finding the top-k result over knowledge bases in a fuzzy generalization of *DL-Lite* [23] (note that [210,211] is subsumed by [260], though in [210,211] the storage systems is no-longer a database, but a RDF storage system).

Fuzzy logic has numerous practical applications in general (see, e.g., [124]). Related to fuzzy description logics, we point out that they have first been proposed for *logic-based information retrieval* [192], which originated from the idea to annotate textual documents with graded description logic sentences, which goes back to [193]. The idea has been reconsidered in [240, 266, 288]. In particular, (i) Zhang et al. [288] describe a semantic portal that is based on fuzzy description logics; (ii) Li et al. [136] present an improved semantic search model by integrating inference and information retrieval and an implementation in the security domain; (iii) Straccia and Visco [266] report on a multimedia information retrieval system based on a fuzzy DLR-Lite description logic, which is capable to deal with hundreds of thousands of images. D'Aquin et al. [42] provide a use case in the medical domain, where fuzzy concrete domains are used to identify tumor regions in x-ray images. Agarwal and Lamparter [1] use fuzzy description logics to improve searching and comparing products in electronic markets. They provide a more expressive search mechanism that is closer to human reasoning and that aggregates multiple search criteria to a single value (ranking of an offer relative to the query), thus enabling a better selection of offers to be considered for the negotiation. Liu et al. [140] use a fuzzy description logic to model the management part in project selection tasks. Finally, [14] shows also how to use fuzzyDLs for e-Commerce Matchmaking and Semantic Fuzzy Control.

3.2   The Case of Logic Programs

In logic programming, the management of imperfect information has attracted the attention of many researchers and numerous frameworks have been proposed. Addressing all of them is almost impossible, due to both the large number of works published in this field (early works date back to early 80-ties [236]) and the different approaches proposed (see the appendix for a list of references). Like for the DL case, essentially they differ in the underlying notion of uncertainty theory and vagueness theory (probability theory, possibilistic logic, fuzzy logic and multi-valued logic) and how uncertainty/vagueness values, associated to rules and facts, are managed.

Basically [141], a logic program $\mathcal{P}$ is made out by a set of rules and a set of facts. *Facts* are *atoms* of the form $P(t_1, \ldots, t_n)$, where t_i is a *term* (usually, a constant or a variable). In most cases, facts are ground. On the other hand rules are of the form $A \leftarrow B_1, \ldots, B_n$, where each A and B_i is an atom. $B_1, \ldots, B_n$ is called *body*, while A is called head of the rule. The intended meaning of a rules is that "if all B_i are true, then also A is true". From a FOL perspective, a rule is just a FOL formula $\forall \mathbf{x}.B_1 \wedge \ldots \wedge B_n \rightarrow A$, where $\mathbf{x}$ are all the variables occurring in the rule. Such logic programs are called *positive* as no literal occurs. In case a literal occurs in the body, then we speak about *normal logic programs*. We may also have a disjunction of atoms in the head, and then we talk about *disjunctive logic programs* ([234]). In the most general setting, literals are allowed in the head as well and from a semantics point of view, the *stable model semantics* [84] is widely adopted.

Probabilistic Uncertainty and Logic Programs. The variety of proposals of logic programming under probability theory is huge and an description of most of them is out of the scope of this work. We describe here some groups of works.

In probabilistic generalizations of (annotated) logic programs (see [122]) based on probabilistic logic fall works such as [44, 45, 46, 47, 48, 201, 202], where rules have the form of annotated logic programming rules. Facts are expressions of the form $A : \mu$, where μ is an interval in $[0, 1]$. The intended meaning of an expression $A : [m, n]$ is "the probability of the event corresponding to A to occur (have occurred) lies in the interval $[m, n]$". Rules have the form $A : \mu \leftarrow B_1 : \mu_1, \ldots, B_n : \mu_2$, where μ, μ_i are intervals in $[0, 1]$.

In probabilistic generalizations of logic programs based on Bayesian networks / causal models fall works such as [11, 117, 118, 204, 215, 216]. Interesting is Poole's Independent Choice Logic (ICL) approach. It is based on acyclic logic programs $\mathcal{P}$ under different "choices". Each choice along with $\mathcal{P}$ produces a first-order model. By placing a probability distribution over the different choices, one then obtains a distribution over the set of first-order models. Roughly, rules and facts are as for classical logic programs. Additionally, there is a set C of choices of the form $\{(A_1 : \alpha_1), \ldots, (A_n : \alpha_n)\}$, where A_i is an atom and the α_i sum-up to 1. A *total choice* T_C is a set of atoms such that from each choice $C_j \in C$ there is exactly one atom $A_i^i \in C_j$ in T_C. The probability of a query q w.r.t. to $\mathcal{P}$ is the sum of the probabilities p_C of total choices T_C such that $\mathcal{P} \cup T_C \models q$, where p_C is the product of the α_i^j, for $C_i^j \in T_C$. It is worth to note that the ICL approach generalizes Bayesian networks, influence diagrams, Markov decision processes, and normal form games.

In the third group fall first-order generalization of probabilistic knowledge bases in probabilistic logic (based on logical entailment, lexicographic entailment, and maximum entropy entailment) and comprises works such as [153, 160, 162]. In these works, similarly to P-$\mathcal{SHOIN}(\mathbf{D})$, expressions are of the form $(\psi|\phi)[l, u]$, but now ψ, ϕ are formulae rather than concepts. The development of the semantics parallels to the case of P-$\mathcal{SHOIN}(\mathbf{D})$.

For the sake of a concrete example, let us here formally introduce Poole's ICL-based approach. Let us denote with HB_Φ (resp., HU_Φ) the Herbrand base (resp., universe) over Φ, where Φ is a function-free first-order vocabulary Φ with finite nonempty sets of constant symbols and predicate symbols.

A *choice space* C is a set of pairwise disjoint and nonempty sets $A \subseteq HB_\Phi$. Any $A \in C$ is an *alternative* of C and any $a \in A$ an *atomic choice* of C. Intuitively, every $A \in C$ represents a random variable and every $a \in A$ one of its possible values. A *total choice* of C is a set $B \subseteq HB_\Phi$ such that $|B \cap A| = 1$ for all $A \in C$. Intuitively, every total choice B of C represents an assignment of values to all the random variables. A *probability* μ on a choice space C is a probability function on the set of all total choices of C. Intuitively, every μ is a probability distribution over the set of all variable assignments. Since C and all its alternatives are finite, μ can be defined by (i) a mapping $\mu\colon \bigcup C \to [0, 1]$ such that $\sum_{a \in A} \mu(a) = 1$ for all $A \in C$, and (ii) $\mu(B) = \Pi_{b \in B} \mu(b)$ for all total choices B of C. Intuitively, (i) defines a probability over the values of each random variable of C, and (ii) assumes independence between the random variables.

A *probabilistic logic program* $KB = (P, C, \mu)$ consists of a logic program P, and a choice space C such that (i) $\bigcup C \subseteq HB_\Phi$ and (ii) no atomic choice in C coincides with the head of any rule in $ground(P)$, and a probability μ on C. Intuitively, since the total choices of C select subsets of P, and μ is a probability distribution on the total choices of C, every probabilistic logic program compactly represents a probability distribution on a finite set of logic programs. A *probabilistic query* to KB is defined as follows. A formula is inductively defined as (i) and atom; (ii) if ϕ, ψ are formulae, so are $\phi \vee \psi, \phi \wedge \psi, \neg\psi, \phi \to \psi$. If ϕ is a formula and $l, u \in [0, 1]$ then $\exists\phi[l, u]$, is a probabilistic query.

Semantics. A *world* I is an interpretation over HB_Φ. We denote by $\mathcal{I}_\Phi$ the set of all worlds over Φ. A *variable assignment* σ maps each variable x to some $t \in HU_\Phi$. It is extended to all terms by $\sigma(c) = c$ for all constant symbols c from Φ. A world I under σ is a model of an atom A, denoted $I \models_\sigma A$, iff $A\sigma \in I$. The extension of I under σ is a model of a formula ϕ is as usual. A world I under σ is a model of a rule $A \leftarrow B_1, \ldots, B_n$ iff $I \models_\sigma B_1 \wedge \ldots \wedge B_n \to A$.

A *probabilistic interpretation* Pr is a probability function on $\mathcal{I}_\Phi$ (that is, a mapping $Pr\colon \mathcal{I}_\Phi \to [0, 1]$ such that (i) the set of all $I \in \mathcal{I}_\Phi$ with $Pr(I) > 0$ is denumerable, and (ii) all $Pr(I)$ with $I \in \mathcal{I}_\Phi$ sum up to 1). The *probability* of a formula ϕ in Pr under a variable assignment σ, denoted $Pr_\sigma(\phi)$ (or $Pr(\phi)$ when ϕ is ground), is the sum of all $Pr(I)$ such that $I \in \mathcal{I}_\Phi$ and $I \models_\sigma \phi$.

A probabilistic interpretation Pr is a *model* of a query $\exists\phi[l, u]$ iff $Pr_\sigma(\phi) \in [l, u]$ for every variable assignment σ. We say Pr is the *canonical model* of a probabilistic logic program $KB = (P, C, \mu)$ iff every world $I \in \mathcal{I}_\Phi$ with $Pr(I) > 0$ is the minimal model of $P \cup \{p \leftarrow | p \in B\}$ for some total choice B of C with $Pr(I) = \mu(B)$. Notice that every KB has a unique canonical model Pr. We say that a query $\exists\phi[l, u]$ is a *consequence* of KB, denoted $KB \Vdash \exists\phi[l, u]$, iff the canonical model of KB is also a model of $\exists\phi[l, u]$. A query $\exists\phi[l, u]$ is a *tight consequence* of KB, denoted $KB \Vdash_{tight} \exists\phi[l, u]$, iff l (resp., u) is the infimum (resp., supremum) of $Pr_\sigma(\phi)$ subject to the canonical model Pr of KB and all σ. A *correct answer* to $\exists\phi[l, u]$ is a substitution σ such that

$\exists\phi\sigma[l,u]$ is a consequence of KB. A *tight answer* to $\exists\phi[l,u]$ is a substitution σ such that $\exists\phi\sigma[l,u]$ is a tight consequence of KB.

As in Section 2.1, we introduce *conditional formulae* of the form $\phi \mid \psi$, where ϕ and ψ are formulae, and *conditional probabilistic queries* of the form $\exists(\phi \mid \psi)[l,u]$. A probabilistic interpretation Pr is a *model* of a conditional probabilistic query $\exists(\phi \mid \psi)[l,u]$ iff $Pr_\sigma(\phi \mid \psi) \in [l,u]$ for every variable assignment σ, where $Pr_\sigma(\phi \mid \psi)$ is defined similarly as in Eq. 2:

$$Pr_\sigma(\phi \mid \psi) = \begin{cases} \frac{Pr_\sigma(\phi\wedge\psi)}{Pr_\sigma(\psi)} & \text{if } Pr_\sigma(\psi) \neq 0 \\ 1 & \text{otherwise .} \end{cases}$$

Example 3.4. Let us show how we may encode the BN in Example 2.1 into probabilistic logic programs. For each variable a we consider an unary predicate $a(x)$, where the variable x will take either the value T or F. If a node a has no parents then we can encode its associated probability table as follows: we consider the rule

$$a(x) \leftarrow h_a(x)$$

and we consider the alternative C_a in the choice space C,

$$C_a = \{h_a(T), h_a(F)\}$$

with $\mu(h_a(T)) = Pr(a(T)), \mu(h_a(F)) = Pr(a(F)) = 1 - Pr(a(T))$. For instance, related to Fig. 1, we will have

$$Rain(x) \leftarrow h_{Rain}(x)$$
$$C_{Rain} = \{h_{Rain}(T), h_{Rain}(F)\}$$
$$\mu(h_{Rain}(T)) = 0.2$$
$$\mu(h_{Rain}(F)) = 0.8 .$$

If a node a has parents $b_1, \ldots, b_n$, we encode its associated conditional probability table using a rule and an alternative in the choice space:

$$a(x) \leftarrow b_1(x_1), \ldots, b_n(x_n), h_a(x, x_1, \ldots, x_n)$$

and we consider the alternative C_a in the choice space C,

$$C_a = \{h_a(v, v_1, \ldots, v_n) \mid v, v_i \in \{T, F\}\} .$$

with

$$\mu(h_a(v, v_1, \ldots, v_n)) = Pr(a = v \mid b_1 = v_1, \ldots, b_n = v_n) .$$

For instance, related to Fig. 1, we will have

$$Sprinkler(x) \leftarrow Rain(x_1), h_{Sprinkler}(x, x_1)$$
$$C_{Sprinkler} = \{h_{Sprinkler}(T, F), h_{Sprinkler}(T, T),$$
$$h_{Sprinkler}(F, F), h_{Sprinkler}(F, T)\}$$
$$\mu(h_{Sprinkler}(T, F)) = 0.4$$
$$\mu(h_{Sprinkler}(T, T)) = 0.01$$
$$\mu(h_{Sprinkler}(F, F)) = 0.6$$
$$\mu(h_{Sprinkler}(F, T)) = 0.99 .$$

The encoding for the node *GrassWet* is similar.

Then, we may infer that

$$KB \; \Vdash_{tight} \; GrassWet(T)[0.4484, 0.4484]$$
$$KB \; \Vdash_{tight} \; (Rain(T) \wedge GrassWet(T))[0.1604, 0.1604]$$
$$KB \; \Vdash_{tight} \; (Rain(T) \mid GrassWet(T))[0.3577, 0.3577] \,,$$

Note that $0.3577 = 0.1604/0.4484$. □

Possibilistic Uncertainty and Logic Programs. In possibilistic logic programs [57], facts are of the form $(P(t_1, \ldots, t_n), \mathsf{N}\, l)$, while rules are of the form $(A \leftarrow B_1, \ldots, B_n, \mathsf{N}\, l)$. The meaning of them is given directly by the possibilistic FOL formulae, $\mathsf{N}\, P$ $(t_1, \ldots, t_n), \geqslant l$ and $\mathsf{N}\, (\forall \mathbf{x}. B_1 \wedge \ldots \wedge B_n \rightarrow A) \geqslant l$, respectively (the necessity of the formula is greater or equal than l). This basic form has been extended in [206] (which describes also an implementation) to the case of disjunctive logic programming under the stable model semantics, while [2, 3, 4, 25] allow explicitly to deal with fuzzy sets in the language.

Vagueness and Logic Programs. While there is a large literature related to the management of vagueness in logic programs, there are rule forms that are general enough to cover a large amount of them (see e.g., [174, 250, 276]). Roughly, rules are of the form $A \leftarrow f(B_1, ..., B_n)$, where A, B_i are atoms and f is a total function $f : \mathcal{S}^n \rightarrow \mathcal{S}$ over a truth space $\mathcal{S}$. Computationally, given an assignment/interpretation I of values to the B_i, the value of A is computed by stating that A is at least as true as $f(I(B_1), ..., I(B_n))$. The form of the rules is sufficiently expressive to encompass many approaches to many-valued logic programming. [174] provides an even more general setting as the function f may also depend on the variables occurring in the rule body. On the other hand there are also some extensions to many-valued disjunctive logic programs [186, 187, 253]. In some cases, e.g. [130] there is also a function g, which dictates how to aggregate the truth values in case an atom is head of several rules.

Most works deal with logic programs without negation and some may provide some technique to answer queries in a top-down manner, as e.g. [35, 122, 130, 252, 276]. On the other hand, there are very few works dealing with normal logic programs [38, 78, 80, 142, 143, 144, 145, 146, 147, 148, 173, 186, 250, 253, 258, 263], and little is know about top-down query answering procedures. The only exceptions are [250, 258, 263].

Another rising problem is the problem to compute the top-k ranked answers to a query, without computing the score of all answers. This allows to answer queries such as "find the top-k closest hotels to the conference location". Solutions to this problem can be found in [174, 259, 264].

For illustrative purposes, we formally present a quite general logic programming formalism dealing with vagueness.

The truth space that we consider here is the finite set $[0,1]_m = \{ \frac{0}{m}, \frac{1}{m}, \ldots, \frac{m-1}{m}, \frac{m}{m} \}$ (for a natural number $m > 0$), which is pretty common in fuzzy logic. Throughout the paper, we assume $m = 100$ in the examples with usual decimal rounding (e.g., 0.375 becomes 0.38, while 0.374 becomes 0.37).

ID	MODEL	TYPE	PRICE	KM	COLOR	AIRBAG	INTERIOR TYPE	AIR COND	ENGINE FUEL
455	MAZDA 3	Sedan	12500	10000	Red	0	VelvetSeats	1	Gasoline
34	ALFA 156	Sedan	12000	15000	Black	1	LeatherSeats	0	Diesel
1812	FORD FOCUS	StationVagon	11000	16000	Gray	1	LeatherSeats	1	Gasoline

Fig. 3. The car table

A *knowledge base KB* consists of a *facts component F* and an *LP component P*, which are defined below.

Facts Component. F is a finite set of expressions of the form

$$\langle R(c_1, \ldots, c_n), s \rangle ,$$

where R is an n-ary relation, every c_i is a constant, and s is a degree of truth (or simply *score*) in $[0, 1]_m$. For each R, we may represent the facts $\langle R(c_1, \ldots, c_n), s \rangle$ in F by means of a relational $n + 1$-ary table T_R, containing the records $(c_1, \ldots, c_n, s)$. We assume that there cannot be two records $(c_1, \ldots, c_n, s_1)$ and $(c_1, \ldots, c_n, s_2)$ in T_R with $s_1 \neq s_2$ (if there are, then we remove the one with the lower score). Each table is sorted in descending order with respect to the scores. For ease, we may omit the score component and in such cases the value 1 is assumed.

Example 3.5 ([221]). Suppose we have a car selling site, and we would like to buy a car. The cars belong to the relation *CarTable* shown in Fig. 3. Here, the score is implicitly assumed to be 1 in each record. For instance, the first record corresponds to the fact

$$\langle CarTable(455, MAZDA3, Sedan, 12500, 10000, Red, 0, VelvetSeats, 1, Gasoline), 1 \rangle .$$

□

LP Component. P is a finite set of *vague rules* of the form (an example of a rule is shown in Example 3.7 below.)

$$R(\mathbf{x}) \leftarrow \exists \mathbf{y}. f(R_1(\mathbf{z}_1), \ldots, R_l(\mathbf{z}_l), p_1(\mathbf{z}'_1), \ldots, p_h(\mathbf{z}'_h)) ,$$

where

1. R is an n-ary relation, every R_i is an n_i-ary relation,
2. $\mathbf{x}$ are the *distinguished variables*;
3. $\mathbf{y}$ are existentially quantified variables called the *non-distinguished variables*;
4. $\mathbf{z}_i, \mathbf{z}'_j$ are tuples of constants or variables in $\mathbf{x}$ or $\mathbf{y}$;
5. p_j is an n_j-ary *fuzzy predicate* assigning to each n_j-ary tuple $\mathbf{c}_j$ a *score* $p_j(\mathbf{c}_j) \in [0, 1]_m$. Such predicates are called *expensive predicates* in [26] as the score is not pre-computed off-line, but is computed on query execution. We require that an n-ary fuzzy predicate p is *safe*, that is, there is not an m-ary fuzzy predicate p' such that $m < n$ and $p = p'$. Informally, all parameters are needed in the definition of p;
6. f is a *scoring* function $f: ([0, 1]_m)^{l+h} \rightarrow [0, 1]_m$, which combines the scores of the l relations $R_i(\mathbf{c}'_i)$ and the n fuzzy predicates $p_j(\mathbf{c}''_j)$ into an overall *score*

$Vehicles(x) \leftarrow Cars(x)$
$Vehicles(x) \leftarrow Trucks(x)$
$Vehicles(x) \leftarrow Vans(x)$
$Cars(x) \leftarrow LuxuryCars(x)$
$Cars(x) \leftarrow PassengerCars(x)$
$Cars(x_1) \leftarrow CarTable(x_1, \ldots, x_{10})$
$Cars(x) \leftarrow Sedan(x)$
$Cars(x) \leftarrow StationWagon(x)$
$Seats(x_8) \leftarrow CarTable(x_1, \ldots, x_{10})$

$Seats(x) \leftarrow LeatherSeats(x)$
$Seats(x) \leftarrow VelvetSeats(x)$
$PassengerCars(x) \leftarrow MidSizeCars(x)$
$PassengerCars(x) \leftarrow SportyCars(x)$
$PassengerCars(x) \leftarrow CompactCars(x)$
$hasPrice(x_1, x_4) \leftarrow CarTable(x_1, \ldots, x_{10})$
$hasKm(x_1, x_5) \leftarrow CarTable(x_1, \ldots, x_{10})$
$FuelType(x_1, x_{10}) \leftarrow CarTable(x_1, \ldots, x_{10})$

Fig. 4. Excerpt of a car selling ontology

to be assigned to the rule head $R(\mathbf{c})$. We assume that f is *monotone*, that is, for each $\mathbf{v}, \mathbf{v}' \in ([0,1]_m)^{l+h}$ such that $\mathbf{v} \leqslant \mathbf{v}'$, it holds $f(\mathbf{v}) \leqslant f(\mathbf{v}')$, where $(v_1, \ldots, v_{l+h}) \leqslant (v_1', \ldots, v_{l+h}')$ iff $v_i \leqslant v_i'$ for all i. We also assume that the computational cost of f and all fuzzy predicates p_i is bounded by a constant.

We call $R(\mathbf{x})$ the *head* and $\exists \mathbf{y}.f(R_1(\mathbf{z}_1), \ldots, R_l(\mathbf{z}_l), p_1(\mathbf{z}_1'), \ldots, p_h(\mathbf{z}_h'))$ the *body* of the rule. We assume that relations occurring in F do not occur in the head of rules (so, we do not allow that the fact relations occurring in F can be redefined by P). As usual in deductive databases, the relations in F are called *extensional* relations, while the others are *intensional* relations.

Example 3.6. Consider again Example 3.5. An excerpt of the domain ontology is described in Fig. 4 and partially encodes the web directory behind the car selling site www.autos.com. □

Semantically, the notion of Herbrand universe HU_{KB} and Herbrand base HB_{KB} are defined as usual as the set of individual constants occurring in KB and the set of ground atoms that can be formed using constants in HU_{KB} and atoms occurring in KB, respectively. An *interpretation* $\mathcal{I}$ maps every n-ary relation R to a partial function $R^{\mathcal{I}} \colon HU_{KB}^n \to [0,1]_m$ and every constant to an element of HU_{KB} such that $a^{\mathcal{I}} \neq b^{\mathcal{I}}$ if $a \neq b$ (unique name assumption). Note that, since $R^{\mathcal{I}}$ may be a partial function, some tuples may not have a score. Alternatively, we may assume $R^{\mathcal{I}}$ to be a total function. We use the former formulation to distinguish the case where a tuple $\mathbf{c}$ may be retrieved, even though the score is 0, from the case where a tuple is not retrieved, since it does not satisfy the query. In particular, if a tuple does not belong to an extensional relation, then its score is assumed to be undefined, while if $R^{\mathcal{I}}$ is total, then the score of this tuple would be 0.

An interpretation $\mathcal{I}$ is a *model* of (or *satisfies*) a fact $\langle R(c_1, \ldots, c_n), s \rangle$, denoted $\mathcal{I} \models \langle R(c_1, \ldots, c_n), s \rangle$, iff $R^{\mathcal{I}}(c_1, \ldots, c_n) \geqslant s$ whenever $R^{\mathcal{I}}(c_1, \ldots, c_n)$ is defined.

An interpretation $\mathcal{I}$ is a *model* of a rule r of the form $R(\mathbf{x}) \leftarrow \exists \mathbf{y}.\phi(\mathbf{x}, \mathbf{y})$, where $\phi(\mathbf{x}, \mathbf{y}) = \exists \mathbf{y}.f(R_1(\mathbf{z}_1), \ldots, R_l(\mathbf{z}_l), p_1(\mathbf{z}_1'), \ldots, p_h(\mathbf{z}_h'))$, denoted $\mathcal{I} \models r$, iff for all $\mathbf{c} \in HU_{KB}^n$ such that $R^{\mathcal{I}}(\mathbf{c})$ is defined, the following holds (where $\phi^{\mathcal{I}}(\mathbf{c}, \mathbf{c}')$ is obtained from $\phi(\mathbf{c}, \mathbf{c}')$ by replacing every R_i by $R_i^{\mathcal{I}}$ and every constant c by $c^{\mathcal{I}}$):

$$R^{\mathcal{I}}(\mathbf{c}) \geqslant \sup_{\mathbf{c}' \in HU_{KB} \times \cdots \times HU_{KB}, \; \phi^{\mathcal{I}}(\mathbf{c}, \mathbf{c}') \text{ is defined}} \phi^{\mathcal{I}}(\mathbf{c}, \mathbf{c}').$$

$$Pref1(x, p) \leftarrow \min(Cars(x), hasPrice(x, p), ls(10000, 14000)(p)) ; \quad (1)$$
$$Pref2(x, k) \leftarrow \min(Cars(x), hasKM(x, k), ls(13000, 17000)(k)) ; \quad (2)$$
$$Buy(x, p, k) \leftarrow 0.7 \cdot Pref1(x, p) + 0.3 \cdot Pref2(x, k) . \quad (3)$$

Fig. 5. The car buying rules

We say $\mathcal{I}$ is a *model* of a knowledge base KB, denoted $\mathcal{I} \models KB$, iff $\mathcal{I}$ is a model of each expression $E \in F \cup P$. We say KB entails $R(\mathbf{c})$ to degree s, denoted $KB \models \langle R(\mathbf{c}), s \rangle$, iff for each model $\mathcal{I}$ of KB, it is true that $R^{\mathcal{I}}(\mathbf{c}) \geqslant s$ whenever $R^{\mathcal{I}}(\mathbf{c})$ is defined. The *greatest lower bound* of $R(\mathbf{c})$ relative to KB is $glb(KB, R(\mathbf{c})) = \sup\{s \mid KB \models \langle R(\mathbf{c}), s \rangle\}$.

Example 3.7. Consider again Example 3.6. Now, suppose that in buying a car, preferably we would like to pay around \$12000 and the car should have less than 15000 km. Of course, our constraints on price and kilometers are not crisp as we may still accept to some degree, e.g., a car's cost of \$12200 and with 16000 km. Hence, these constraints are rather *vague*. We model this by means of left-shoulder functions (see Fig. 2). We may model the vague constraint on the cost with $ls(10000, 14000)(x)$ dictating that we are definitely satisfied if the price is less than \$10000, but can pay up to \$14000 to a lesser degree of satisfaction. Similarly, we may model the vague constraint on the kilometers with $ls(13000, 17000)(x)$.[3] We also set some preference (weights) on these two vague constraints, say the weight 0.7 to the price constraint and 0.3 to the kilometers constraint, indicating that we give more priority to the price rather than to the car's kilometers. The rules encoding the above conditions are represented in Fig. 5. Rule (1) in Fig. 5 encodes the preference on the price. Here, $ls(10000, 14000)(p)$ is the function that given a price p returns the degree of truth provided by the left-shoulder function $ls(10000, 14000)(p)$ evaluated on the input p. Similarly, for rule (2). Rule (3) encodes the combination of the preferences by taking into account the weight given to each preference. The table below reports the instances of $Buy(x, p, k)$ together with their greatest lower bound.

ID	PRICE	KM	$\|s$
455	12500	10000	0.56
34	12000	15000	0.50
1812	11000	16000	0.60 .

□

The basic inference problem that we are interested in here is the top-k retrieval problem, which is formulated as follows.

Top-k Retrieval. Given a knowledge base KB, retrieve k tuples $(\mathbf{c}, s)$ that instantiate the query relation R with maximal scores (if k such tuples exist), and rank them in decreasing order relative to the score s, denoted

$$ans_k(KB, R) = Top_k\{(\mathbf{c}, s) \mid s = glb(KB, R(\mathbf{c}))\} .$$

---

[3] Recall that in our setting, all fuzzy membership functions provide a truth value in $[0, 1]_m$.

Example 3.8. It can be verified that the answer to the top-2 problem for Example 3.7 is

ID	PRICE	KM	s
1812	*11000*	16000	0.60
455	*12500*	10000	0.56 .

□

3.3 Description Logic Programs

Description Logic Programs [87, 134, 195, 225] are a combination of description logics with logic programming. [4] There is a large body of work on integrating rules and ontologies, which is a key requirement of the layered architecture of the Semantic Web. Significant research efforts focus on hybrid integrations of rules and ontologies, called *description logic programs* (or *dl-programs*), which are of the form $KB = (L, P)$, where L is a description logic knowledge base and P is a finite set of rules involving either queries to L in a loose integration (see especially [71, 72, 68, 69, 70]) or concepts and roles from L as unary resp. binary predicates in a tight integration (see especially [134, 223, 224, 168, 195, 196]). Roughly, in the loosely coupled approach, DL atoms may appear in rule bodies and act as queries to an underlying DL system, while in the tightly coupled approach the integration is more involved.

In parallel to these to approaches (loosely coupled vs. tightly coupled) there has been some works on the extension of these approaches towards the management of imperfect information: (i) under probability fall works such as [20, 21, 164, 169, 170]; (ii) under vagueness fall the works [166, 173, 174, 178, 255, 257, 261, 274]; while a combination of probability and vagueness in description logic programs can be found in the work (unique so far) [172].

References

1. Agarwal, S., Lamparter, S.: Smart: A semantic matchmaking portal for electronic markets. In: CEC 2005: Proceedings of the Seventh IEEE International Conference on E-Commerce Technology (CEC 2005), pp. 405–408. IEEE Computer Society Press, Washington (2005)
2. Alsinet, T., Godo, L.: Towards an automated deduction system for first-order possibilistic logic programming with fuzzy constants. International Journal of Intelligent Systems 17(9), 887–924 (2002)
3. Alsinet, T., Godo, L., Sandri, S.: On the semantics and automated deduction fo PLFC, a logic of possibilistic uncertainty and fuzzyness. In: Proceedings of the 15th Annual Conference on Uncertainty in Artificial Intelligence (UAI 1999) (1999)
4. Alsinet, T., Godo, L.G.L.: A complete calcultis for possibilistic logic programming with fuzzy propositional variables with fuzzy propositional variables. In: Proceedings of the 16th Conference in Uncertainty in Artificial Intelligence (UAI 2000), pp. 1–10. Morgan Kaufmann, San Francisco (2000)
5. Amarger, S., Dubois, D., Prade, H.: Constraint propagation with imprecise conditional probabilities. In: Proceedings UAI 1991, pp. 26–34. Morgan Kaufmann, San Francisco (1991)

---

[4] The term Description Logic Programs was introduced for the specific approach of [87]. We use it here to address any kind of combination of description logics with logic programming.

6. Baader, F., Calvanese, D., McGuinness, D., Nardi, D., Patel-Schneider, P.F. (eds.): The Description Logic Handbook: Theory, Implementation, and Applications. Cambridge University Press, Cambridge (2003)
7. Baldwin, J.F.: Evidential support of logic programming. Fuzzy Sets and Systems 24(1), 1–26 (1987)
8. Baldwin, J.F.: A theory of mass assignments for artificial intelligence. In: Driankov, D., L. Ralescu, A., Eklund, P.W. (eds.) IJCAI-WS 1991. LNCS, vol. 833, pp. 22–34. Springer, Heidelberg (1994)
9. Baldwin, J.F., Martin, T.P., Pilsworth, B.W.: Fril - Fuzzy and Evidential Reasoning in Artificial Intelligence. Research Studies Press Ltd (1995)
10. Baldwin, J.F., Martin, T.P., Pilsworth, B.W.: Applications of fuzzy computation: Knowledge based systems: Knowledge representation. In: Ruspini, E.H., Bonnissone, P., Pedrycz, W. (eds.) Handbook of Fuzzy Computing, IOP Publishing (1998)
11. Baral, C., Gelfond, M., Rushton, N.: Probabilistic reasoning with answer sets. In: Lifschitz, V., Niemelä, I. (eds.) LPNMR 2004. LNCS (LNAI), vol. 2923, pp. 21–33. Springer, Heidelberg (2003)
12. Bobillo, F., Delgado, M., Gómez-Romero, J.: A crisp representation for fuzzy $\mathcal{SHOIN}$ with fuzzy nominals and general concept inclusions. In: Proceedings of the 2th Workshop on Uncertainty Reasoning for the Semantic Web (URSW 2006) (November 2006)
13. Bobillo, F., Straccia, U.: A fuzzy description logic with product t-norm. In: Proceedings of the IEEE International Conference on Fuzzy Systems (Fuzz-IEEE 2007), pp. 652–657. IEEE Computer Society Press, Los Alamitos (2007)
14. Bobillo, F., Straccia, U.: fuzzyDL: An expressive fuzzy description logic reasoner. In: 2008 International Conference on Fuzzy Systems (FUZZ 2008), pp. 923–930. IEEE Computer Society Press, Los Alamitos (2008)
15. Bobillo, F., Straccia, U.: Towards a crisp representation of fuzzy description logics under Łukasiewicz semantics. In: An, A., Matwin, S., Raś, Z.W., Ślęzak, D. (eds.) Foundations of Intelligent Systems. LNCS (LNAI), vol. 4994, pp. 309–318. Springer, Heidelberg (2008)
16. Bonatti, P., Tettamanzi, A.: Some complexity results on fuzzy description logics. In: Di Gesú, V., Masulli, F., Petrosino, A. (eds.) WILF 2003. LNCS (LNAI), vol. 2955. Springer, Heidelberg (2006)
17. Boole, G.: An Investigation of the Laws of Thought, on which are Founded the Mathematical Theories of Logic and Probabilities. Walton and Maberley, London (1854); (reprint: Dover Publications, New York, 1958)
18. Brachman, R.J., Levesque, H.J.: The tractability of subsumption in frame-based description languages. In: Proceedings of AAAI 1984, 4th Conference of the American Association for Artificial Intelligence, Austin, TX, pp. 34–37 (1984); [a] An extended version appears as [133]
19. Bueno, F., Cabeza, D., Carro, M., Hermenegildo, M., López-García, P., Puebla, G.: The Ciao prolog system. Reference manual. Technical Report CLIPS3/97.1, School of Computer Science, Technical University of Madrid (UPM) (1997), http://www.cliplab.org/Software/Ciao/
20. Calì, A., Lukasiewicz, T.: Tightly integrated probabilistic description logic programs for the semantic web. In: Dahl, V., Niemelä, I. (eds.) ICLP 2007. LNCS, vol. 4670, pp. 428–429. Springer, Heidelberg (2007)
21. Calì, A., Lukasiewicz, T., Predoiu, L., Stuckenschmidt, H.: Tightly integrated probabilistic description logic programs for representting ontology mappings. In: Hartmann, S., Kern-Isberner, G. (eds.) FoIKS 2008. LNCS, vol. 4932, pp. 178–198. Springer, Heidelberg (2008)
22. Calmet, J., Lu, J., Rodriguez, M., Schü, J.: Signed formula logic programming: operational semantics and applications. In: Michalewicz, M., Raś, Z.W. (eds.) ISMIS 1996. LNCS, vol. 1079, pp. 202–211. Springer, Berlin (1996)

23. Calvanese, D., De Giacomo, G., Lembo, D., Lenzerini, M., Rosati, R.: DL-Lite: Tractable description logics for ontologies. In: Proc. of the 20th Nat. Conf. on Artificial Intelligence (AAAI 2005). AAAI Press, Menlo Park (2005)

24. Cao, T.H.: Annotated fuzzy logic programs. Fuzzy Sets and Systems 113(2), 277–298 (2000)

25. Carlos, C., Guillermo, S., Teresa, A., Lluis, G.: A logic programming framework for possibilistic argumentation with vague knowledge. In: Proceedings of the 20th Annual Conference on Uncertainty in Artificial Intelligence (UAI 2004), Arlington, Virginia, pp. 76–84. AUAI Press (2004)

26. Chang, K.C.-C., won Hwang, S.: Minimal probing: Supporting expensive predicates for top-k queries. In: SIGMOD Conference (2002)

27. Chortaras, A., Stamou, G.B., Stafylopatis, A.: Integrated query answering with weighted fuzzy rules. In: Mellouli, K. (ed.) ECSQARU 2007. LNCS (LNAI), vol. 4724, pp. 767–778. Springer, Heidelberg (2007)

28. da Costa, P.C.G.: Bayesian semantics for the Semantic Web. PhD thesis, George Mason University, Fairfax, VA, USA (2005)

29. da Costa, P.C.G., Laskey, K.B.: PR-OWL: A framework for probabilistic ontologies. In: Proceedings FOIS 2006, pp. 237–249. IOS Press, Amsterdam (2006)

30. da Costa, P.C.G., Laskey, K.B., Laskey, K.J.: PR-OWL: A Bayesian ontology language for the Semantic Web. In: Proceedings URSW 2005, pp. 23–33 (2005)

31. Damásio, C., Medina, J., Ojeda-Aciego, M.: Termination of logic programs with imperfect information: applications and query procedure. Journal of Applied Logic (to appear 2006)

32. Damásio, C., Medina, M., Ojeda-Aciego, J.: A tabulation procedure for first-order residuated logic programs. In: Proceedings of the 11th International Conference on Information Processing and Managment of Uncertainty in Knowledge-Based Systems (IPMU 2006) (2006)

33. Damásio, C., Medina, M., Ojeda-Aciego, J.: Termination of logic programs with imperfect information: applications and query procedure. Journal of Applied Logic 7(5), 435–458 (2007)

34. Damásio, C.V., Medina, J., Ojeda Aciego, M.: Sorted multi-adjoint logic programs: Termination results and applications. In: Alferes, J.J., Leite, J.A. (eds.) JELIA 2004. LNCS (LNAI), vol. 3229, pp. 252–265. Springer, Heidelberg (2004)

35. Damásio, C.V., Medina, J., Ojeda Aciego, M.: A tabulation proof procedure for residuated logic programming. In: Proceedings of the 6th European Conference on Artificial Intelligence (ECAI 2004) (2004)

36. Damásio, C.V., Medina, J., Ojeda Aciego, M.: Termination results for sorted multi-adjoint logic programs. In: Proceedings of the 10th International Conference on Information Processing and Managment of Uncertainty in Knowledge-Based Systems (IPMU 2004), pp. 1879–1886 (2004)

37. Damásio, C.V., Pereira, L.M.: A survey of paraconsistent semantics for logic programs. In: Gabbay, D., Smets, P. (eds.) Handbook of Defeasible Reasoning and Uncertainty Management Systems, pp. 241–320. Kluwer Academic Publishers, Dordrecht (1998)

38. Damásio, C.V., Pereira, L.M.: Antitonic logic programs. In: Eiter, T., Faber, W., Truszczyński, M. (eds.) LPNMR 2001. LNCS (LNAI), vol. 2173. Springer, Heidelberg (2001)

39. Damásio, C.V., Pereira, L.M.: Monotonic and residuated logic programs. In: Benferhat, S., Besnard, P. (eds.) ECSQARU 2001. LNCS (LNAI), vol. 2143, pp. 748–759. Springer, Heidelberg (2001)

40. Damásio, C.V., Pereira, L.M.: Hybrid probabilistic logic programs as residuated logic programs. Studia Logica 72(1), 113–138 (2002)

41. Damásio, C.V., Pereira, L.M.: Sorted monotonic logic programs and their embeddings. In: Proceedings of the 10th International Conference on Information Processing and Management of Uncertainty in Knowledge-Based Systems (IPMU 2004), pp. 807–814 (2004)

42. d'Aquin, M., Lieber, J., Napoli, A.: Towards a semantic portal for oncology using a description logic with fuzzy concrete domains. In: Sanchez, E. (ed.) Fuzzy Logic and the Semantic Web, pp. 379–393. Elsevier, Amsterdam (2006)

43. Dazhou Kang, J.L.: Baowen Xu and Y. Li. Reasoning for a fuzzy description logic with comparison expressions. In: Proceeedings of the International Workshop on Description Logics (DL 2006). CEUR (2006)

44. Dekhtyar, A., Dekhtyar, M.I.: Possible worlds semantics for probabilistic logic programs. In: Demoen, B., Lifschitz, V. (eds.) ICLP 2004. LNCS, vol. 3132, pp. 137–148. Springer, Heidelberg (2004)

45. Dekhtyar, A., Dekhtyar, M.I.: Revisiting the semantics of interval probabilistic logic programs. In: Baral, C., Greco, G., Leone, N., Terracina, G. (eds.) LPNMR 2005. LNCS (LNAI), vol. 3662, pp. 330–342. Springer, Heidelberg (2005)

46. Dekhtyar, A., Dekhtyar, M.I., Subrahmanian, V.S.: Temporal probabilistic logic programs. In: Schreye, D.D. (ed.) Logic Programming: The 1999 International Conference, Las Cruces, New Mexico, USA, November 29 - December 4, 1999, pp. 109–123 (1999)

47. Dekhtyar, A., Subrahmanian, V.: Hybrid probabilistic programs. Journal of Logic Programming 43(3), 187–250 (2000)

48. Dekhtyar, M.I., Dekhtyar, A., Subrahmanian, V.S.: Hybrid probabilistic programs: Algorithms and complexity. In: Laskey, K.B., Prade, H. (eds.) Proceedings of the 15th Conference on Uncertainty in Artificial Intelligence (UAI 1999), January 30, 1999, pp. 160–169. Morgan Kaufmann, San Francisco (1999)

49. Denecker, M., Marek, V., Truszczyński, M.: Approximations, stable operators, well-founded fixpoints and applications in nonmonotonic reasoning. In: Minker, J. (ed.) Logic-Based Artifical Intelligence, pp. 127–144. Kluwer Academic Publishers, Dordrecht (2000)

50. Denecker, M., Marek, V.W., Truszczyński, M.: Uniform semantic treatment of default and autoepistemic logics. In: Cohn, A., Giunchiglia, F., Selman, B. (eds.) Proceedings of the 7th International Conference on Principles of Knowledge Representation and Reasoning, pp. 74–84. Morgan Kaufmann, San Francisco (2000)

51. Denecker, M., Marek, V.W., Truszczyński, M.: Ultimate approximations. Technical Report CW 320, Katholieke Iniversiteit Leuven (September 2001)

52. Denecker, M., Marek, V.W., Truszczyński, M.: Ultimate approximations in nonmonotonic knowledge representation systems. In: Fensel, D., Giunchiglia, F., McGuinness, D., Williams, M. (eds.) Principles of Knowledge Representation and Reasoning: Proceedings of the 8th International Conference, pp. 177–188. Morgan Kaufmann, San Francisco (2002)

53. Denecker, M., Pelov, N., Bruynooghe, M.: Ultimate well-founded and stable semantics for logic programs with aggregates. In: Codognet, P. (ed.) ICLP 2001. LNCS, vol. 2237. Springer, Heidelberg (2001)

54. Ding, Z., Peng, Y.: A probabilistic extension to ontology language OWL. In: Proceedings of the 37th Hawaii International Conference on Systems Sciences. IEEE, Los Alamitos (2004)

55. Ding, Z., Peng, Y., Pan, R.: BayesOWL: Uncertainty modeling in Semantic Web ontologies. In: Ma, Z. (ed.) Soft Computing in Ontologies and Semantic Web. Studies in Fuzziness and Soft Computing, vol. 204. Springer, Heidelberg (2006)

56. Dubois, D., Foulloy, L., Mauris, G., Prade, H.: Probability-possibility transformations, triangular fuzzy sets, and probabilistic inequalities. Reliable Computing 10(4), 273–297 (2004)

57. Dubois, D., Lang, J., Prade, H.: Towards possibilistic logic programming. In: Proc. of the 8th Int. Conf. on Logic Programming (ICLP 1991), pp. 581–595. MIT Press, Cambridge (1991)

58. Dubois, D., Mengin, J., Prade, H.: Possibilistic uncertainty and fuzzy features in description logic. a preliminary discussion. In: Sanchez, E. (ed.) Capturing Intelligence: Fuzzy Logic and the Semantic Web. Elsevier, Amsterdam (2006)

59. Dubois, D., Prade, H.: Possibilistic logic. In: Gabbay, D.M., Hogger, C.J. (eds.) Handbook of Logic in Artificial Intelligence, vol. 3, pp. 439–513. Clarendon Press, Oxford (1986)

60. Dubois, D., Prade, H.: On fuzzy syllogisms. Computational Intelligence 4(2), 171–179 (1988)

61. Dubois, D., Prade, H.: When upper probabilities are possibility measures. Fuzzy Sets and Systems 49, 65–74 (1992)

62. Dubois, D., Prade, H.: Can we enforce full compositionality in uncertainty calculi? In: Proc. of the 12th Nat. Conf. on Artificial Intelligence (AAAI 1994), pp. 149–154. AAAI Press, Menlo Park (1994)

63. Dubois, D., Prade, H.: Possibility theory, probability theory and multiple-valued logics: A clarification. Annals of Mathematics and Artificial Intelligence 32(1-4), 35–66 (2001)

64. Dubois, D., Prade, H., Godo, L., de Màntaras, R.L.: Qualitative reasoning with imprecise probabilities. J. Intell. Inf. Syst. 2, 319–363 (1993)

65. Dubois, D., Prade, H., Touscas, J.-M.: Inference with imprecise numerical quantifiers. In: Ras, Z.W., Zemankova, M. (eds.) Intelligent Systems, ch. 3, pp. 53–72. Ellis Horwood (1990)

66. Dürig, M., Studer, T.: Probabilistic ABox reasoning: Preliminary results. In: Proceedings DL 2005, pp. 104–111 (2005)

67. Ebrahim, R.: Fuzzy logic programming. Fuzzy Sets and Systems 117(2), 215–230 (2001)

68. Eiter, T., Ianni, G., Schindlauer, R., Tompits, H.: Nonmonotonic description logic programs: Implementation and experiments. In: Baader, F., Voronkov, A. (eds.) LPAR 2004. LNCS (LNAI), vol. 3452, pp. 511–527. Springer, Heidelberg (2005)

69. Eiter, T., Ianni, G., Schindlauer, R., Tompits, H.: A uniform integration of higher-order reasoning and external evaluations in answer-set programming. In: Proceedings of the Nineteenth International Joint Conference on Artificial Intelligence (IJCAI 2005), pp. 90–96. Professional Book Center (2005)

70. Eiter, T., Ianni, G., Schindlauer, R., Tompits, H.: Effective integration of declarative rules with external evaluations for semantic-web reasoning. In: Sure, Y., Domingue, J. (eds.) ESWC 2006. LNCS, vol. 4011, pp. 273–287. Springer, Heidelberg (2006)

71. Eiter, T., Lukasiewicz, T., Schindlauer, R., Tompits, H.: Combining answer set programming with description logics for the semantic web. In: Proceedings of the 9th International Conference on Principles of Knowledge Representation and Reasoning (KR 2004). AAAI Press, Menlo Park (2004)

72. Eiter, T., Lukasiewicz, T., Schindlauer, R., Tompits, H.: Well-founded semantics for description logic programs in the semantic web. In: Antoniou, G., Boley, H. (eds.) RuleML 2004. LNCS, vol. 3323, pp. 81–97. Springer, Heidelberg (2004)

73. Fagin, R.: Combining fuzzy information: an overview. SIGMOD Rec. 31(2), 109–118 (2002)

74. Fagin, R., Halpern, J.Y., Megiddo, N.: A logic for reasoning about probabilities. Inf. Comput. 87, 78–128 (1990)

75. Fitting, M.: A Kripke-Kleene-semantics for general logic programs. Journal of Logic Programming 2, 295–312 (1985)

76. Fitting, M.: Pseudo-Boolean valued Prolog. Studia Logica XLVII(2), 85–91 (1987)

77. Fitting, M.: Bilattices and the semantics of logic programming. Journal of Logic Programming 11, 91–116 (1991)

78. Fitting, M.C.: The family of stable models. Journal of Logic Programming 17, 197–225 (1993)

79. Fitting, M.C.: Bilattices are nice things. In: Conference on Self-Reference, Copenhagen, Denmark (2002)
80. Fitting, M.C.: Fixpoint semantics for logic programming - a survey. Theoretical Computer Science 21(3), 25–51 (2002)
81. Frisch, A.M., Haddawy, P.: Anytime deduction for probabilistic logic. Artif. Intell. 69(1–2), 93–122 (1994)
82. Fuhr, N.: Probabilistic Datalog: Implementing logical information retrieval for advanced applications. Journal of the American Society for Information Science 51(2), 95–110 (2000)
83. Fukushige, Y.: Representing probabilistic knowledge in the Semantic Web. In: Proceedings of the W3C Workshop on Semantic Web for Life Sciences (2004)
84. Gelfond, M., Lifschitz, V.: Classical negation in logic programs and disjunctive databases. New Generation Computing 9(3/4), 365–386 (1991)
85. Ginsberg, M.L.: Multi-valued logics: a uniform approach to reasoning in artificial intelligence. Computational Intelligence 4, 265–316 (1988)
86. Giugno, R., Lukasiewicz, T.: P-$\mathcal{SHOQ}(\mathbf{D})$: A probabilistic extension of $\mathcal{SHOQ}(\mathbf{D})$ for probabilistic ontologies in the Semantic Web. In: Flesca, S., Greco, S., Leone, N., Ianni, G. (eds.) JELIA 2002. LNCS (LNAI), vol. 2424, pp. 86–97. Springer, Heidelberg (2002)
87. Grosof, B.N., Horrocks, I., Volz, R., Decker, S.: Description logic programs: combining logic programs with description logic. In: Proceedings of the twelfth international conference on World Wide Web, pp. 48–57. ACM Press, New York (2003)
88. Guller, D.: Procedural semantics for fuzzy disjunctive programs. In: Baaz, M., Voronkov, A. (eds.) LPAR 2002. LNCS (LNAI), vol. 2514, pp. 247–261. Springer, Heidelberg (2002)
89. Guller, D.: Semantics for fuzzy disjunctive programs with weak similarity. In: Abraham, A., Köppen, M. (eds.) Hybrid Information Systems, Proceedings of First International Workshop on Hybrid Intelligent Systems, Adelaide, Australia, December 11-12, 2001. Advances in Soft Computing, pp. 285–299. Physica-Verlag (2002)
90. Hadjali, A., Kaci, S., Prade, H.: Database preference queries — a possibilistic logic approach with symbolic priorities. In: Hartmann, S., Kern-Isberner, G. (eds.) FoIKS 2008. LNCS, vol. 4932. Springer, Heidelberg (2008)
91. Hähnle, R.: Uniform notation of tableaux rules for multiple-valued logics. In: Proc. International Symposium on Multiple-Valued Logic, Victoria, pp. 238–245. IEEE Press, Los Alamitos (1991)
92. Hähnle, R.: Many-valued logics and mixed integer programming. Annals of Mathematics and Artificial Intelligence 3,4(12), 231–264 (1994)
93. Hähnle, R.: Advanced many-valued logics. In: Gabbay, D.M., Guenthner, F. (eds.) Handbook of Philosophical Logic, 2nd edn. Kluwer Academic Publishers, Dordrecht (2001)
94. Hailperin, T.: Sentential Probability Logic: Origins, Development, Current Status, and Technical Applications. Associated University Presses, London, UK (1996)
95. Hájek, P.: Metamathematics of Fuzzy Logic. Kluwer Academic Publishers, Dordrecht (1998)
96. Hájek, P.: Making fuzzy description logics more expressive. Fuzzy Sets and Systems 154(1), 1–15 (2005)
97. Hájek, P.: What does mathematical fuzzy logic offer to description logic. In: Sanchez, E. (ed.) Fuzzy Logic and the Semantic Web, Capturing Intelligence, ch. 5, pp. 91–100. Elsevier, Amsterdam (2006)
98. Hansen, P., Jaumard, B., Nguetsé, G.-B.D., de Aragão, M.P.: Models and algorithms for probabilistic and Bayesian logic. In: Proceedings IJCAI 1995, pp. 1862–1868. Morgan Kaufmann, San Francisco (1995)
99. Heinsohn, J.: Probabilistic description logics. In: Proceedings UAI 1994, pp. 311–318. Morgan Kaufmann, San Francisco (1994)

100. Hinde, C.: Fuzzy prolog. International Journal Man.-Machine Stud. (24), 569–595 (1986)
101. Holi, M., Hyvönen, E.: A method for modeling uncertainty in Semantic Web taxonomies. In: Proceedings WWW 2004, pp. 296–297. ACM Press, New York (2004)
102. Holi, M., Hyvönen, E.: Modeling degrees of conceptual overlap in Semantic Web ontologies. In: Proceedings URSW 2005, pp. 98–99 (2005)
103. Hölldobler, S., Khang, T.D., Störr, H.-P.: A fuzzy description logic with hedges as concept modifiers. In: Phuong, N.H., Nguyen, H.T., Ho, N.C., Santiprabhob, P. (eds.) Proceedings InTech/VJFuzzy', Hanoi, Vietnam, Institute of Information Technology, Vietnam Center for Natural Science and Technology, Science and Technics Publishing House, Hanoi, Vietnam, pp. 25–34 (2002)
104. Hölldobler, S., Nga, N.H., Khang, T.D.: The fuzzy description logic ALC_{FH}. In: Proceeedings of the International Workshop on Description Logics (DL 2005) (2005)
105. Hölldobler, S., Störr, H.-P., Khang, T.D.: The fuzzy description logic ALC_{FH} with hedge algebras as concept modifiers. Journal of Advanced Computational Intelligence (2003)
106. Hölldobler, S., Störr, H.-P., Khang, T.D.: The subsumption problem of the fuzzy description logic ALC_{FH}. In: Proceedings of the 10th International Conference on Information Processing and Managment of Uncertainty in Knowledge-Based Systems (IPMU 2004) (2004)
107. Hollunder, B.: An alternative proof method for possibilistic logic and its application to terminological logics. International Journal of Approximate Reasoning 12, 85–109 (1995)
108. Horrocks, I., Sattler, U.: A tableaux decision procedure for $\mathcal{SHOIQ}$. In: Proc. of the 19th Int. Joint Conf. on Artificial Intelligence (IJCAI 2005) (2005)
109. Hung, E., Deng, Y., Subrahmanian, V.S.: TOSS: An extension of TAX with ontologies and similarity queries. In: Proceedings ACM SIGMOD 2004, pp. 719–730. ACM Press, New York (2004)
110. Ilyas, I.F., Aref, W.G., Elmagarmid, A.K.: Supporting top-k join queries in relational databases. In: Proceedings of 29th International Conference on Very Large Data Bases (VLDB 2003), pp. 754–765 (2003)
111. Ishizuka, M., Kanai, N.: Prolog-ELF: incorporating fuzzy logic. In: Proceedings of the 9th International Joint Conference on Artificial Intelligence (IJCAI 1985), Los Angeles, CA, pp. 701–703 (1985)
112. Jaeger, M.: Probabilistic reasoning in terminological logics. In: Proceedings KR 1994, pp. 305–316. Morgan Kaufmann, San Francisco (1994)
113. Jaeger, M.: Probabilistic role models and the guarded fragment. In: Proceedings IPMU-2004, pp. 235–242 (2004); Extended version in International Journal of Uncertainty, Fuzziness and Knowledge-Based Systems 14(1), 43–60 (2006)
114. Jaumard, B., Hansen, P., de Aragão, M.P.: Column generation methods for probabilistic logic. ORSA J. Comput. 3, 135–147 (1991)
115. Kaplunova, A., Möller, R.: Probabilistic LCS in a P-Classic Implementation. Technical report, Institute for Software Systems (STS), Hamburg University of Technology, Germany (2007), http://www.sts.tu-harburg.de/tech-reports/papers.html
116. Kern-Isberner, G., Lukasiewicz, T.: Combining probabilistic logic programming with the power of maximum entropy. Artificial Intelligence 157(1-2), 139–202 (2004)
117. Kersting, K., Raedt, L.D.: Bayesian logic programs. In: Cussens, J., Frisch, A.M. (eds.) ILP Work-in-progress reports, 10th International Conference on Inductive Logic Programming, CEUR Workshop Proceedings. CEUR-WS.org (2000)
118. Kersting, K., Raedt, L.D.: Bayesian logic programming: Theory and tools. In: Getoor, L., Taskar, B. (eds.) An Introduction to Statistical Relational Learning. MIT Press, Cambridge (2005)
119. Khamsi, M., Misane, D.: Disjunctive signed logic programs. Fundamenta Informaticae 32, 349–357 (1996)

120. Khamsi, M., Misane, D.: Fixed point theorems in logic programming. Annals of Mathematics and Artificial Intelligence 21, 231–243 (1997)
121. Kifer, M., Li, A.: On the semantics of rule-based expert systems with uncertainty. In: Gyssens, M., Van Gucht, D., Paredaens, J. (eds.) ICDT 1988. LNCS, vol. 326, pp. 102–117. Springer, Heidelberg (1988)
122. Kifer, M., Subrahmanian, V.: Theory of generalized annotated logic programming and its applications. Journal of Logic Programming 12, 335–367 (1992)
123. Klawonn, F., Kruse, R.: A Łukasiewicz logic based Prolog. Mathware & Soft Computing 1(1), 5–29 (1994)
124. Klir, G.J., Yuan, B.: Fuzzy sets and fuzzy logic: theory and applications. Prentice-Hall, Inc., Upper Saddle River (1995)
125. Koller, D., Levy, A., Pfeffer, A.: P-Classic: A tractable probabilistic description logic. In: Proceedings AAAI 1997, pp. 390–397. AAAI Press/MIT Press (1997)
126. Kulmann, P., Sandri, S.: An annotaded logic theorem prover for an extended possibilistic logic. Fuzzy Sets and Systems 144, 67–91 (2004)
127. Lakshmanan, L.: An epistemic foundation for logic programming with uncertainty. In: Thiagarajan, P.S. (ed.) FSTTCS 1994. LNCS, vol. 880, pp. 89–100. Springer, Heidelberg (1994)
128. Lakshmanan, L.V., Sadri, F.: Uncertain deductive databases: a hybrid approach. Information Systems 22(8), 483–508 (1997)
129. Lakshmanan, L.V., Shiri, N.: Probabilistic deductive databases. In: Int'l Logic Programming Symposium, pp. 254–268 (1994)
130. Lakshmanan, L.V., Shiri, N.: A parametric approach to deductive databases with uncertainty. IEEE Transactions on Knowledge and Data Engineering 13(4), 554–570 (2001)
131. Lakshmanan, L.V.S., Sadri, F.: On a theory of probabilistic deductive databases. Theory and Practice of Logic Programming 1(1), 5–42 (2001)
132. Lehmann, D.: Another perspective on default reasoning. Ann. Math. Artif. Intell. 15(1), 61–82 (1995)
133. Levesque, H.J., Brachman, R.J.: Expressiveness and tractability in knowledge representation and reasoning. Computational Intelligence 3, 78–93 (1987)
134. Levy, A.Y., Rousset, M.-C.: Combining horn rules and description logics in CARIN. Artificial Intelligence 104, 165–209 (1998)
135. Li, C., Chang, K.C.-C., Ilyas, I.F., Song, S.: RankSQL: query algebra and optimization for relational top-k queries. In: Proceedings of the 2005 ACM SIGMOD International Conference on Management of Data (SIGMOD 2005), pp. 131–142. ACM Press, New York (2005)
136. Li, R., Wen, K., Lu, Z., Sun, X., Wang, Z.: An improved semantic search model based on hybrid fuzzy description logic. In: Workshop on Frontier of Computer Science and Technology (FCST 2006), pp. 139–146. IEEE Press, Los Alamitos (2006)
137. Li, Y., Xu, B., Lu, J., Kang, D., Wang, P.: Extended fuzzy description logic ALCN. In: Khosla, R., Howlett, R.J., Jain, L.C. (eds.) KES 2005. LNCS (LNAI), vol. 3684, pp. 896–902. Springer, Heidelberg (2005)
138. Li, Y., Xu, B., Lu, J., Kang, D., Wang, P.: A family of extended fuzzy description logics. In: 29th Annual International Computer Software and Applications Conference (COMPSAC 2005), pp. 221–226. IEEE Computer Society Press, Los Alamitos (2005)
139. Liau, C.-J., Yao, Y.Y.: Information retrieval by possibilistic reasoning. In: Mayr, H.C., Lazanský, J., Quirchmayr, G., Vogel, P. (eds.) DEXA 2001. LNCS, vol. 2113, pp. 52–61. Springer, Heidelberg (2001)
140. Liu, O., Tian, Q., Ma, J.: A fuzzy description logic approach to model management in R&D project selection. In: Proceedings of the 8th Pacific Asia Conference on Information Systems (PACIS 2004) (2004)

141. Lloyd, J.W.: Foundations of Logic Programming. Springer, Heidelberg (1987)
142. Loyer, Y., Straccia, U.: Uncertainty and partial non-uniform assumptions in parametric deductive databases. In: Flesca, S., Greco, S., Leone, N., Ianni, G. (eds.) JELIA 2002. LNCS (LNAI), vol. 2424, pp. 271–282. Springer, Heidelberg (2002)
143. Loyer, Y., Straccia, U.: The well-founded semantics in normal logic programs with uncertainty. In: Hu, Z., Rodríguez-Artalejo, M. (eds.) FLOPS 2002. LNCS, vol. 2441, pp. 152–166. Springer, Heidelberg (2002)
144. Loyer, Y., Straccia, U.: The approximate well-founded semantics for logic programs with uncertainty. In: Rovan, B., Vojtáš, P. (eds.) MFCS 2003. LNCS, vol. 2747, pp. 541–550. Springer, Heidelberg (2003)
145. Loyer, Y., Straccia, U.: Default knowledge in logic programs with uncertainty. In: Palamidessi, C. (ed.) ICLP 2003. LNCS, vol. 2916, pp. 466–480. Springer, Heidelberg (2003)
146. Loyer, Y., Straccia, U.: Epistemic foundation of the well-founded semantics over bilattices. In: Fiala, J., Koubek, V., Kratochvíl, J. (eds.) MFCS 2004. LNCS, vol. 3153, pp. 513–524. Springer, Heidelberg (2004)
147. Loyer, Y., Straccia, U.: Any-world assumptions in logic programming. Theoretical Computer Science 342(2-3), 351–381 (2005)
148. Loyer, Y., Straccia, U.: Epistemic foundation of stable model semantics. Journal of Theory and Practice of Logic Programming 6, 355–393 (2006)
149. Lu, J., Li, Y., Zhou, B., Kang, D., Zhang, Y.: Distributed reasoning with fuzzy description logics. In: 7th International International Conference on Computational Science, pp. 196–203 (2007)
150. Lu, J.J.: Logic programming with signs and annotations. Journal of Logic and Computation 6(6), 755–778 (1996)
151. Lu, J.J., Calmet, J., Schü, J.: Computing multiple-valued logic programs. Mathware % Soft Computing 2(4), 129–153 (1997)
152. Lukasiewicz, T.: Many-valued first-order logics with probabilistic semantics. In: Gottlob, G., Grandjean, E., Seyr, K. (eds.) CSL 1998. LNCS, vol. 1584, pp. 415–429. Springer, Heidelberg (1999)
153. Lukasiewicz, T.: Probabilistic logic programming. In: Proc. of the 13th European Conf. on Artificial Intelligence (ECAI 1998), Brighton, England, August 1998, pp. 388–392 (1998)
154. Lukasiewicz, T.: Local probabilistic deduction from taxonomic and probabilistic knowledge-bases over conjunctive events. Int. J. Approx. Reasoning 21(1), 23–61 (1999)
155. Lukasiewicz, T.: Many-valued disjunctive logic programs with probabilistic semantics. In: Gelfond, M., Leone, N., Pfeifer, G. (eds.) LPNMR 1999. LNCS (LNAI), vol. 1730, pp. 277–289. Springer, Heidelberg (1999)
156. Lukasiewicz, T.: Probabilistic and truth-functional many-valued logic programming. In: The IEEE International Symposium on Multiple-Valued Logic, pp. 236–241 (1999)
157. Lukasiewicz, T.: Probabilistic deduction with conditional constraints over basic events. J. Artif. Intell. Res. 10, 199–241 (1999)
158. Lukasiewicz, T.: Fixpoint characterizations for many-valued disjunctive logic programs with probabilistic semantics. In: Eiter, T., Faber, W., Truszczyński, M. (eds.) LPNMR 2001. LNCS (LNAI), vol. 2173, pp. 336–350. Springer, Heidelberg (2001)
159. Lukasiewicz, T.: Probabilistic logic programming under inheritance with overriding. In: Proceedings UAI 2001, pp. 329–336. Morgan Kaufmann, San Francisco (2001)
160. Lukasiewicz, T.: Probabilistic logic programming under inheritance with overriding. In: Proceedings of the 17th Conference in Uncertainty in Artificial Intelligence (UAI 2001), pp. 329–336. Morgan Kaufmann Publishers Inc., San Francisco (2001)
161. Lukasiewicz, T.: Probabilistic logic programming with conditional constraints. ACM Trans. Comput. Log. 2(3), 289–339 (2001)

162. Lukasiewicz, T.: Probabilistic logic programming with conditional constraints. ACM Transactions on Computational Logic 2(3), 289–339 (2001)

163. Lukasiewicz, T.: Probabilistic default reasoning with conditional constraints. Ann. Math. Artif. Intell. 34(1–3), 35–88 (2002)

164. Lukasiewicz, T.: Probabilistic description logic programs. In: Godo, L. (ed.) ECSQARU 2005. LNCS (LNAI), vol. 3571. Springer, Heidelberg (2005)

165. Lukasiewicz, T.: Weak nonmonotonic probabilistic logics. Artif. Intell. 168(1–2), 119–161 (2005)

166. Lukasiewicz, T.: Fuzzy description logic programs under the answer set semantics for the semanticweb. In: Second International Conference on Rules and Rule Markup Languages for the Semantic Web (RuleML 2006), pp. 89–96. IEEE Computer Society Press, Los Alamitos (2006)

167. Lukasiewicz, T.: Probabilistic description logics for the Semantic Web. Technical Report INFSYS RR-1843-06-04, Institut für Informationssysteme, Technische Universität Wien (submitted for journal publication) (June 2006)

168. Lukasiewicz, T.: A novel combination of answer set programming with description logics for the semantic web. In: Franconi, E., Kifer, M., May, W. (eds.) ESWC 2007. LNCS, vol. 4519, pp. 384–398. Springer, Heidelberg (2007)

169. Lukasiewicz, T.: Probabilistic description logic programs. International Journal of Approximate Reasoning 42(2), 288–307 (2007)

170. Lukasiewicz, T.: Tractable probabilistic description logic programs. In: Prade, H., Subrahmanian, V.S. (eds.) SUM 2007. LNCS (LNAI), vol. 4772, pp. 143–156. Springer, Heidelberg (2007)

171. Lukasiewicz, T.: Expressive probabilistic description logics. Artificial Intelligence 172(6-7), 852–883 (2008)

172. Lukasiewicz, T., Straccia, U.: Description logic programs under probabilistic uncertainty and fuzzy vagueness. In: Mellouli, K. (ed.) ECSQARU 2007. LNCS (LNAI), vol. 4724, pp. 187–198. Springer, Heidelberg (2007)

173. Lukasiewicz, T., Straccia, U.: Tightly integrated fuzzy description logic programs under the answer semantics for the semantic web. In: Marchiori, M., Pan, J.Z. (eds.) RR 2007. LNCS, vol. 4524, pp. 289–298. Springer, Heidelberg (2007)

174. Lukasiewicz, T., Straccia, U.: Top-k retrieval in description logic programs under vagueness for the semantic web. In: Prade, H., Subrahmanian, V.S. (eds.) SUM 2007. LNCS (LNAI), vol. 4772, pp. 16–30. Springer, Heidelberg (2007)

175. Lukasiewicz, T., Straccia, U.: Uncertainty and vagueness in description logic programs for the semantic web. INFSYS Research Report 1843-07-02, Institut für Informationssysteme, Arbeitsbereich wissensbasierte Systeme, Technische Universität Wien (2007)

176. Lutz, C.: Description logics with concrete domains—a survey. In: Advances in Modal Logics, vol. 4, King's College Publications (2003)

177. Magrez, P., Smets, P.: Fuzzy modus ponens: a new model suitable for applications in knowledge-based systems. International Journal of Intelligent Systems 4, 181–200 (1989)

178. Mailis, T.P., Stoilos, G., Stamou, G.B.: Expressive reasoning with horn rules and fuzzy description logics. In: Marchiori, M., Pan, J.Z., d Marie, C.S. (eds.) RR 2007. LNCS, vol. 4524, pp. 43–57. Springer, Heidelberg (2007)

179. Majkic, Z.: Coalgebraic semantics for logic programs. In: 18th Workshop on (Constraint) Logic Programming (W(C)LP 2005), Ulm, Germany (2004)

180. Majkic, Z.: Many-valued intuitionistic implication and inference closure in a bilattice-based logic. In: 35th International Symposium on Multiple-Valued Logic (ISMVL 2005), pp. 214–220 (2005)

181. Majkic, Z.: Truth and knowledge fixpoint semantics for many-valued logic programming. In: 19th Workshop on (Constraint) Logic Programming (W(C)LP 2005), Ulm, Germany, pp. 76–87 (2005)
182. Mantay, T., Möller, R., Kaplunova, A.: Computing Probabilistic Least Common Subsumers in Description Logics. In: Burgard, W., Christaller, T., Cremers, A.B. (eds.) KI 1999. LNCS (LNAI), vol. 1701, pp. 89–100. Springer, Heidelberg (1999)
183. Marek, V.W., Truszczyński, M.: Logic programming with costs. Technical report, University of Kentucky (2000),
ftp://al.cs.engr.uky.edu/cs/manuscripts/lp-costs.ps
184. Martin, T.P.: Soft computing, logic programming and the semantic web. In: Proceedings of the 10th International Conference on Information Processing and Managment of Uncertainty in Knowledge-Based Systems (IPMU 2004), pp. 815–822 (2004)
185. Martin, T.P., Baldwin, J.F., Pilsworth, B.W.: The implementation of FProlog –a fuzzy prolog interpreter. Fuzzy Sets Syst. 23(1), 119–129 (1987)
186. Mateis, C.: Extending Disjunctive Logic Programming by t-norms. In: Gelfond, M., Leone, N., Pfeifer, G. (eds.) LPNMR 1999. LNCS (LNAI), vol. 1730, pp. 290–304. Springer, Heidelberg (1999)
187. Mateis, C.: Quantitative disjunctive logic programming: Semantics and computation. AI Communications 13, 225–248 (2000)
188. Medina, J., Ojeda-Aciego, M.: Multi-adjoint logic programming. In: Proceedings of the 10th International Conference on Information Processing and Managment of Uncertainty in Knowledge-Based Systems (IPMU 2004), pp. 823–830 (2004)
189. Medina, J., Ojeda-Aciego, M., Vojtáš, P.: Multi-adjoint Logic Programming with Continuous Semantics. In: Eiter, T., Faber, W., Truszczyński, M. (eds.) LPNMR 2001. LNCS (LNAI), vol. 2173, pp. 351–364. Springer, Heidelberg (2001)
190. Medina, J., Ojeda-Aciego, M., Vojtáš, P.: A procedural semantics for multi-adjoint logic programming. In: Proceedings of the 10th Portuguese Conference on Artificial Intelligence on Progress in Artificial Intelligence, Knowledge Extraction, Multi-agent Systems, Logic Programming and Constraint Solving, pp. 290–297. Springer, Heidelberg (2001)
191. Medina, J., Ojeda-Aciego, M., Vojtáš, P.: Similarity-based unification: a multi-adjoint approach. Fuzzy sets and systems 1(146), 43–62 (2004)
192. Meghini, C., Sebastiani, F., Straccia, U.: A model of multimedia information retrieval. Journal of the ACM 48(5), 909–970 (2001)
193. Meghini, C., Sebastiani, F., Straccia, U., Thanos, C.: A model of information retrieval based on a terminological logic. In: Proceedings of the 16th Annual International ACM SIGIR Conference on Research and Development in Information Retrieval (ACM SIGIR 1993), Pittsburgh, USA, pp. 298–307 (1993)
194. Mitra, P., Noy, N.F., Jaiswal, A.: OMEN: A probabilistic ontology mapping tool. In: Gil, Y., Motta, E., Benjamins, V.R., Musen, M.A. (eds.) ISWC 2005. LNCS, vol. 3729, pp. 537–547. Springer, Heidelberg (2005)
195. Motik, B., Horrocks, I., Rosati, R., Sattler, U.: Can OWL and Logic Programming Live Together Happily Ever After? In: Cruz, I., Decker, S., Allemang, D., Preist, C., Schwabe, D., Mika, P., Uschold, M., Aroyo, L.M. (eds.) ISWC 2006. LNCS, vol. 4273, pp. 501–514. Springer, Heidelberg (2006)
196. Motik, B., Rosati, R.: A Faithful Integration of Description Logics with Logic Programming. In: Proc. of the 20th Int. Joint Conf. on Artificial Intelligence (IJCAI 2007). Morgan Kaufmann Publishers, San Francisco (2007)
197. Muggleton, S.: Stochastic logic programs. In: De Raedt, L. (ed.) Proceedings of the 5th International Workshop on Inductive Logic Programming, p. 29. Department of Computer Science, Katholieke Universiteit Leuven (1995)

198. Mukaidono, M.: Foundations of fuzzy logic programming. In: Advances in Fuzzy Systems – Application and Theory, vol. 1. World Scientific, Singapore (1996)
199. Mukaidono, M., Shen, Z., Ding, L.: Fundamentals of fuzzy prolog. Int. J. Approx. Reasoning 3(2), 179–193, (1989)
200. Naeth, T.H.: Analysis of the average-case behavior of an inference algorithm for probabilistic description logics. Diplomarbeit, TU Hamburg-Harburg, Germany, (February 2007)
201. Ng, R., Subrahmanian, V.: Probabilistic logic programming. Information and Computation 101(2), 150–201, (1993)
202. Ng, R., Subrahmanian, V.: Stable model semantics for probabilistic deductive databases. Information and Computation 110(1), 42–83, (1994)
203. Ngo, L.: Probabilistic disjunctive logic programming. In: Uncertainty in Artificial Intelligence: Proceedings of the Twelfeth Conference (UAI 1996), pp. 397–404. Morgan Kaufmann, San Francisco (1996)
204. Ngo, L., Haddawy, P.: Probabilistic logic programming and bayesian networks. In: Kanchanasut, K., Levy, J.-J. (eds.) ACSC 1995. LNCS, vol. 1023, pp. 286–300. Springer, Heidelberg (1995)
205. Ngo, L., Haddawy, P.: Answering queries from context-sensitive probabilistic knowledge bases. Theoretical Computer Science 171(1-2), 147–177 (1997)
206. Nicolas, P., Garcia, L., Stéphan, I.: Possibilistic stable models. In: Proceedings of the 19th International Joint Conference on Artificial Intelligence (IJCAI 2005), pp. 248–253. Morgan Kaufmann, San Francisco (2005)
207. Nilsson, N.J.: Probabilistic logic. Artif. Intell. 28(1), 71–88 (1986)
208. Nottelmann, H., Fuhr, N.: Adding probabilities and rules to OWL Lite subsets based on probabilistic Datalog. International Journal of Uncertainty, Fuzziness and Knowledge-Based Systems 14(1), 17–42 (2006)
209. Novák, V.: Which logic is the real fuzzy logic? Fuzzy Sets and Systems, 635–641 (2005)
210. Pan, J.Z., Stamou, G., Stoilos, G., Thomas, E.: Expressive querying over fuzzy dl-lite ontologies. In: 20th International Workshop on Description Logics, Brixen-Bressanone, Italy (2007)
211. Pan, J.Z., Stamou, G., Stoilos, G., Thomas, E., Taylor, S.: Scalable querying service over fuzzy ontologies. In: International World Wide Web Conference (WWW 2008), Beijing (2008)
212. Pan, R., Ding, Z., Yu, Y., Peng, Y.: A Bayesian network approach to ontology mapping. In: Gil, Y., Motta, E., Benjamins, V.R., Musen, M.A. (eds.) ISWC 2005. LNCS, vol. 3729, pp. 563–577. Springer, Heidelberg (2005)
213. Paulik, L.: Best possible answer is computable for fuzzy sld-resolution. In: Hajék, P. (ed.) Gödel 1996: Logical Foundations of Mathematics, Computer Science, and Physics. Lecture Notes in Logic, vol. 6, pp. 257–266. Springer, Heidelberg (1996)
214. Pool, M., Aikin, J.: KEEPER and Protégé: An elicitation environment for Bayesian inference tools. In: Proceedings of the Workshop on Protégé and Reasoning held at the 7th International Protégé Conference (2004)
215. Poole, D.: Probabilistic horn abduction and bayesian networks. Artificial Intelligence 64(1), 81–129 (1993)
216. Poole, D.: The independent choice logic for modelling multiple agents under uncertainty. Artificial Intelligence 94(1-2), 7–56 (1997)
217. Qi, G., Pan, J.Z., Ji, Q.: Extending description logics with uncertainty reasoning in possibilistic logic. In: Mellouli, K. (ed.) ECSQARU 2007. LNCS (LNAI), vol. 4724, pp. 828–839. Springer, Heidelberg (2007)
218. Qi, G., Pan, J.Z., Ji, Q.: Extending description logics with uncertainty reasoning in possibilistic logic. In: Mellouli, K. (ed.) ECSQARU 2007. LNCS (LNAI), vol. 4724, Springer, Heidelberg (2007)

219. Qi, G., Pan, J.Z., Ji, Q.: A possibilistic extension of description logics. In: Proceedings DL 2007 (2007)
220. Ragone, A., Straccia, U., Bobillo, F., Noia, T.D., Sciascio, E.D.: Fuzzy description logics for bilateral matchmaking in e-marketplaces. In: Proceedings of the 21st International Workshop on Description Logics (DL 2008) (2008)
221. Ragone, A., Straccia, U., Noia, T.D., Sciascio, E.D., Donini, F.M.: Vague knowledge bases for matchmaking in p2p e-marketplaces. In: Franconi, E., Kifer, M., May, W. (eds.) ESWC 2007. LNCS, vol. 4519, pp. 414–428. Springer, Heidelberg (2007)
222. Rhodes, P.C., Menani, S.M.: Towards a fuzzy logic programming system: a clausal form fuzzy logic. Knowledge-Based Systems 8(4), 174–182 (1995)
223. Rosati, R.: On the decidability and complexity of integrating ontologies and rules. Journal of Web Semantics 3(1), 61–73, (2005)
224. Rosati, R.: Dl+log: Tight integration of description logics and disjunctive datalog. In: Tenth International Conference on Principles of Knowledge Representation and Reasoning (KR 2006), pp. 68–78. AAAI Press, Menlo Park (2006)
225. Rosati, R.: On the decidability and finite controllability of query processing in databases with incomplete information. In: PODS 2006: Proceedings of the twenty-fifth ACM SIGMOD-SIGACT-SIGART symposium on Principles of database systems, pp. 356–365. ACM Press, New York (2006)
226. Rounds, W.C., Zhang, G.-Q.: Clausal logic and logic programming in algebraic domains. Information and Computation 171, 183–200 (2001)
227. Sanchez, D., Tettamanzi, A.G.: Generalizing quantification in fuzzy description logics. In: Proceedings 8th Fuzzy Days in Dortmund, (2004)
228. Sanchez, D., Tettamanzi, A.G.: Reasoning and quantification in fuzzy description logics. In: Bloch, I., Petrosino, A., Tettamanzi, A.G.B. (eds.) WILF 2005. LNCS (LNAI), vol. 3849, pp. 81–88. Springer, Heidelberg (2006)
229. Sanchez, D., Tettamanzi, A.G.: Fuzzy quantification in fuzzy description logics. In: Sanchez, E. (ed.) Capturing Intelligence: Fuzzy Logic and the Semantic Web. Elsevier, Amsterdam (2006)
230. Schmidt-Schauß, M., Smolka, G.: Attributive concept descriptions with complements. Artificial Intelligence 48, 1–26 (1991)
231. Schroeder, M., Schweimeier, R.: Fuzzy argumentation and extended logic programming. In: Proceedings of ECSQARU Workshop Adventures in Argumentation (2001)
232. Schroeder, M., Schweimeier, R.: Arguments and misunderstandings: Fuzzy unification for negotiating agents. In: Proceedings of the ICLP workshop CLIMA 2002. Elsevier, Amsterdam (2002)
233. Schroeder, M., Schweimeier, R.: Fuzzy unification and argumentation for well-founded semantics. In: Van Emde Boas, P., Pokorný, J., Bieliková, M., Štuller, J. (eds.) SOFSEM 2004. LNCS, vol. 2932, pp. 102–121. Springer, Heidelberg (2004)
234. Seipel, D., Minker, J., Ruiz, C.: Model generation and state generation for disjunctive logic programs. Journal of Logic Programming 32(1), 49–69 (1997)
235. Sessa, M.I.: Approximate reasoning by similarity-based sld resolution. Theoretical Computer Science 275, 389–426 (2002)
236. Shapiro, E.Y.: Logic programs with uncertainties: A tool for implementing rule-based systems. In: Proceedings of the 8th International Joint Conference on Artificial Intelligence (IJCAI 1983), pp. 529–532 (1983)
237. Shen, Z., Ding, L., Mukaidono, M.: A Theoretical Framework of Fuzzy Prolog Machine. In: Fuzzy Computing, pp. 89–100. Elsevier Science Publishers B.V, Amsterdam (1988)
238. Stoilos, G., Stamou, G., Pan, J.: D2.5.6: Fuzzy reasoning extensions. Knowledge Web Technical Report (2007)

239. Stoilos, G., Stamou, G., Pan, J., Tzouvaras, V., Horrocks, I.: The fuzzy description logic f-SHIN. In: International Workshop on Uncertainty Reasoning For the Semantic (Web 2005) (2005)

240. Stoilos, G., Stamou, G., Tzouvaras, V., Pan, J.Z., Horrock, I.: A Fuzzy Description Logic for Multimedia Knowledge Representation. In: Proc. of the International Workshop on Multimedia and the Semantic Web (2005)

241. Stoilos, G., Stamou, G.B., Pan, J.Z., Tzouvaras, V., Horrocks, I.: Reasoning with very expressive fuzzy description logics. Journal of Artificial Intelligence Research 30, 273–320 (2007)

242. Stoilos, G., Straccia, U., Stamou, G., Pan, J.: General concept inclusions in fuzzy description logics. In: Proceedings of the 17th Eureopean Conference on Artificial Intelligence (ECAI 2006), pp. 457–461. IOS Press, Amsterdam (2006)

243. Straccia, U.: A fuzzy description logic. In: Proc. of the 15th Nat. Conf. on Artificial Intelligence (AAAI 1998), pp. 594–599. AAAI Press, Menlo Park (1998)

244. Straccia, U.: A framework for the retrieval of multimedia objects based on four-valued fuzzy description logics. In: Crestani, F., Pasi, G. (eds.) Soft Computing in Information Retrieval: Techniques and Applications, pp. 332–357. Springer, Heidelberg (2000)

245. Straccia, U.: Reasoning within fuzzy description logics. Journal of Artificial Intelligence Research 14, 137–166 (2001)

246. Straccia, U.: Transforming fuzzy description logics into classical description logics. In: Alferes, J.J., Leite, J.A. (eds.) JELIA 2004. LNCS (LNAI), vol. 3229, pp. 385–399. Springer, Heidelberg (2004)

247. Straccia, U.: Uncertainty in description logics: a lattice-based approach. In: Proceedings of the 10th International Conference on Information Processing and Managment of Uncertainty in Knowledge-Based Systems (IPMU 2004), pp. 251–258 (2004)

248. Straccia, U.: Description logics with fuzzy concrete domains. In: Bachus, F., Jaakkola, T. (eds.) 21st Conference on Uncertainty in Artificial Intelligence (UAI 2005), Edinburgh, Scotland, pp. 559–567. AUAI Press (2005)

249. Straccia, U.: Fuzzy alc with fuzzy concrete domains. In: Proceeedings of the International Workshop on Description Logics (DL 2005), Edinburgh, Scotland, pp. 96–103 (2005)

250. Straccia, U.: Query answering in normal logic programs under uncertainty. In: Godo, L. (ed.) ECSQARU 2005. LNCS (LNAI), vol. 3571, pp. 687–700. Springer, Heidelberg (2005)

251. Straccia, U.: Towards a fuzzy description logic for the semantic web (preliminary report). In: Gómez-Pérez, A., Euzenat, J. (eds.) ESWC 2005. LNCS, vol. 3532, pp. 167–181. Springer, Heidelberg (2005)

252. Straccia, U.: Uncertainty management in logic programming: Simple and effective top-down query answering. In: Khosla, R., Howlett, R.J., Jain, L.C. (eds.) KES 2005. LNCS (LNAI), vol. 3682, pp. 753–760. Springer, Heidelberg (2005)

253. Straccia, U.: Annotated answer set programming. In: Proceedings of the 11th International Conference on Information Processing and Managment of Uncertainty in Knowledge-Based Systems (IPMU 2006), pp. 1212–1219. E.D.K, Paris (2006)

254. Straccia, U.: Answering vague queries in fuzzy dl-lite. In: Proceedings of the 11th International Conference on Information Processing and Managment of Uncertainty in Knowledge-Based Systems (IPMU 2006), pp. 2238–2245. E.D.K., Paris (2006)

255. Straccia, U.: Description logics over lattices. International Journal of Uncertainty, Fuzziness and Knowledge-Based Systems 14(1), 1–16 (2006)

256. Straccia, U.: A fuzzy description logic for the semantic web. In: Sanchez, E. (ed.) Fuzzy Logic and the Semantic Web, Capturing Intelligence, vol. 4, pp. 73–90. Elsevier, Amsterdam (2006)

257. Straccia, U.: Fuzzy description logic programs. In: Proceedings of the 11th International Conference on Information Processing and Managment of Uncertainty in Knowledge-Based Systems (IPMU 2006), pp. 1818–1825. E.D.K., Paris (2006)

258. Straccia, U.: Query answering under the any-world assumption for normal logic programs. In: Proceedings of the 10th International Conference on Principles of Knowledge Representation (KR 2006), pp. 329–339. AAAI Press, Menlo Park (2006)

259. Straccia, U.: Towards top-k query answering in deductive databases. In: Proceedings of the 2006 IEEE International Conference on Systems, Man and Cybernetics (SMC 2006), pp. 4873–4879. IEEE, Los Alamitos (2006)

260. Straccia, U.: Towards top-k query answering in description logics: the case of DL-Lite. In: Fisher, M., van der Hoek, W., Konev, B., Lisitsa, A. (eds.) JELIA 2006. LNCS (LNAI), vol. 4160, pp. 439–451. Springer, Heidelberg (2006)

261. Straccia, U.: Uncertainty and description logic programs over lattices. In: Sanchez, E. (ed.) Fuzzy Logic and the Semantic Web, Capturing Intelligence, vol. 7, pp. 115–133. Elsevier, Amsterdam (2006)

262. Straccia, U.: Reasoning in l-$\mathcal{SHIF}$: an expressive fuzzy description logic under łukasiewicz semantics. Technical Report TR-2007-10-18, Istituto di Scienza e Tecnologie dell'Informazione, Consiglio Nazionale delle Ricerche, Pisa, Italy (2007)

263. Straccia, U.: A top-down query answering procedure for normal logic programs under the any-world assumption. In: Mellouli, K. (ed.) ECSQARU 2007. LNCS (LNAI), vol. 4724, pp. 115–127. Springer, Heidelberg (2007)

264. Straccia, U.: Towards vague query answering in logic programming for logic-based information retrieval. In: Melin, P., Castillo, O., Aguilar, L.T., Kacprzyk, J., Pedrycz, W. (eds.) IFSA 2007. LNCS (LNAI), vol. 4529, pp. 125–134. Springer, Heidelberg (2007)

265. Straccia, U., Bobillo, F.: Mixed integer programming, general concept inclusions and fuzzy description logics. Mathware & Soft Computing 14(3), 247–259 (2007)

266. Straccia, U., Visco, G.: DLMedia: an ontology mediated multimedia information retrieval system. In: Proceeedings of the International Workshop on Description Logics (DL 2007), Insbruck, Austria, vol. 250, CEUR (2007)

267. Subramanian, V.: On the semantics of quantitative logic programs. In: Proc. 4th IEEE Symp. on Logic Programming, pp. 173–182. IEEE Computer Society Press, Los Alamitos (1987)

268. Thomas, C., Sheth, A.: On the expressiveness of the languages for the Semantic Web — Making a case for "A little more". In: Sanchez, E. (ed.) Fuzzy Logic and the Semantic Web, Capturing Intelligence, pp. 3–20. Elsevier, Amsterdam (2006)

269. Tresp, C., Molitor, R.: A description logic for vague knowledge. In: Proc. of the 13th European Conf. on Artificial Intelligence (ECAI 1998), Brighton, England (August 1998)

270. Turner, H.: Signed logic programs. In: Bruynooghe, M. (ed.) Logic Programming: Proc. of the 1994 International Symposium, pp. 61–75. MIT Press, Cambridge (1994)

271. Udrea, O., Deng, Y., Hung, E., Subrahmanian, V.S.: Probabilistic ontologies and relational databases. In: Meersman, R., Tari, Z. (eds.) OTM 2005. LNCS, vol. 3760, pp. 1–17. Springer, Heidelberg (2005)

272. Udrea, O., Subrahmanian, V.S., Majkic, Z.: Probabilistic rdf. In: Proceedings of the 2006 IEEE International Conference on Information Reuse and Integration, IRI 2006: Heuristic Systems Engineering, pp. 172–177. IEEE Systems, Los Alamitos (2006)

273. van Emden, M.: Quantitative deduction and its fixpoint theory. Journal of Logic Programming 4(1), 37–53 (1986)

274. Venetis, T., Stoilos, G., Stamou, G., Kollias, S.: f-dlps: Extending description logic programs with fuzzy sets and fuzzy logic. In: IEEE International Conference on Fuzzy Systems (Fuzz-IEEE 2007), London (2007)

275. Vennekens, J., Verbaeten, S., Bruynooghe, M.: Logic programs with annotated disjunctions. In: Demoen, B., Lifschitz, V. (eds.) ICLP 2004. LNCS, vol. 3132, pp. 431–445. Springer, Heidelberg (2004)

276. Vojtáš, P.: Fuzzy logic programming. Fuzzy Sets and Systems 124, 361–370 (2001)

277. Vojtáš, P., Paulík, L.: Soundness and completeness of non-classical extended SLD-resolution. In: Herre, H., Dyckhoff, R., Schroeder-Heister, P. (eds.) ELP 1996. LNCS, vol. 1050, pp. 289–301. Springer, Heidelberg (1996)

278. Vojtáš, P., Vomelelová, M.: Transformation of deductive and inductive tasks between models of logic programming with imperfect information. In: Proceedings of the 10th International Conference on Information Processing and Managment of Uncertainty in Knowledge-Based Systems (IPMU 2004), pp. 839–846 (2004)

279. Wagner, G.: Negation in fuzzy and possibilistic logic programs. In: Martin, T., Arcelli, F. (eds.) Logic programming and Soft Computing. Research Studies Press (1998)

280. Weikum, G., Graupmann, J., Schenkel, R., Theobald, M.: Towards a statistically Semantic Web. In: Atzeni, P., Chu, W., Lu, H., Zhou, S., Ling, T.-W. (eds.) ER 2004. LNCS, vol. 3288, pp. 3–17. Springer, Heidelberg (2004)

281. Wüttrich, B.: Probabilistic knowledge bases. IEEE Transactions on Knowledge and Data Engineering 7(5), 691–698 (1995)

282. Yang, Y., Calmet, J.: OntoBayes: An ontology-driven uncertainty model. In: Proceedings IAWTIC 2005, pp. 457–463. IEEE Press, Los Alamitos (2005)

283. Li, J.L.Y., Xu, B., Kang, D.: Discrete tableau algorithms for shi. In: Proceeedings of the International Workshop on Description Logics (DL 2006). CEUR (2006)

284. Yasui, H., Hamada, Y., Mukaidono, M.: Fuzzy prolog based on lukasiewicz implication and bounded product. IEEE Trans. Fuzzy Systems 2, 949–954 (1995)

285. Yelland, P.M.: An alternative combination of Bayesian networks and description logics. In: Proceedings KR 2000, pp. 225–234. Morgan Kaufmann, San Francisco (2000)

286. Yen, J.: Generalizing term subsumption languages to fuzzy logic. In: Proceedings of the 12th International Joint Conference on Artificial Intelligence (IJCAI 1991), Sydney, Australia, pp. 472–477 (1991)

287. Zadeh, L.A.: Fuzzy sets. Information and Control 8(3), 338–353 (1965)

288. Zhang, L., Yu, Y., Zhou, J., Lin, C., Yang, Y.: An enhanced model for searching in semantic portals. In: WWW 2005: Proceedings of the 14th international conference on World Wide Web, pp. 453–462. ACM Press, New York (2005)

A   Some References Related to Logic Programming, Uncertainty and Vagueness

Below a list of references and the underlying imprecision and uncertainty theory in logic programming frameworks. The list of references is by no means intended to be all-inclusive. The author apologizes both to the authors and with the readers for all the relevant works, which are not cited here.

Probability theory:[11,7,8,40,46,48,44,45,47,82,117,118,116,129,131,152,153,155] [156,158,162,160,184,197,201,202,203,205,215,216,275,281]
Possibilistic logic: [3,4,2,25,57,206]
Fuzzy set theory: [185,9,10,19,24,27,67,100,111,123,89,88,185,199,198,213] [222,235,236,237,177,267,273,277,276,278,279,284]

Multi-valued logic: [22, 34, 35, 36, 31, 32, 37, 38, 39, 41, 33, 53, 49, 52, 50, 51]
[78, 80, 75, 76, 77, 91, 119, 120, 121, 122, 126, 127, 128, 130]
[142, 143, 144, 145, 146, 147, 148, 150, 151, 179, 181, 180, 183, 186, 187, 190, 190, 188, 189, 191]
[226, 231, 232, 233, 252, 250, 253, 258, 259, 264, 263, 270]

Attempto Controlled English for Knowledge Representation

Norbert E. Fuchs, Kaarel Kaljurand, and Tobias Kuhn

Department of Informatics & Institute of Computational Linguistics
University of Zurich, Switzerland
{fuchs,kalju,tkuhn}@ifi.uzh.ch
http://attempto.ifi.uzh.ch

Abstract. Attempto Controlled English (ACE) is a controlled natural language, i.e. a precisely defined subset of English that can automatically and unambiguously be translated into first-order logic. ACE may seem to be completely natural, but is actually a formal language, concretely it is a first-order logic language with an English syntax. Thus ACE is human and machine understandable. ACE was originally intended to specify software, but has since been used as a general knowledge representation language in several application domains, most recently for the semantic web. ACE is supported by a number of tools, predominantly by the Attempto Parsing Engine (APE) that translates ACE texts into Discourse Representation Structures (DRS), a variant of first-order logic. Other tools include the Attempto Reasoner RACE, the AceRules system, the ACE View plug-in for the Protégé ontology editor, AceWiki, and the OWL verbaliser.

1 Introduction

Traditionally human knowledge is presented informally, predominantly in natural language. Everybody knows and understands natural language that takes no extra learning effort, is highly expressive, and provides domain-specific words and phrases. Concerning knowledge representation the disadvantages of natural language are its ambiguity, vagueness and potential inconsistency. To represent knowledge in computers people use formal languages. These languages have a well-defined syntax and an unambiguous semantics, and support formal methods, specifically reasoning. However, many domain specialists are unfamiliar or uneasy with formal languages and formal methods. Furthermore, in order to express domain-specific knowledge in a formal language we need to bridge a conceptual distance. Thus there exists a conflict between the wish to use natural languages and the need to use formal languages. Controlled natural languages[1] have been proposed as a way to resolve this conflict.

Attempto Controlled English (ACE) is a controlled English, i.e. a precisely defined, tractable subset of full English that can automatically and unambiguously be translated into first-order logic. ACE seems completely natural, but is

---

[1] http://www.ics.mq.edu.au/~rolfs/controlled-natural-languages/

C. Baroglio et al. (Eds.): Reasoning Web 2008, LNCS 5224, pp. 104–124, 2008.

actually a formal language defined by a small set of construction and interpretation rules. One could say that ACE is a first-order logic language with the syntax of a subset of English. As a consequence, ACE is understandable both by humans and by machines. Most importantly, ACE texts can be read by anybody who knows English.

Like any formal language ACE has to be learned. Teaching the construction and interpretation rules takes — according to our experience — about two days. Of course, getting fluent with ACE takes longer. This process is supported by ACE tools that provide feedback like paraphrases and reasoning results. To relieve users of having to learn ACE's construction rules, we are developing a predictive editor that guides users in constructing syntactically correct ACE texts.

The Attempto Parsing Engine (APE) that embodies ACE's construction and interpretation rules translates ACE texts unambiguously into discourse representation structures (DRS). DRSs are a variant of first-order logic, and can be easily translated into any formal language equivalent to (a subset of) first-order logic. For the current version 6 of ACE, we developed an extended form of discourse representation structures that allows us to express complex linguistic features, for instance plurals and generalised quantifiers, in first-order logic, and that furthermore facilitates logical deductions on ACE texts.

As a DRS can get a model-theoretic or a proof-theoretic semantics, we can assign the same formal semantics, i.e. unique meaning, to the ACE text from which the DRS was derived. Thus, every ACE sentence is unambiguous, even if people may perceive the sentence as ambiguous in full English.

ACE is supported by a number of tools, predominantly the Attempto Parsing Engine (APE) already mentioned above. Besides translating an ACE text into discourse representation structures, APE also offers translations into various other forms of first-order logic, into OWL, SWRL, and into RuleML. Furthermore, APE can generate ACE paraphrases of DRSs derived from ACE texts.

To support automatic reasoning in ACE, we have developed the Attempto Reasoner (RACE). RACE can prove that one ACE text is the logical consequence of another one, and give a justification for the success or the failure of the proof in ACE.

Recently, ACE has found several applications within the semantic web. Therefore, we have developed translations of ACE into and from semantic web languages. Concretely, there are the translations ACE ↔ OWL/SWRL and ACE → rules. Also, there are various tools that use these translations: AceWiki (uses ACE → OWL/SWRL), ACE View (uses ACE ↔ OWL/SWRL), and AceRules (uses ACE → rules). The tool AceWiki combines controlled natural language with the ideas and technologies of the semantic web and with the concepts of wikis. AceWiki also incorporates a predictive editor that enables users to construct syntactically correct ACE sentences from a restricted vocabulary. ACE View is a plug-in for the ontology editor Protégé. Finally, AceRules is a forward chaining rule system that offers three different semantics.

Applications of ACE include software and hardware specifications, data base integrity constraints, agent control, legal and medical regulations, and ontologies. Furthermore, ACE served as natural language interface to semantic web languages like OWL, SWRL, RuleML, Protune, R2ML and as query language for MIT's Process Handbook.

In the following we give an overview of the language ACE, and then briefly present the tools Attempto Parsing Engine (APE), Attempto Reasoner (RACE), ACE View, AceRules, AceWiki, and OWL verbaliser.

2 Overview of ACE

This section is a brief introduction into ACE 6. For a full account please consult the ACE documentation found at the Attempto website[2].

Sections 2.1 to 2.6 describe the syntax of ACE 6, sections 2.8 to 2.10 summarise the handling of ambiguity, and section 2.11 explains anaphoric references.

2.1 Vocabulary

The vocabulary of ACE comprises

- Predefined function words (e.g. determiners, conjunctions, prepositions), and some predefined phrases (*there is/are, it is false that, ...*)
- Content words (nouns, verbs, adjectives, and adverbs)

2.2 Grammar

The grammar of ACE defines and constrains the form and the meaning of ACE sentences and texts. ACE's grammar is expressed as a small set of construction rules[3]. The meaning of ACE texts is defined by a small set of interpretation rules[4].

2.3 ACE Texts

An ACE text is a sequence of declarative sentences that can be anaphorically interrelated. Furthermore, ACE supports questions that allow users to interrogate the contents of an ACE text, and commands for the interactive control of agents.

Declarative sentences are categorised as simple sentences, and composite sentences.

2.4 Simple Sentences

A simple sentence describes that something is the case — a fact, an event, a state.

> *A customer inserts 2 cards.*
> *The temperature is -2 °C.*
> *At least 3 cards and exactly 2 codes are valid.*

---

[2] http://attempto.ifi.uzh.ch

[3] http://attempto.ifi.uzh.ch/site/docs/ace_constructionrules.html

[4] http://attempto.ifi.uzh.ch/site/docs/ace_interpretationrules.html

Simple ACE sentences have the following general structure:

subject + verb + complements + adjuncts

Every simple sentence has a subject and a verb. Complements (direct and indirect objects) are necessary for transitive verbs (*insert something*) and ditransitive verbs (*give something to somebody, give somebody something*), whereas adjuncts (adverbs, prepositional phrases) are optional.

All elements of a simple sentence can be elaborated upon to describe the situation in more detail. To further specify the nouns *customer* and *card* of the first example sentence, we could add adjectives

A trusted customer inserts two valid cards.

possessive nouns and *of*-prepositional phrases

John's customer inserts 2 cards of Mary.

or variables as appositions

The customer X inserts 2 cards Y.

Other modifications of nouns are possible through relative sentences

A customer who is new inserts 2 cards that he owns.

We can also detail the insertion event, e.g. by adding an adverb

A customer inserts two cards manually.

or equivalently

A customer manually inserts two cards.

or by adding prepositional phrases, e.g.

A customer inserts two cards into a slot.

We can combine all of these elaborations to arrive at

John's customer who is new inserts 2 valid cards of Mary manually into a slot X.

2.5   Composite Sentences

Composite sentences are recursively built from simpler sentences through coordination, subordination, quantification, and negation. Note that ACE composite sentences overlap with what linguists call compound sentences and complex sentences.

Coordination by *and* is possible between sentences and between phrases of the same syntactic type.

A customer inserts a card and the machine checks the code.
There is a customer who inserts a card and who enters a code.
A customer inserts a card and enters a code.
An old and trusted customer enters a card and a code.

Note that the coordination of the noun phrases *a card and a code* represents a plural object.

Coordination by *or* is possible between sentences, relative clauses and verb phrases.

A customer inserts a card or the machine checks the code.
A customer owns a card that is invalid or that is damaged.
A customer inserts a card or enters a code.

Coordination by *and* and *or* is governed by the standard binding order of logic, i.e. *and* binds stronger than *or*. Commas can be used to override the standard binding order. Thus the sentence

A customer inserts a VisaCard or inserts a MasterCard, and inserts a code.

means that the customer inserts a VisaCard and a code or, alternatively a MasterCard and a code.

There are three constructs of subordination: *if-then* sentences, modality, and sentence subordination.

With the help of *if-then* sentences we can specify conditional or hypothetical situations, e.g.

If a card is valid then a customer inserts it.

Note the anaphoric reference via the pronoun *it* in the *then*-part to the noun phrase *a card* in the *if*-part.

Modality allows us to express possibility and necessity.

A trusted customer can insert a card.
A trusted customer must insert a card.
It is possible that a trusted customer inserts a card.
It is necessary that a trusted customer inserts a card.

Sentence subordination comes in various forms.

It is true that a customer inserts a card. (= A customer inserts a card.)
It is false that a customer inserts a card.
It is not provable that a customer inserts a card.
A clerk believes that a customer inserts a card.

Quantification allows us to speak about all objects of a certain class (universal quantification), or to denote explicitly the existence of at least one object of this class (existential quantification). The textual occurrence of a universal or existential quantifier opens its scope that extends to the end of the sentence, or in coordinations to the end of the respective coordinated sentence.

To express that all customers insert cards, we can write

Every customer inserts a card.

Alternatively, with exactly the same meaning

All customers insert a card.

This sentence means that each customer inserts a card that may, or may not, be the same as the one inserted by another customer. To specify that all customers insert the same card — however unrealistic that situation seems — we can write

There is a card that every customer inserts.

or, equivalently

A card is inserted by every customer.

To state that every card is inserted by a customer, we write

Every card is inserted by a customer.

or, somewhat indirectly

For every card there is a customer who inserts it.

Negation allows us to express that something is not the case, e.g.

A customer does not insert a card.
A card is not valid.

To negate something for all objects of a certain class one uses *no*

No customer inserts more than 2 cards.

or, equivalently, *there is no*

There is no customer who inserts more than 2 cards.

To negate a complete statement one uses sentence negation

It is false that a customer inserts a card.

2.6   Query Sentences

Query sentences permit us to interrogate the contents of an ACE text, data bases etc. ACE supports two forms of queries: *yes/no*-queries and *wh*-queries. Note that interrogative sentences need always a question mark at the end.

Yes/no-queries establish the existence or non-existence of a specified situation. If we specified

A customer inserts a card.

then we can ask

Does a customer insert a card?

to get a positive answer.

With the help of *wh*-queries, i.e. queries with query words, we can interrogate a text for details of the specified situation. If we specified

A new customer inserts a valid card manually.

we can ask for each constituent of the sentence with the exception of the verb.

Who inserts a card?
Which customer inserts a card?
What does a customer insert?
How does a customer insert a card?

Queries can also be constructed by a sequence of declarative sentences followed by one interrogative sentence. Here is an example.

A customer uses a card that is valid and that is owned by the customer. The customer has an account that is activated. The card belongs-to the account. What is the code of the card?

2.7   Commands

ACE also supports commands intended to be used in interactive environments. Some examples:

John, go to the bank!
John and Mary, wait!
Every dog, bark!
The brother of John, give the book to Mary!

A command always consists of a noun phrase (the addressee), followed by a comma, followed by an uncoordinated verb phrase. Furthermore, a command has to end with an exclamation mark.

2.8   Constraining Ambiguity

To constrain the ambiguity of full natural language, ACE employs three simple means

- some ambiguous constructs are not part of the language; unambiguous alternatives are available in their place
- all remaining ambiguous constructs are interpreted deterministically on the basis of a small number of interpretation rules
- users can either accept the assigned interpretation — shown for example in the paraphrase generated by APE — or they must rephrase the input to obtain another one

2.9   Avoidance of Ambiguity

Here is an example how ACE replaces ambiguous constructs by unambiguous constructs. In full natural language relative sentences combined with coordinations can introduce ambiguity, e.g.

A customer inserts a card that is valid and opens an account.

In ACE the sentence has the unequivocal meaning that the customer opens an account. This is reflected by the paraphrase

A card is valid. A customer inserts the card. The customer opens an account.

To express the alternative — though not very realistic — meaning that the card opens an account the relative pronoun *that* must be repeated, thus yielding a coordination of relative sentences.

A customer inserts a card that is valid and that opens an account.

with the paraphrase

A card is valid. The card opens an account. A customer inserts the card.

2.10   Interpretation Rules

However, not all ambiguities can be safely removed from ACE without rendering it artificial. To deterministically interpret otherwise syntactically correct ACE sentences we use a small set of interpretation rules. For example, if we write

The customer inserts a card with a code.

then *with a code* attaches to the verb *inserts*, but not to *a card*. However, this is probably not what we meant to say. To express that the code is associated with the card we can employ the interpretation rule that a relative clause always modifies the immediately preceding noun phrase, and rephrase the input as

A customer inserts a card that carries a code.

yielding the paraphrase

A card carries a code. A customer inserts the card.

or — to specify that the customer inserts a card and a code — as

The customer inserts a card and a code.

Another example. Adverbs can precede or follow the verb. To disambiguate the sentence

The customer who inserts a card manually enters a code.

where in full English *manually* could modify *insert* or *enter*, we employ the interpretation rule that the postverbal position has priority. This is exhibited in the paraphrase

There is a customer. The customer enters a code. The customer inserts a card manually.

2.11   Anaphoric References

Usually ACE texts consist of more than one sentence, e.g.

> *A customer enters a card and a code. If a code is valid then SimpleMat accepts a card. If a code is not valid then SimpleMat rejects a card.*

To express that all occurrences of *card* and *code* should mean the same card and the same code, ACE provides anaphoric references via the definite article, i.e.

> *A customer enters a card and a code. If the code is valid then SimpleMat accepts the card. If the code is not valid then SimpleMat rejects the card.*

During the processing of the ACE text, all anaphoric references are replaced by the most recent and most specific accessible noun phrase that agrees in gender and number, yielding the paraphrase

> *There is a customer X1. The customer X1 enters a card X2 and a code X3. If the code X3 is valid then SimpleMat accepts the card X2. If it is false that the code X3 is valid then SimpleMat rejects the card X2.*

where the variables *X1*, *X2*, and *X3* are introduced to clearly show the anaphoric references.

What does "most recent and most specific" mean? Given the sentence

> *A customer enters a red card and a blue card.*

then

> *The card is correct.*

refers to the second card, since it is "most recent" reference to *a card*, while

> *The red card is correct.*

refers to the first card, since it is "most recent" reference to *a red card*.

What does "accessible" mean? In accordance with standard English, noun phrases introduced in *if-then* sentences, universally quantified sentences, negations, modality, and subordinated sentences, and noun phrase preceded by the generalised quantifiers *less than* and *at most* cannot be used anaphorically in subsequent sentences. Thus for each of the sentences

> *If a customer owns a card then he enters it.*
> *Every customer enters a card.*
> *A customer does not enter a card.*
> *A customer can enter a card.*
> *A clerk believes that a customer enters a card.*
> *A customer enters less than 2 cards.*
> *A customer enters at most 2 cards.*

we cannot refer to *a card*, *less than 2 cards* or *at most 2 cards* with, for instance

The card is correct.

Anaphoric references are also possible via personal pronouns

A customer enters a card and a code. If it is valid then SimpleMat accepts the card. If it is not valid then SimpleMat rejects the card.

or via variables

A customer enters a card X and a code Y. If Y is valid then SimpleMat accepts X. If Y is not valid then SimpleMat rejects X.

Anaphoric references via definite articles and variables can be combined.

A customer enters a card X and a code Y. If the code X is valid then SimpleMat accepts the card X. If the code Y is not valid then SimpleMat rejects the card X.

Note that proper names like *SimpleMat* always refer to the same object.

2.12   Other Controlled Natural Languages

Traditionally, controlled natural languages fall into two major types: those that improve readability for human readers, and those that enable reliable automatic semantic analysis of the language. The first type of languages, for example ASD Simplified Technical English[5], Caterpillar Technical English, IBM's Easy English, are used in the industry to increase the quality of technical documentation. The second type of languages have a formal logical basis, i.e. they have a formal syntax and semantics, and can be mapped to an existing formal language, such as first-order logic. Thus, languages of the second type can be used for knowledge representation and reasoning.

Since ACE falls into the second type we will focus here only on other languages of the second type. Expressive and recently developed versions of controlled English include PENG [23, 24, 27, 28], Common Logic Controlled English [29], Boeing's Computer Processable Language [1], and E2V [21]. For an exhaustive list of controlled natural languages see footnote 1 and [20] that lists 32 languages altogether.

Rolf Schwitter's PENG[6] branched out from the research done on ACE. Therefore the designs of the two languages are quite similar. In recent years, more features have been added to ACE, making it both syntactically and semantically more expressive than PENG. Research on PENG, on the other hand, stresses the need for syntax-aware editing tools for controlled natural languages, and has focused on the development of ECOLE [26], a predictive text editor that guides the user in constructing only syntactically acceptable PENG sentences. A similar predictive editor is being developed in the AceWiki system (see section 3.5) for a subset of ACE.

Another ACE-like controlled English is John Sowa's CLCE [29, 30], which has been designed as a "human interface" to the ISO standard Common Logic[7].

---

[5] http://www.asd-ste100.org
[6] http://www.ics.mq.edu.au/~rolfs/peng/
[7] http://cl.tamu.edu/

However, there is only a partial specification of CLCE available, and a parser for CLCE has not yet been published.

CPL [1] is a controlled English developed at Boeing, and used experimentally for various purposes, e.g. to rephrase texts on chemistry. CPL is closer to everyday English than ACE, PENG, or CLCE, in the sense that it uses fewer strict rules and its interpreter is expected to "smartly" resolve various ambiguities. The interpreter also handles nominalizations, and guesses the word senses of nouns and verbs with the help of the WordNet[8] lexicon. Errors are handled by sophisticated error resolution. The result of parsing is a logical formula in a frame-based knowledge representation language Knowledge Machine [2] on which a reasoner can be applied.

E2V [21] is a fragment of English that corresponds to the decidable two-variable fragment of first-order logic ($\mathcal{L}^2$). Syntactically, E2V is a subset of ACE. However, its treatment of pronominal references is different — pronouns always refer to the closest noun in the syntax tree, and not to the closest noun in the surface order of words. This makes a difference if the preceding noun phrase contains a relative clause. This different treatment seems to be mainly motivated by better reasoning properties. In general, E2V, as well as its extensions have been developed to study the computational properties of certain linguistic structures. The intention of the authors has not been to develop a real-world knowledge representation language by adding features which would increase the usability of the language. Instead, only language features that introduce interesting computational problems have been added.

2.13   Decidablility of ACE

ACE texts are translated into a subset of first-order logic. Since first-order logic is not decidable the question arises whether ACE is decidable.

To answer this question, we rely on results of Ian Pratt-Hartmann and Allan Third (see [22]) who investigated the decidability of various fragments of English.

In their paper, Pratt-Hartmann & Third use the following abbreviations to describe English constructs: Cop (singular, existentially/universally quantified nouns, predicative adjectives, copula with and without negation), Rel (relative clauses), TV (transitive verbs without and with negation), DTV (ditransitive verbs without and with negation), RA (reflexive and non-reflexive pronouns as anaphors, resolution of anaphors to closest antecedent noun phrase in phrase structure), GA (reflexive and non-reflexive pronouns as anaphors, resolution of anaphors by coindexing pronouns and antecedent noun phrases).

From the results of Pratt-Hartmann & Third it follows that ACE is not decidable since it is a superset of the fragment Cop + Rel + TV + GA that Pratt-Hartmann & Third proved to be undecidable.

However, Pratt-Hartmann & Third identified 4 decidable fragments that are also fragments of ACE, namely

- Cop + TV + DTV
- Cop + Rel

---

[8] http://wordnet.princeton.edu

- Cop + Rel + TV
- Cop + Rel + TV + DTV

As [14] shows, there is one further decidable ACE fragment that differs from the ones identified by Pratt-Hartmann & Third. This ACE fragment can be translated into OWL 2 and vice versa (see section 3.3). Since OWL 2 is decidable, the respective ACE fragment is also decidable.

Interestingly, none of these decidable ACE fragments contains adverbs or prepositional phrases. Thus verbs cannot be readily modified.

The so-called AE subset of first order logic — that consists of formulas without functions symbols and with no universal quantifier occurring in the scope of an existential one — is decidable [5]. This means that any ACE sentence that can be mapped to an AE formula is also decidable. This defines a further decidable fragment of ACE that consists of simple sentences and *if-then* sentences with rather intricate restrictions on the use of negation and universal quantification.

As can be seen, each of the decidable fragments of ACE introduces some restrictions on the syntactic structures that can be used. It depends on the respective application whether or not this limitation of expressivity matters, and also on the willingness of the users to cope with syntactic restrictions. To relieve users of these considerations, the ACE reasoner RACE (see section 3.2) accepts all of ACE — of course with the exception of negation as failure that is outside of first-order logic — and controls undecidability by introducing a time-out.

3   ACE Tools

3.1   Attempto Parsing Engine APE

The Attempto Parsing Engine (APE) implements the ACE construction and interpretation rules in Prolog as a Definite Clause Grammar enhanced with feature structures. APE uses a built-in lexicon of function words and a basic lexicon of content words with approximately 100'000 entries. Users can import additional, e.g. domain specific, content word lexicons. Words found in user-imported lexicons take precedence over the same words found in the basic lexicon. Alternatively, users can let the ACE parser guess unknown words, or users can prefix unknown words by their word-class, for instance *n:kitkat, p:Thomas, v:google, a:trusted, a:undeviatingly.*

APE is available as open source under the LGPL license. Alternatively, users can access APE via a web service[9] or via a web client[10] that provides a graphical front-end to the web service.

APE takes an ACE text and optionally a user lexicon as input, and can generate a large number of various outputs: the tokens of the input text, various representations of the syntax tree of the input text, several representations of the DRS of the

---

[9] http://attempto.ifi.uzh.ch/site/docs/ape_webservice.html
[10] http://attempto.ifi.uzh.ch/ape/

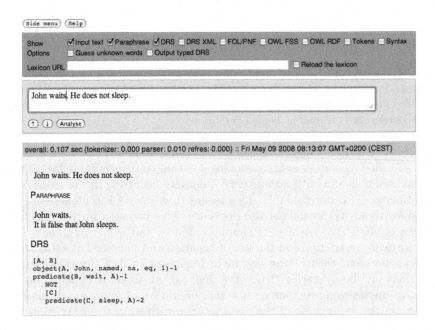

Fig. 1. Screenshot of the APE web client translating a simple ACE text into a DRS

input text, different paraphrases of the input text derived from its DRS, several first-order representations of the DRS, and two syntaxes of OWL/SWRL derived from the DRS.

If parsing fails, APE generates warning and error messages that identify the cause and the approximate location of the problems encountered, and suggest remedies for the problems. An ACE text can be erroneous because the input contained an unknown word, the input violated the ACE syntax rules, and finally, the input was syntactically correct but anaphoric references could not be resolved.

APE is sufficiently fast and parses approximately 100 ACE sentences per second.

Figure 1 shows a screenshot of the APE web client translating a simple text into a DRS.

3.2 ACE Reasoner RACE

The Attempto Reasoner RACE proves that one ACE text — the theorems — is the logical consequence of another one — the axioms — and gives a justification for the proof in ACE. Variations of the basic deduction mode permit query answering and consistency checking.

RACE is implemented in Prolog. The implementation is based on the model generator Satchmo [18] that tries to find a minimal model of a set of range-restricted clauses. Satchmo had to be extended in various ways to fulfil the requirements of RACE.

Since RACE's input is given in ACE, axioms and theorems are translated by APE into discourse representation structures that are then further translated into Satchmo clauses. To generate output in ACE, RACE keeps track of which axioms are needed to prove the theorems, and reports these axioms as result of the proof.

Satchmo stops once it found that a set of clauses is unsatisfiable. RACE, however, finds all proofs, i.e. all possibilities in which subsets of a set of ACE axioms combined with the negation of a set of ACE theorems is unsatisfiable.

Some proofs require domain-independent linguistic and mathematical knowledge that cannot be expressed in ACE, for instance the relation between plurals and singulars or the ordering of natural numbers. To express this knowledge RACE uses auxiliary first-order and Prolog axioms.

Users can access RACE via its web service[11] or via a web client[12] that provides a graphical front-end to the web service.

RACE offers three deduction modes: consistency checking, proving and query answering. All three modes can be controlled by parameters that allow various deductions from collective plurals, enable RACE to check for additional proofs once the first proof was found, and allow users to display auxiliary axioms used in a deduction.

Figure 2 shows a screenshot of the RACE web client proving an ACE theorem from ACE axioms using auxiliary axioms.

RACE applies several means to perform deductions efficiently. Basically, RACE executes its clauses by forward chaining. The worst-case complexity of forward chaining is $O(N^2)$ where N is the number of clauses. Thus an important goal is to reduce the number of clauses that participate in forward chaining. This number was already enormously reduced by simplifications that we introduced in the DRS language. The number of clauses is further reduced by clause compaction, i.e. by a more complex clause form that combines several clauses into one clause. Furthermore, RACE executes rules derived from facts — i.e. rules with the body "true" — only once. Another speed-up is achieved by intelligently selecting the rules that participate in any forward chaining step. Further efficiency is gained by complement splitting of disjunctions — an effective way to prune the search space. Finally, even more efficiency is achieved by expressing auxiliary axioms in Prolog instead of in first-order logic.

3.3   ACE View Protégé Plug-In

ACE View is a novel ontology and rule editor. The goal of ACE View is to simplify the exploration and editing of expressive and syntactically complex OWL 2 [19] ontologies and SWRL [13] rulesets by basing the user interface on ACE. This makes ACE View radically different from current OWL/SWRL editors which are based on standard graphical user interface widgets and formal logic syntaxes, and which are often seen as too complicated and misleading for domain experts

---

[11] http://attempto.ifi.uzh.ch/site/docs/race_webservice.html
[12] http://attempto.ifi.uzh.ch/race/

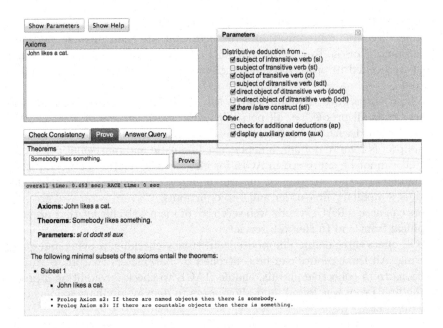

Fig. 2. Screenshot of the RACE web client proving an ACE theorem from ACE axioms using auxiliary axioms

with no background in formal methods. ACE View integrates two mappings, ACE→OWL/SWRL and OWL→ACE (both discussed in detail in [14]), and is implemented as a plug-in for the widely-used Protégé OWL editor [12].

Current OWL editors/viewers (e.g. Protégé[13], OwlSight[14], TopBraid Composer[15]) attempt to hide the complexity resulting from the various ontology, rule, and query formalisms by offering a graphical front-end based on forms, trees, wizards, etc. to enable the entering and viewing of ontologies. This is effective for simple structures like class and property assertions, and the subclass hierarchy between named classes. However, for complex structures like negation, property restrictions, general class inclusion axioms, and SWRL rules, visual methods fail and the tools fall back to one of the native syntaxes of OWL (e.g. Manchester OWL Syntax is used to present OWL class expressions). Thus, in general, current tools fail to hide the complexities of OWL. [4] compared TopBraid Composer and Protégé and found several problems that both novices and experts encountered.

An alternative and less explored approach is to base ontology editing on the use of controlled natural language (CNL) [3, 10, 14]. Several studies have shown that controlled English can offer an improvement in usability over existing approaches for domain experts viewing and editing OWL statements [6, 16, 25]. However, ontology

---

[13] http://protege.stanford.edu
[14] http://pellet.owldl.com/owlsight/
[15] http://www.topbraidcomposer.com

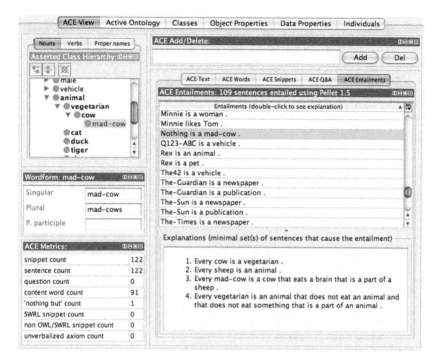

Fig. 3. ACE View offers a controlled English front-end to ontology and rule editing and viewing. The "entailments view" (shown on the screenshot) lists sentences that follow from the entered ACE text. Each of such entailments can be explained by listing a smaller fragment of the text that causes the entailment. The screenshot shows the explanation of why "Nothing is a mad-cow."

editors offering CNL editing as their main component are still in their infancy and their possible architecture has not been agreed upon.

ACE View offers one unified syntax for OWL axioms, SWRL rules and DL queries — axioms and rules are hidden behind English declarative sentences and queries behind English interrogative sentences. ACE View is implemented as an extension to the popular ontology editor Protégé. This greatly simplifies the implementation of our approach as we can leverage the integrated OWL API [11], reasoners, rule and query support that Protégé provides and just concentrate on providing the CNL front-end to these tools. Also, we can easily fall back to the Protégé solutions for e.g. annotation editing, etc. that we do not intend to express in ACE. Being based on Protégé also simplifies the evaluation of our approach, e.g. one sensible way to evaluate ACE View is to let people complete an ontology engineering task and observe for how much of it they want to fall back to Protégé.

3.4   AceRules

AceRules [15] is a multi-semantics rule system prototype using ACE as input and output language. AceRules is designed for forward-chaining interpreters that

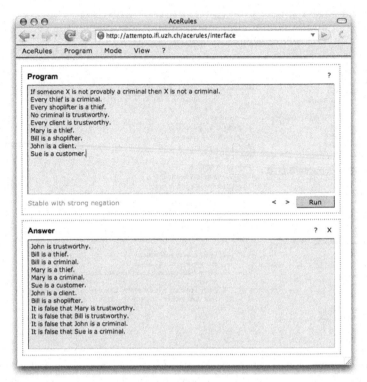

Fig. 4. Screenshot of the AceRules web interface showing an exemplary program (i.e. rule set) and the answer that is inferred from it

calculate the complete answer set. The general approach of AceRules, however, could easily be adopted for backward-chaining interpreters. Figure 4 shows a screenshot of the AceRules interface. The upper text box is the input component and contains the program to be executed. The result of the program is then displayed in the text box below.

At the moment, AceRules incorporates three different semantics: courteous logic programs [9], stable models [7], and stable models with strong negation [8]. Depending on the semantics, AceRules supports negation as failure, strong negation, labelled rules, and priorities between rules. Furthermore, it has an internal grouping mechanism that transforms certain logical statements that do not have a rule structure into valid rules.

3.5   AceWiki

The goal of AceWiki [17] is to show that semantic wikis can be more natural and at the same time more expressive than existing semantic wikis.

Naturalness is achieved by representing the formal statements in ACE. In order to enable easy creation of ACE sentences, AceWiki provides a predictive editor that shows step-by-step the words and phrases that are syntactically possible at a given position in the sentence. Figure 5 shows a screenshot of the AceWiki interface.

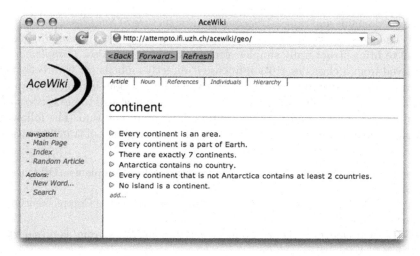

Fig. 5. Screenshot of the web interface of the AceWiki prototype showing an article about continents

AceWiki makes use of the high expressivity of ACE that goes beyond OWL and SWRL. AceWiki integrates the OWL reasoner Pellet[16] which considers only the sentences that are OWL-compliant. The reasoner is used to ensure that the ontology is always consistent and it calculates the class memberships and class hierarchies which are then displayed in ACE again. Furthermore, the reasoner is used to answer questions formulated in ACE.

We conducted a user experiment [16] that proved that ordinary people with no background in logic are able to deal with AceWiki. The participants — without being instructed how to interact with the interface — were asked to add knowledge to AceWiki. About 80% of the created sentences were correct and sensible. This is remarkable since most of the sentences were quite complex: more than 60% of them contained an implication or a negation or both. Using the predictive editor which the participants had never seen before, they needed on average only five minutes to create their first correct sentence.

3.6   OWL Verbaliser

The OWL verbaliser performs a mapping of the logical content of an OWL ontology into ACE. The OWL verbaliser accepts an OWL ontology in OWL 2 XML serialization as input and produces a plain ACE text as output. The OWL verbaliser is implemented in SWI-Prolog.

The verbalisation of an OWL axiom is done in three steps, two of which perform a set of semantics preserving transformations on the axiom and the third maps the resulting structure directly to ACE. First, the axiom is rewritten into a different form which is either one of *SubClassOf*, *SubPropertyOf*, *DisjointProperties*. This step removes a lot of syntactic sugar (such as axioms dedicated to

---

[16] http://pellet.owldl.com

expressing domains and ranges). Secondly, the structure of *SubClassOf*-axioms is slightly changed, e.g. elements in coordination (*IntersectionOf, UnionOf*) are re-ordered to bring structurally simpler elements to the front. Also, *ComplementOf* is removed from a class description in case it directly embeds (or is directly embedded in) a property restriction. Third, the modified axiom is directly mapped to ACE via a simple Definite Clause Grammar. The purpose of the first two steps is to improve the readability of the eventual ACE representation. The following example demonstrates how an axiom in OWL is via a sequence of transformations translated into a sentence in ACE.

1. ClassAssertion(Sarkozy AllValuesFrom(is-president-of ComplementOf(OneOf(USA))))
2. SubClassOf(OneOf(Sarkozy) AllValuesFrom(is-president-of ComplementOf(OneOf(USA))))
3. SubClassOf(OneOf(Sarkozy) ComplementOf(SomeValuesFrom(is-president-of OneOf(USA))))
4. It is false that Sarkozy is-president-of USA.

4   Conclusions

Attempto Controlled English (ACE) is a language with a dual face — because of its natural language heritage humans can read it easily and because of its logical foundations machines can process it in various ways. The attributes of ACE — specifically its ability to express relations, rules, commands and queries in one and the same language — make it a prime candidate for knowledge representation in almost any application domain including the semantic web. The flexibility and power of ACE becomes apparent when used in tools like APE, RACE, ACE View, AceRules, AceWiki, and OWL verbaliser.

References

1. Clark, P., Harrison, P., Jenkins, T., Thompson, J., Wojcik, R.H.: Acquiring and Using World Knowledge Using a Restricted Subset of English. In: FLAIRS 2005, pp. 506–511 (2005)
2. Clark, P., Porter, B.: KM — The Knowledge Machine 2.0: Users Manual. Technical report (2004), http://www.cs.utexas.edu/users/mfkb/km/userman.pdf
3. Cregan, A., Schwitter, R., Meyer, T.: Sydney OWL Syntax — towards a Controlled Natural Language Syntax for OWL 1.1. In: Golbreich, C., Kalyanpur, A., Parsia, B. (eds.) CEUR Proceedings of 3rd OWL Experiences and Directions Workshop (OWLED 2007), vol. 258 (2007)
4. Dzbor, M., Motta, E., Buil, C., Gomez, J., Görlitz, O., Lewen, H.: Developing ontologies in OWL: An observational study. In: 2nd OWL Experiences and Directions Workshop (OWLED 2006) (2006)
5. Fitting, M.: First-Order Logic and Automated Theorem Proving. Springer, Heidelberg (1996)

6. Funk, A., Tablan, V., Bontcheva, K., Cunningham, H., Davis, B., Handschuh, S.: CLOnE: Controlled Language for Ontology Editing. In: Aberer, K., Choi, K.-S., Noy, N., Allemang, D., Lee, K.-I., Nixon, L., Golbeck, J., Mika, P., Maynard, D., Mizoguchi, R., Schreiber, G., Cudré-Mauroux, P. (eds.) ASWC 2007 and ISWC 2007. LNCS, vol. 4825, Springer, Heidelberg (2007)

7. Gelfond, M., Lifschitz, V.: The stable model semantics for logic programming. In: Proceedings of the 5th International Conference on Logic Programming, pp. 1070–1080. MIT Press, Cambridge (1988)

8. Gelfond, M., Lifschitz, V.: Classical negation in logic programs and disjunctive databases. New Generation Computing 9, 365–385 (1990)

9. Grosof, B.N.: Prioritized conflict handling for rules. Technical Report RC 20836, IBM Research, IBM T.J. Watson Research Center (December 1997)

10. Hart, G., Dolbear, C., Goodwin, J.: Lege Feliciter: Using Structured English to represent a Topographic Hydrology Ontology. In: Golbreich, C., Kalyanpur, A., Parsia, B. (eds.) CEUR Proceedings of 3rd OWL Experiences and Directions Workshop (OWLED 2007), vol. 258 (2007)

11. Horridge, M., Bechhofer, S., Noppens, O.: Igniting the OWL 1.1 Touch Paper: The OWL API. In: Golbreich, C., Kalyanpur, A., Parsia, B. (eds.) CEUR Proceedings of 3rd OWL Experiences and Directions Workshop (OWLED 2007), vol. 258 (2007)

12. Horridge, M., Jupp, S., Moulton, G., Rector, A., Stevens, R., Wroe, C.: A Practical Guide To Building OWL Ontologies Using Protégé 4 and CO-ODE Tools. The University Of Manchester (2007), http://www.co-ode.org/resources/tutorials/

13. Horrocks, I., Patel-Schneider, P.F., Boley, H., Tabet, S., Grosof, B., Dean, M.: SWRL: A Semantic Web Rule Language Combining OWL and RuleML. W3C Member Submission May 21, 2004. Technical report, W3C (2004), http://www.w3.org/Submission/2004/SUBM-SWRL-20040521/

14. Kaljurand, K.: Attempto Controlled English as a Semantic Web Language. PhD thesis, Faculty of Mathematics and Computer Science, University of Tartu (2007)

15. Kuhn, T.: AceRules: Executing Rules in Controlled Natural Language. In: Marchiori, M., Pan, J.Z., d Marie, C.S. (eds.) RR 2007. LNCS, vol. 4524, pp. 299–308. Springer, Heidelberg (2007)

16. Kuhn, T.: AceWiki: A Natural and Expressive Semantic Wiki. In: Semantic Web User Interaction at CHI 2008: Exploring HCI Challenges (2008)

17. Kuhn, T.: AceWiki: Collaborative Ontology Management in Controlled Natural Language. In: SemWiki 2008 —The Wiki Way of Semantics (2008)

18. Manthey, R., Bry, F.: SATCHMO: A Theorem Prover Implemented in Prolog. In: Lusk, E.L., Overbeek, R.A. (eds.) CADE 1988. LNCS, vol. 310, pp. 415–434. Springer, Heidelberg (1988)

19. Motik, B., Patel-Schneider, P.F., Horrocks, I.: OWL 2 Web Ontology Language: Structural Specification and Functional-Style Syntax. Technical report, W3C (2008), http://www.w3.org/TR/2008/WD-owl2-syntax-20080411/

20. Pool, J.: Can Controlled Languages Scale to the Web? In: 5th International Workshop on Controlled Language Applications (2006)

21. Pratt-Hartmann, I.: A two-variable fragment of English. Journal of Logic, Language and Information 12(1), 13–45 (2003)

22. Pratt-Hartmann, I., Third, A.: More fragments of language: the case of ditransitive verbs. Notre Dame Journal of Formal Logic 47(2), 151–177 (2006)

23. Schwitter, R.: A Controlled Natural Language Layer for the Semantic Web. In: Zhang, S., Jarvis, R. (eds.) AI 2005. LNCS (LNAI), vol. 3809, pp. 425–434. Springer, Heidelberg (2005)

24. Schwitter, R.: Controlled Natural Language as Interface Language to the Semantic Web. In: 2nd Indian International Conference on Artificial Intelligence (IICAI 2005), Pune, India, December 20–22 (2005)
25. Schwitter, R., Kaljurand, K., Cregan, A., Dolbear, C., Hart, G.: A Comparison of three Controlled Natural Languages for OWL 1.1. In: 4th OWL Experiences and Directions Workshop (OWLED, DC), Washington, April 1–2, 2008, p. 10 (2008)
26. Schwitter, R., Ljungberg, A., Hood, D.: ECOLE — A Look-ahead Editor for a Controlled Language. In: Controlled Translation, Proceedings of EAMT-CLAW 2003, Joint Conference combining the 8th International Workshop of the European Association for Machine Translation and the 4th Controlled Language Application Workshop, Dublin City University, Ireland, May 15–17, 2003, pp. 141–150 (2003)
27. Schwitter, R., Tilbrook, M.: Controlled Natural Language meets the Semantic Web. In: Wan, S., Asudeh, A., Paris, C. (eds.) Australasian Language Technology Workshop 2004, Macquarie University, December 2004, pp. 55–62 (2004)
28. Schwitter, R., Tilbrook, M.: Let's Talk in Description Logic via Controlled Natural Language. In: Logic and Engineering of Natural Language Semantics 2006 (LENLS 2006), Tokyo, Japan, June 5–6 (2006)
29. Sowa, J.F.: Common Logic Controlled English. Technical report, 2004. Draft (February 24, 2004), http://www.jfsowa.com/clce/specs.htm
30. Sowa, J.F.: Common Logic Controlled English. Technical report, 2007. Draft (March 15, 2007), http://www.jfsowa.com/clce/clce07.htm

Semantic Multimedia

Steffen Staab[1], Ansgar Scherp[1], Richard Arndt[1], Raphael Troncy[2],
Marcin Grzegorzek[1], Carsten Saathoff[1], Simon Schenk[1], and Lynda Hardman[2]

[1] ISWeb Research Group, University of Koblenz-Landau
http://isweb.uni-koblenz.de
[2] Semantic Media Interfaces, CWI Amsterdam
http://www.cwi.nl

Abstract. Multimedia constitutes an interesting field of application for
Semantic Web and Semantic Web reasoning, as the access and management of multimedia content and context depends strongly on the
semantic descriptions of both. At the same time, multimedia resources
constitute complex objects, the descriptions of which are involved and
require the foundation on sound modeling practice in order to represent
findings of low- and high level multimedia analysis and to make them
accessible via Semantic Web querying of resources. This tutorial aims
to provide a red thread through these different issues and to give an
outline of where Semantic Web modeling and reasoning needs to further
contribute to the area of semantic multimedia for the fruitful interaction
between these two fields of computer science.

1 Semantics for Multimedia

Multimedia objects are ubiquitous, whether found via web search (e.g., Google[1]
or Yahoo![2] images), or via dedicated sites (e.g., Flickr[3] or YouTube[4]) or in the
repositories of private users or commercial organizations (film archives, broad-
casters, photo agencies, etc.). The media objects are produced and consumed
by professionals and amateurs alike. Unlike textual assets, whose content can
be searched for using text strings, media search is dependent on, *(i)*, complex
analysis processes, *(ii)*, manual descriptions of multimedia resources, *(iii)*, representation of these results and contributions in a widely understandable format
for, *(iv)* later retrieval and/or querying by the consumer of this data.

In the past, this process has not been supported by an interoperable and easily
extensible machinery of processing tools, applications and data formats, but only
by idiosyncratic combinations of system components into sealed off applications
such that effective sharing of their semantic metadata remained impossible and
the linkage to semantic data and ontologies found on the Semantic Web remained
far off.

---

[1] http://images.google.com/
[2] http://images.search.yahoo.com/
[3] http://www.flickr.com/
[4] http://www.youtube.com/

C. Baroglio et al. (Eds.): Reasoning Web 2008, LNCS 5224, pp. 125–170, 2008.
© Springer-Verlag Berlin Heidelberg 2008

MPEG-7 [52, 57] is an international standard defined by the Moving Picture Experts Group (MPEG) that specifies how to connect descriptions to parts of a media asset. The standard includes descriptors representing low-level media-specific features that can often be automatically extracted from media types. Unfortunately, MPEG-7 is not fully suitable for describing multimedia content, because i) it is not open to standards that represent knowledge and make use of existing controlled vocabularies for describing the subject matter and (ii) its XML Schema[5] based nature has led to design decisions that leave the annotations conceptually ambiguous and therefore prevent direct machine processing of semantic content descriptions.

In order to avoid such problems, we advocate the use of Semantic Web languages and a core ontology for multimedia annotations throughout the manual and automatic processing of multimedia content and its retrieval. For this purpose, we build on rich ontological foundations provided by an ontology such as the Descriptive Ontology for Linguistic and Cognitive Engineering[6] (DOLCE) and sound ontology engineering principles. The result presented in this tutorial is COMM, a core ontology for multimedia, which is able to accommodate results from manual annotation of data (cf. Section 6) as well as from automated processing (cf. Section 4).

The remainder of this document is organized as follows: In the next Section 2, we illustrate by an example scenario the main problems when using MPEG-7 for describing multimedia resources. Subsequently, we define in Section 3 the requirements that a multimedia ontology should meet. We review work in image and video processing in Section 4, before we present COMM, an MPEG-7 based ontology, in Section 5 and discuss our design decisions based on our requirements. In Section 6, we illustrate how to use COMM in a manual annotation tool. In Section 7, we demonstrate the use of the ontology with the scenario from Section 2 and in Section 8 we indicate challenges and solutions for querying metadata based on COMM. Further and future issues of semantic multimedia are considered in Section 9, before we summarize and conclude the paper.

2   Annotating Multimedia Assets

For annotating multimedia assets, let us imagine Nathalie, a student in history, who wants to create a multimedia presentation of the major international conferences and summits held in the last 60 years. Her starting point is the famous "Big Three" picture, taken at the Yalta (Crimea) Conference, showing the heads of government of the United States, the United Kingdom, and the Soviet Union during World War II. Nathalie uses an MPEG-7 compliant authoring tool for detecting and labeling relevant multimedia objects automatically. On the Internet, she finds three different face recognition web services that provide very good results for detecting Winston Churchill, Franklin D. Roosevelt, and Josef Stalin, respectively. Having these tools, she would like to run the face recognition web

---

[5] http://www.w3.org/XML/Schema

[6] http://wonderweb.semanticweb.org/deliverables/documents/D18.pdf

```
<Mpeg7>
 <Description xsi:type="ContentEntityType">
  <MultimediaContent xsi:type="ImageType">
   <Image id="IMG1">
    <SpatialDecomposition>

     <StillRegion id="SR1">
      <Semantic>
       <Label><Name> Roosevelt </Name></Label>
      </Semantic>
     </StillRegion>

     <StillRegion id="SR2">
      <TextAnnotation>      <!-- TextAnnotationType -->
       <KeywordAnnotation><Keyword> Churchill </Keyword></KeywordAnnotation>
      </TextAnnotation>
     </StillRegion>

     <StillRegion id="SR3">
      <Semantic>
       <Definition>    <!-- Also TextAnnotationType -->
        <StructuredAnnotation><Who><Name> Stalin </Name></Who></StructuredAnnotation>
       </Definition>
      </Semantic>
     </StillRegion>
     ...
```

Fig. 1. MPEG-7 annotation example of an image adapted from Wikipedia, http://en.wikipedia.org/wiki/Yalta_Conference

services on images and import the extraction results into the authoring tool in order to automatically generate links from the detected face regions to detailed textual information about Churchill, Roosevelt, and Stalin (image in Fig. 1-A).

Nathalie would then like to describe a recent video from a G8 summit, such as the retrospective *A history of G8 violence* made by Reuters[7]. She uses again an MPEG-7 compliant segmentation tool for detecting the seven main sequences of this 2'26 minutes report: the various anti-capitalist protests during the Seattle (1999), Melbourne (2000), Prague (2000), Gothenburg (2001), Genoa (2001), St Petersburg (2006), Heiligendamm (2007) World Economic Forums, EU and G8 Summits. Finally, Nathalie plans to deliver her multimedia presentation in an Open Document Format (ODF) document embedding the image and video previously annotated. However, this scenario causes several problems with

---

[7] http://www.reuters.com/news/video/summitVideo?videoId=56114

existing solutions. These problems refer to fragment identification, semantic annotation, web interoperability, and embedding semantic annotations into compound documents.

Fragment identification. Particular regions of the image need to be localized (anchor value in [29]). However, the current web architecture does not provide a means for uniquely identifying sub-parts of media assets, in the same way that the fragment identifier in the URI can refer to a part of an HTML or XML document. Indeed, for almost any other media type such as audio, video, and image, the semantics of the fragment identifier has not been defined or is not commonly accepted. Providing an agreed upon way to localize sub-parts of multimedia objects (e.g., sub-regions of images, temporal sequences of videos, or tracking moving objects in space and in time) is fundamental[8] [25]. For images, one can use either MPEG-7 or SVG snippet code to define the bounding box coordinates of specific regions. For temporal locations, one can use MPEG-7 code or the TemporalURI RFC[9]. MPEG-21 specifies a normative syntax to be used in URIs for addressing parts of any resource but whose media type is restricted to MPEG [51]. The MPEG-7 approach requires an indirection: an annotation is *about* a fragment of an XML document that *refers* to a multimedia document, whereas the MPEG-21 approach does not have this limitation [90].

Semantic annotation. MPEG-7 is a natural candidate for representing the extraction results of multimedia analysis software such as a face recognition web service. The language, standardized in 2001, specifies a rich vocabulary of multimedia descriptors, which can be represented in either XML or a binary format. While it is possible to specify very detailed annotations using these descriptors, it is not possible to guarantee that MPEG-7 metadata generated by different agents will be mutually understood due to the lack of formal semantics of this language [32, 87]. The XML code of Fig. 1-B illustrates the inherent interoperability problems of MPEG-7: several descriptors, semantically equivalent and representing the same information while using different syntax can coexist [88]. As Nathalie used three different face recognition web services, the extraction results of the regions SR1, SR2, and SR3 differ from each other even though they are all syntactically correct. While the first service uses the MPEG-7 `SemanticType` for assigning the `<Label>` *Roosevelt* to still region SR1, the second one makes use of a `<KeywordAnnotation>` for attaching the keyword *Churchill* to still region SR2. Finally the third service uses a `<StructuredAnnotation>` (which can be used within the `SemanticType`) in order to label still region SR3 with *Stalin*. Consequently, alternative ways for annotating the still regions render almost impossible the retrieval of the face recognition results within the authoring tool since the corresponding XPath[10] query has to deal with these syntactic variations. As a result, the authoring tool will not link occurrences of Churchill in

---

[8] See also the forthcoming W3C Media Fragments Working Group:
  http://www.w3.org/2008/01/media-fragments-wg.html
[9] http://www.annodex.net/TR/URI_fragments.html
[10] http://www.w3.org/TR/xpath20/

the images with, e.g., his biography as it does not expect semantic labels of still regions as part of the `<KeywordAnnotation>` element.

Web interoperability. Nathalie would like to link the multimedia presentation to historical information about the key figures of the Yalta Conference or the various G8 summits that is already available. She has also found semantic metadata about the relationships between these figures that could improve the automatic generation of the multimedia presentation. However, she realizes that MPEG-7 cannot be combined with these concepts defined in domain-specific ontologies because of its closing to the web. As this example demonstrates, although MPEG-7 provides ways of associating semantics with (parts of) non-textual media assets, it is incompatible with (semantic) web technologies and has no formal description of the semantics encapsulated implicitly in the standard.

Embedding into compound documents. Nathalie needs to compile the semantic annotations of the images, videos, and textual stories into a semantically annotated compound document. However, the current state of the art does not provide a framework which allows the semantic annotation of compound documents. MPEG-7 solves only partially the problem as it is restricted to the description of audiovisual compound documents. Bearing the growing number of multimedia office documents in mind, this limitation is a serious drawback.

Querying. Eventually, Nathalie and other consumers of Nathalie's compound document may want to pick out specific events, related to specific persons or locations. Depending on such a condition and depending on what they want to pick out, e.g., a 2 minute video stream or a key frame out of a video, they need to formulate a query and receive the corresponding results. The query language and corresponding engine receiving such a request must be able to drill down into the compound document at an arbitrary level of granularity. For instance, if a person like Churchill appears in a keyframe that is part of a video scene that is part of a video shot, Churchill will also appear in the video shot as a whole. The engine must return results also at the desired level of granularity, e.g., the video scene.

3   Requirements for Designing a Multimedia Ontology

Requirements for designing a multimedia ontology have been gathered and reported in the literature, e.g., in [35]. Here, we compile these and use our scenario from the previous section to present a list of requirements for a web-compliant multimedia ontology.

MPEG-7 compliance. As an international standard, MPEG-7 is used both in the signal processing and the broadcasting communities. It contains a wealth of accumulated experience that needs to be included in a web-based multimedia ontology. In addition, existing annotations in MPEG-7 should be easily expressible in this multimedia ontology.

Semantic interoperability. Annotations are only re-usable when the captured semantics can be shared among multiple systems and applications. Obtaining similar results from reasoning processes about terms in different environments can only be guaranteed if the semantics is sufficiently explicitly described. A multimedia ontology has to ensure that the intended meaning of the captured semantics can be shared among different systems.

Syntactic interoperability. Systems are only able to share the semantics of annotations if there is a means of conveying this in some agreed-upon syntax. Given that the (semantic) web is an important repository of both media assets and annotations, a semantic description of the multimedia ontology should be expressible in a web language such as OWL, RDF/XML, or RDFa[11].

Separation of concerns. Clear separation of subject matter (i.e., knowledge about depicted entities, such as the person Winston Churchill) from knowledge that is related to the administrative management or the structure and the features of multimedia documents (e.g., Churchill's face is to the left of Roosevelt's face) is required. Reusability of multimedia annotations can only be achieved if the connection between both ontologies is clearly specified by the multimedia ontology.

Modularity. As demonstrated by MPEG-7, a complete multimedia ontology can be very large. The design of a multimedia ontology should thus be made modular, to minimize the execution overhead when used for multimedia annotation. Modularity is also a good engineering principle.

Extensibility. While we intend to construct a comprehensive multimedia ontology, as ontology development methodologies demonstrate, this can never be complete. New concepts will always need to be added to the ontology. This requires a design that can always be extended, without changing the underlying model and assumptions and without affecting legacy annotations.

4   Low Level Multimedia Processing and Classification

In this section, chosen low-level methods (in the sense of signal processing) for describing and classifying multimedia assets are reviewed. Section 4.1 presents briefly some multimedia description techniques with the focus on visual information, while in Section 4.2 few algorithms for automatic classification of multimedia assets are discussed.

4.1   Multimedia Content Description

Multimedia assets can be represented by features in order to reduce and simplify the amount of resources required to describe a large set of data accurately.

---

[11] RDFa allows for representing structured information in XHTML documents such as calendar items, business contact information, licenses of the document, or creator and camera settings of images. It is available from `http://www.w3.org/2006/07/SWD/RDFa/primer/`.

Fig. 2. Example of two objects with identical shape and different texture

According to current state of the art, for analysis with a large number of variables a large amount of memory and computation power is needed. For this reason, feature computation is a very important and unavoidable step in the multimedia processing chain.

Considering visual media assets, the feature computation techniques can be divided into two categories, namely the shape-based and the texture-based. Shape-based methods make use of geometric features such as lines or corners extracted by segmentation operations. These features and their relationships are then used for visual content description [7, 31, 39, 44]. However, the segmentation-based approach often suffers from errors due to loss of image details or other inaccuracies resulting from the segmentation process. Texture-based approaches avoid these disadvantages by directly using the visual data on the pixel level without a previous segmentation step [53, 70, 72]. Depending on the problem definition, both approaches have their advantages and disadvantages. For instance, objects depicted in Figure 2 can only be distinguished by texture features.

On the other hand, shape features of only one of the cups already describe fully the whole general class "cup". Concluding, shape-based description of multimedia contents seems to be more useful for classification into general categories, while texture-based features allow to distinguish visual contents belonging to the same general category from each other.

In the last decades many different algorithms for feature extraction from multimedia content have been proposed. Therefore, the MPEG-7 standard has been introduced to describe multimedia assets. Among many other things, the MPEG-7 standard defines visual descriptions for elementary features, such as color, texture, shape, and motion. Subsequently, we briefly present these descriptors.

MPEG-7 Color Descriptors. Color is the most basic attribute of visual media assets. MPEG-7 Visual defines five different description methods, each of which represents a different aspect of the color attribute. Color distribution includes a representative color description (Dominant Color), basic color distribution description (Scalable Color) and an advanced color distribution description (Color Structure). The remaining extraction techniques include Color Layout describing spatial distribution of colors, and Color Temperature describing perceptual feeling of illumination color.

Dominant Color. The Dominant Color descriptor characterizes an image or region by a small number of representative colors. These are selected by quantizing pixel colors into (up to seven) principal clusters. The description then consists of the fraction of the image represented by each color cluster and the variance of each one. A measure of overall spatial coherency of the clusters is also defined. This descriptor is a very compact description of the color distribution in the image.

Scalable Color. The Scalable Color descriptor is a color Histogram in the HSV Color Space [65], which is encoded by a Haar transform [65]. It has a binary representation that is scalable, in terms of bin numbers and bit representation accuracy, over a broad range of granularity. Retrieval accuracy can therefore be balanced against descriptor size. Inversion of the Haar transform [65] is not necessary for consumption of the description, since similarity matching is also effective in the transform domain.

Color Layout. The Color Layout descriptor represents the spatial layout of color images in a very compact form. It is based on generating a tiny (8 × 8) thumbnail of an image, which is encoded via Discrete Cosinus Transformation (DCT) and quantized. As well as efficient visual matching, this also offers a quick way to visualize the appearance of an image.

Color Structure. The Color Structure descriptor captures both color content and information about the spatial arrangement of the colors. Specifically, it is a histogram that counts the number of times a color is present in an 8 × 8 windowed neighborhood, as this window progresses over the image rows and columns. This enables it to distinguish, e.g., between an image in which pixels of each color are distributed uniformly and an image in which the same colors occur in the same proportions but are located in distinct blocks.

MPEG-7 Texture Descriptors

Edge Histogram. The Edge Histogram descriptor represents the spatial distribution of five types of edges (four directional edges and one non-directional). It consists of local histograms of these edge directions, which may optionally be aggregated into global or semi-global histograms.

Homogeneous Texture. The Homogeneous Texture descriptor is designed to characterize the properties of texture in an image (or region), based on the assumption that the texture is homogeneous, i.e., the visual properties of the texture are relatively constant over the region. It consists of the mean, the standard deviation value of an image, energy, and energy deviation values of Fourier transform [65] of the image.

Texture Browsing. The Texture Browsing descriptor is useful for representing homogeneous texture for browsing type applications, and requires only 12 bits (maximum). It provides a perceptual characterization of texture, similar to a human characterization, in terms of regularity, coarseness and directionality. The computation of this descriptor proceeds similarly as the Homogeneous Texture descriptor. First, the image is filtered with a bank of orientation and scale tuned filters (modeled using Gabor functions) [97]; from the filtered outputs, two dominant texture orientations are identified. Three bits are used to represent each of the dominant orientations. This is followed by analyzing the filtered image projections along the dominant orientations to determine the regularity (quantified to 2 bits) and coarseness (2 bits × 2). The second dominant orientation and second scale feature are optional. This descriptor, combined with the Homogeneous Texture descriptor, provide a scalable solution to representing homogeneous texture regions in images.

MPEG-7 Shape Descriptors

Region Shape. The shape of an object may consist of either a single region or a set of regions as well as some holes in the object. Since the Region Shape descriptor makes use of all pixels constituting the shape within a frame, it can describe any shapes, i.e. not only a simple shape with a single connected region but also a complex shape that consists of holes in the object or several disjoint regions. The Region Shape descriptor not only can describe such diverse shapes efficiently in a single descriptor, but is also robust to minor deformation along the boundary of the object.

Contour Shape. The Contour Shape descriptor captures characteristic shape features of an object or region based on its contour. It uses so-called Curvature Scale Space representation [50], which captures perceptually meaningful features of the shape. The Contour Shape descriptor has a number of important properties, namely: (i) it captures very well characteristic features of the shape, enabling similarity-based retrieval; (ii) it reflects properties of the perception of human visual system and offers good generalization; (iii) it is robust to non-rigid motion; (iv) it is robust to partial occlusion of the shape; (v) it is robust to perspective transformations which result from the changes of the camera parameters and are common in images and video; (vi) it is compact.

MPEG-7 Motion Descriptors

Camera Motion. This descriptor characterizes 3D camera motion parameters. It is based on 3D camera motion parameter information, which can be automatically extracted or generated by capture devices. The camera motion descriptor supports the following well-known basic camera operations: fixed, panning, tracking, tilting, booming, zooming, dollying, and rolling.

Motion Trajectory. The motion trajectory of an object is a simple feature defined as the localization in time and space of one representative point of this object. This descriptor is useful for content-based retrieval in object-oriented visual databases.

Parametric Motion. The parametric motion is associated with arbitrary (foreground or background) objects, defined as regions (group of pixels) in the image over a specified time interval. Such an approach leads to a very efficient description of several types of motions, including simple translation, rotation and zoom, or more complex motions such as combinations of the above-mentioned elementary motions.

Motion Activity. The Motion Activity descriptor captures the intuitive notion of "intensity of action" or "pace of action" in a video segment. This descriptor is useful for applications such as video re-purposing, surveillance, fast browsing, dynamic video summarization, content-based querying, and others.

4.2 Multimedia Content Classification

In the previous section, we introduced how media assets can be described by feature vectors, sometimes referred to as histograms. In this section, we present how these assets can be classified using automatic computer-aided approaches. In order to classify multimedia assets into concepts (classes), computers need to model sample data of these concepts. This process is called training. In the training phase, annotated and representative training data for all concepts (e.g., images for visual concepts, or music samples for audio concepts) is required. Once the concepts have been modeled in the training phase, unknown and not annotated multimedia assets can be assigned to the trained concepts by classification algorithms (classifiers). Considering visual media assets, the most known classification techniques are: Template Matching [5, 26, 71], Artificial Neural Networks [60, 64, 86, 97, 99], Support Vector Machines (SVM) [9, 96], and the Eigenspace Approach [27, 48, 49, 94]. Today, the SVM algorithm is widely applied to classify multimedia content. Thus, it is elaborated in more detail in the following using the example of object classification in images.

Support Vector Machines have been proposed as a very effective method for general purpose pattern recognition [9, 96]. Intuitively, given a set of points which belong to either of two classes, a SVM finds the hyperplane leaving the largest possible fraction of points of the same class on the same side, while maximizing the distance of either class from the hyperplane. In the sense of object classification in digital images, a simple two-class problem has to be solved for all objects $\Omega_{\kappa=1,\ldots,N_\Omega}$ considered in the task. The first class is the object class Ω_κ itself. The second class represents everything which is not the class Ω_κ. It can be denoted by Ω'_κ. For the training of the class Ω_κ images of this object Ω_κ from different viewpoints are taken into account, while for the learning of the anti-class Ω'_κ images of all other objects $\Omega_{i\neq\kappa}$ are used. In the recognition phase, the SVM decides which of the objects $\Omega_{\kappa=1,\ldots,N_\Omega}$ occurs in a test scene. The two-class problem is regarded for each object class Ω_κ, i.e., N_Ω times. It is expected that $N_\Omega - 1$ times the anti-class $\Omega'_{\hat{\kappa}}$ wins the two-class problem. The actual classification result $\Omega_{\hat{\kappa}}$ is supposed to win the two-class problem only once[12].

---

[12] Assuming that exactly one of the trained objects $\Omega_{\kappa=1,\ldots,N_\Omega}$ occurs in the scene.

In the following, we present a simple example where the object class Ω_κ and its anti-class Ω'_κ are linearly separable. Let the feature vectors $c_{j=1,\ldots,N_S}$ representing all object classes $\Omega_{\kappa=1,\ldots,\kappa}$ build a set S, where

$$S = \{c_1, c_2, \ldots, c_j, \ldots, c_{N_S}\} \quad . \tag{1}$$

Each feature vector c_j from S belongs either to the class Ω_κ or to the anti-class Ω'_κ, which is given with the corresponding labels $y_j = \{-1, 1\}$. The goal is to establish the equation of a hyperplane that divides the set S leaving all the feature vectors describing Ω_κ on its one side and all the feature vectors belonging to Ω'_κ on the other side of the hyperplane. Moreover, both the distance of the class Ω_κ and the anti-class Ω'_κ to the hyperplane has to be maximized. For this purpose, some preliminary definitions are needed.

Definition 1. *The set S is linearly separable if there exist a vector $v \in \mathbb{R}^{N_c}$ and scalar $b \in \mathbb{R}$ such that*

$$y_j(v \cdot c_j + b) \geq 1 \tag{2}$$

for all $j = 1, 2, \ldots, N_S$. Note that $c_j \in \mathbb{R}^{N_c}$.

The pair (v, b) defines a hyperplane of equation

$$v \cdot c + b = 0 \quad , \tag{3}$$

named *separating hyperplane*. If with $|v|$ the norm of the vector v is denoted, the distance d_j of a point c_j (feature vector) to the separating hyperplane (v, b) is given by

$$d_j = \frac{v \cdot c_j + b}{|v|} \quad . \tag{4}$$

Combining inequality (2) and equation (4) for all $c_j \in S$ we have

$$y_j d_j \geq \frac{1}{|v|} \quad . \tag{5}$$

Therefore, $|v|^{-1}$ is the lower bound on the distance between the feature vectors c_j and the separating hyperplane (v, b). A *canonical representation* of the separating hyperplane is obtained by rescaling the pair (v, b) into the pair (v', b') in such a way that the distance of the closest feature vector equals $|v'|^{-1}$. For the canonical representation (v', b') of the hyperplane it can be written considering the equation (2) that

$$\min_{c_j \in S}\{y_j(v' \cdot c_j + b')\} = 1 \quad . \tag{6}$$

Consequently, for a separating hyperplane in the canonical representation, the bound in inequality (5) is tight. The discussion comes to the point where the *optimal separating hyperplane* has to be defined.

Definition 2. *Given a linearly separable set S, the optimal separating hyperplane is the separating hyperplane, for which the distance to the closest point of S is maximum.*

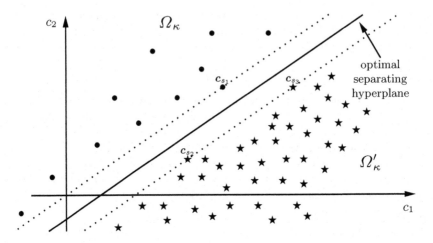

Fig. 3. Optimal separating hyperplane for two-dimensional feature space. With • feature vectors of the object class Ω_κ are denoted. By ★ the remaining feature vectors of all other object classes are represented. Three feature vectors c_{s_1}, c_{s_2}, and c_{s_3} lie in the minimum distance to the optimal separating hyperplane and are called support vectors.

Such an optimal separating hyperplane for a two-dimensional feature space, i. e., for $c = (c_1, c_2)^T$, is depicted in Figure 3. In this case, it is just a straight line. The feature vectors c_{s_1}, c_{s_2}, and c_{s_3}, which are closest to the optimal separating hyperplane, are called *support vectors*. For object modeling (i.e., the training phase) it is sufficient to store the support vectors for each class Ω_κ, which significantly reduces the data amount. In the recognition phase, the classification algorithm starts with the extraction of feature vectors from a scene. Subsequently, it determines for each object class on which side of the optimal separating hyperplane the corresponding feature vectors lie. In this way, the objects which occur in the scene are found. A detailed discussion of object classification methods using the SVM approach can be found in [8].

So far, we considered the classification of single objects. Here, it is generally assumed that the probability of appearance of objects in the scene is equal (all objects have the same a priori probability). For example, if we consider ten objects for classification, we assume an a priori probability of 10 percent for all objects. If there is contextual information about the scene available, one can leverage this information to improve the classification results. For example, Grzegorzek and Izquierdo [28] are showing object classification at the example of three different contextual scenes: kitchen, office, and nursery. However, we can also imagine a scenario where we have to classify multiple objects in a scene. For example, in a tennis match we may detect a tennis player. In addition, we may detect another object being either a lemon or a tennis ball due to similar shape and texture. Taking contextual information into account and knowing that the probability of appearance for the two relations "player and ball" is higher than "player and lemon", we can rank the first classification higher and improve the overall classification quality. In another example, we may analyze a picture and identify a blue part at the top as sea or sky. Another part in the middle is also classified as sea or sky. Here, we can take contextual information about the spatial distribution into account saying that sky is typically above sea. This example of taking contextual information into account for object classification is presented in [74]. It pursues a knowledge-based approach for reasoning using the degree of classification confidence for the single objects as input to achieve overall annotation of the picture.

5   A Formal Ontological Foundation for Multimedia

As introduced in Section 1, MPEG-7 can be used to specify the connection between semantic annotations and parts of media assets. In Section 4, we presented concrete examples of different kinds of semantic annotations supported by MPEG-7. Here, we are aiming at defining a formal core ontology for multimedia called COMM (Core Ontology of MultiMedia). Based on early work [37, 87], COMM has been designed manually by re-engineering completely MPEG-7 according to the intended semantics of the written standard. We satisfy our semantic interoperability not by aligning our ontology to the XML Schema definition of MPEG-7 but by providing a formal semantics for MPEG-7. The foundational ontology DOLCE serves as the basis of COMM. More precisely, the Description and Situation (D&S) and Ontology of Information Objects (OIO) patterns are extended into various multimedia patterns that formalize the MPEG-7 concepts. For designing COMM, we employ a methodology by Sure et al. [85] that bases on a foundational, or top level, ontology. This provides a domain independent vocabulary that explicitly includes formal definitions of foundational categories, such as processes or physical objects, and eases the linkage of domain-specific ontologies because of the shared definitions of top level concepts.

COMM covers the most important part of MPEG-7 that is commonly used for describing the structure and the content of multimedia documents. Current investigations show that parts of MPEG-7 that have not yet been considered (e.g., navigation & access) can be formalized analogously to the other descriptors through the definition of other multimedia patterns.

COMM is an OWL DL ontology that can be viewed using Protégé. Its consistency has been validated using Fact++-v1.1.5. Other reasoners failed to classify it due to the enormous amount of DL axioms that are present in DOLCE. The presented OWL DL version of the core module is just an approximation of the intended semantics of COMM since the use of OWL 1.1 (e.g., qualified cardinality restrictions for number restrictions of MPEG-7 low-level descriptors) and even more expressive logic formalisms are required for capturing its complete semantics[13].

Firstly, we briefly introduce our chosen foundational ontology in Section 5.1. The multimedia ontology COMM is presented in Sections 5.2 and 5.3. Subsequently,

---

[13] The reification schema of DOLCE D&S is even not completely expressible in OWL 1.1.

we discuss why our ontology satisfies all the requirements stated in Section 5.4. Finally, we discuss related work in Section 5.5 and provide a comparison to COMM. Please note that the interested reader may also download the COMM ontology and its documentation from http://multimedia.semanticweb.org/COMM/.

5.1 DOLCE as Modeling Basis

Using the review in [61], we select the Descriptive Ontology for Linguistic and Cognitive Engineering (DOLCE) (cf. [18]) as a modeling basis. Our choice is influenced by two of the main design patterns: *Descriptions & Situations* (D&S) and *Ontology of Information Objects* (OIO) [17]. The former can be used to formalize contextual knowledge, while the latter, based on D&S, implements a semiotics model of communication theory. We consider that the annotation process is a *situation* (i.e., a reified context) that needs to be described.

5.2 Multimedia Patterns

The patterns for D&S and OIO need to be extended for representing MPEG-7 concepts since they are not sufficiently specialized to the domain of multimedia annotation. This section introduces these extended multimedia design patterns, while Section 5.3 details two central concepts underlying these patterns: digital data and algorithms (cf. [61]). In order to define design patterns, one has to identify repetitive structures and describe them at an abstract level. The two most important functionalities provided by MPEG-7 are: the *decomposition* of media assets and the (semantic) *annotation* of their parts, which we include in our multimedia ontology.

Decomposition. MPEG-7 provides descriptors for spatial, temporal, spatio-temporal and media source decompositions of multimedia content into segments. A segment is the most general abstract concept in MPEG-7 and can refer to a region of an image, a piece of text, a temporal scene of a video or even to a moving object tracked during a period of time.

Annotation. MPEG-7 defines a very large collection of descriptors that can be used to annotate a segment. These descriptors can be low-level visual features, audio features or more abstract concepts. They allow the annotation of the content of multimedia documents or the media asset itself.

In the following, we first introduce the notion of multimedia data and then present the patterns that formalize the decomposition of multimedia content into segments, or allow the annotation of these segments. The decomposition pattern handles the structure of a multimedia document, while the media annotation pattern, the content annotation pattern, and the semantic annotation pattern are useful for annotating the media, the features, and the semantic content of the multimedia document respectively.

Multimedia Data. This encapsulates the MPEG-7 notion of multimedia content and is a subconcept of digital-data[14] (introduced in more detail in Section 5.3). multimedia-data is an abstract concept that has to be further specialized for concrete multimedia content types (e.g., image-data corresponds to the pixel matrix of an image). According to the OIO pattern, multimedia-data is realized by some physical media (e.g., an image). This concept is needed for annotating the physical realization of multimedia content.

Decomposition Pattern. Following the D&S pattern, we consider that a decomposition of a multimedia-data entity is a situation (a segment-decomposition) that satisfies a description such as a segmentation-algorithm or a method (e.g., a user drawing a bounding box around a depicted face), which has been applied to perform the decomposition, see Fig. 4-B. Of particular importance are the roles that are defined by a segmentation-algorithm or a method. The output-segment-roles express that some multimedia-data entities are segments of a multimedia-data entity that plays the role of an input segment (input-segment-role). These data entities have as setting a segment-decomposition situation that satisfies the roles of the applied segmentation-algorithm or method. The output-segment-roles as well as segment-decompositions are then specialized according to the segment and decomposition hierarchies of MPEG-7 ([52], part 5, section 11). In terms of MPEG-7, unsegmented (complete) multimedia content also corresponds to a segment. Consequently, annotations of complete multimedia content start with a root segment. In order to designate multimedia-data instances that correspond to these root segments the decomposition pattern provides the root-segment-role concept. Note that root-segment-roles are not defined by methods which describe segment-decompositions. They are rather defined by methods which cause the production of multimedia content. These methods as well as annotation modes which allow the description of the production process (e.g., [52], part 5, section 9) are currently not covered by our ontology. Nevertheless, the prerequisite for enhancing COMM into this direction is already given.

The decomposition pattern also reflects the need for localizing segments within the input segment of a decomposition as each output-segment-role requires a mask-role. Such a role has to be played by one or more digital-data entities which express one localization-descriptor. An example of such a descriptor is an ontological representation of the MPEG-7 RegionLocatorType[15] for localizing regions in an image (see Fig. 4-C). Hence, the mask-role concept corresponds to the notion of a mask in MPEG-7.

The specialization of the pattern for describing image decompositions is shown in Fig. 5-F. According to MPEG-7, an image or an image segment (image-data) can be composed into still regions. Following this modeling, the concepts output-segment-role and root-segment-role are specialized by the concepts still-region-role and root-still-region-role respectively. Note, that root-still-region-role is a subconcept of still-region-role *and* root-segment-role. The MPEG-7 decomposition mode which can be applied to

---

[14] Sans serif font indicates ontology concepts.

[15] Italic type writer font indicates MPEG-7 language descriptors.

140   S. Staab et al.

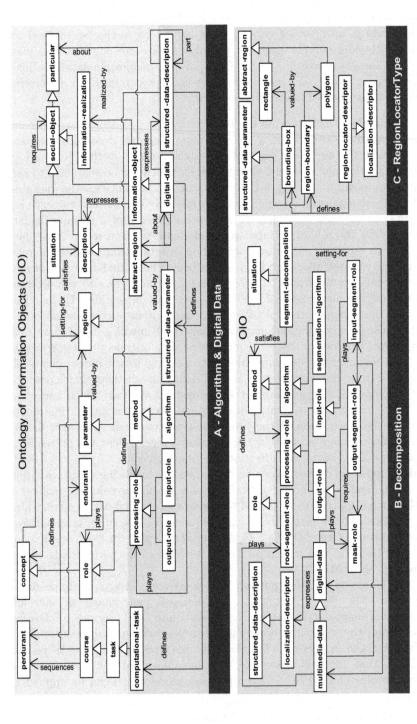

Fig. 4. COMM: Design patterns in UML notation: Basic design patterns (A), multimedia patterns Decomposition (B) and modeling example (C)

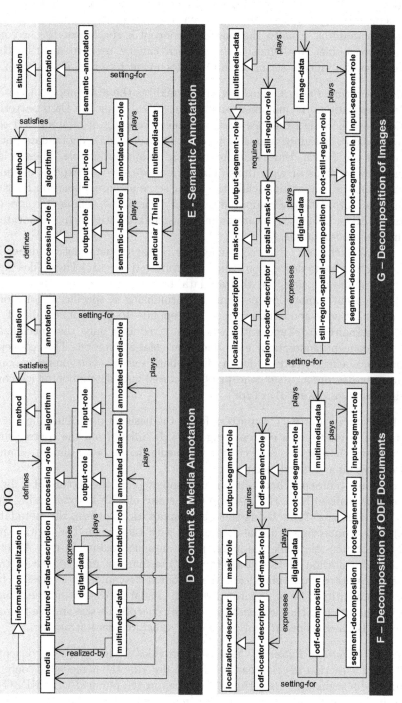

Fig. 5. COMM: Design patterns in UML notation continued: Multimedia patterns Content & Media Annotation and Semantic Annotation (D and E) and modeling example (F)

still regions is called `StillRegionSpatialDecompositionType`. Consequently, the concept still-region-spatial-decomposition is added as a subconcept of segment-decomposition. Finally, the mask-role concept is specialized by the concept spatial-mask-role. Analogously, the pattern can be used to describe the decomposition of a video asset or of an ODF document (see Fig. 7).

Content Annotation Pattern. This pattern formalizes the attachment of metadata (i.e., annotations) to multimedia-data (Fig. 5-D). Using the D&S pattern, annotations also become situations that represent the state of affairs of all related digital-data (metadata and annotated multimedia-data). digital-data entities represent the attached metadata by playing an annotation-role. These roles are defined by methods or algorithms. The former are used to express manual (or semi-automatic) annotation while the latter serve as an explanation for the attachment of automatically computed features such as the dominant colors of a still region. It is mandatory that the multimedia-data entity being annotated plays an annotated-data-role.

The actual metadata that is carried by a digital-data entity depends on the structured-data-description that is expressed by it. These descriptions are formalized using the digital data pattern (see Section 5.3). Applying the content annotation pattern for formalizing a specific annotation, e.g., a dominant-color-annotation which corresponds to the connection of a MPEG-7 `DominantColorType` with a segment, requires only the specialization of the concept annotation, e.g., dominant-color-annotation. This concept is defined by being a setting for a digital-data entity that expresses one dominant-color-descriptor (a subconcept of structured-data-description which corresponds to the `DominantColorType`).

Media Annotation Pattern. This pattern forms the basis for describing the physical instances of multimedia content (Fig. 5-D). It differs from the content annotation pattern in only one respect: it is the media that is being annotated and therefore plays an annotated-media-role.

One can thus represent that some visual content (e.g., the picture of a digital camera) is realized by a JPEG image with a size of 462848 bytes, using the MPEG-7 `MediaFormatType`. Using the media annotation pattern, the metadata is attached by connecting a digital-data entity with the image. The digital-data plays an annotation-role while the image plays an annotated-media-role. An ontological representation of the `MediaFormatType`, namely an instance of the structured-data-description subconcept media-format-descriptor, is expressed by the digital-data entity. The tuple formed with the scalar "462848" and the string "JPEG" is the value of the two instances of the concepts file-size and file-format respectively. Both concepts are subconcepts of structured-data-parameter.

Semantic Annotation Pattern. MPEG-7 provides some general concepts (see [52], part 5, section 12) that can be used to describe the perceivable content of a multimedia segment. It is germane to the approach pursued with MPEG-7 that the real world objects appearing in a multimedia document are modeled within the realm of MPEG-7, too. We argue that it is indeed useful to create an ontology specific to multimedia. However, we decline that it was useful to try to model the real world within the very same approach. An ontology-based multimedia annotation framework should rely on domain-specific ontologies for the representation of the real world entities that might be depicted in multimedia content. Consequently, this pattern specializes the content annotation pattern to allow the connection of multimedia descriptions with domain descriptions provided by independent world ontologies (Fig. 5-E).

An OWL Thing or a DOLCE particular (belonging to a domain-specific ontology) that is depicted by some multimedia content is not directly connected to it but rather through the way the annotation is obtained. Actually, a manual annotation method or its subconcept algorithm, such as a classification algorithm, has to be applied to determine this connection. It is embodied through a semantic-annotation that satisfies the applied method. This description specifies that the annotated multimedia-data has to play an annotated-data-role and the depicted Thing/particular has to play a semantic-label-role. The pattern also allows the integration of features which might be evaluated in the context of a classification algorithm. In that case, digital-data entities that represent these features would play an input-role.

5.3   Basic Patterns

Specializing the D&S and OIO patterns for defining multimedia design patterns is enabled through the definition of basic design patterns, which formalize the notion of digital data and algorithm.

Digital Data Pattern. Within the domain of multimedia annotation, the notion of digital data is central—both the multimedia content being annotated and the annotations themselves are expressed as digital data. We consider digital-data entities of arbitrary size to be information-objects, which are used for communication between machines. The OIO design pattern states that descriptions are expressed by information-objects, which have to be about facts (represented by particulars). These facts are settings for situations that have to satisfy the descriptions that are expressed by information-objects. This chain of constraints allows the modeling of complex data structures to store digital information. Our approach is as follows (see Fig. 4-A): digital-data entities express descriptions, namely structured-data-descriptions, which define meaningful labels for the information contained by digital-data. This information is represented by numerical entities such as scalars, matrices, strings, rectangles, or polygons. In DOLCE terms, these entities are abstract-regions. In the context of a description, these regions are described by parameters. structured-data-descriptions thus define structured-data-parameters for which abstract-regions carried by digital-data entities assign values.

The digital data pattern can be used to formalize complex MPEG-7 low-level descriptors. Fig. 4-C shows the application of this pattern by formalizing the MPEG-7 `RegionLocatorType`, which mainly consists of two elements: a `Box` and a `Polygon`. The concept region-locator-descriptor corresponds to the `RegionLocatorType`. The element `Box` is represented by the structured-data-parameter subconcept BoundingBox while the element Polygon is represented by the region-boundary concept.

The MPEG-7 code example given in Fig. 1 highlights that the formalization of data structures is not sufficient so far. Complex MPEG-7 types can include nested types that again have to be represented by structured-data-descriptions. In our example, the MPEG-7 SemanticType contains the element Definition which is of complex type TextAnnotationType. The digital data pattern covers such cases by allowing a digital-data instance dd1 to be about a digital-data instance dd2 that expresses a structured-data-description corresponding to a nested type (see Fig. 4-A). In this case, the structured-data-description of instance dd2 would be a part of the one expressed by dd1.

Algorithm Pattern. The production of multimedia annotation can involve the execution of algorithms or the application of computer assisted methods which are used to produce or manipulate digital-data. The recognition of a face in an image region is an example of the former, while manual annotation of the characters is an example of the latter.

We consider algorithms to be methods that are applied to solve a computational problem (see Fig. 4-A). The associated (DOLCE) situations represent the work that is being done by algorithms. Such a situation encompasses digital-data[16] involved in the computation, regions that represent the values of parameters of an algorithm, and perdurants[17] that act as computational-tasks (i.e., the processing steps of an algorithm). An algorithm defines roles that are played by digital-data. These roles encode the meaning of data. In order to solve a problem, an algorithm has to process input data and return some output data. Thus, every algorithm defines at least one input-role and one output-role that both have to be played by digital-data.

5.4   Comparison with Requirements

In the previous sections, we have introduced COMM as a formal ontological foundation for multimedia. We now discuss whether the requirements stated in Section 3 are satisfied with our proposed modeling of the multimedia ontology.

MPEG-7 compliance. The ontology is MPEG-7 compliant since the patterns have been designed with the aim of translating the standard into DOLCE. It covers the most important part of MPEG-7 that is commonly used for describing the structure and the content of multimedia documents. Our current investigation shows that parts of MPEG-7 that have not yet been considered (e.g., navigation & access) can be formalized analogously to the other descriptors through the definition of further patterns. The technical realization of the basic MPEG-7 data types (e.g., matrices and vectors) is not within the scope of the multimedia ontology. They are represented as ontological concepts, because

---

[16] digital-data entities are DOLCE endurants, i.e., entities that exist in time and space.

[17] Events, processes, or phenomena are examples of perdurants. endurants participate in perdurants.

the about relationship that connects digital-data with numerical entities is only defined between concepts. Thus, the definition of OWL data type properties is required to connect instances of data type concepts (subconcepts of the DOLCE abstract-region) with the actual numeric information (e.g., xsd:string). Currently, simple string representation formats are used for serializing data type concepts (e.g., rectangle) that are currently not covered by W3C standards. Future work includes the integration of the extended data types of OWL 1.1.

Semantic and syntactic interoperability. The syntactic and semantic interoperability of our multimedia ontology is achieved by an OWL DL formalization[18]. Similar to DOLCE, we provide a rich axiomatization of each pattern using first order logic. Our ontology can be linked to any web-based, domain-specific ontology through the semantic annotation pattern.

Separation of concerns. A clear separation of concerns is ensured through the use of the multimedia patterns: the decomposition pattern for handling the structure and the annotation pattern for dealing with the metadata.

Modularity. The decomposition and annotation patterns form the core of the modular architecture of the multimedia ontology. We follow the various MPEG-7 parts and organize the multimedia ontology into modules which cover *i)* the descriptors related to a specific media type (e.g., visual, audio or text) and *ii)* the descriptors that are generic to a particular media (e.g., media descriptors). We also design a separate module for data types in order to abstract from their technical realization.

Extensibility. Through the use of multimedia design patterns, our ontology is also extensible. It allows inclusion of further media types and descriptors (e.g., new low-level features) using the same patterns. As our patterns are grounded in the D&S pattern, it is straightforward to include further contextual knowledge (e.g., about provenance) by adding roles or parameters. Such extensions will not change the patterns, so that legacy annotations will remain valid.

5.5   Related Work

In the field of semantic image understanding, using a multimedia ontology infrastructure is regarded to be the first step for closing the, so-called, semantic gap between low-level signal processing results and explicit semantic descriptions of the concepts depicted in images. Furthermore, multimedia ontologies have the potential to increase the interoperability of applications producing and consuming multimedia annotations. The application of multimedia reasoning techniques on top of semantic multimedia annotations is also a research topic which is currently investigated [59]. A number of drawbacks of MPEG-7 have been reported [58, 63]. As a solution, multimedia ontologies based on MPEG-7 have been proposed.

---

[18] Examples of the axiomatization are available on the COMM website.

Table 1. Summary of the different MPEG-7 based Multimedia Ontologies

	Hunter	DS-MIRF	Rhizomik	COMM
Foundations	ABC	none	none	DOLCE
Complexity	OWL-Full[a]	OWL-DL[b]	OWL-DL[c]	OWL-DL[d]
Coverage	MDS+Visual	MDS+CS	All	MDS+Visual
Reference	[32]	[92]	[19]	[3]
Applications	Digital Libraries, e-Research	Digital Libraries, e-Learning	Digital Rights Management, e-Business	Multimedia Analysis and Annotations

[a]http://metadata.net/mpeg7/
[b]http://www.music.tuc.gr/ontologies/MPEG703.zip
[c]http://rhizomik.net/ontologies/mpeg7ontos
[d]http://multimedia.semanticweb.org/COMM/

From 2001 until the present time, there are four main ontologies that formalize the MPEG-7 standard using Semantic Web languages. Besides COMM, these are the ontology by Hunter, DS-MIRF and the ontology by Rhizomik. In the following, we describe these four ontologies, and the main characteristics as well as the context in which they have been developed are summarized in the Table 1.

Hunter's MPEG-7 ontology. In 2001, Hunter proposed an initial manual translation of MPEG-7 into RDFS (and then into DAML+OIL) and provided a rationale for its use within the Semantic Web [32]. This multimedia ontology was translated into OWL, extended and harmonized using the ABC upper ontology [43] for applications in the digital libraries [33, 34] and eResearch fields [36].

The current version is an OWL Full ontology containing classes defining the media types (Audio, AudioVisual, Image, Multimedia, Video) and the decompositions from the MPEG-7 Multimedia Description Schemes (MDS) part [52]. The descriptors for recording information about the production and creation, usage, structure, and the media features are also defined. The ontology can be viewed in Protégé[19] and has been validated using the WonderWeb OWL Validator[20].

This ontology has usually been applied to describe the decomposition of images and their visual descriptors for use in larger semantic frameworks. Harmonizing through an upper ontology, such as ABC, enables queries for abstract concepts such as subclasses of *events* or *agents* to return media objects or segments of media objects. While the ontology has most often been applied in conjunction with the ABC upper model, it is independent of that ontology and can also be harmonized with other upper ontologies such as SUMO [66] or DOLCE [18].

DS-MIRF ontology. In 2004, Tsinaraki et al. have proposed the DS-MIRF ontology that fully captures in OWL DL the semantics of the MPEG-7 MDS and the Classification Schemes. The ontology can be visualized with GraphOnto or Protégé and has been validated and classified with the WonderWeb OWL

---

[19] http://protege.stanford.edu/
[20] http://www.mygrid.org.uk/OWL/Validator

Validator. The ontology has been integrated with OWL domain ontologies for soccer and Formula 1 [93] in order to demonstrate how domain knowledge can be systematically integrated in the general-purpose constructs of MPEG-7. This ontological infrastructure has been utilized in several applications, including audiovisual digital libraries and e-learning.

The DS-MIRF Ontology has been conceptualized manually, according to the methodology outlined in [92]. The XML Schema simple datatypes defined in MPEG-7 are stored in a separate XML Schema to be imported in the DS-MIRF ontology. The naming of the XML elements are generally kept in the rdf:IDs of the corresponding OWL entities, except when two different XML Schema constructs have the same names. The mapping between the original names of the MPEG-7 descriptors and the rdf:IDs of the corresponding OWL entities is represented in an OWL DL mapping ontology. Therefore, this ontology will represent, e.g., that the Name element of the MPEG-7 type TermUseType is represented by the TermName object property, while the Name element of the MPEG-7 type PlaceType is represented by the Name object property in the DS-MIRF ontology. The mapping ontology also captures the semantics of the XML Schemas that cannot be mapped to OWL constructs such as the sequence element order or the default values of the attributes. Hence, it is possible to return to an original MPEG-7 description from the RDF metadata using this mapping ontology. This process has been partially implemented in GraphOnto [68], for the OWL entities that represent the SemanticBaseType and its descendants.

The generalization of this approach has led to the development of a transformation model for capturing the semantics of any XML Schema in an OWL DL ontology [91]. The original XML Schema is converted into a main OWL DL ontology while a OWL DL mapping ontology keeps trace of the constructs mapped in order to allow circular conversions.

Rhizomik Ontology. In 2005, Garcia and Celma have presented the Rhizomik approach that consists in mapping XML Schema constructs to OWL constructs following a generic XML Schema to OWL together with an XML to RDF conversion [19]. Applied to the MPEG-7 schemas, the resulting ontology covers the whole standard as well as the Classification Schemes and TV Anytime[21]. It can be visualized with Protégé or Swoop[22] and has been validated and classified using the Wonderweb OWL Validator and Pellet.

The Rhizomik ontology was originally expressed in OWL Full, since 23 properties must be modeled using an rdf:Property as they have both a data type and object type range, i.e., the corresponding elements are both defined as containers of complex types and simple types. An OWL DL version of the ontology has been produced, solving this problem by creating two different properties (owl:DatatypeProperty and owl:ObjectProperty) for each of them. This change is also incorporated into the XML2RDF step in order to map the affected input XML elements to the appropriate OWL property (object or datatype) depending on the kind of content of the input XML element.

---

[21] http://www.tv-anytime.org
[22] http://code.google.com/p/swoop

The main contribution of this approach is that it benefits from the great amount of metadata that has been already been produced by the XML community. Moreover, it is implemented in the ReDeFer project[23], which allows to automatically map input XML Schemas to OWL ontologies and XML data based on them to RDF metadata following the resulting ontologies. This approach has been used with other large XML Schemas in the Digital Rights Management domain such as MPEG-21 and ODRL [21] or in the E-Business domain [20].

Comparison and Summary. These ontologies have been recently compared with COMM according to three criteria:[24] *i)* the way the multimedia ontology is linked with domain semantics, *ii)* the MPEG-7 coverage of the multimedia ontology, and *iii)* the scalability and modeling rationale of the conceptualization [89]. Unlike COMM, all the other ontologies perform a one to one translation of MPEG-7 types into OWL concepts and properties. However, this translation does not guarantee that the intended semantics of MPEG-7 is fully captured and formalized. On the contrary, the syntactic interoperability and conceptual ambiguity problems illustrated in Section 2 remain. Although COMM is based on a foundational ontology, the annotations proved to be no more verbose than those in MPEG-7.

Finally, general models for annotations of non-multimedia content have been proposed by librarians. The Functional Requirements for Bibliographic Records (FRBR)[25] model specifies the conventions for bibliographic description of traditional books. The CIDOC Conceptual Reference Model (CRM)[26] defines the formal structure for describing the concepts and relationships used in cultural heritage documentation. Hunter has described how an MPEG-7 ontology could specialize CIDOC-CRM for describing multimedia objects in museums [33]. Interoperability with such models is an issue, but interestingly, the design rationale used in these models are often comparable and complementary to foundational ontologies approach.

6   KAT—The K-Space Annotation Tool

The K-Space Annotation Tool (KAT) is a platform for an efficient, semi-automatic semantic annotation of multimedia content. It provides a plugin infrastructure to integrate different annotation support. KAT further consists of a core that allows for instantiation, communication, visualization, and threaded execution of plugins. Plugins communicate using a message mechanism and exchange metadata based on COMM (cf. Section 5). The development of KAT is based on the tool M-Ontomat Annotizer [4], which was developed as a tool for extracting features from multimedia content and linking those features to domain ontologies. However, M-Ontomat did not provide the same flexible

---

[23] http://rhizomik.net/redefer

[24] Available from: http://mklab.iti.gr/mareso/files/proceedings.pdf

[25] http://www.ifla.org/VII/s13/frbr/index.htm

[26] http://cidoc.ics.forth.gr/

infrastructure, was not geared towards annotation and retrieval, and was further not based on such a generic multimedia ontology as COMM.

Within the KAT, a plugin is required to understand COMM annotations in order to determine whether and how it has to process a certain content item and to produce its output according to COMM. There are two major types of plugins, the analysis plugins and visual plugins.

Analysis plugins provide automatic or semi-automatic analysis functionalities of media assets. Examples of analysis plugins could be an image segmentation algorithm that decomposes an image into regions or a key-frame extraction algorithm that extracts the most important frames from a video. The location, size, or boundaries of both segments or key-frames are described as COMM annotations. Since a key-frame is a kind of image data, a key-frame can be processed by the image segmentation algorithm (given that the key-frame data, i.e., the pixels are stored in an appropriate format). The resulting segments are added as annotations to the key-frame in the same way as it was done for an image. In other words, an algorithm does not have to distinguish between key-frames or images. It only has to check the COMM annotations whether the data provides all information that it requires. Besides this, all image-data is treated equally. The fact that a key-frame is part of a video is only important in the context of video processing.

Visual plugins provide the means for visualization of COMM annotations and the associated content. They are responsible for any kind of user interaction. A plugin might register a view, which is responsible for displaying a certain type of content and certain types of annotations. One of the standard plugins delivered with the KAT is the Image Annotation Tool, which is capable of displaying images and their decompositions. A user might add additional regions using different drawing tools and regions might be annotated with ontology concepts and instances. The concepts and instances are displayed by another default plugin, the ontology browser. Using a simple drag&drop mechanism, a region is dropped on a concept or an instance of the ontology, which creates an according annotation. Another visual plugin is the annotation browser, which provides a more structured and media-type independent view on the resulting COMM graph. It does not display the content itself but only the COMM annotation in a tree view.

One might also consider other types of plugins, e.g., plugins to browse and import content from Web 2.0 sites such as Flickr or plugins that provide retrieval functionalities. The plugin architecture of KAT is kept very simple and generic in order to provide for implementing also unforeseen semantic multimedia applications. The foundation on the formally defined and extensible COMM offers easy extension to other types of annotations and content.

A screenshot of the current version of KAT is depicted in Figure 6 showing the image of the "Big Three". Each of them is marked with a bounding box (a type of a segment) and annotated with an instance of the concept Man identifying the specific person. The ontology is displayed on the left-hand side, while the annotation browser is displayed in the lower right corner. In the screenshot, the left most bounding box (referring to Churchill) is selected and all concepts and instances associated with the selected region are displayed in the annotation

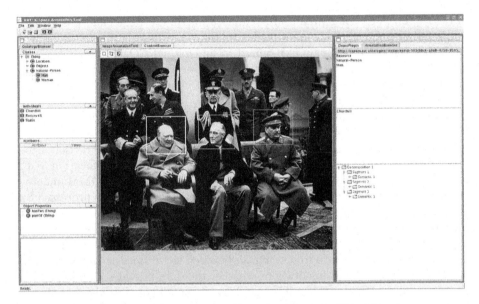

Fig. 6. The KAT showing the annotation of the "Big Three"

browser. The latest information about the KAT as well as binary and source releases are available from `http://www.uni-koblenz.de/FB4/Institutes/IFI/AGStaab/Research/kat`.

7   Expressing the "Big Three" Scenario in COMM

The interoperability problem with which Nathalie is faced in Section 2 can be solved by using a tool like KAT employing the COMM ontology for representing the metadata of all relevant multimedia objects and the presentation itself throughout the whole creation workflow. The student is shielded from details of the multimedia ontology by embedding it in authoring tools like KAT and feature analysis web services.

The application of the Winston Churchill face recognizer results in an annotation RDF graph that is depicted in the upper part of Fig. 7 (visualized by an UML object diagram[27]). The decomposition of Fig. 1-A, whose content is represented by id0, into one still region (the bounding box of Churchill's face) is represented by the lighter middle part of the UML diagram. The segment is represented by the image-data instance id1 that plays the still-region-role srr1. It is located by the digital-data instance dd1 which expresses the region-locator-descriptor rld1 (lower part of the diagram). Using the semantic annotation pattern, the face recognizer can annotate the still region by connecting it with the URI `http://en.wikipedia.org/wiki/Winston_Churchill`. An instance of an arbitrary domain ontology concept could also have been used for identifying the resource.

---

[27] The scheme used in Fig. 7 is instance:Concept, the usual UML notation.

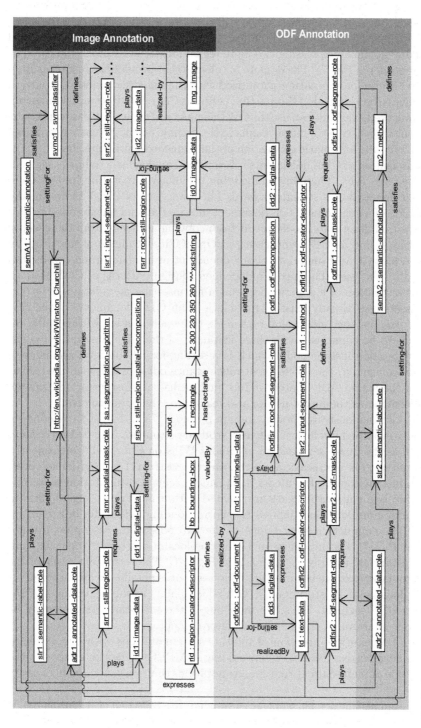

Fig. 7. Annotation of one segment of the Yalta picture and its embedding into an ODF document which contains a text segment that is also about Winston Churchill

Running the two remaining face recognizers for Roosevelt and Stalin will extend the decomposition further by two still regions, i.e., the image-data instances id2 and id3 as well as the corresponding still-region-roles, spatial-mask-roles, and digital-data instances expressing two more region-locator-descriptors (indicated at the right border of Fig. 7). The domain ontologies that provide the instances Roosevelt and Stalin for annotating id2 and id3 with the semantic annotation pattern do not have to be identical to the one that contains Churchill. If several domain ontologies are used, Nathalie can use the OWL sameAs and equivalentClass constructs to align the three face recognition results to the domain ontology that is best suited for enhancing the automatic generation of the multimedia presentation.

Decomposition of ODF documents is formalized analogously to image segmentation (see Fig. 5-F). Therefore, embedding the image annotation into an ODF document annotation is straightforward. The lower part of Fig. 7 shows the decomposition of a compound ODF document into textual and image content. This decomposition description could result from copying an image from the desktop and pasting it into an ODF editor such as OpenOffice. A plugin of this program could produce COMM metadata of the document in the background while it is produced by the user. The media independent design patterns of COMM allow the implementation of a generic mechanism for inserting metadata of arbitrary media assets into already existing metadata of an ODF document. In the case of Fig. 7, the instance id0 (which represents the whole content of the Yalta image) needs to be connected with three instances of the ODF annotation: *i)* the odf-decomposition instance odfd which is a setting-for all top level segments of the odf-document, *ii)* the odf-segment-role instance odfsr1 which identifies id0 as a part of the whole ODF content md (a multimedia-data instance), and *iii)* the instance odfdoc as the image now is also realized-by the odf-document.

Fig. 7 also demonstrates how a domain ontology[28] can be used to define semantically meaningful relations between arbitrary segments. The textual content td as well as the image segment id1 are about Winston Churchill. Consequently, the URI http://en.wikipedia.org/wiki/Winston_Churchill is used for annotating both instances using the media independent semantic annotation pattern.

The two segments td and id1 are located within md by two digital-data instances (dd2 and dd3) that express two corresponding odf-locator-descriptor instances. The complete instantiations of the two odf-locator-descriptors are not shown in Fig. 7. The modeling of the region-locator-descriptor, which is completely instantiated in Fig. 7, is shown in Fig. 4-C. The technical details of the odf-locator-descriptor are not presented. However, it is possible to locate segments in ODF documents by storing an XPath which points to the beginning and the end of an ODF segment. Thus, the modeling of the odf-locator-descriptor can be carried out analogously to the region-locator-descriptor.

In order to ease the creation of multimedia annotations with our ontology, we have developed a Java API[29] providing a MPEG-7 class interface for the construction of meta-data at runtime. Annotations that are generated in memory

---

[28] In this example, the domain ontology corresponds to a collection of Wikipedia URI's.
[29] The Java API is available at http://multimedia.semanticweb.org/COMM/api/.

can be exported to Java-based RDF triple stores such as Sesame. To this end, the API translates the objects of the MPEG-7 classes into instances of the COMM concepts. The API also facilitates the implementation of multimedia retrieval tools as it is capable of loading RDF annotation graphs (e.g., the complete annotation of an image including the annotation of arbitrary regions) from a store and converting them back to the MPEG-7 class interface. Using this API, the face recognition web service will automatically create the annotation which is depicted in the upper part of Fig. 7 by executing the code described below.

First of all an image has to be created. In the COMM, an image is formalized as some image-data, that plays a root-segment-role. This is abstracted in the API by creating an image object and assigning a still region (which refers to the image-data) to it (lines 1–3). The bounding box that refers to the recognized face is added as a decomposition to the root still region representing the image. The resulting regions are added as output segments to decomposition object (lines 4–14). Finally the semantic annotation is performed by creating a Semantic object. This is assigned a label, which has to be an individual of the domain ontology (in this case the individual representing Winston Churchill). This semantic annotation is then added to the segment (lines 15–18).

```
1   Image img0 = new Image();
2   StillRegion isr0 = new StillRegion();
3   img0.setImage(isr0);
4   StillRegionSpatialDecomposition srsd1 =
5     new StillRegionSpatialDecomposition();
6   isr0.addSpatialDecomposition(srsd1);
7   srsd1.setDescription(new SegmentationAlgorithm());
8   StillRegion srr1 = new StillRegion();
9   srsd1.addStillRegion(srr1);
10  SpatialMask smr1 = new SpatialMask();
11  srr1.setSpatialMask(smr1);
12  RegionLocatorDescriptor rld1 = new RegionLocatorDescriptor();
13  smr1.addSubRegion(rld1);
14  rld1.setBox(new Rectangle(300, 230, 50, 30));
15  Semantic s1 = new Semantic();
16  s1.addLabel("http://en.wikipedia.org/wiki/Winston_Churchill");
17  s1.setDescription(new SVMClassifier());
18  srr1.addSemantic(s1);
```

8 Querying for Semantic Multimedia

So far, we have presented sophisticated support for processing, classifying, and semantically annotating media assets. To be of actual use, these annotations and metadata shall be leveraged to query for media assets. In the K-Space project[30] a database based on Sesame[31] has been developed that allows for storing and querying over RDF triples describing the semantics of media assets. Queries on

---

[30] http://www.k-space.eu/

[31] Available from http://www.openrdf.org/

semantically-enriched media assets vary from navigating the decomposition of a video into shots and keyframes to retrieving all documents annotated with a certain pattern. Sophisticated queries may even take background knowledge into account. In the scenario presented in Section 2, we might be interested, e.g., in all images showing the heads of the United States and the Soviet Union together. To answer this query, we need to take decompositions of images, semantic annotations, and domain-specific knowledge into account in order to determine whether the persons depicted are heads of the USA or USSR.

In order to process and answering such queries, we are faced with various challenges with respect to the potential size of the dataset, complexity of queries, recursiveness of queries, and interactive access to media asset annotations. These challenges are elaborated below.

Large Datasets. The queried datasets may become extremely large. We estimate annotations of one million triples for one hour of video, which is decomposed into keyframes and annotated region based. If basic inferencing is done to compute subclass and instance relations, this may easily result in an increase by a large constant factor. On the other hand, most state of the art RDF repositories scale to tens or hundreds of million of statements[32]. Only at the time of writing this report, the billion triples border is being attacked [30, 62]. However, such repositories usually require powerful hardware or even clusters of repositories. Compared to this scale, typical datasets of background world knowledge, like DBPedia[33], can almost be considered small.

Complex queries. Queries can become extremely complex. A typical instantiation of a COMM pattern results in up to 20 statements. This complexity is not COMM specific, but typical for multimedia annotation, in order to capture the necessary expressivity [89]. In turn, this results in a query with 20 statement patterns and 19 joins. Given the size of the datasets, this is a challenge that also most existing relational databases fail to meet. Special care needs to be taken to find a very good query execution plan for this kind of queries. In order to avoid errors, it is desirable to hide these complex queries from application developers. In the case of COMM, COMM-API provides an abstraction layer for developers, which allows to access COMM items as Java objects without writing SPARL queries.

Complex recursive queries. Annotations to multimedia items can be done on a variety of levels of decomposition. For example, a whole image can be annotated with a concept but also only a segment showing the concept or a compound ODF document containing the image. Hence, retrieval queries need to recursively follow the decompositions. Standard query languages like the Semantic Web Query Language[34] (SPARQL) do not allow for formulating such recursion. There are extensions to SPARQL that add support for regular path expressions [42, 67].

---

[32] See http://esw.w3.org/topic/RdfStoreBenchmarking for a good overview of RDF benchmarks.

[33] http://wiki.dbpedia.org/Datasets

[34] http://www.w3.org/2001/sw/DataAccess/

However, such regular expressions are not expressive enough to capture the patterns used in COMM to annotate media assets. For this reason, a metadata repository must additionally support a specialized set of rules that allows to (recursively) follow decompositions during retrieval.

Interactive access to annotations. Multimedia data is often browsed in interactive manner. Hence, drill down and query refinement must be supported for querying semantic multimedia. Given the potential complexity of the dataset and the queries, it must be possible to start a new query from any given point in the annotation graph. For example, if we want to drill down into the annotation of a keyframe in a shot of a video, we should start from the already known shot instead of searching the whole database again. This is facilitated by using RDF for media assets annotations, as in RDF everything is assigned to an URI, e.g., a label, a segment, or a situation.

To illustrate these challenges, we consider two example queries. The first query selects all media assets that show both an US and an USSR leader (lines 10–18 and 28, lines 19–27 and 29). In addition, the direct types, e.g., the image or ODF document and the URLs of realizations of the assets are selected (lines 3 and 5). Please note that we do not specify what an US or USSR leader is. Hence, the query makes use of additional inferencing done over a domain ontology. However, the semantics of all concepts is still clear; in contrast to annotation done in MPEG-7, where the link to a domain ontology can be missing.

```
 1  SELECT ?ITEM ?URI ?TYPE
 2  WHERE {
 3  ?ITEM                custom:directInstanceOf ?TYPE;
 4                       a                 core:multimedia-data;
 5                       core:plays        core:root-segment-role;
 6                       core:realized-by ?URI;
 7                       core:plays        ?annotated-data-role1.
 8                       core:plays        ?annotated-data-role2.
 9  ?annotated-data-role  a                core:annotated-data-role.
10  ?annotation1         a                 core:semantic-annotation;
11                       core:setting-for ?ITEM;
12                       core:setting-for ?label1;
13                       core:satifies     [
14                           a core:method;
15                           core:defines ?annotated-data-role1;
16                           core:defines ?semantic-label-role1].
17  ?label1              core:plays        ?semantic-label-role1.
18  ?semantic-label-role1 a                core:semantic-label-role.
19  ?annotation2         a                 core:semantic-annotation;
20                       core:setting-for ?ITEM;
21                       core:setting-for ?label2;
22                       core:satifies     [
23                           a core:method;
24                           core:defines ?annotated-data-role2;
25                           core:defines ?semantic-label-role2].
26  ?label2              core:plays        ?semantic-label-role2.
```

```
27   ?semantic-label-role2 a              core:semantic-label-role.
28   ?label1              a               ex:USLeader.
29   ?label2              a               ex:USSRLeader.
30   }
```

The second query selects all subsegments of any input segment (lines 13–25) and propagates the semantic annotation of the subsegment (selected in lines 26–34) to the input segment. Here, new COMM annotations are generated using SPARQL construct queries (lines 1–11). If this rule is evaluated recursively, e.g., using Networked Graphs [75], the first query can ignore decompositions and can be formulated in a much shorter way.

```
1    CONSTRUCT {
2    ?ITEM                core:plays          _:annotated-data-role.
3    _:annotation         a                   core:semantic-annotation;
4                         core:setting-for    ?ITEM;
5                         core:setting-for    ?LABEL;
6                         core:satifies       [
7                               a core:method;
8                               core:defines _:annotated-data-role;
9                               core:defines _:semantic-label-role].
10   ?LABEL               core:plays          _:semantic-label-role.
11   _:semantic-label-role a                  core:semantic-label-role }
12   WHERE {
13   ?ITEM                a                   core:multimedia-data;
14                        core:plays          ?input-segment-role.
15   ?input-segment-role  a                   core:input-segment-role.
16   ?decomposition       a                   core:decomposition;
17                        core:setting-for    ?ITEM;
18                        core:settingFor     ?segment;
19                        core:satisfies      [
20                              a core:method;
21                              core:defines ?segment-role;
22                              core:defines ?input-segment-role].
23   ?segment             core:plays          ?segment-role;
24                        core:plays          ?annotated-data-role.
25   ?segment-role        a                   core:segment-role.
26   ?annotation          a                   core:semantic-annotation;
27                        core:setting-for    ?segment
28                        core:setting-for    ?label;
29                        core:satifies       [
30                              a core:method;
31                              core:defines ?annotated-data-role;
32                              core:defines ?semantic-label-role].
33   ?LABEL               core:plays          ?semantic-label-role.
34   ?semantic-label-role a                   core:semantic-label-role.
35   }
```

Having presented the challenges of querying multimedia semantics and demonstrated these challenges at the example of two representative queries, we now propose a selection of approaches to deal with the enormous amounts of data we are faced with here.

Partitioning Datasets. In contrast to many sources of world knowledge, multimedia metadata can easily be split horizontally. This means that annotations of two media assets are to a very large degree independent of each other. The links between them are usually indirect, specified through world knowledge. For example, two images could show the same scenery from different angles. However, the scenery is not part of the actual multimedia annotation but world knowledge. As a result, one possible approach to scaling querying of multimedia metadata is to distinguish between multimedia annotation and world knowledge and to accordingly split the datasets and queries. This allows us to come up with easier problems due to shorter queries and a smaller dataset. On the other hand, new challenges arise when splitting queries and datasets such as determining relevant fragments for answering (a part of) a query or joining query results like efficiently handling distributed joins. Even though many of these challenges are well known from distributed and federated relational databases, they are more problematic for RDF as schema information is not reflected in the structure of data and an extremely high number of joins has to be handled compared to relational databases. For illustration, please remember that in relational databases the table structure implicitly reflects the schema of the data. In contrast, in RDF we have triples as the only structure and schema information is expressed explicitly using special predicates.

Appropriate Expressiveness of Languages. State of the art reasoners are not able to deal with the very large datasets we are facing here. To alleviate this issue, again intelligent splitting of data can be applied, using different expressiveness when reasoning with different parts of the dataset. For example, the COMM ontology can still be classified by some OWL-DL reasoners. While this takes a long time, it can be precomputed. Using a pre-classified COMM and some comparable simple query rewriting, we are able to completely avoid reasoning at runtime for many queries. Similar strategies can be used when including knowledge from domain ontologies. We also use a small extension of SPARQL to query for meta-knowledge such as fuzzy values or provenance [82] in order to determine what is more recent, reliable, and so on. Another approach uses fuzzy logic and probabilities to express and manage uncertainty and vagueness, respectively [84].

On Demand Access to Annotation. Due to the enormous size of the metadata, applications cannot hold whole annotation graphs even for moderately complex problems in the main memory. For this reason, we are pursuing a RDF persistence framework to rebuild the COMM API upon. Similar to approaches like Hibernate[35] for relational databases, this allows to read and write only fractions of multimedia annotations on demand. Consequently, we avoid to deal with the whole, very large dataset in memory.

Related Work on Querying. Besides the approach described above for querying media assets by the use of a semantic database, there are also other

---

[35] http://www.hibernate.org/

approaches and solutions to query semantic multimedia. For example, the commercial database Oracle with its Oracle Multimedia[36] feature provides for retrieving images, audio, and video. The Multimedia package is an extension of the relational Oracle database. It supports the extraction of metadata from media assets and allows querying for media assets by specific indices. The Digital Memory Engineering group at the Research Studios in Austria developed with the multimedia database METIS a sophisticated storage and management solution for structured multimedia content and its semantics [40, 73]. The METIS database provides a flexible concept for the definition and management of arbitrary media elements and their semantics. It is adaptable and extensible to the requirements of a concrete application domain by integrating application-specific plugins and defining domain-specific (complex) media types. For it, the semantic relationship of specific media elements and their semantics can be described to form new, independent multimedia data types. Those domain-specific media types can be bundled up and distributed in form of so-called *semantic packs*. The research approach QBIC [16] from IBM is known to be one of the first databases that supports content-based features for querying the content.[37] QBIC supports queries with respect to content-based attributes of images such as color distribution, color layout, and specific textures in the images. Both approaches, Oracle's Intermedia and IBM's QBIC use a relational database and do not provide support for a fully-fledged semantic description of the content such as supported by the K-Space database.

The multimedia presentation algebra (MPA) by Adali et al. [1] extends the relational model of data and allows for dynamically creating new presentations from (parts of) existing presentations. With the MPA, a page-oriented view on multimedia content is given. A multimedia presentation is considered as an interactive presentation that consists of a tree, which is stored in a database. Each node of this tree represents a non-interactive presentation, e.g., a sequence of slides, a video element, or a HTML page. The branches of the tree reflect different possible playback variants of a set of presentations. A transition from a parent node to a child node in this tree corresponds to an interaction. The proposed MPA allows for specifying a query on the database based on the contents of individual nodes as well as querying based on the presentation's tree structure. For it, the MPA provides extensions and generalizations of the `select` and `project` operations in the relational algebra. However, it also allows to author new presentations based on the nodes and tree structure stored in the database. For it, the MPA defines operations such as `merge`, `join`, `path-union`, `path-intersection`, and `path-difference`. These extend the algebraic join operation to tree structures and allow to author new presentations by combining existing presentations and parts of presentations. Another approach comprises a multimedia calculus and algebra allowing for querying on tree-based multimedia content stored in multimedia databases [46, 47]. Here, the new multimedia presentations are created on basis of a given query and a set of inclusion and

---

[36] http://www.oracle.com/technology/products/intermedia/index.html
[37] http://wwwqbic.almaden.ibm.com/

exclusion constraints stored in the database. The main advantage of these approaches based on algebras is that the requested multimedia content is specified as a query in a formal language. However, typically high effort is necessary to learn the algebra and their operators and it is very difficult to apply such a formal approach. Consequently, the presented algebras remain purely academic so far.

9 Further and Future Issues of Semantic Multimedia

In this section, we reconsider selected aspects of multimedia semantics. We briefly motivate and summarize them in order to give an outlook to future work.

Semantics for Multimedia. Multimedia semantics exhibits multiple semantics influenced by many different factors like time and contextual use. As motivated in Section 1 and described in Section 4, researchers are looking into the bits and bytes of multimedia content in order to determine its semantics. They also take contextual information about the media assets into account such as EXIF[38] information provided by digital still cameras. In recent time, there is also much research that aims at combining both content-based analysis and context-based analysis in order to improve the results. However, today's approaches and systems typically only look at particular factors that influence multimedia semantics and do not consider the problem in its entirety. Thus, they only look at particular aspects that determine the semantics of multimedia. In order to better understand, describe, and communicate multimedia semantics, a holistic approach is needed that describes and embraces this complex and challenging problem.

A multimedia ontology like COMM presented in Section 5 is an annotation model that can be used to organize and structure multimedia semantics. However, it does not provide support in terms of a method or "high-level" model that helps one in understanding the different factors that make the semantics of multimedia content. Thus, it does not provide for a holistic view we are looking for to better understand multimedia semantics.

The WeKnowIt project[39] aims at understanding the semantics of social media for personal, organizational, and social use through a so-called collective intelligence. The goal of the project is to develop novel techniques for exploiting multiple layers of intelligence from user-generated content. These multiple layers of intelligence together form the collective intelligence that emerges from the collaboration and competition among many individuals. To this end, various sources of information from digital content items and contextual information (media intelligence), massive user feedback (mass intelligence), and users' social interaction (social intelligence) so as to benefit end-users (personal intelligence) as well as organizations (organizational intelligence) will be we analyzed and combined. Thus, it aims at understanding different factors that influence multimedia semantics.

---

[38] http://www.exif.org/
[39] http://www.weknowit.eu/

With semiotics, we find a general philosophical theory for understanding signs and symbols.[40] It especially deals with the function of signs and symbols in languages and can be broken up into three branches: semantics, syntactics, and pragmatics. Semantics describes the relation between signs and the things they refer to. Syntactics deals with the relation of signs in formal structures. Finally, pragmatics describes the relation of signs to their users and the environment in which they occur. Prominent work in the field of semantics is, e.g., the classification of ten fundamental visual codes by Eco [12]. These codes are an instrument to shape images: codes of perception, codes of transmission, codes of recognition, tonal codes, iconic codes, iconographic codes, codes of taste and sensibility, rhetorical codes, stylistic codes, and codes of the unconscious.[41] Based on this work, concrete systems like the semiotic-aware architecture for hypermedia [56] and the automated video editing tool AUTEUR [55] have been developed, providing valuable achievements in order to understand multimedia semantics.

Finally, we find with the semantics ecosystem a theoretical approach for understanding and modeling semantics [79]. The ecosystem bases on work from the philosopher Popper [69] and defines five different types of semantics (natural, analytical, user, expressive, and emergent semantics) and their relationships. It aims at integrating existing work in the field rather than reinventing it. With natural semantics, we understand the semantics of the non-living physical objects, living things, and events of our physical world. It is the result of the long-term natural language communication between humans. Natural semantics associates basic objects and actions with symbols. Analytical semantics bases on natural semantics. It aims at understanding more complex objects, concepts, and situations. Analytical semantics is applied to dismantle these more complex objects, identify the individual parts, and interpreted them by applying natural semantics. User semantics is the human's perception of the physical world based on his or her personal background. It is the perception of the items, biological objects, and events of the physical world based on a multitude of very different aspects. Among them are the individual's knowledge, preferences, interests, needs, and cultural background [6, 15, 41] and the location, time, used end device, and social situation [10, 80, 81]. With expressive semantics, we consider how the products of the physical world are created. A product can be a gesture, a spoken sentence, or any kind of a non-living object like a book, CD, or multimedia presentation. Expressive semantics describes the intention of the creator when creating such a product (why is the product created in that certain way and what is the intention of the creator in creating it like this). The expressive semantics heavily depends on the individual's background and contextual situation as introduced above. Thus, it depends on the user semantics. Finally, emergent semantics considers the change of semantics over time and use. This means that the individual's semantics and observation of a physical world item, biological object, or event can and will change over time and will change through the different contexts in which it is used. Emergent semantics can be

---

[40] http://www.merriam-webster.com/dictionary/semiotics
[41] http://www.aber.ac.uk/media/Documents/S4B/sem08.html

short-termed (a couple of seconds up to some minutes) or very long-termed (like a couple of years). However, the key to emergent semantics is the interaction of expressive semantics and analytical semantics. This interaction leads to a modification of user semantics, i.e., the personal ontologies and understanding of the physical world of the individual. Early results of applying parts of the ecosystem in the area of authoring semantically-rich multimedia albums are very promising. However, the ecosystem is still in an early stage and requires maturation. In a future work, it will be very interesting to elaborate how the work on the five types of semantics defined in the ecosystem, the layers of intelligence considered in the WeKnowIt project, and the work in the field of semiotics can be integrated. Thus, what we need is bringing the different ideas and approaches together to provide a better understanding of multimedia semantics.

Organizing, Sharing, and Communicating semantically-rich Multimedia Content. Looking at the field of multimedia semantics and understanding the different contextual factors that determine the multimedia content's semantics raises the question of an appropriate support to organize, share, and communicate such semantically-rich content. Here, we find different systems and applications like Flickr, Picasa[42], and YouTube. The goal of these applications is to provide the users a means to organize and share their experiences. However, these systems and applications focus on the media assets that accompany these experiences, thus they are media-centric. In recent years, it has been reinforced that events are a much better abstraction of human experience [98]. Thus, events are much better for managing media assets captured during events. As a consequence, we find today approaches and applications like SenseCam [23], MyLifeBits [22], PhotoCompas [54], World Explorer [2], FotoFiti [45], PhotoFinder [38, 83], and many more that integrate the concept of events into their media management solution. These are very important and valuable steps towards an event-centric media management. However, the existing approaches and applications typically consider events only as second-class entities, i.e., as some semantics that can be extracted from the media assets and attached to them as additional metadata. Thus, in media-centric approaches, events are considered only one concept among many such as the actual media management, a social network support, and others to describe the multimedia semantics. However, an event-centric management of media assets promises strong advantages over a media-centric approach [76]. Thus, it would be a much better approach for managing the multimedia content's semantics. Early work in this area has been done such as the EMMA system [76]. However, extensive user studies have to be conducted to further underpin this claim.

Annotating Multimedia Assets. Annotating multimedia assets has been introduced in Section 2 at the example of the "Big Three" picture. Looking at today's support for annotating multimedia assets, we typically find support for adding tags (Flickr and YouTube), attaching geo-positions to photos (Zonetag[43]

---

[42] http://picasa.google.com/
[43] http://zonetag.research.yahoo.com/

and Locr[44]), defining and annotating regions of interest (ROI) on Flickr, detecting faces with Riya[45], or manually writing and adding comments. Most of these systems are mono-media and allow only for annotations that refer to entire media assets like images and videos. Only a few approaches and systems actually look into fragments of the media assets like ROIs in Flickr and face detection in Riya. For modeling the annotations, typically proprietary formats are used rather then employing standards. This is very unfortunate as many of these standards exist for the different media types (examples are listed in [3]). So far there has not been a broad uptake of these standards for annotating multimedia assets.

In addition, there is a huge lack in providing appropriate annotation support for structured multimedia content such as Flash[46], SMIL[47], SVG[48], or LASeR[49] presentations. Although today's systems and approaches like the Cuypers Multimedia Transformation Engine [24, 95] and the Semi-automatic Multimedia Presentation Generation Environment [13, 14] generate rich multimedia content, exploit semantically-rich annotations and metadata, and even derive further information while authoring the content, this valuable source of information is thrown away once the content creation task is finished. Thus, the created multimedia presentations carry none or only very few annotations.

An approach to (semi-)automatically annotate structured multimedia content during the multimedia authoring process is provided with the SemanticMM4U framework [77, 78]. The framework itself does not define a model for semantic annotation but provides the ability to integrate and use arbitrary ones. These can be simple models like Dublin Core[50] but also complex ones like MPEG-7 or the COMM model introduced in Section 5.

Low Level Multimedia Processing and Classification. We find research in the field of low level multimedia processing and classification already for a couple of decades. A good introduction to this field gives Section 4. The related work shows that classification can be done to a certain degree of accuracy using the different technologies described. However, despite the long-term research in the field there is until today no approach that overcomes the semantic gap. Shape-based approaches can be used to classify arbitrary media assets into a set of classes. However, they remain on the concept level like people/faces, landscapes, nature, and so on. This approach has not reached high-level semantics and annotations of the media assets by proper nouns like determining the peoples' names in the "Big Three" example and identifying that the picture has been taken at the Yalta Conference. Classification using textures allows for identifying objects on the proper noun level (if the objects have been assigned one in the training phase). However, this approach is only applicable for a limited set of objects

---

[44] http://www.locr.com/
[45] http://www.riya.com/
[46] http://www.adobe.com/devnet/swf/
[47] http://www.w3.org/AudioVideo/
[48] http://www.w3.org/Graphics/SVG/
[49] http://www.mpeg-laser.org/html/techSection_laserSpec.htm
[50] http://dublincore.org/

to classify. To alleviate the problem, researchers recently combine traditional content-based classification with additional contextual information such as location, compass, calendar, weather station, and so on. Another promising step to enhance the current state of the art is to combine the so-far uncombined research areas of shape-based processing and texture-based processing.

Most of the work we find today on low level multimedia processing and classification focuses on single media assets like images, video, and audio. However, only little work has been done on analyzing and classifying structured multimedia content such as Flash presentations. An example of low level processing and classification of Flash presentations is by Ding et al. [11].

A Formal Ontological Foundation for Multimedia. MPEG-7 is one of the most renowned metadata standards for annotating media assets. However, as elaborated in Section 1 it became semantically ambiguous due to its complexity. Thus, it lacks from a formal semantics that provides guidelines to the users of the standard how to apply it. With COMM presented in Section 5, we find an approach to describe parts of MPEG-7 using formal semantics based on DOLCE. With the example of expressing complex semantics in the "Big Three" scenario by using the annotation tool KAT in Section 6 and manually applying COMM in Section 7, applicability of COMM for rich semantic annotations is shown. A major challenge for COMM is the high burden and effort needed to start using it. In future, it is to become more practicable and applicable. Thus, what is missing are methods and guidelines how to apply an ontology like COMM to annotate multimedia content and providing tools working with COMM. A fundamental issue here is introducing the concept of modules into ontologies. By this, the complex problem is broken down into smaller bricks and at the same time allows for providing very domain-specific and thus easier to use ontologies. On top of such modularized ontologies we can then define appropriate methods and tools. Enhancing the state of the art here is a key research issue of the NEON project[51].

Querying for Semantic Multimedia. For querying semantic multimedia, we presented in Section 8 a database based on Sesame providing for storing and querying over RDF triples. We also considered related approaches and systems in the field of querying for semantic multimedia. Looking at the current state of the art, a future research issue is providing efficient support for a recursive querying in structured multimedia content over a large dataset. For it, we need effective query optimization algorithms taking pattern similarities of the queries into account. The further, current research allows for querying using fuzzy logic and provenance [82, 84]. Feasibility of this approach is shown by first systems that actually integrate fuzzy logic. However, it remains future challenge to proof real benefit of using fuzzy logic. With respect to provenance, a future challenge is to leverage this information to make decisions about the trustworthiness of specific statements made about the multimedia content. Thus, to establish trust to the user. Finally, we can state that querying for semantic multimedia is a vehicle to bring a vitally needed, sophisticated expressiveness to multimedia metadata.

---

[51] http://www.neon-project.org/

However, as we could only sketch in Section 8, this sophisticated expressiveness also puts very high demands on the semantic infrastructure used. Consequently, we expect that the demands of semantic multimedia applications significantly drive the development of a semantic web infrastructure in the next years, both in terms of scaleability but also with respect to the expressivity of query languages.

10   Summary and Outlook

In this paper, we presented current research in multimedia semantics. We looked into the field of annotating media assets and elaborated the drawbacks of todays support for annotation such as fragment identification, semantic annotation, web interoperability, and embedding semantic annotations into compound documents. Research in the area low level multimedia processing and classification has been been presented. We identified requirements for designing a multimedia ontology and introduced a formal ontological foundation for multimedia with the multimedia ontology COMM. The multimedia ontology COMM has been used for implementing the multimedia annotation tool KAT and has been applied to annotate the "Big Three" scenario. We investigated the retrieval of multimedia semantics based on SPARQL and considered further and future aspects of multimedia semantics.

As a quintessence of the discussion in Section 9, we conclude with identifying the major challenges for future research in semantic multimedia. These are combining existing research approaches and streams and providing semantics support for structured multimedia content.

Combining research approaches and streams. Recent approaches of combing, e.g., content-based analysis with context-based analysis of media assets have shown that the results achieved here are much better compared to applying the techniques solitary. To further enhance the state of the art in annotating, processing, and classifying media assets, a big challenge for the future is to bring different fields and streams of research and thus different approaches together. Current efforts towards integration of content-based and context-based media understanding reflects this trend. Another example is the so far uncombined research in shape-based classification and texture-based classification. It seems very promising to combine both approaches to bring the field one step further.

Support for structured multimedia content. Most approaches for annotating, processing, and classifying is focused on single media assets such as images, video, and audio. The challenge for the research results in these areas is to extend and to apply it to rich, structured multimedia content.

Acknowledgment. The research that lead to this paper was partially supported by the European Commission under contract FP6-027026, Knowledge Space of semantic inference for automatic annotation and retrieval of multimedia content (K-Space), and under contract FP6-026978, X-Media Integrated Project.

References

1. Adali, S., Sapino, M.L., Subrahmanian, V.S.: An algebra for creating and querying multimedia presentations. Multimedia Syst. 8(3), 212–230 (2000)
2. Ahern, S., Naaman, M., Nair, R., Yang, J.H.-I.: World explorer: visualizing aggregate data from unstructured text in geo-referenced collections. In: Proceedings of the 7th ACM/IEEE joint conference on Digital libraries, pp. 1–10. ACM Press, New York (2007)
3. Arndt, R., Troncy, R., Staab, S., Hardman, L., Vacura, M.: COMM: Designing a Well-Founded Multimedia Ontology for the Web. In: 6th Int. Semantic Web Conference (2007)
4. Blöhdorn, S., Petridis, K., Saathoff, C., Simou, N., Tzouvaras, V., Avrithis, Y., Handschuh, S., Kompatsiaris, Y., Staab, S., Strintzis, M.: Semantic Annotation of Images and Videos for Multimedia Analysis. In: 2nd European Semantic Web Conference (2005)
5. Brunelli, R., Poggio, T.: Template matching: Matched spatial filters and beyond. Pattern Recognition 30(5), 751–768 (1997)
6. Brusilovsky, P., Maybury, M.T.: From adaptive hypermedia to the adaptive Web. Communications of the ACM 45(5), 30–33 (2002)
7. Chen, H., Shimshoni, I., Meer, P.: Model based object recognition by robust information fusion. In: 17th International Conference on Pattern Recognition, Cambrige, UK (August 2004)
8. Christianini, N., Shawe-Taylor, J.: An Introduction to Support Vector Machines. Cambridge University Press, Cambridge (2000)
9. Cortes, C., Vapnik, V.N.: Support vector networks. Machine Learning 20, 273–297 (1995)
10. Dey, A.K., Abowd, G.D.: Towards a Better Understanding of Context and Context-Awareness. Technical Report GIT-GVU-99-22, Graphics, Visualization and Usability Center and College of Computing, Georgia Institute of Technology, Atlanta, GA, USA (June 1999)
11. Ding, D., Yang, J., Li, Q., Liu, W., Wang, L.: What can expressive semantics tell: Retrieval model for a flash-movie search engine. In: Leow, W.-K., Lew, M., Chua, T.-S., Ma, W.-Y., Chaisorn, L., Bakker, E.M. (eds.) CIVR 2005. LNCS, vol. 3568, pp. 123–133. Springer, Heidelberg (2005)
12. Eco, U.: Einfuehrung in die Semiotik. Wilhelm Fink Verlag, Munich (1985)
13. Falkovych, K., Nack, F.: Context Aware Guidance for Multimedia Authoring: Harmonizing domain and discourse knowledge. Multimedia Systems Journal 11(3) (2006)
14. Falkovych, K., Nack, F., van Ossenbruggen, J., Rutledge, L.: Sample: Towards a framework for system-supported multimedia authoring. In: Multimedia Modelling, p. 362. IEEE Computer Society, Los Alamitos (2004)
15. Fink, J., Kobsa, A., Schreck, J.: Personalized hypermedia information through adaptive and adaptable system features: User modeling, privacy and security issues. In: Mullery, A., Besson, M., Campolargo, M., Gobbi, R., Reed, R. (eds.) Intelligence in Services and Networks: Technology for Cooperative Competition, pp. 459–467. Springer, Heidelberg (1997)
16. Flickner, M., Sawhney, H., Niblack, W., Ashley, J., Huang, Q., Dom, B., Gorkani, M., Hafner, J., Lee, D., Petkovic, D., Steele, D., Yanker, P.: Query by image and video content: the QBIC system. In: Readings in multimedia computing and networking, pp. 255–264. Morgan Kaufmann, San Francisco (2001)

17. Gangemi, A., Borgo, S., Catenacci, C., Lehmann, J.: Task Taxonomies for Knowledge Content. Technical report, Metokis Deliverable 7, (2004)
18. Gangemi, A., Guarino, N., Masolo, C., Oltramari, A., Schneider, L.: Sweetening ontologies with dolce. In: Gómez-Pérez, A., Benjamins, V.R. (eds.) EKAW 2002. LNCS (LNAI), vol. 2473, pp. 166–181. Springer, Heidelberg (2002)
19. Garcia, R., Celma, O.: Semantic Integration and Retrieval of Multimedia Metadata. In: 5th International Workshop on Knowledge Markup and Semantic Annotation (2005)
20. García, R., Gil, R.: Facilitating Business Interoperability from the Semantic Web. In: Abramowicz, W. (ed.) BIS 2007. LNCS, vol. 4439, pp. 220–232. Springer, Heidelberg (2007)
21. Garcia, R., Gil, R., Delgado, J.: A Web Ontologies Framework for Digital Rights Management. Journal of Artificial Intelligence and Law 15, 137–154 (2007)
22. Gemmell, J., Bell, G., Lueder, R.: Mylifebits: a personal database for everything. Commun. ACM 49(1), 88–95 (2006)
23. Gemmell, J., Williams, L., Wood, K., Lueder, R., Bell, G.: Passive capture and ensuing issues for a personal lifetime store. In: Proceedings of the the 1st ACM workshop on Continuous archival and retrieval of personal experiences, pp. 48–55. ACM Press, New York (2004)
24. Geurts, J., van Ossenbruggen, J., Hardman, L.: Application-specific constraints for multimedia presentation generation. In: Multimedia Modeling. IEEE, Los Alamitos (2001)
25. Geurts, J., van Ossenbruggen, J., Hardman, L.: Requirements for practical multimedia annotation. In: Workshop on Multimedia and the Semantic Web (2005)
26. Gonzalez, R.C., Woods, R.E.: Digital Image Processing. Prentice Hall, Englewood Cliffs (2001)
27. Gräßl, C., Deinzer, F., Nieman, H.: Continuous parametrization of normal distribution for improving the discrete statistical eigenspace approach for object recognition. In: Krasnoproshin, V., Ablameyko, S., Soldek, J. (eds.) Pattern Recognition and Information Processing 2003, Minsk, Belarus, May 2003, pp. 73–77 (2003)
28. Grzegorzek, M., Izquierdo, E.: Statistical 3d object classification and localization with context modeling. In: Domanski, M., Stasinski, R., Bartkowiak, M. (eds.) 15th European Signal Processing Conference, pp. 1585–1589. PTETiS, Poznan (2007)
29. Halasz, F., Schwartz, M.: The Dexter Hypertext Reference Model. Communications of the ACM 37(2), 30–39 (1994)
30. Harth, A., Umbrich, J., Hogan, A., Decker, S.: Yars2: A federated repository for searching and querying graph structured data. Technical report, Digital Enterprise Research Institute, Galway, 4 (2007)
31. Hornegger, J.: Statistische Modellierung, Klassifikation und Lokalisation von Objekten. Shaker Verlag, Aachen (1996)
32. Hunter, J.: Adding Multimedia to the Semantic Web - Building an MPEG-7 Ontology. In: 1st International Semantic Web Working Symposium, pp. 261–281 (2001)
33. Hunter, J.: Combining the CIDOC/CRM and MPEG-7 to Describe Multimedia in Museums. In: 6th Museums and the Web Conference (2002), http://www.archimuse.com/mw2002/papers/hunter/hunter.html
34. Hunter, J.: Enhancing the semantic interoperability of multimedia through a core ontology. IEEE Transactions on Circuits and Systems for Video Technology 13(1), 49–58 (2003)
35. Hunter, J., Armstrong, L.: A Comparison of Schemas for Video Metadata Representation. In: 8th International World Wide Web Conference, pp. 1431–1451 (1999)

36. Hunter, J., Little, S.: A Framework to Enable the Semantic Inferencing and Querying of Multimedia Content. International Journal of Web Engineering and Technology – Special Issue on the Semantic Web 2(2/3), 264–286 (2005)
37. Isaac, A., Troncy, R.: Designing and Using an Audio-Visual Description Core Ontology. In: Workshop on Core Ontologies in Ontology Engineering (2004)
38. Kang, H., Shneiderman, B.: Visualization methods for personal photo collections: Browsing and searching in the photofinder. In: IEEE International Conference on Multimedia and Expo (III), pp. 1539–1542 (August 2000)
39. Kerr, J., Compton, P.: Toward generic model-based object recognition by knowledge acquisition and machine learning. In: Proceedings of the Eighteenth International Joint Conference on Artificial Intelligence, Acapulco, Mexico, pp. 9–15 (2003)
40. King, R., Popitsch, N., Westermann, U.: METIS: a flexible database foundation for unified media management. In: Proc.of the 12th annual ACM Int. Conf. on Multimedia, pp. 744–745. ACM Press, New York (2004)
41. Kobsa, A., Koenemann, J., Pohl, W.: Personalized Hypermedia Presentation Techniques for Improving Online Customer Relationships. In: The Knowledge Engineering Review, vol. 16, pp. 111–155. Cambridge University Press, Cambridge (2001)
42. Kochut, K., Janik, M.: Sparqler: Extended sparql for semantic association discovery. In: Franconi, E., Kifer, M., May, W. (eds.) ESWC 2007. LNCS, vol. 4519, pp. 145–159. Springer, Heidelberg (2007)
43. Lagoze, C., Hunter, J.: The ABC Ontology and Model (v3.0). Journal of Digital Information 2(2) (2001)
44. Latecki, L.J., Lakaemper, R., Wolter, D.: Optimal partial shape similarity. Image and Vision Computing Journal 23, 227–236 (2005)
45. Lee, B.N., Chen, W., Chang, E.Y.: Fotofiti: web service for photo management. In: Proceedings of the 14th annual ACM international conference on Multimedia, pp. 485–486. ACM Press, New York (2006)
46. Lee, T., Sheng, L., Balkir, N.H., Al-Hamdani, A., Özsoyoglu, G., Özsoyoglu, Z.M.: Query Processing Techniques for Multimedia Presentations. Multimedia Tools Appl. 11(1), 63–99 (2000)
47. Lee, T., Sheng, L., Bozkaya, T., Balkir, N.H., Özsoyoglu, Z.M., Özsoyoglu, G.: Querying Multimedia Presentations Based on Content. IEEE Trans. on Knowledge and Data Engineering 11(3), 361–385 (1999)
48. Leonardis, A., Bischof, H.: Dealing with occlusions in the eigenspace approach. In: Pelillo, M., Hancock, E.R. (eds.) EMMCVPR 1997. LNCS, vol. 1223, pp. 453–458. Springer, Heidelberg (1997)
49. Moghaddam, B., Pentland, A.: Probabilistic visual learning for object representation. PAMI 19(7), 696–710 (1997)
50. Mokhtarian, F., Bober, M.: Curvature Scale Space Representation: Theory, Applications, and MPEG7-Standardization. Springer, Heidelberg (2003)
51. MPEG-21. Part 17: Fragment Identification of MPEG Resources. Standard No. ISO/IEC 21000-17 (2006)
52. MPEG-7. Multimedia Content Description Interface. Standard No. ISO/IEC 15938 (2001)
53. Murase, H., Nayar, S.K.: Visual learning and recognition of 3-d objects from appearance. International Journal of Computer Vision 14(1), 5–24 (1995)
54. Naaman, M., Yeh, R.B., Garcia-Molina, H., Paepcke, A.: Leveraging context to resolve identity in photo albums. In: Proceedings of the 5th ACM/IEEE-CS joint conference on Digital libraries, pp. 178–187. ACM Press, New York (2005)

55. Nack, F.: AUTEUR: The Application of Video Semantics and Theme Representation for Automated Film Editing. PhD thesis, Lancaster University, UK (September 1996)

56. Nack, F., Hardman, L.: Denotative and connotative semantics in hypermedia: proposal for a semiotic-aware architecture. New Rev. Hypermedia Multimedia 7(1), 7–37 (2002)

57. Nack, F., Lindsay, A.T.: Everything you wanted to know about MPEG-7 (Parts I & II). IEEE Multimedia 6(3-4) (1999)

58. Nack, F., van Ossenbruggen, J., Hardman, L.: That Obscure Object of Desire: Multimedia Metadata on the Web (Part II). IEEE Multimedia 12(1) (2005)

59. Neumann, B., Möller, R.: On Scene Interpretation with Description Logics. In: Cognitive Vision Systems, pp. 247–275. Springer, Heidelberg (2006)

60. Niemann, H.: Klassifikation von Mustern. Springer, Heidelberg (1983)

61. Oberle, D., Lamparter, S., Grimm, S., Vrandecic, D., Staab, S., Gangemi, A.: Towards Ontologies for Formalizing Modularization and Communication in Large Software Systems. Journal of Applied Ontology 1(2), 163–202 (2006)

62. Sirma Group Corp Ontotext Lab. Bigowlim: System documentation (2006) [15-05-2008], http://www.ontotext.com/owlim/big/BigOWLIMSysDoc.pdf

63. van Ossenbruggen, J., Nack, F., Hardman, L.: That Obscure Object of Desire: Multimedia Metadata on the Web (Part I). IEEE Multimedia 11(4) (2004)

64. Park, S., Lee, J., Kim, S.: Content-based image classification using a neural network. Pattern Recognition Letters 25(3), 287–300 (2004)

65. Paulus, D., Hornegger, J.: Applied Pattern Recognition. Friedr. Vieweg & Sohn Verlagsgesellschaft GmbH, Braunschweig (2003)

66. Pease, A., Niles, I., Li, J.: The Suggested Upper Merged Ontology: A Large Ontology for the Semantic Web and its Applications. In: Working Notes of the AAAI-2002 Workshop on Ontologies and the Semantic Web (2002)

67. Polleres, A., Scharffe, F., Schindlauer, R.: Sparql++ for mapping between rdf vocabularies. In: OTM Conferences (1), pp. 878–896 (2007)

68. Polydoros, P., Tsinaraki, C., Christodoulakis, S.: GraphOnto: OWL-based ontology management and multimedia annotation in the DS-MIRF framework. Journal of Digital Information Management (JDIM) 4(4), 214–219 (2006)

69. Popper, K.: Three worlds [the tanner lecture on human values: Delivered at the university of michigan], April (1978), http://www.tannerlectures.utah.edu/lectures/documents/popper80.pdf

70. Pösl, J.: Erscheinungsbasierte, statistische Objekterkennung. Shaker Verlag, Aachen (1999)

71. Pratt, W.K.: Digital Image Processing. John Wiley & Sons Ltd., New York (2001)

72. Reinhold, M.: Robuste, probabilistische, erscheinungsbasierte Objekterkennung. Logos Verlag, Berlin (2004)

73. Ross, K., Westermann, G.U., Popitsch, N.: METIS - A Flexible Database Solution for the Management of Multimedia Assets. In: Proc. of the 10th Int. Workshop on Multimedia Information Systems, College Park, MD, USA (August 2004)

74. Saathoff, C., Staab, S.: Exploiting Spatial Context in Images Using Fuzzy Constraint Reasoning. In: 9th Int. Workshop on Image Analysis for Multimedia Interactive Services, Klagenfurt, Austria. IEEE, Los Alamitos (2008)

75. Schenk, S., Staab, S.: Networked graphs: A declarative mechanism for sparql rules, sparql views and rdf data integration on the web. In: Proceedings of the 17th International World Wide Web Conference, WWW2008, Bejing, China (2008)

76. Scherp, A., Agaram, S., Jain, R.: Event-centric media management. In: Gevers, T., Jain, R.C., Santini, S. (eds.) Multimedia Content Access: Algorithms and Systems II. Proceedings of the SPIE Society of Photo-Optical Instrumentation Engineers (SPIE) Conference, vol. 6820, pp. 68200C-68200C-15 (January 2008)

77. Scherp, A.: Semantics support for personalized multimedia content. In: Int. Conf. Internet and Multimedia Systems and Applications, Innsbruck, Austria, March 2008, pp. 57–65. IASTED (2008)

78. Scherp, A., Boll, S., Cremer, H.: Emergent semantics in personalized multimedia content. J. of Digital Information Management 5(2) (April 2007)

79. Scherp, A., Jain, R.: Towards an ecosystem for semantics. In: MS 2007: Workshop on multimedia information retrieval on The many faces of multimedia semantics, pp. 3–12. ACM Press, New York (2007)

80. Schilit, B., Adams, N., Want, R.: Context-Aware Computing Applications. In: Workshop on Mobil Computing Systems and Applications, Santa Cruz, CA, USA, pp. 85–90. IEEE, Los Alamitos (1994)

81. Schmidt, A., Beigl, M., Gellersen, H.-W.: There is more to context than location. Computers & Graphics 23(6), 893–901 (1999)

82. Schueler, B., Sizov, S., Staab, S., Tran, D.T.: Querying for meta knowledge. In: WWW 2008: Proceeding of the 17th international conference on World Wide Web, pp. 625–634. ACM, New York (2008)

83. Shneiderman, B., Kang, H.: Direct annotation: A drag-and-drop strategy for labeling photos. In: Proceedings of the International Conference on Information Visualisation, p. 88. IEEE Computer Society, Washington (2000)

84. Straccia, U.: Managing Uncertainty and Vagueness in Description Logics, Logic Programs and Description Logic Programs. Springer, Heidelberg (2008)

85. Sure, Y., Staab, S., Studer, R.: Methodology for development and employment of ontology based knowledge management applications. SIGMOD Rec. 31(4), 18–23 (2002)

86. Tadeusiewicz, R.: Introduction to Practice of Application of Neural Networks (in Neuron Networks) StatSoft, Warsaw, Poland (1999)

87. Troncy, R.: Integrating Structure and Semantics into Audio-visual Documents. In: 2nd International Semantic Web Conference, pp. 566–581 (2003)

88. Troncy, R., Bailer, W., Hausenblas, M., Hofmair, P., Schlatte, R.: Enabling Multimedia Metadata Interoperability by Defining Formal Semantics of MPEG-7 Profiles. In: 1st International Conference on Semantics And digital Media Technology, pp. 41–55 (2006)

89. Troncy, R., Celma, Ó., Little, S., García, R., Tsinaraki, C.: MPEG-7 based Multimedia Ontologies: Interoperability Support or Interoperability Issue? In: 1st International Workshop on Multimedia Annotation and Retrieval enabled by Shared Ontologies, pp. 2–15 (2007)

90. Troncy, R., Hardman, L., van Ossenbruggen, J., Hausenblas, M.: Identifying Spatial and Temporal Media Fragments on the Web. In: W3C Video on the Web Workshop (2007), http://www.w3.org/2007/08/video/positions/Troncy.pdf

91. Tsinaraki, C., Christodoulakis, S.: Interoperability of XML Schema Applications with OWL Domain Knowledge and Semantic Web Tools. In: 6th International Conference on Ontologies, DataBases, and Applications of Semantics (ODBASE) (2007)

92. Tsinaraki, C., Polydoros, P., Christodoulakis, S.: Interoperability support for Ontology-based Video Retrieval Applications. In: 3rd International Conference on Image and Video Retrieval (CIVR), pp. 582–591 (2004)

93. Tsinaraki, C., Polydoros, P., Christodoulakis, S.: Interoperability support between MPEG-7/21 and OWL in DS-MIRF. Transactions on Knowledge and Data Engineering (TKDE) 19(2), 219–232 (2007) (Special Issue on the Semantic Web Era)

94. Turk, M., Pentland, A.: Face recognition using eigenfaces. In: Conference on Computer Vision and Pattern Recognition, Maui, USA, pp. 586–591 (June 1991)

95. van Ossenbruggen, J., Hardman, L., Geurts, J., Rutledge, L.: Towards a multimedia formatting vocabulary. In: World Wide Web. ACM, New York (2003)

96. Vapnik, V.N.: The Nature of Statistical Learning Theory. Springer, New York (1995)

97. Walter, J., Arnrich, B.: Gabor filters for object localization and robot grasping. In: Proceedings of the 15th International Conference on Pattern Recognition, Barcelona, Spain, September 2000. ICSP, pp. 124–127 (2000)

98. Westermann, U., Jain, R.: Toward a common event model for multimedia applications. IEEE MultiMedia 14(1), 19–29 (2007)

99. Yuan, C., Niemann, H.: Neural networks for the recognition and pose estimation of 3-d objects from a single 2-d perspective view. International Journal of Image and Vision Computing 19, 585–592 (2001)

Applications of Semantic Web Methodologies and Techniques to Social Networks and Social Websites

Sheila Kinsella[1], John G. Breslin[1], Alexandre Passant[2], and Stefan Decker[1]

[1] DERI, National University of Ireland, Galway, Ireland
firstname.lastname@deri.org
[2] LaLIC, Université Paris-Sorbonne, France
alexandre.passant@paris4.sorbonne.fr

Abstract. One of the most visible trends on the Web is the emergence of "Social Web" sites which facilitate the creation and gathering of knowledge through the simplification of user contributions via blogs, tagging and folksonomies, wikis, podcasts, and the deployment of online social networks. The Social Web has enabled community-based knowledge acquisition with efforts like the Wikipedia demonstrating the "wisdom of the crowds" in creating the world's largest online encyclopaedia. Although it is difficult to define the exact boundaries of what structures or abstractions belong to the Social Web, a common property of such sites is that they facilitate collaboration and sharing between users with low technical barriers, although usually on single sites. As more social websites form around the connections between people and their objects of interest, and as these "object-centred networks" grow bigger and more diverse, more intuitive methods are needed for representing and navigating the content items in these sites: both within and across social websites. Also, to better enable user access to multiple sites, interoperability among social websites is required in terms of both the content objects and the person-to-person networks expressed on each site. This requires representation mechanisms to interconnect people and objects on the Social Web in an interoperable and extensible way. The Semantic Web provides such representation mechanisms: it can be used to link people and objects by representing the heterogeneous ties that bind us all to each other (either directly or indirectly). In this paper, we will describe methods that build on agreed-upon Semantic Web formats to describe people, content objects, and the connections that bind them together explicitly or implicitly, enabling social websites to interoperate by appealing to some common semantics. We will also focus on how developers can use the Semantic Web to augment the ways in which they create,reuse, and link content on social networking sites and social websites.

Keywords: Social web, Semantic Web, social networks, social media, FOAF, SIOC, object-centred networks.

1 Introduction

Since the foundations of the Web, it has been used to facilitate communication not only between computers but also between people. Usenet mailing lists and web forums allowed people to connect with each other and communities to form, often

C. Baroglio et al. (Eds.): Reasoning Web 2008, LNCS 5224, pp. 171–199, 2008.
© Springer-Verlag Berlin Heidelberg 2008

around topics of interest. The social networks formed via these technologies were not explicitly stated, but were implicitly defined by the interactions of the people involved. Later, technologies such as IRC, instant messaging and blogging continued the trend of using the Internet to build communities. Social networking sites - where explicitly-stated networks of friendship form a core part of the website - began to appear around 2002. Since then, the popularity of these sites has grown hugely and continues to do so.

Social networking sites such as Friendster, orkut, LinkedIn and MySpace have become part of the daily lives of millions of users, and generated huge amounts of investment. Boyd and Ellison [8] recently described the history of social networking sites (SNSs), and suggested that in the early days of SNSs, when only the SixDegrees service existed, there simply were not enough users: "While people were already flocking to the Internet, most did not have extended networks of friends who were online". A graph from Internet World Stats[1] shows the growth in the number of Internet users over time. Between 2000 (when SixDegrees shut down) and 2003 (when Friendster became the first successful SNS), the number of Internet users had doubled.

Content-sharing sites with social networking functionality such as YouTube, Flickr and last.fm have enjoyed similar popularity. The basic features of a social networking site are profiles, friend's listings and commenting, often along with other features such as private messaging, discussion forums, blogging, and media uploading and sharing. Many content-sharing sites, such as Flickr and YouTube also include some social networking functionality. In addition to SNSs, other forms of social websites include wikis, forums and blogs. Some of these publish content in structured formats enabling them to be aggregated together.

A limitation of current social websites is that they are isolated from one another like islands in a sea. For example, different online discussions may contain complementary knowledge and topics, segmented parts of an answer that a person may be looking for, but people participating in one discussion do not have ready access to information about related discussions elsewhere. As more and more Social Web sites, communities and services come online, the lack of interoperation among them becomes obvious: a set of single data silos or "stovepipes" has been created, i.e., there are many sites, communities and services that can not interoperate with each other, where synergies are expensive to exploit, and where reuse and interlinking of data is difficult and cumbersome. The main reason for this lack of interoperation is that for the most part in the Social Web, there are still no common standards for knowledge and information exchange and interoperation available. RSS could be a first solution for interoperability among social websites, but it has various limitations that make it difficult to be used efficiently in such a context, as we will see later.

However, the Semantic Web effort aims to provide the tools that are necessary to define extensible and flexible standards for information exchange and interoperability. The Scientific American article from Berners-Lee et al. [3] defined the Semantic Web as "an extension of the current Web in which information is given well-defined meaning, better enabling computers and people to work in cooperation". The last couple of years have seen large efforts going into the definition of the foundational standards supporting data interchange and interoperation, and currently a well-defined

---

[1] http://www.internetworldstats.com/emarketing.htm

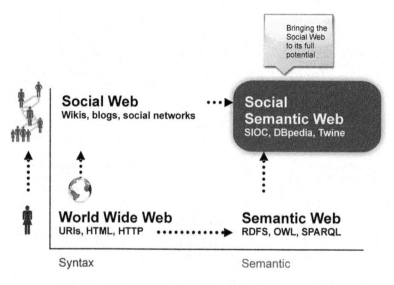

Fig. 1. The Social Semantic Web

Semantic Web technology stack exists, enabling the creation of defining metadata and associated vocabularies. The Semantic Web effort is in an ideal position to make Social Web sites interoperable. The application of the Semantic Web to the Social Web can lead to a "Social Semantic Web" (Figure 1), creating a network of interlinked and semantically-rich knowledge. This vision of the Web will consist of interlinked documents and data created by the end users themselves as the result of various social interactions, and it is modelled using machine-readable formats so that it can be used for purposes that the current state of the Social Web cannot achieve without difficulty.

A semantic data "food chain" (see Figure 2), i.e. producers, collectors and consumers of semantic data from social networks and social websites can lead to something greater than the sum of its parts: a Social Semantic Web where the islands of the Social Web can be interconnected with semantic technologies, and Semantic Web applications are enhanced with the wealth of knowledge inherent in user-generated content.

Applying semantic technologies to social websites can greatly enhance the value and functionality of these sites. The information within these sites is forming vast and diverse networks which can benefit from Semantic Web technologies for representation and navigation. Additionally, in order to easily enable navigation and data portability across sites, mechanisms are required to represent data in an interoperable and extensible way. These are termed semantic data producers.

An intermediary step which may or may not be required is for the collection of semantic data. In very large sites, this may not be an issue as the information in the site may be sufficiently linked internally to warrant direct consumption after production, but in general, may users make small contributions across a range of services which can benefit from an aggregate view through some collection service. Collection services can include aggregation and consolidation systems, semantic search engines or data lookup indexes.

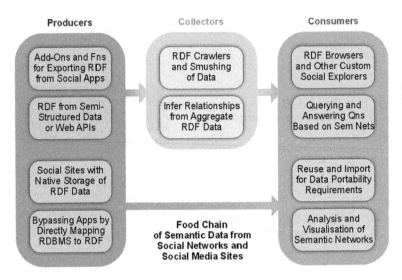

Fig. 2. A food chain for semantic data on the Social Web

The final step involves consumers of semantic data. Social networking technologies enable people to articulate their social network via friend connections. A social network can be viewed as a graph where the nodes represent individuals and the edges represent relations. Methods from graph theory can be use to study these networks, and we will describe how social network analysis can consume semantic data from the food chain.

Also, representing social data in RDF enables us to perform queries on a network to locate information relating to a person or people. Interlinking social data from multiple sources may give an enhanced view of information in distributed communities, and we will describe applications to consume this interlinked data.

In this paper, we will begin by describing various social networking sites and social websites, along with some of their limitations and initial approaches to leverage semantics in social networks, blogs and wikis. We will then describe each of the stages in the semantic data food chain in more detail, giving examples of queries that can be used to consolidate data or extract information from aggregates of data from social websites. Finally, we will give our conclusions and ideas for future work.

2 Social Websites and Approaches to Add Semantics

2.1 Social Networks

The "friend-of-a-friend effect" often occurs when someone tells someone something and they then tell you - linked to the theory that anybody is connected to everybody else (on average) by no more than six degrees of separation. This number of six degrees came from a sociologist called Stanley Milgram who conducted an experiment in the late 1960s. Random people from Nebraska and Kansas were told to send a letter (via intermediaries) to a stock broker in Boston. However, they could only give the letter to someone that they knew on a first-name basis. Amongst the letters that found their target (around 20%), the average number of links was around 5.5 (rounded up to 6). Some other related ideas include the Erdös number (the number of links required to connect scholars to mathematician Paul Erdös, a prolific writer who co-authored over 1500 papers with more than 500 authors), and the Kevin Bacon game (the goal is to connect any actor to Kevin Bacon, by linking actors who have acted in the same movie).

It is often found that even though one route is followed to get in contact with a particular person, after talking to them there is another obvious connection that was not previously known about. This is part of the small-world network theory [28], which says that most nodes in a network exhibiting small-world characteristics (such as a social network) can be reached from every other node by a small number of hops or steps.

There has been a proliferation of social networking sites (SNSs) which Boyd and Ellison [8] define as a category of websites consisting of user profiles, which other users can comment on, and a traversable social network originating from publicly articulated lists of friends. The idea behind such services is to make people's real-world relationships explicitly defined online - whether they be close friends, business colleagues or just people with common interests. Most SNSs allow one to surf from a list of friends to find friends-of-friends, or friends-of-friends-of-friends for various purposes. While the majority of these sites are for purely social reasons, others have additional purposes such as LinkedIn which is targeted towards professionals.

Before 2002, most people networked using online services such as OneList, ICQ or eVite. The first big SNS in 2002 was Friendster; in 2003, LinkedIn (a SNS for professionals) and MySpace (a band-oriented service) appeared; then in 2004, orkut (Google's SNS) and Facebook (by a college student for college students) were founded; these were followed by Bebo (targeting both high school and college students) in 2005. Social networking services usually offer the same basic functionalities: network of friends listings (showing a person's "inner circle"), person surfing, private messaging, discussion forums or communities, events management, blogging, commenting (sometimes as endorsements on people's profiles), and media uploading. In general, these sites do not usually work together and therefore require you to re-enter your profile and redefine your connections when you register for each new site.

Some motivations for SNS usage include building friendships and relationships, arranging offline meetings, curiosity about others, arranging business opportunities, or job hunting. People may want to meet with local professionals, create a network for parents, network for social (dating) purposes, get in touch with a venture capitalist, or find out if they can link to any famous people via their friends.

A key feature of these sites is community-contributed content that may be tagged and can be commented on by others. That content can be virtually anything: blog entries, board posts, videos, audio, images, wiki pages, user profiles, bookmarks, events, etc. Already, sites are being proposed where live multiplayer video games will appear in browser-embedded windows just as YouTube does for videos, with running commentaries going on about the games in parallel. Tagging is common to many social networking websites - a tag is a keyword that acts like a subject or category for the associated content. Folksonomies - collaboratively generated, open-ended labelling systems - emerge from the use of tagging on a given platform and enable users of these sites to categorise content using the tags system, and to thereby visualise popular tag usages via "tag clouds" (visual depictions of the tags used on a particular website, similar to a weighted list in visual design, that provides an overview of the different categories and topics used within a community).

Even in a small-sized SNS, there can be a lot of links available for analysis, and this data is usually meaningless when viewed as a whole, so one usually needs to apply some social network analysis (SNA) techniques[2]. Apart from comprehensive textbooks in this area [27], there are many academic tools for examining social networks and performing common SNA routines. For example, the tool Pajek[3] [2] can be used to drill down into various social networks. A common method is to reduce the amount of relevant social network data by clustering. One can choose to cluster people by common friends, by shared interests, by geography, by tags, etc.

In social network analysis, people are modelled as nodes or "actors". Relationships (such as acquaintanceship, co-authorship, friendship, etc.) between actors are represented by lines or edges. This model allows analysis using existing tools from mathematical graph theory and mapping, with target domains such as movie actors, scientists and mathematicians (as already mentioned), sexual interaction, phone call patterns or terrorist activity. There are some useful tools for visualising these models, such as Vizster[4] by Heer and Boyd [19], based on the Prefuse[5] open-source toolkit.

2.2 Leveraging Semantics in "Object-Centred" Social Networks

Jyri Engeström, co-founder of the micro-blogging site Jaiku, has theorised[6] that the longevity of social websites is proportional to the "object-centred sociality" occurring in these networks, i.e. the degree to which people are connecting via items of interest related to their jobs, workplaces, favourite hobbies, etc. On the Web, social connections are formed through the actions of people - via the content they create together, comment on, link to, or for which they use similar annotations. For many of the social websites, success has come from enabling communities formed around common interests, where the users are active participants who as well as consuming information also provide content and metadata. In this way, it is probable that people's SNS methods will continue to move closer towards simulating their real-life social interaction, so that people will meet others via something they have in common, not by randomly approaching each other- eventually leading towards more realistic interaction methods with friends à la virtual worlds like Second Life.

As more social networks form around connections between people and their objects of interest, and as these object-centred social networks grow bigger and more diverse, more intuitive methods are needed for representing and navigating the information in these networks - within and across social networking sites. Also, to better enable navigation across sites, interoperability among SNSs is required in terms of both the content objects and the person-to-person networks expressed on each site. That requires representation mechanisms to interconnect people and objects on the Web in an interoperable, extensible way [10].

---

[2] http://lrs.ed.uiuc.edu/tse-portal/analysis/social-network-analysis/
[3] http://vlado.fmf.uni-lj.si/pub/networks/pajek/
[4] http://jheer.org/vizster/
[5] http://prefuse.org/
[6] http://www.zengestrom.com/blog/2005/04/why_some_social.html

Semantic Web representation mechanisms are ideally suited to describing people and the objects that link them together in such object-centred networks, by recording and representing the heterogeneous ties that bind each to the other. By using agreed-upon Semantic Web formats to describe people, content objects, and the connections that bind them together, social networks can also interoperate by appealing to common semantics. Developers are already using Semantic Web technologies to augment the ways in which they create, reuse, and link content on social networking and social websites. These efforts include the Friend-of-a-Friend (FOAF) project[7], the Nepomuk social semantic desktop[8], and the Semantically-Interlinked Online Communities (SIOC) initiative[9]. Some SNSs, such as Facebook, are also starting to provide query interfaces to their data, which others can reuse and link to via the Semantic Web[10].

The Semantic Web is a useful platform for linking and for performing operations on diverse person- and object-related data gathered from heterogeneous social networking sites. In the other direction, object-centred networks can serve as rich data sources for Semantic Web applications. This linked data can provide an enhanced view of individual or community activity in localised or distributed object-centred social networks. In fact, since all this data is semantically interlinked using well-given semantics (e.g. using the FOAF and SIOC ontologies), in theory it makes no difference whether the content is distributed or localised. All of this data can be considered as a unique interlinked machine-understandable graph layer (with nodes as users and related data and arcs as relationships) over the existing Web of documents and hyperlinks, i.e. a Giant Global Graph as Tim Berners-Lee recently coined[11]. Moreover, such interlinked-data allows advanced querying capabilities, for example, "show me all the content that Alice has acted on in the past three months".

As Tim Berners-Lee said in a 2005 podcast[12], Semantic Web technologies can support online communities even as "online communities ... support Semantic Web data by being the sources of people voluntarily connecting things together". For example, SNS users are already creating extensive vocabularies and annotations through folksonomies [24]. Because a consensus of community users is defining the meaning, these terms are serving as the objects around which those users form more tightly-connected social networks.

2.3 Blogs

A blog, or weblog, is a user-created website consisting of journal style entries displayed in reverse-chronological order. Entries may contain text, links to other websites, and images or other media. Often there is a facility for readers to leave comments on individual entries. Blogs may be written by individuals, or by groups of contributors. A blog may function as a personal journal, or it may provide news or opinions on a particular subject.

---

[7] http://www.foaf-project.org/
[8] http://nepomuk.semanticdesktop.org/
[9] http://sioc-project.org/
[10] http://www.openlinksw.com/blog/~kidehen/?id=1237
[11] http://dig.csail.mit.edu/breadcrumbs/node/215
[12] http://esw.w3.org/topic/IswcPodcast

The growth and takeup of blogs over the past five years has been impressive, with a doubling in the size of the "blogosphere" every six or so months (according to statistics from Technorati[13]). Over 100,000 blogs are created every day, working out at about one a second. Nearly 1.5 million blog posts are being made each day, with over half of bloggers still contributing to their sites three months after the blog's creation.

RSS feeds are also a useful way of accessing information from your favourite blogs, but they are usually limited to the last 15 entries, and do not provide much information on exactly who wrote or commented on a particular post, or what the post is talking about. Some approaches like SIOC (more later) aim to enhance the semantic metadata provided about blogs, forums and posts, but there is also a need for more information about what exactly a person is writing about. Blog entries often refer to resources on the web and these resources will usually have a context in which they are being used could be described. For example a post which critiques a particular resource could incorporate a rating, or a post announcing an event could include start and end times.

When searching for particular information in or across blogs, it is often not that easy to get it because of "splogs" (spam blogs) and also because of the fact that the virtue of blogs so far has been their simplicity - apart from the subject field, everything and anything is stored in one big text field for content. Keyword searches may give some relevant results, but useful questions such as "find me all the Chinese restaurants that bloggers reviewed in Dublin with a rating of at least 5 out of 10" cannot be posed, and you cannot easily drag-and-drop events or people or anything (apart from URLs) mentioned in blog posts into your own applications.

2.4 Adding Semantics to Blogs

There have been some approaches to tackle the issue of adding more information to blog posts, so that queries can be made and the things that people talk about can be reused in other posts or applications (because not everyone is being served well by the lowest common denominator that we currently have in blogs). One approach is called "structured blogging"[14] and the other is "semantic blogging".

Structured blogging is an open-source community effort that has created tools to provide microcontent (including microformats[15] like hReview) from popular blogging platforms such as WordPress and Moveable Type. Although the original effort has tapered off, structured blogging is continuing through services like LouderVoice[16]. In structured blogging, packages of structured data are becoming post components. Sometimes (not all of the time) a person will have a need for more structure in their posts - if they know a subject deeply, or if their observations or analyses recur in a similar manner throughout their blog - then they may best be served by filling in a form (which has its own metadata and model) during the post creation process. For example, someone may be writing a review of a film they went to see, or reporting on a sports game they attended, or creating a guide to tourist attractions they saw on their travels. Not only do people get to express themselves more clearly, but blogs can start to interoperate with enterprise applications through the microcontent that is being created in the background.

---

[13] http://technorati.com/weblog/2007/04/328.html

[14] http://structuredblogging.org/

[15] http://microformats.org

[16] http://www.loudervoice.com/

Take the scenario where someone (or a group of people) is reviewing some soccer games that they watched. Their after-game soccer reports will typically include information on which teams played, where the game was held and when, who were the officials, what were the significant game events (who scored, when and how, or who received penalties and why, etc.) - it would be easier for these blog posters if they could use a tool that would understand this structure, presenting an editing form with the relevant fields, and automatically create both HTML and RSS with this structure embedded in it. Then, others reading these posts could choose to reuse this structure in their own posts, and their blog reading / writing application could make this structure available when the blogger is ready to write. As well as this, reader applications could begin to answer questions based on the form fields available – "show me all the matches from South Africa with more than two goals scored", etc.

At the moment, structured blogging tools provide a fixed set of forms that bloggers can fill in for things like reviews, events, audio, video and people - but there is no reason that people could not create custom structures, and news aggregators or readers could auto-discover an unknown structure, notify a user that a new structure is available, and learn the structure for reuse in the user's future posts.

Semantic Web technologies can also be used to ontologise any available post structures for more linkage and reuse. Blog posts are usually only tagged on the blog itself by the post creator, using free-text keywords such as "scotland", "movies", etc. (or can be tagged by others using social bookmarking services like del.icio.us or personal aggregators like Gregarius). Technorati, the blog search engine, aims to use these keywords to build a "tagged web". Both tags and hierarchical categorisations of blog posts can be further enriched using the SKOS framework. However, there is often much more to say about a blog post than simply what category it belongs in.

This is where semantic blogging comes in. Traditional blogging is aimed at what can be called the "eyeball Web" - i.e. text, images or video content that is targeted mainly at people. Semantic blogging aims to enrich traditional blogging with metadata about the structure (what relates to what and how) and the content (what is this post about - a person, event, book, etc.). Already RSS and Atom are used to describe blog entries in a machine-readable way and enable them to be aggregated together. However by augmenting this data with additional structural and content-related metadata, new ways of querying and navigating blog data become possible.

In structured blogging, microcontent such as microformats or RDFa is positioned inline in the HTML (and subsequent syndication feeds) and can be rendered via CSS. Structured blogging and semantic blogging do not compete, but rather offer metadata in slightly different ways (using microcontent and RDF respectively). There are already mechanisms such as GRDDL which can be used to move from one to the other and allows one to provide RDF data from embedded RDFa or microformats. Extracted RDF data can be then reused as would any native RDF data, and so it may be processed using common Semantic Web tools and services.

The question remains as to why one would choose to enhance their blogs and posts with semantics. Current blogging offers poor query possibilities (except for searching by keyword or seeing all posts labelled with a particular tag). There is little or no reuse of data offered (apart from copying URLs or text from posts). Some linking of posts is possible via direct HTML links or trackbacks, but again, nothing can be said about the nature of those links (are you agreeing with someone, linking to an interesting post, or are you quoting someone whose blog post is directly in contradiction with your own opinions?). Semantic blogging aims to tackle some of these issues, by facilitating better (i.e. more precise) querying when compared with keyword matching, by providing more reuse possibilities, and by creating "richer" links between blog posts.

It is not simply a matter of adding semantics for the sake of creating extra metadata, but rather a case of being able to reuse what data a person already has in their desktop or web space and making the resulting metadata available to others. People are already (sometimes unknowingly) collecting and creating large amounts of structured data on their computers, but this data is often tied into specific applications and locked within a user's desktop (e.g. contacts in a person's address book, events in a calendaring application, author and title information in documents, audio metadata in MP3 files). Semantic blogging can be used to "lift" or release this data onto the Web, as in the semiBlog[17] application (now called Shift) which allows users to reuse metadata from Apple Mac desktops in blog posts. For example, Aidan can write a blog post which he annotates using metadata about events and people from his desktop calendaring and address book applications. He publishes this post onto the Web, and John, reading this post, can reuse the embedded metadata in his own desktop applications. As well as semiBlog, other semantic blogging systems have been developed by HP[18], the National Institute of Informatics, Japan[19] and MIT[20].

Also, conversations often span multiple blog sites in blog posts and their comments, and bloggers may respond to the entries of other users in their own blogs. The use of semantic technologies can also enable the tracking of these distributed conversations. Links between units of conversation could even be enhanced to include sentiment information, e.g. who agrees or disagrees with the initial opinion.

2.5 Wikis

A wiki is a website which allows users to edit content through the same interface they use to browse it, usually a web browser, while some desktop-based wikis also exist. This facilitates collaborative authoring in a community, especially since editing a wiki does not require advanced technical skills. A wiki consists of a set of web pages which can be connected together by links. Users can create new pages, and change existing ones, even those created by other members. As well as the Wikipedia online encyclopaedia, wikis are being used for free dictionaries, book repositories, event organisation, and software development. They have become increasingly used in enterprise environments for collaborative purposes: research projects, papers and proposals, coordinating meetings, etc. SocialText[21] produced the first commercial open-source wiki solution, and many companies now use wikis as one of their main intranet collaboration tools.

There are hundreds of wiki software systems now available, ranging from MediaWiki, the software used on the Wikimedia family of sites, and PurpleWiki, where fine grained elements on a wiki page are referenced by purple numbers, to OddMuse,

---

[17] http://semiblog.semanticweb.org/
[18] http://www.hpl.hp.com/personal/Steve_Cayzer/semblog.htm
[19] http://www.semblog.org/
[20] http://theory.csail.mit.edu/~dquan/iswc2004-blog.ppt
[21] http://www.socialtext.com/

a single Perl script wiki install, and WikidPad, a desktop-based wiki for managing personal information. Many are open source, free, and will often run on multiple operating systems. The differences between wikis are usually quite small but can include the development language used (Java, PHP, Python, Perl, Ruby, etc.), the database required (MySQL, flat files, etc.), whether attachment file uploading is allowed or not, spam prevention mechanisms, page access controls, RSS feeds, etc.

The Wikipedia project consists of over 250 different wikis, corresponding to a variety of languages. The English-language one is currently the biggest, with over 2 million pages, but there are wikis in languages ranging from Gaelic to Chinese. A typical wiki page will have two buttons of interest: "Edit" and "History". Normally, anyone can edit an existing wiki article, and if the article does not exist on a particular topic, anyone can create it. If someone messes up an article (either deliberately or erroneously), there is a revision history so that the contents can be reverted or fixed by the community. Thus, while there is no pre-defined hierarchy in most wikis, content is auto-regulated thanks to an emergent consensus within the community, ideally in a democratic way (for instance, most wikis include discussions pages where people can discuss sensible topics). There is a certain amount of ego-related motivation in contributing to a wiki - people like to show that they know things, to fix mistakes and fill in gaps in underdeveloped articles (stubs), and to have a permanent record of what they have contributed via their registered account. By providing a template structure to input facts about certain things (towns, people, etc.), wikis also facilitate this user drive to populate wikis with information.

2.6 Adding Semantics to Wikis

Typical wikis usually enable the description of resources in natural language. By additionally allowing the expression of knowledge in a structured way, wikis can provide advantages in querying, managing and reusing information. Wikis such as the Wikipedia have contained structured metadata in the form of templates for some time now (to provide a consistent look to the content placed within article texts), but there is still a growing need for more structure in wikis. Templates can also be used to provide a structure for entering data, so that it is easy to extract metadata about the topic of an article (e.g. from a template field called "population" in an article about London). Semantic wikis bring this to the next level by allowing users to create semantic annotations anywhere within a wiki article text for the purposes of structured access and finer-grained searches, inline querying, and external information reuse. Generally, those annotations are designed to create instances and properties of domain ontologies (either explicit ontologies or ontologies that will emerge from the usage of the wiki itself), whereas other wikis use semantic annotations to provide advanced metadata regarding wiki pages. There are already about 20 semantic wikis in existence, and one of the largest ones is Semantic MediaWiki, based on the popular MediaWiki system. Semantic MediaWiki allows for the expression of semantic data describing the connection from one page to another, and attributes or data relating to a particular page.

Let us take an example of providing structured access to information in wikis. There is a Wikipedia page about JK Rowling that has a link to "Harry Potter and the Philosopher's Stone" (and to other books that she has written), to Edinburgh because she lives there, and to Scholastic Press, her publisher. In a traditional wiki, you cannot perform fine-grained searches on the Wikipedia dataset such as "show me all the books written by JK Rowling", or "show me all authors that live in the UK", or "what authors are signed to Scholastic", because the type of links (i.e. the relationship type) between wiki pages are not defined. In Semantic MediaWiki, you can do this by linking with [[author of::Harry Potter and the Philosopher's Stone]] rather than just the name of the novel. There may also be some attribute such as [[birthdate:=1965-07-31]] which is defined in the JK Rowling article. Such attributes could be used for answering questions like "show me authors over the age of 40" or for sorting articles, since this wiki syntax is translated into RDF annotations when saving the wiki page. Moreover, page categories are used to model the related class for the created instance.

Since Semantic MediaWiki is completely open in terms of the wiki syntax for annotating content, extracted data may be subject to heterogeneity problems. For instance, some users will use [[author of:xxx]] while others will prefer [[has written:xxx]], leading to problems when querying data. Other wikis such as OntoWiki, IkeWiki or UfoWiki assist the user when modelling semantic annotations, in order to avoid those heterogeneity issues and provide data that is based on pre-defined ontologies.

Some semantic wikis also provide what is called inline querying. A question such as "?page dc:creator EyalOren" (or find me all pages where the creator is Eyal Oren) is processed as a query when the page is viewed and the results are shown in the wiki page itself. Also, when defining some relationships and attributes for a particular article (e.g. "foaf:gender Male"), other articles with matching properties can be displayed along with the article. Moreover, some wikis feature reasoning capabilities, for example, retrieving all instances of foaf:Person when querying for a list of all foaf:Agent(s) since the first class subsumes the second one in the FOAF ontology.

Finally, just as in the semantic blogging scenario, wikis can enable the Web to be used as a clipboard, by allowing readers to drag structured information from wiki pages into other applications (for example, geographic data about locations on a wiki page could be used to annotate information on an event or a person in your calendar application or address book software respectively).

2.7 Tags, Tagging and Folksonomies

Apart from providing a means to define and manage social networks, one of the most important features of social websites is the ability to upload and share content with others, either with anyone subscribed to (or just browsing) the website or else within a restricted community. Various media files can be shared, such as pictures, videos, bookmarks, slides, etc. In order to make this content more easily discoverable, users can add free-text keywords, or tags, to any content that they upload. For example, this chapter could be tagged with 'semanticweb', 'socialnetworks', 'sioc' on a scientific bibliography management system such as bibsonomy.org. While the same content can be tagged by various users on the same system, anyone can use their own tags. Yet, most services suggest existing tags for a given item when someone begins tagging it.

The main advantage of tagging for end-users is that one does not have to learn a predefined organisation scheme (such as a hierarchy or taxonomy) and one can use the keywords that exactly fit with his or her needs. Websites that support tagging benefit from the "wisdom of the crowds" effect. Tags evolve quickly according to the needs of the users, and these tags, combined with the tagging actions and the frequency with which they are used, lead to the emergence of a folksonomy, i.e. a user-driven, open and evolving classification scheme. Moreover, tags can be used for various purposes and [17] has identified seven different functions that tags can play for end users, from topic definition to opinion forming and even self-reference.

In spite of its advantages when annotating content, tagging leads to various issues in information retrieval. Since a single tag can refer to various concepts, it can lead to ambiguity. For instance, 'paris' can refer to a city in France, a city in the USA or even a person. Moreover, various tags can be used to define the same idea, so that a user must run various queries to get the content related to a given concept. Such heterogeneity is mainly caused by the multilingual nature of tags (e.g. 'semanticweb' and 'websemantique') but also due to the fact people will use acronyms or shortened versions ('sw' and 'semweb'), as well as linguistic and morpho-syntactic variations (synonyms, plurals, case, etc.). Finally, since a folksonomy is essentially a flat organisation of tags, the lack of relationships between tags makes it difficult to suggest related content.

2.8 Adding Semantics to Tags and Related Objects

Numerous works related to the links between tags, the tagging process, folksonomies and the Semantic Web have been published during the last couple of years. We can divide these into two general approaches: the ones aiming to define, mine or automatically link to ontologies from existing folksonomies, and works based on defining Semantic Web models for tags and related objects (e.g., tagging, tag clouds, etc.).

The first set of approaches is based on the idea that emergent semantics naturally appears through the use of tags, relying on various methods to achieve this goal. For example, [26] combines automatic tag filtering, clustering and mapping with ontologies already available on the Web in order to extract ontologies from existing folksonomies in a completely-automated approach. Another approach involving a social aspect is the one defined by [24], which uses social network analysis to extract ontologies from the Flickr folksonomy, based on the way that the community shares and uses tags.

Regarding the second approach, various models have been proposed to define Semantic Web vocabularies for tagging. Representing tags using Semantic Web technologies offer various advantages: providing a uniform, machine-readable and extendable way to represent tags as well as other concepts such as tagging actions, tag clouds, the relationships between tags and the meanings that they carry. While tag-based search is the only way to retrieve tagged content at the moment (and leads to the aforementioned problems), these new models allow advanced querying capabilities such as "retrieve all the content tagged with something relevant to the Semantic Web field" or "give me all the tags used by Bob on Flickr and Alice on del.icio.us". Moreover, having tags and tagged content published in RDF allows one to easily link to it from other Semantic Web data, and to reuse it across applications.

The Tag Ontology[22] provides an initial model to represent tags and tagging actions in RDF, based on the ideas of Gruber [18] and on a common mathematical model of tagging that defines it as a tripartite relationship involving a "Tag", a "User", and a tagged "Resource". This ontology defines the Tag class by sub-classing skos:Concept,

---

[22] http://www.holygoat.co.uk/projects/tags/

which means that each tag has a given URI. This offers the ability to interlink tags together with semantic relationships, as this model permits. SCOT [20] aims to represent tag clouds, and so defines a model to represent the use and co-occurrence of tags on a given social platform, allowing one to move his or her tags from one service to another and to share tags with others. Finally, MOAT [30] aims to represent the meaning of tags using URIs of existing domain ontology instances from existing public knowledge bases (such as Geonames or DBPedia). It also provides a framework using this model, the goal of which is to let people easily bridge the gap between simple free-text tagging and semantic indexing.

Some tools already used some of these models to provide advanced and more precise querying tag-based capabilities to their users, including Gnizr, SweetWiki and int.ere.st.

3   Producers of Social Semantic Data

Applying Semantic Web technologies to online social spaces allows for the expression of different types of relationships between people, objects and concepts. By using common, machine-readable ways of expressing individuals, profiles, social connections, and content, they provide a way to interconnect people and objects on the Web in an interoperable, extensible way.

On the conventional Web, navigation of social data across sites can be a major challenge. Communities are often dispersed across numerous different sites and platforms. For example, a group of people interested in a particular topic may share photos on Flickr, bookmarks on del.icio.us and hold conversations on a discussion forum. Additionally, a single person may hold several separate online accounts, and may have a different network of friends on each. The information existing in these spaces is generally disconnected, lacking in semantics, and centrally controlled by single organisations. Individuals generally lack control or ownership of their own data.

Social spaces on the Web are becoming bigger and more distributed. This presents new challenges for navigating such data. Machine-readable descriptions of people and objects, and the use of common identifiers, would allow for linking diverse information from heterogeneous social networking sites. This would create a starting point for easy navigation across the information in these networks.

The use of common formats allows interoperability across sites, enabling users to reuse and link to content across different platforms. This also provides a basis for data portability, where users could have ownership and control over their own data and could move profile and content information between services as they wish. Recently there has been a push within the web community to make data portability a reality.

Additionally, the Social Web and social networking sites can contribute to the Semantic Web effort. Users of these sites often provide metadata in the form of annotations and tags on photos, links, blogs posts etc. social networks and semantics can complement each other. Already within online communities, common vocabularies or folksonomies for tagging are emerging through of a consensus of community members.

There are also a number of semantically-enabled social applications appearing that have been enhanced with extra features due to the rich content being created in social software tools by users. The Twine application from Radar Networks is a recent example of a system that leverages both the explicit (tags and metadata) and implicit semantics (auto tagging of text) associated with content items. Twine is a "knowledge networking" application that allows users to share, organise, and find information with people they trust. People create and join "twines" (community containers) around certain topics of interest, and items (documents, bookmarks, media files, etc., that can be commented on) are posted to these containers through a variety of methods. The underlying semantic data can be exposed as RDF by appending "?rdf" to any Twine URL. The DBpedia represents structured content from the collaboratively-edited Wikipedia in semantic form, leveraging the semantics from many social content contributions by multiple users. DBpedia allows you to perform semantic queries on this data, and enables the linking of this socially-created data to other datasets on the Web by exposing it via RDF. Revyu.com combines Web 2.0 interfaces and principles such as tagging with Semantic Web modelling principles to provide a reviews website that is integrated with Linked Data principles. Anyone can review objects defined on other services (such as a movie from DBpedia), and the whole content of the website is available in RDF, therefore it is available for reuse by other applications.

3.1 FOAF

Semantic Web technologies allow for a more expressive description of a social network, enabling the use of heterogeneous nodes and link denoting different types of objects and different types of relationships. This enables us to express a model of an object-centred network where content and other items of interest can be described along with people.

The Friend-of-a-Friend (FOAF) project was started in 2000 and defines a widely-used vocabulary for describing people and the relationships between them, as well

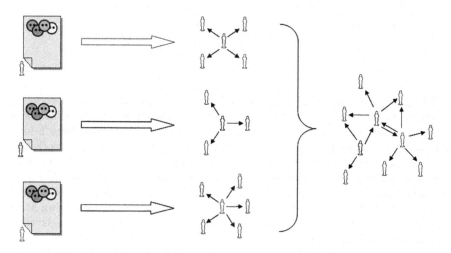

Fig. 3. Integrating social networks by using FOAF as a common representation format and having unique URIs for people

as the things they create and do. Anyone can create their own FOAF file describing themselves and their social network, and the information from multiple FOAF files can easily be combined to obtain a higher-level view of the network across various sources, as shown in Figure 3. This means that a group of people can articulate their social network without the need for a single centralised database.

FOAF can be integrated with any other Semantic Web vocabularies, such as SIOC, SKOS, etc. Some prominent social networking services that expose data using FOAF include hi5, LiveJournal, Vox, Pownce and MyBlogLog. People can also create their own FOAF document and link to it from their homepage, and exporters are available for some major social websites as Flickr, Twitter an Facebook. Such FOAF documents usually contain personal information, links to friends, and other related resources.

The knowledge representation of a person and their friends would be achieved through a FOAF fragment similar to that below.

```
<foaf:Person rdf:about="#JB">
  <foaf:name>John Breslin</foaf:name>
  <foaf:mbox rdf:resource="mailto:john.breslin@deri.org" />
  <foaf:homepage rdf:resource="http://www.johnbreslin.com/" />
  <foaf:nick>Cloud</foaf:nick>
  <foaf:depiction
rdf:resource="http://www.johnbreslin.com/images/foaf_photo.jpg" />
  <foaf:interest>
    <rdf:Description rdf:about=" http://dbpedia.org/resource/SIOC"
rdfs:label="SIOC" />
  </foaf:interest>
  <foaf:knows>
    <foaf:Person>
      <foaf:name>Sheila Kinsella</foaf:name>
      <foaf:mbox rdf:resource="mailto:sheila.kinsella@deri.org" />
    </foaf:Person>
  </foaf:knows>
  <foaf:knows>
    <foaf:Person>
      <foaf:name>Stefan Decker</foaf:name>
      <foaf:mbox rdf:resource="mailto:stefan.decker@deri.org" />
    </foaf:Person>
  </foaf:knows>
</foaf:Person>
```

The evolving requirement for distributed social networks and reusable profiles, as highlighted by efforts such as DataPortability.org, DiSo and Google's Social Graph API, can be realised through open standards like FOAF. There have been a lot of complaints in recent years about the walled gardens that are social network sites. Some of the most popular SNSs would not exist without the walled garden approach, but some flexibility would be useful. Users may have many identities on different social networks, where each identity was created from scratch. A reusable profile would allow a user to import their existing identity and connections (from their own homepage or from another site they are registered on), thereby forming a single global identity with different views.

The structure of the social network formed by relations expressed in FOAF documents on the Web has been studied in [11], particularly the small-world characteristics of the graph.

3.2 SIOC

The SIOC initiative is aimed at interlinking related online community content from platforms such as blogs, message boards, and other social websites. In combination with the FOAF vocabulary for describing people and their friends, and the Simple Knowledge Organisation Systems (SKOS) model for organizing knowledge, SIOC lets developers link discussion posts and content items to other related discussions and items, people (via their associated user accounts), and topics (using specific "tags" or hierarchical categories). As discussions begin to move beyond simple text-based conversations to include audio and video content, SIOC is evolving to describe not only conventional discussion platforms but also new Web-based communication and content-sharing mechanisms.

Since disconnected social websites require ontologies for interoperation, and due to the fact that there is a lot of social data with inherent semantics contained in these sites, there is potential for high impact through the successful deployment of SIOC. Many online communities still use mailing lists and message boards as their main communication mechanisms, and the SIOC initiative has created a number of data producers for such systems in order to lift these communities to the Semantic Web. As well as having applications to social websites, there is a parallel lack of integration between social software and other systems in enterprise intranets. So far, SIOC has been adopted in a framework of 50 applications or modules[23] deployed on over 400 sites.

A sample fragment of SIOC RDF is shown below, representing a blog post, its metadata and associated follow-up comments.

```
    <sioc:Post
rdf:about="http://johnbreslin.com/blog/2006/09/07/creating-connections-
between-discussion-clouds-with-sioc/">
    <dc:title>Creating connections between discussion clouds with
SIOC</dc:title>
    <dcterms:created>2006-09-07T09:33:30Z</dcterms:created>
    <sioc:has_container
rdf:resource="http://johnbreslin.com/blog/index.php?sioc_type=site#weblo
g"/>
    <sioc:has_creator>
      <sioc:User rdf:about="http://johnbreslin.com/blog/author/cloud/"
rdfs:label="Cloud">
        <rdfs:seeAlso
rdf:resource="http://johnbreslin.com/blog/index.php?sioc_type=user&sioc_
id=1"/>
      </sioc:User>
    </sioc:has_creator>
    <sioc:content>SIOC provides a unified vocabulary for content and
interaction description: a semantic layer that can co-exist with exist-
ing discussion platforms.</sioc:content>
    <sioc:topic rdfs:label="Semantic Web"
rdf:resource="http://johnbreslin.com/blog/category/semantic-web/"/>
    <sioc:topic rdfs:label="Blogs"
rdf:resource="http://johnbreslin.com/blog/category/blogs/"/>
    <sioc:has_reply>
```

---

[23] http://rdfs.org/sioc/applications

```
        <sioc:Post
rdf:about="http://johnbreslin.com/blog/2006/09/07/creating-connections-
between-discussion-clouds-with-sioc/#comment-123928">
            <rdfs:seeAlso
rdf:resource="http://johnbreslin.com/blog/index.php?sioc_type=comment&si
oc_id=123928"/>
        </sioc:Post>
    </sioc:has_reply>
</sioc:Post>
```

So far, work on SIOC has focussed on producing social semantic data, but the augmentation of this data with rules to aid with reasoning is the next step (for example, as discussed by the ExpertFinder initiative[24]). By combining information from one's explicitly defined social network and from implicit connections that may be derived through common activities (e.g. commenting on each other's content, participating in the same community areas), the suggestion of experts can be enhanced.

4   Collectors of Social Semantic Data

The semantic social data available on the web is distributed across numerous sources and is stored in many different formats. In some cases, this data may be published in such a way that it can be consumed directly by applications, for example in an RDF store with a SPARQL endpoint. Alternatively it may be necessary to first gather and process the data, for example when it is stored in documents which need to be crawled and indexed. In the following we describe issues with interpreting social data from mined the web, inferring relations from semantic data, and technical aspects of collecting data.

4.1   The Web as a Source of Social Network Data

Common traditional methods of collecting social network information include administering questionnaires, conducting interviews or performing observational studies, and studying archival records. There are some fundamental differences between the networks acquirable by these methods and the networks retrievable from the Internet. Extracting data from the Web presents a different set of challenges but also offers some advantages over traditional methods.

A major advantage of mining online social networks for analysis is the much lower cost of acquiring data due to the reduced time and effort involved. Also, the scale of the social information available online is unprecedented. In the past, acquisition of social network data of the order of millions of nodes would have been impossible; with the social data now freely available on the Internet it is easy. In addition, networks collected from the Web are evidence-based and objective. Unlike interviews or questionnaires, results are not dependant on the accurate recall of the subjects, who may interpret questions differently, or may be unwilling to cooperate. Furthermore, while it is unlikely you will get a 100% participation rate in a survey, especially on a large network, if you have access to a full web dataset you can analyse a whole

---

[24] http://expertfinder.info/

network. Finally, electronic data collection easily enables longitudinal studies, allowing the dynamics of networks to be investigated, as opposed to surveying, where repeated data collection would be time-consuming and maybe impossible if the subjects are unwilling or unable to repeat the survey.

However, the accuracy of social network data mined from the Internet can be highly questionable. People can easily misrepresent themselves or others. Depending on Internet usage habits, some people will have far more information available about them online than others. This means that the social networks extracted from the Web may not give a balanced representation of real-life social networks. There is also the question of how exactly to interpret information from the Internet, e.g. the strength of the relationship implied. The people on an individual's contact list on a social networking site may encompass a spectrum from close friends to distant acquaintances or even strangers. Another problem is that there are likely to be errors in Web data, for example resulting from typos, inconsistent spelling of names, and variations on names.

Semantic Web technologies can greatly assist the process of harvesting social networks. The use of common, structured formats means that social network data can easily be aggregated from multiple, heterogeneous sources. References to the same person or resource can be identified across multiple sources and consolidated. Much of the effort needed to construct a model of a social network is removed and the need for human effort is lessened. It is possible to do reasoning on the data and infer relations from certain properties. Additionally, it is possible to extract a network of typed nodes and links.

Harvesting and analysing social data from the Web raises important ethical issues. It involves using data for purposes which were not intended by the users who uploaded for their use and that of their friends. Trust and provenance of information are important aspects that should be taken into consideration. At a technical level, the ability to confirm the origin of data is important, and at a more social level, a means to express trust in sources is also required [16].

4.2 Collecting and Aggregating Data

Data on the Semantic Web is published in different ways, so different methods may be required to collect it. Additional processing may also be required to merge data from multiple sources.

Crawling. Due to the linked nature of social networks, given URIs to seed members of the network, we can follow links from these nodes to their friends, and then their friends-of-friends and so on. This can be done by simply following rdf:seeAlso links. Additional knowledge about the structure of the data can be used to improve the task. For example, the SIOC Crawler [4] uses knowledge of the ontology's structure to incrementally retrieve new SIOC data in threads.

Exporters. For some platforms, exporters are available which generate a structured RDF representation of the data. These allow information in a relational database or other structured stores to be automatically transformed into RDF. Exporters make it easy for users to maintain semantic representations of their data. For example, there are SIOC exporters available for platforms including mailing lists [12], web forums and blogs [9], and existing Web 2.0 services such as Flickr.

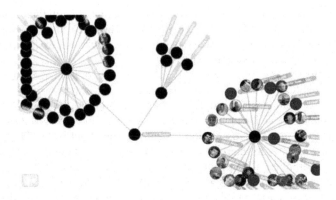

Fig. 4. Identity consolidation and social network browsing using data exported from various social websites[25]

Object Consolidation. An important task in extracting social data from the web is merging identifiers of equivalent instances occurring across different sources. This involves identifying instances representing the same object, and unifying them into one entity. Object consolidation (or "smushing") can be performed for instances which share the same value for inverse functional properties, for example foaf:mbox [23][26]. Another option is to provide explicit identification using owl:sameAs links between various resources that identify the same person or data, in spite of various URIs. This best practice allows one to unify all of their identities from various exporters (e.g. Flickr, Twitter, Facebook, etc.) and to then query their complete social network with a single entry point, as the schema below shows. Finally, it can also be achieved by considering various alternative criteria and if a certain threshold is reached in similarity between two instances, they can be considered equal [1]. Yet, while one can define such rules within his or her own restricted social graph, it may lead to unexpected results on the complete Web (for instance, since different people will sometimes have the same name) and identity management on the Semantic Web is a vast research topic.

4.3   Inferring Relationships from Aggregate Data

The simplest way of extracting a social network from the Web is to look at explicitly stated connections. Social networking sites and other types of social software allow users to express lists of friends. Blogging platforms may allow users to add a blogroll which is a list of favourite blogs. Depending on the platform, these connections may indicate a directed or undirected link between users. For example, blogroll links are frequently unreciprocated, and are therefore directed, but many social networking sites require both users to consent to the link, creating undirected ties. A sample query

---

[25] http://apassant.net/home/2008/01/foafgear

[26] Defining a property as inverse functional (owl:InverseFunctionalProperty) implies that if two resources share the same value for that property, they are the same even if they have different URIs. FOAF defines various IFPs (foaf:mbox, foaf:opened).

for extracting the social network formed by explicit foaf:knows relationships follows using the SPARQL query language.

```
PREFIX rdf: <http://www.w3.org/1999/02/22-rdf-syntax-ns#>
PREFIX foaf: <http://xmlns.com/foaf/0.1/>

SELECT ?s ?o
WHERE {
    ?s rdf:type foaf:Person .
    ?o rdf:type foaf:Person .
    ?s foaf:knows ?o .
}
```

In addition to explicitly stated person-to-person links, there are many implicit social connections present on the Web. Links between people may be inferred due to links to some common objects, for example appearing in the same pictures, tagging the same documents, replying to each others blog posts. These connections indicate relationships of varying strengths - for example, e-mail communication may be interpreted as stronger evidence of a real tie than the case of one person replying to another's blog post. Co-occurrence of names in documents would be an even weaker sign of a relation. A sample query for extracting the implicit social network formed by replies to posts follows.

```
PREFIX rdf: <http://www.w3.org/1999/02/22-rdf-syntax-ns#>
PREFIX sioc: <http://rdfs.org/sioc/ns#>
PREFIX foaf: <http://xmlns.com/foaf/0.1/>

SELECT ?author1 ?author2
WHERE {
    ?post1 rdf:type sioc:Post .
    ?post1 foaf:maker ?author1 .
    ?post1 sioc:has_reply ?post2 .
    ?post2 rdf:type sioc:Post .
    ?post2 foaf:maker ?author2 .
}
```

Instead of running queries to retrieve those implicit relationships, we can define rules to make them explicit and to state the acquaintance of users on a weblog. For instance, we can consider that there is a formal agreement relationship between two users (modelled with an arg:agreedWith relationship) as soon as one replies to a post from the other one using "I agree" in his or her answer[27]. To model this rule, we rely here on the SPARQL CONSTRUCT pattern, which can be used to produce new statements from existing ones. Thus, we can apply the following query on our triple store, and then put the created RDF graph in the store itself, so that the relationship will become explicit. The produced statements may then be used to extract a more precise social network within a blogging community when querying data.

```
PREFIX rdf: <http://www.w3.org/1999/02/22-rdf-syntax-ns#>
PREFIX sioc: <http://rdfs.org/sioc/ns#>
PREFIX foaf: <http://xmlns.com/foaf/0.1/>
```

---

[27] Ideally, more advanced pattern matching and NLP methods should be used to define agreement between two users on a weblog.

```
CONSTRUCT {
    ?author2 arg:agreedWith ?author1 .
} WHERE {
    ?post1 rdf:type sioc:Post .
    ?post1 foaf:maker ?author1 .
    ?post1 sioc:has_reply ?post2 .
    ?post2 rdf:type sioc:Post .
    ?post2 foaf:maker ?author2 .
    FILTER REGEX(?post2, "I agree", "i") .

}
```

While the above examples result in simple networks of people and untyped ties, more complex social networks consisting of multiple node and link types can also be studied. These examples are only possible through linking people and content in and across sites. Traditional, non-semantic queries like in SQL would be limited to one site and would require some kind of join on a user / content table. However the use of shared semantically-rich vocabularies makes it possible to perform operations like these on data originating from many different sources.

5 Consumers of Social Semantic Data

Once data has been collected and aggregated, or made directly accessible through a SPARQL endpoint, it can be studied or used in applications. As the information is in a structured format, it can easily be converted into the formats required by popular so-cial network analysis and visualisation tools. RDF data can also be queried directly to return some set of items that fit certain criteria that a user is interested in. In the fol-lowing we describe these two ways of using semantic social data.

5.1 Social Network Analysis

Social network analysis uses methods from graph theory to study networks of indi-viduals and the relationships between them. The individuals are often referred to as nodes or actors, and they may represent people, groups, countries, organisations or any other type of social unit. The relations between them can be called edges or ties, and can indicate any type of link, for example acquaintance, friendship, co-authorship and information exchange. Ties may be undirected, in which case the relationship is symmetric, or directed, in which case the relationship has a specific direction and may not be reciprocated.

The nodes in a social network can be seen as analogous to entities in an RDF graph, where a <subject, predicate, object> triple indicates a directed tie from the subject node to an object node, and the predicate indicates the type of the relationship. While social network analysis methods are generally applied to social networks, they can be used to analyse any kind of networked data.

We can apply mathematical measures from social network analysis to get interesting information about a social network. The more complex methods of network analysis cannot be performed directly on a graph in RDF format, but must be converted to a representation more suited to network analysis. An RDF graph can be loaded into a network analysis program such as Pajek or UCINET [7] which can perform various measures and visualisations. Alternatively, a library like JUNG [25], which provides analysis and visualisation methods, can be used to develop custom analytic or visual tools.

Locating important individuals. Centrality measures can be used to locate key players in a network [27]. Degree centrality is based on the number of connections a person has. This measure locates individuals who are connected to a large number of others. In a directed graph, indegree is the number of incoming connections and outdegree is the number of outgoing connections. Closeness centrality is calculated based on the total shortest distance to all other nodes in the network. This measure can be an indicator of people who can most quickly communicate information to the whole network. Betweenness centrality is based on the number of shortest paths on which a node lies. A node which scores highly according to this metric may occupy a strategic position and function as a bridge between different parts of the network. Flink [23] applies these measures to a social network of Semantic Web researchers in order to investigate whether the network position of a scientist is related to their performance.

Extracting communities. We may be interested in finding subgraphs or small communities within a larger graph. This enables the restriction of network to a manageable size for performing further analysis. Algorithms exist for partitioning a network into different groups, for example that of Girvan and Newman [15]. Alternatively, if there is a particular individual of interest we can extract their ego network, the area of the graph focussed around them. For example, spreading activation algorithms can activate an input node or nodes, and propagate the activation from these in order to locate those individuals which are most strongly connected and therefore receive the most activation [21].

Characterising a social network. There are some interesting whole network properties that can be investigated in order to gain an understanding of the overall structure of the network [27]. Centralisation measures the degree to which the network has a leader. Cohesiveness measures the well-connectedness of the network. These measures can also be used to make comparisons between different networks.

Visualising a social network. By creating a pictorial image of a social network, it may be possible to get an improved insight into the structure of the graph. A visual representation can help analysts to understand the network better themselves, and also aid in explaining features of the network to others [13]. Flink provides visualisations of the ego-networks of individual researchers and allows users to browse members of the Semantic Web research community.

5.2 Querying an RDF Graph

By representing social data in RDF and putting it in a store with a SPARQL endpoint, we can perform queries to extract interesting information about users, communities and content. In the following we discuss some example scenarios and illustrate them with sample queries.

Finding a person's ego-network. Identifying an ego-centric network centred around a focus person involves finding all people to whom they are connected to online. This means searching over all their accounts, and across all social networking sites of which they are a member. Below is a simple example query over FOAF data to get all friends of Persons with a particular e-mail address sha1sum. We use the hash of an e-mail address as an identifier (since the foaf:mbox_sha1sum is defined as an owl:InverseFunctionalProperty in FOAF), as the focus person is likely to have different URIs on different sites.

```
PREFIX foaf: <http://xmlns.com/foaf/0.1/>

SELECT DISTINCT ?o
WHERE {
    ?s foaf:mbox_sha1sum "9a348bd34fe67b15f388c95c2cb9b4bfc9073797" .
    ?s foaf:knows ?o .
}
```

Finding a person's implicit social links. While locating a person's explicitly stated connections goes some way to locating their social network, they may have more acquaintances with whom they are implicitly linked. It is possible to identify additional potential acquaintances of a person via objects to which they are both connected. The example below shows a query to find all people with the same workplace, school or project as the focus person. We could also consider people who are co-authors of some documents, or who have replied to each others SIOC-enabled posts.

```
PREFIX foaf: <http://xmlns.com/foaf/0.1/>

SELECT DISTINCT ?s
WHERE { {
    <http://sw.deri.org/~sheila/foaf.rdf#me> foaf:workplaceHomepage ?o

    ?s foaf:workplaceHomepage ?o .
} UNION {
    <http://sw.deri.org/~sheila/foaf.rdf#me> foaf:schoolHomepage ?o .
    ?s foaf:schoolHomepage ?o .
} UNION {
    <http://sw.deri.org/~sheila/foaf.rdf#me> foaf:project ?o .
    ?s foaf:project ?o .
} }
```

We can carry out simple reasoning by expressing a set of rules to describe when such implicit links create a social connection between people and when they may not. For example, we may decide that two people are socially connected if one posts a comment on someone else's blog post; alternatively, we may conclude that a weak link exists if two people posted on the same lengthy discussion thread and that no social connection exists.

Aggregating a person's web contribution. This means retrieving content that a person has contributed to various sources on the web; for example, all blog posts and comments on other blogs, chat logs, mailing list and forum posts. This is a difficult problem to perform with a normal search engine as people may share their name with other people, or may use different account names on different sites. A sample query over SIOC data is shown below, to get all posts created by a particular user.

```
PREFIX rdf: <http://www.w3.org/1999/02/22-rdf-syntax-ns#>
PREFIX foaf: <http://xmlns.com/foaf/0.1/>
PREFIX sioc: <http://rdfs.org/sioc/ns#>

SELECT DISTINCT ?post
WHERE {
        ?post rdf:type sioc:Post .
        ?post sioc:has_creator
<http://www.mindswap.org/blog/author/hendler/#foaf> .
    }
```

Yet, since this query is based on a precise URI, it will not retrieve content created by the same user while using another URI (for instance, http://example.org/hendler). One option to retrieve this content is to define owl:sameAs statements between this URIs and other URIs of the same user, such as:

```
    <http://example.org/hendler> owl:sameAs
<http://www.mindswap.org/blog/author/hendler/#foaf> .
```

Then, by adding these statements in the triple store that holds the data, and assuming it supports reasoning based on owl:sameAs, the query will also retrieve posts that have http://example.org/hendler as a sioc:has_creator.

A second way to do retrieve the person's contributions is to run the query not based on the URI, but based on an inverseFunctionalProperty, such as the foaf:mbox or foaf:openid. Since OpenID aims to become a standard for authentication on the web, this can be a useful way to retrieve all the contributions of a given user no matter which social website it comes from - providing the person signs in using the same OpenID URL - and this method is shown in the following query:

```
PREFIX rdf: <http://www.w3.org/1999/02/22-rdf-syntax-ns#>
PREFIX foaf: <http://xmlns.com/foaf/0.1/>
PREFIX sioc: <http://rdfs.org/sioc/ns#>

SELECT DISTINCT ?post
WHERE {
        ?post rdf:type sioc:Post .
        ?post sioc:has_creator ?user .
        ?user foaf:openid <http://example.org/hendleropenid> .
    }
```

Locating a community around a topic. We may be interested in extracting a community centred around a certain topic, using tags, keywords and other metadata to find people who are talking about a certain thing. The query below locates posts with the topic "semantic web" and returns the URIs of the authors of these posts.

```
PREFIX rdf: <http://www.w3.org/1999/02/22-rdf-syntax-ns#>
PREFIX rdfs: <http://www.w3.org/2000/01/rdf-schema#>
PREFIX sioc: <http://rdfs.org/sioc/ns#>
PREFIX foaf: <http://xmlns.com/foaf/0.1/>

SELECT DISTINCT ?author
WHERE {
    ?post rdf:type sioc:Post .
    ?post foaf:maker ?author .
    ?post sioc:topic ?post_topic .
    ?post_topic rdfs:label "semantic web" .
    }
```

Yet, this query will not retrieve posts written in French, for example, using a "web seman-
tique" string instead of the "semantic web" phrase. However, if people were encouraged to
use a precise URI instead of the simple tag, such as http://dbpedia.org/resource/Category:
Semantic_Web, we would then be able to retrieve all related posts. Moreover, using those
URIs, we can run even more advanced queries, as in the example of retrieving all posts related to the Semantic Web, we could also show those for which the topic is directly related
to this URI (e.g. RDFa, SKOS, etc.), as the following query does, emphasising the benefits
of combining data from various datasets, interlinked together in the whole Semantic Web
graph.

```
PREFIX rdf: <http://www.w3.org/1999/02/22-rdf-syntax-ns#>
PREFIX rdfs: <http://www.w3.org/2000/01/rdf-schema#>
PREFIX sioc: <http://rdfs.org/sioc/ns#>
PREFIX foaf: <http://xmlns.com/foaf/0.1/>

SELECT DISTINCT ?author
WHERE {
    ?post rdf:type sioc:Post .
    ?post foaf:maker ?author .
    ?post sioc:topic ?topic .
    ?topic ?rel <http://dbpedia.org/resource/Category:Semantic_Web> .
}
```

As with the example queries in Section 4, the queries above can be performed on data
originating from various diverse sources.

6 Future Work

A key feature of the new Social Web is the change in the role of user from just a consumer of content, to an active participant in the creation of content. For example,
Wikipedia articles are written and edited by volunteers; Amazon.com uses information
about what users view and purchase to recommend products to other users; Slashdot
moderation is performed by the readers. One area of future work in relation to social
networks on the Semantic Web is the application of semantic techniques to take even
more advantage of community input to provide useful functionality. As an example, we
will look at the area of multimedia management.

There is an ever increasing amount of multimedia of various formats becoming
available on the Internet. Current techniques to retrieve, integrate and present these media to users are deficient and would benefit from improvement. Semantic technologies
make it possible to give rich descriptions to media, facilitating the process of locating
and combining diverse media from various sources. Making use of online communities
can give additional benefits. Two main areas in which social networks and semantic
technologies can assist multimedia management are annotation and recommendation.

Social bookmarking systems like del.icio.us allow users to assign shared free-form
tags to resources, thus generating annotations for objects with a minimum amount of effort. The informal nature of tagging means that semantic information cannot be directly
inferred from an annotation, as any user can tag any resource with whatever strings they
wish. However, studying the collective tagging behaviour of a large number of users

allows emergent semantics to be derived [29]. Through a combination of such mass collaborative "structural" semantics (via tags, geo-temporal information, ratings, etc.) and extracted multimedia "content" semantics (which can be used for clustering purposes, e.g. image similarities or musical patterns), relevant annotations can be suggested to users when they contribute multimedia content to a community site by comparing new items with related semantic items in one's implicit / explicit network.

Another way in which the wisdom of crowds can be harnessed in semantic multimedia management is in providing personalised social network-based recommender systems. Liu et al. [22] presents an approach for semantic mining of personal tastes and a model for taste-based recommendation. [14] explores how a group of people with similar interests can share documents / metadata and can provide each other with semantically-rich recommendations. The same principles can be applied to multimedia recommendation, and these recommendations can be augmented with the semantics derived from the multimedia content itself (e.g. the information on those people depicted or carrying out actions in multimedia objects[28]).

Some challenges must also be overcome regarding the online identity aspect and authentication / privacy for users of social websites. An interesting aspect of social networking and media sharing websites is that most people use various websites because they want to fragment their online identity: uploading pictures of friends on MySpace, forming business contacts on LinkedIn, etc. While the Semantic Web and in particular reasoning principles (such as leveraging IFPs) allow us to merge this data and provide vocabularies, methods and tools for data portability among social websites [5], [6], this identity fragmentation must be taken into account. It implies a need for new ways to authenticate queries or carry out inferencing, by delivering data in different manners depending on which social subgraph the person requesting the data belongs to.

7 Conclusions

In this paper, we have described the significance of community-oriented and content-sharing sites on the Web, the shortcomings of many of these sites as they are now, and the benefits that semantic technologies can bring to social networks and social websites. Online social spaces encouraging content creation and sharing have resulted in the formation of massive and intricate networks of people and associated content. However the lack of integration between sites means that these networks are disjoint and users are unable to reuse data across sites. Semantic Web technologies can solve some of these issues and improve the value and functionality of online social spaces. The process of creating and using semantic data in the Social Web can be viewed as a sort of food chain of producers, collectors and consumers. Semantic data producers publish information in structured, common formats, such that it can be easily integrated with data from other diverse sources. Collectors, if necessary, aggregate and consolidate heterogeneous data from other diverse sources. Consumers may use this data for analysis or in end-user applications.

In this way, it becomes possible to integrate diverse information from heterogeneous sites, enabling improved navigation and the ability to query over data. There are

---

[28] http://acronym.deri.org/

also advantages for those interested in studying social networks, as the Semantic Web makes freely available large-scale, multi-relational datasets for analysis. In this paper, we described some methods by which consolidated facts and content can be extracted from people and content networks aggregated from multiple social networks and social websites, and we presented our ideas for future work as the focus of these sites moves more towards the provision of multimedia content.

Acknowledgments. This work was supported by Science Foundation Ireland under Grant No. SFI/02/CE1/I131.

References

1. Aleman-Meza, B., Nagarajan, M., Ramakrishnan, C., Ding, L., Kolari, P., Sheth, A.P., Arpinar, I.B., Joshi, A., Finin, T.: Semantic Analytics on Social Networks: Experiences in Addressing the Problem of Conflict of Interest Detection. In: Proceedings of the 15th International Conference on the World Wide Web, Edinburgh, Scotland (2006)
2. Batagelj, V., Mrvar, A.: Pajek - Program for Large Network Analysis. Connections 21(2), 47–57 (1998)
3. Berners-Lee, T., Hendler, J.A., Lassila, O.: The Semantic Web. Scientific American 284(5), 34–43 (2001)
4. Bojārs, U., Heitmann, B., Oren, E.: A Prototype to Explore Content and Context on Social Community Sites. In: The SABRE Conference on Social Semantic Web (CSSW 2007), Leipzig, Germany (September 2007)
5. Bojārs, U., Breslin, J.G., Finn, A., Decker, S.: Using the Semantic Web for Linking and Reusing Data Across Web 2.0 Communities; Special Issue on the Semantic Web and Web 2.0, The Journal of Web Semantics (2008)
6. Bojārs, U., Passant, A., Breslin, J.G., Decker, S.: Social Network and Data Portability using Semantic Web Technologies. In: Proceedings of the BIS 2008 Workshop on Social Aspects of the Web, Innsbruck, Austria (May 2008)
7. Borgatti, S.P., Everett, M.G., Freeman, L.C.: UCINET for Windows: Software for Social Network Analysis. Analytic Technologies, Harvard (2002)
8. Boyd, D.M., Ellison, N.B.: Social Network Sites: Definition, History, and Scholarship. The Journal of Computer-Mediated Communication 13(1) (2007)
9. Breslin, J.G., Harth, A., Bojārs, U., Decker, S.: Towards Semantically-Interlinked Online Communities. In: Gómez-Pérez, A., Euzenat, J. (eds.) ESWC 2005. LNCS, vol. 3532, pp. 500–514. Springer, Heidelberg (2005)
10. Breslin, J.G., Decker, S.: The Future of Social Networks on the Internet: The Need for Semantics. IEEE Internet Computing 11, 86–90 (2007)
11. Ding, L., Zhou, L., Finin, T., Joshi, A.: How the Semantic Web is Being Used: An Analysis of FOAF Documents. In: Proceedings of the 38th Hawaii International Conference on System Sciences (HICSS 2005) (2005)
12. Fernandez, S., Berrueta, D., Labra, J.E.: Mailing Lists Meet the Semantic Web. In: Proceedings of the BIS 2007 Workshop on Social Aspects of the Web, Poznan, Poland (April 2007)
13. Freeman, L.C.: Visualizing Social Networks. Journal of Social Structure 1(1) (2000)
14. Ghita, S., Nejdl, W., Paiu, W.R.: Semantically Rich Recommendations in Social Networks for Sharing, Exchanging and Ranking Semantic Context. In: Proceedings of the 4th International Semantic Web Conference, Galway, Ireland (November 2005)

15. Girvan, M., Newman, M.E.J.: Community Structure in Social and Biological Networks. Proceedings of the National Academy of Sciences 99(12), 7821–7826 (2002)
16. Golbeck, J., Parsia, B., Hendler, J.: Trust Networks on the Semantic Web. In: Proceedings of Cooperative Intelligent Agents, Helsinki, Finland (August 2003)
17. Golder, S., Huberman, B.A.: The Structure of Collaborative Tagging Systems. Journal of Information Sciences 32(2), 198–208 (2006)
18. Gruber, T.: Ontology of Folksonomy: A Mash-up of Apples and Oranges. International Journal on Semantic Web and Information Systems 3(2) (2007)
19. Heer, J., Boyd, D.: Vizster: Visualizing Online Social Networks. In: IEEE Symposium on Information Visualization (InfoVis 2005), Minneapolis, Minnesota (October 2005)
20. Kim, H.L., Yang, S.K., Breslin, J.G., Kim, H.G.: Simple Algorithms for Representing Tag Frequencies in the SCOT Exporter. In: The IEEE/WIC/ACM International Conference on Intelligent Agent Technology, pp. 536–539. IEEE Computer Society, Los Alamitos (2007)
21. Kinsella, S., Harth, A., Troussov, A., Sogrin, M., Judge, J., Hayes, C., Breslin, J.G.: Navigating and Annotating Semantically-Enabled Networks of People and Associated Objects. In: The 4th Conference on Applications of Social Network Analysis (ASNA 2007), University of Zurich, Switzerland (accepted, September 2007)
22. Liu, H., Maes, P., Davenport, G.: Unraveling the Taste Fabric of Social Networks. International Journal on Semantic Web and Information Systems 2, 42–71 (2006)
23. Mika, P.: Flink: Semantic Web Technology for the Extraction and Analysis of Social Networks. Web Semantics: Science, Services and Agents on the World Wide Web 3(2-3), 211–223 (2005)
24. Mika, P.: Ontologies are Us: A Unified Model of Social Networks and Semantics. In: International Semantic Web Conference. LNCS, pp. 522–536. Springer, Heidelberg (2005)
25. O'Madadhain, J., Fisher, D., White, S., Boey, Y.: The JUNG (Java Universal Network/Graph) Framework. University of California, Irvine (2003)
26. Specia, L., Motta, E.: Integrating Folksonomies with the Semantic Web. In: Franconi, E., Kifer, M., May, W. (eds.) ESWC 2007. LNCS, vol. 4519, pp. 624–639. Springer, Heidelberg (2007)
27. Wasserman, S., Faust, K.: Social Network Analysis: Methods and Applications. Cambridge University Press, Cambridge (1994)
28. Watts, D.J., Strogatz, S.H.: Collective Dynamics of 'Small-World' Networks. Nature 393(6684), 409–410 (1998)
29. Wu, X., Zhang, L., Yu, Y.: Exploring Social Annotations for the Semantic Web. In: Proceedings of the 15th International Conference on World Wide Web, Edinburgh, Scotland (May 2006)
30. Passant, A., Laublet, P.: Meaning Of A Tag: A Collaborative Approach to Bridge the Gap Between Tagging and Linked Data. In: Proceedings of the WWW 2008 Linked Data on the Web Workshop (LDOW 2008), Beijing, China (April 2008)

Applications of Semantic Web Methodologies and Techniques to Biology and Bioinformatics

Paolo Romano[1] and Andrea Splendiani[2]

[1] National Cancer Research Institute,
Largo Rosanna Benzi 10, I-16132 Genova, Italy
paolo.romano@istge.it
[2] University of Rennes 1,
2, rue Henri Le Guilloux, F-35033 Rennes, France
andrea.splendiani@univ-rennes1.fr

Abstract. Semantic Web technologies are appealing for biomedical researchers since they promise to solve many of the daily problems they face while accessing and integrating biological information that is distributed over the Internet and managed by using tools which are extremely heterogeneous and largely not compatible. On the other hand, the complexity of biomedical information and its heterogeneity, together with the need of keeping current production services steadily up and running, make the transition from current semantic-less to future semantic-aware services a huge problem.

In this paper, authors present the characteristics of biomedical information that make adoption of semantic web technologies both desirable and complex at the same time. They then present the tools and the applications that have been developed so far, including biomedical ontologies, RDF/OWL data stores, query systems and semantic-aware tools and browsers. Finally, they present community efforts and the perspectives that can be sought for short- and mid-term developments in the field.

Keywords: biological data integration, molecular biology databases, bio-ontologies, semantic web applications.

1 Introduction

The Life Sciences domain is unparalleled for the challenges that it poses to the development of Semantic Web technologies, and the possible impact of their implementation. First, it is a vast domain of research, that encompasses biomedical research and industrial biotechnology. Second, its impact on society is huge, as it offers the promise for health and industrial improvements, as well as posing important ethical and social problems. Third, it is an heterogeneous field: object of its domain are as varied as clinical records, bio-molecular measurements or mathematical models, and the way information is represented ranges from the biggest corpus of scientific literature, to specialized database systems.

C. Baroglio et al. (Eds.): Reasoning Web 2008, LNCS 5224, pp. 200–239, 2008.

In the Life Sciences, we find a tradition that in biology and medicine can be dated back to Aristotele. At the same time, the whole domain is undergoing a revolution after the discovery of DNA (desoxyribonucleic acid), that dates no more than 60 years ago, and the sequencing of the human genome, that has been drafted only a few years ago. The challenges that this scenario offers to the development of the Semantic Web are multiple.

To begin with, as a new science is being developed, there is the need for the definition of "a language" of this science. The development of ontologies for several knowledge domains of biology, as well as the attention to upper ontologies in this discipline, is a result and an example of this[1].

Furthermore, there is the need for technologies that support the integration of highly heterogeneous data. Semantic integration of data is needed not only because information can come from heterogeneous domains (such as medicine and biology): homogeneous information from different resources still cannot be easily reconciled. It should be noted that in this domain aspects of scalability, correctness and trust are, more than essential, vital.

Finally, a range of technologies relevant to the life sciences can benefit from the Semantic Web and provide use cases for it. This is, for instance, the case of text mining, where ontological knowledge can be used to improve the analysis process (e.g., in the case of anaphora resolution). It is also the case of experiments' data analysis where, as it will be shown later, ontologies can provide a-priori knowledge to improve interpretation of data.

The complexity of biomedical information and its heterogeneity, together with the need of keeping current production services steadily up and running, makes the transition from current semantic-less to future semantic-aware services a huge problem.

In this course, we will introduce the main issues related to the diffusion of the Semantic Web in the Life Sciences. We will first introduce the characteristics of biological information, and discuss the benefits that the Semantic Web can bring to Life Sciences. We will then focus separately on ontologies and on applications, and conclude with a presentation and discussion on the status of the art. To conclude this paragraph, a brief introduction to the core-domain of molecular biology is given.

1.1 A Brief Overview of Molecular Biology

"Life" is a complex system that can be seen at different levels of granularity, ranging from molecular events to ecosystems. Organisms are composed of cells, and within each cell a molecule called "DNA" holds the "genetic information" of that cell.

The "DNA" is a "nucleic acid", a molecule composed by a "sequence" of only four possible distinct components called "nucleotides". "Proteins" are molecules responsible for the main structural properties and functions of cells. They are polymers, composed of a sequence of basic blocks, usually arranged in a very specific three-dimensional structure that is strictly linked to their functionalities. Within a cell, fragments of the DNA called "genes" encode the information that the cell needs to build proteins, and therefore to grow, to process energy, to react to the environment or to communicate with other cells, just to mention some of the actual proteins functions.

---

[1] We refer to [1] for an introduction on the role of ontologies in modern science.

The process by which "genes" are used to build "proteins" is carried out in two steps. First, the sequence of the gene is copied into an intermediate molecule, called "RNA", then this is used to assemble the protein.

While the DNA is almost the same for all the cells of the same organism[2], the amount of proteins that is present in a given time in each cell is very specific to its type, state, context (tissue where it resides) and function. This is possible because "gene expression", that is the production of a given protein from its correspondent gene, is determined by a complex process of "gene regulation" that, again, depends on the above conditions. Our understanding of the basic principles of gene regulation is still evolving. Biochemical reactions that co-occur in a cell and involve a specific subset of proteins can be seen as organized in complex processes that are called "pathways". Examples of pathways include endogenous production of a substance, the processing of some kind of food (metabolism), the reproduction of a cell or its genetic regulation.

The term "genome" is used to refer to the complete set of all genes of an organism. The adjective "post genomic" is then used to characterize biology after the determination of all DNA sequences ("sequencing") of the human genome. Post genomic biology is characterized by a transition from a data poor discipline to a data intensive one, following the availability of high-throughput measurement techniques, that are able to produce a huge amount of data by analyzing hundreds of thousand biological elements at the same time. Typical of post-genomic biology are information such as the "transcriptome" of cells, that is, the amount of all RNA that is present in the cell under given condition ("trancription" is the process that leads from genes to RNA). The amount of RNA is measured by using "microarrays", that are a widespread high-throughput technology.

In general, the suffix "-ome" is used to designate the extensive observations of a feature across all homogenous elements of an organism (such as genome, transcriptome, and proteome, this referring to proteins) or, at large, it is used to designate observations that can be taken on a high-throughput scale (phenome, phsyiome, metabolome, etc...). The suffix "-omics" is used to specify the relative science.

An extensive presentation of the topics of this paragraph can be found in [2].

2   Characteristics of Biological Information

In this chapter, we focus on a subset of the Life Sciences domain that is relative to biology. This allows to offer a tractable overview of the characteristics of the information that is proper to this domain.

Biology has traditionally been based on the observation of real objects. Unlike other sciences, it doesn't focus on a limited number of variables, or on the study of a limited number of basic laws. Instead, biology is characterized by an extensive and

---

[2] Each individual organism has a specific DNA (and hence a unique genetic information encoded in it). The DNA varies minimally among individuals within a species, and the DNA of "relative" species (such as Human and Chimpanzee) are less different than DNA of "distant" species. Within an individual, variations of the DNA are possible among cells, as they differentiate to form tissues and organs.

fragmented description of facts observed in biological systems. Some basic principles and mechanisms are known, but not to the extent that it would be needed to explain or understand all observed phenomena. One of the most relevant characteristics of biological information is hence that its nature is more extensional than intensional.

This means that the number of involved entities is usually high, while the number of relations among them is limited (some figures will be given later for specific types of information). As a partial consequence of this, a disciplined nomenclature for entities is often missing. It is also important to note that "Biology" is not an homogeneous science, but a set of disciplines sharing both a common object of observation (living organisms) and some basic working principles. As some of these disciplines only recently converged, there is not a common language across biology. Let's take the example of the "gene".

The term "gene" was coined by Johannsen in 1909 to indicate the fundamental physical and functional unit of heredity (the word "gene" was derived from De Vries' term "pangen", itself a derivative of the word "pangenesis" which Darwin had coined in 1868). In the context of genetics the term "gene" refers to a unit of information. In 1944, it was demonstrated that genes are encoded in the DNA. A current definition of a gene is the following:

> *"A gene is an ordered sequence of nucleotides located in a particular position (locus) on a particular chromosome that encodes a specific functional product (the gene product, i.e. a protein or RNA molecule). It includes regions involved in regulation of expression and regions that code for a specific functional product".*

This is the definition of a physical entity. The definition of a framework that can represent both these aspects, and hence support the integration of information structured assuming one of the two interpretations, is ongoing. It should also be added that biological information is of different types, including, for example, images, numeric values, sequences, enumerations, structured records. While some kinds of biological information, such as nucleotide sequences, can be seen as inherently digital, since they are composed of four distinct molecules that can simply be represented by four distinct values, some is not (e.g., this is the case of proteomics measurements).

In synthesis, biological information is extensive, heterogeneous, largely without any structuring principles and semantically fragmented. As we will see, it is also rapidly increasing.

We will now present an overview of some specific kind of biological information: literature, databases, ontologies.

3   Which Information Is Out There?

We sketch in this chapter a brief overview of some of the most relevant types of information available in the biomedical domain. More details on ontologies and their role within Life Sciences will be provided later.

3.1 Scientific Literature

Scientific literature still is the most important source of information in biomedical research. Medline[3], the most important bibliographical resource for biomedical research[4], includes more than 16,000,000 references.

Scientific papers remain, by large, unstructured data. At the moment, there is a very limited use of structured information. An example of this are Mesh terms (see http://www.nlm.nih.gov/pubs/factsheets/mesh.html). The possibility of tagging elements and relations with identifiers has been proposed in information retrieval oriented tools (see [3] and [4] as examples). A general discussion on the evolution of the scientific literature towards a structured form can be found in [5] and [6].

It is important to point out a few facts about the scientific literature that are relevant for the diffusion and adoption of Semantic Web standards. First, not all the literature is freely accessible[5]. This situation is slowly changing with the diffusion of journals that adopt an open-access schema[6] [7]. Second, journals have a key role in the adoption of new behaviors, procedures and standards by researchers. For instance, the availability of well annotated microarray data has been fostered by the requirement of major scientific journals to deposit data into public repositories and to link to the resulting identifier in papers as a precondition for their acceptance [8]. Finally, peer reviewing is intrinsically related to collaborative environments and social networks. A few attempts have been made to connect peer-reviewing with methods for collaborative research based on social networks. See, for example, the 'Faculty of 1000 Biology' initiative at http://www.f1000biology.com/ and Nature Network at http://network.nature.com/. It is not clear yet whether these initiatives will be successful in the Life Science domain, where authoritativeness of sources, as well as privacy issues, are extremely relevant.

3.2 Databases

As previously said, in the post-genomic era, a huge amount of biological and medical information is publicly available. Genome projects, most notably the Human Genome project [9], contributed only a fraction of all available data. High-throughput technologies and emerging research domains, like the analysis of mutations of the sequences of DNA and of metabolic pathways, are contributing with even huger amounts of data.

Moreover, this information is increasing at an impressive rate[7]. The size of the EMBL Nucleotide Sequence Database [10], a repository for nucleotide sequence information, reached 131,771,254 entries in its release n. 95. It grew by 15.11% since the previous release and by 35.34% in one year.

---

[3] Medline web site: http://www.nlm.nih.gov/bsd/pmresources.html

[4] Medline is the largest component of the pubmed collection, whose content is accessible at: http://www.ncbi.nlm.nih.gov/pubmed/

[5] Traditionally, only abstracts of scientific papers have been available without the need of a subscription to the respective journal.

[6] The publication of results of research on open-access journals may soon become a requirement from some funding agencies.

[7] As the price of sequencing is dropping, it is foreseeable that in the future genome-wise information will be collected on an individual base, thus enabling personalized medicine.

ArrayExpress [11], a microarray experiments database that is maintained by the European Bioinformatics Institute (EBI), included 4,194 experiments and occupied 2,159,590 Mb in May 2008 with an increase of more than 80% from June 2007.

Biological databases vary significantly in their size and impact, some are maintained by governmental institutions, some are created and maintained by small groups or even by individual researchers. This leads to a high number of heterogeneous databases, the majority of which is of a great interest to researchers. The Nucleic Acids Research Supplement that is yearly devoted to molecular biology databases gives a precise idea of this situation. In its fourteenth edition, in 2007 [12], it listed 968 databases, 110 more than in the previous one. Also, the list of databases that are available in public SRS[8] sites includes more than 1,000 names.

Only a few databases are managed under a coordinated effort. This is the case for three nucleotide sequences data banks: the already mentioned EMBL[9] nucleotide sequence database, GenBank [13] by NCBI[10] and DDBJ [14] by NIG[11]. These three resources exchange data on a peer to peer basis under the framework of the International Nucleotide Sequence Database Collaboration (INSDC).

In general, databases on similar biological objects can be managed without a common information and data structures. For example, the IARC TP53 Somatic Mutation database [15], the UMD-TP53 database [16] and the Catalogue of Somatic Mutations in Cancer (Cosmic) [17] all refer to mutations of the TP53 human gene, but each of them has its data structure, not to mention related contents.

Often, information from specialized databases undergoes a careful procedure for removal of errors and of duplications as well as an extended annotation that is then recorded in secondary databases. This information is of the highest quality and it often represents an essential resource for researchers since it is aimed at special research interests.

It is interesting the case of UniProt [18], a Protein database born from the unification of distinct protein sequence databases and with the specific intent of generating a coherent information resource. A subset of UniProt, UniProtKB, holds accurate, consistent and rich functional annotations: fig. 1 and fig. 2 report extracts from UniProt relative to the protein Interleukin-2. In the specific case of databases involving sequences, the data curation process involves clustering sequences and determining reference sequences and variations. In fact, sequences relative to the same biological entity may vary, both because of obvious inter-individual variations (mutations), and also because of technical problems. In earlier times, sequence databases were collections of sequences experimentally determined where these identities were only partially resolved.

Sequences and microarray databases are examples of databases holding genome-wide, general information on measured entities, such as nucleotide sequences. An example of a database that addresses a specific research area can be found at http://www.immunoepitope.org/ [19]. It is noteworthy since this resource provides

---

[8]   SRS (Sequence Retrieval System) is one well known software for indexing and searching biological databases in parallel. It currently is a commercial software, but there still are academic installations. See, e.g., http://srs.ebi.ac.uk/.

[9]   European Molecular Biology Laboratory.

[10] National Center for Biotechnology Information, USA.

[11] National Institute of Genetics, Japan.

☆ Reviewed, UniProtKB/Swiss-Prot **P60568** (IL2_HUMAN)

— Contribute —
♡ Send feedback

Last modified February 26, 2008. Version 61. 🗎 History...

⁚ ⁚ Clusters with 100%, 90%, 50% identity l   Documents (8) l 🗎 Third-party data l 🔜 Customize display   TEXT XML RDF/XML GFF FASTA

Names and origin · General annotation (Comments) · Ontologies · Sequence annotation (Features) · Sequences · References · Web resources · Cross-references · Entry information · Relevant documents

Names and origin   Hide l Top

Protein names	**Interleukin-2** [Precursor]
	Also known as:
	IL-2
	T-cell growth factor
	TCGF
	Aldesleukin
Gene names	Name: **IL2**
Organism	**Homo sapiens** (Human)

General annotation (Comments)   Hide l Top

| Function | Produced by T-cells in response to antigenic or mitogenic stimulation, this protein is required for T-cell proliferation and other activities crucial to regulation of the immune response. Can stimulate B-cells, monocytes, lymphokine-activated killer cells, natural killer cells, and glioma cells. |

Ontologies   Hide l Top

Keywords

| Biological process | Immune response |
| Cellular component | Secreted |

Gene Ontology (GO)

Biological process	T cell differentiation
	Traceable author statement. Source: UniProtKB
	anti-apoptosis
	Traceable author statement. Source: UniProtKB

Sequence annotation (Features)   Hide l Top

Feature key	Position(s)	Length	Description	Graphical view

Molecule processing

| ☐ Signal peptide | 1 – 20 | 20 | | |
| ☐ Chain | 21 – 153 | 133 | Interleukin-2 | |

Amino acid modifications

| ☐ Glycosylation | 23 | 1 | O-linked (GalNAc...) | |
| ☐ Disulfide bond | 78 ↔ 125 | | | |

Natural variations

| ☐ Natural variant | 21 | 1 | Missing in FT-IL2-A and FT-IL2-B. | |
| ☐ Natural variant | 22 | 1 | Missing in FT-IL2-B. | |

Secondary structure

1   183

▌ Helix ▌ Strand   Turn

Fig. 1. Extracts of information in UniProt relative to Interleukin-2 (note the use of Gene Ontology to annotate the protein related to this database entry)

both datasets and tools useful for the characterization of sequence data in immunological studies.

Other databases are not relative to measured entities, but to information about how these entities (or generalizations of them) interact. This is the case of pathway databases, that contain information on biological processes and on interactions of the

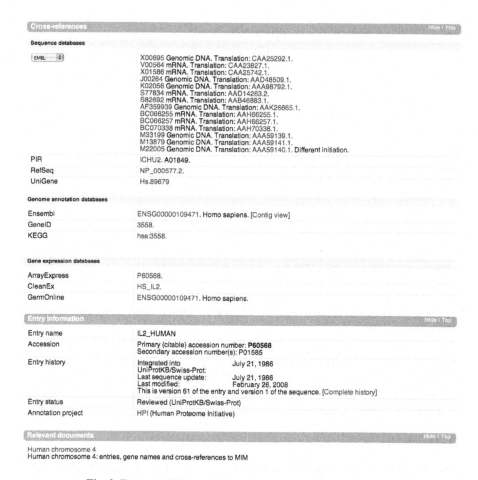

Fig. 2. Extracts of information in UniProt relative to Interleukin-2

involved bio-molecules. Among these, BioCyc [20] automatically predicts pathways for organisms, from their genome and based on information in literature. Pathways are provided on a per-species basis. For some species, the information is manually curated by researchers. Being a database that provides rich information on molecules and their interactions, a rich set of tools and visualization options is provided as interfaces to the user [21, 22]. An extract of the information provided by HumanCyc[12] [23] is presented in fig. 3.

Another relevant example is Reactome [24], where information is edited through a peer-reviewed process. Both Reactome and BioCyc publish their contents in the BioPAX format, that is based on OWL. They also publish their contents in SBML [25] an XML formats designed for biological models, on which the BioModel database is based [26]).

---

[12] HumanCyc is the pathway resource, within the BioCyc collection, dedicated to human.

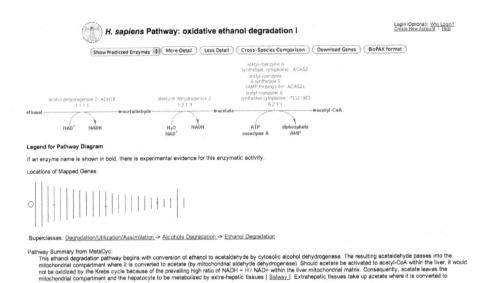

Fig. 3. Extract of the information from the HumanCyc pathway database (generated through PathwayTools v. 12)

Reactome, BioCyc and other pathway databases whose contents can be represented in the BioPAX format participate in the PathwayCommons initiative (see http://www.pathwaycommons.org/), that makes a wide collection of molecular mechanisms, including their contents, available in the OWL format[13].

3.3 Ontologies

Being a science based on an extensive observation of reality, biology (and related sciences) require an extensive terminology. Most of bio-ontologies are large terminologies organized along *"is-a"* and *"part-of"* relations[14]. This is true for traditional ontologies, such as species taxonomy or anatomy, but also for more recent ontologies, such as the Gene Ontology, that was introduced to support the consistent annotation of gene products functions.

It should be noted that although the use of ontologies is extensive, it is not omni-comprehensive: many areas still lack even a systematic nomenclature (this is the case of gene or protein names, for instance).

We have already given a brief introduction to the main characteristics and types of biological information. It is impossible to enter into further details, or to aim at comprehensiveness. The domain of Life Sciences, like Biology itself, has fuzzy boundaries, as it influences many other disciplines. It is important however at least to

---

[13] As it will discussed later, this can only be in partially considered a semantic web resource. One relevant limitation is the lack of a uniform and consistent definition of URIs for described elements.

[14] Often terms in ontologies are represented as classes, and is-a map to the subclass relation.

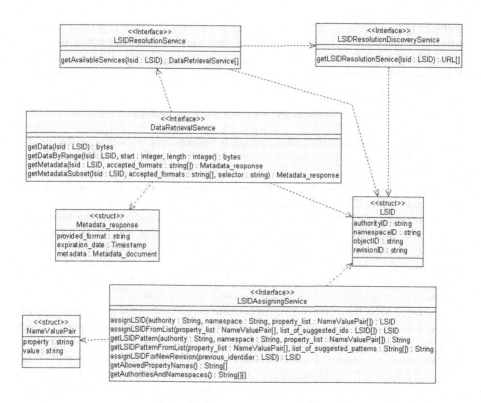

Fig. 4. LSID information data model

mention another kind of information: clinical records (a relevant entry point to this subject can be found at http://www.hl7.org/).

3.4   The Problem of Life Science Identifiers

In the Life Sciences, there are many different types of entities that are manipulated analytically. Typically, each type of entity has at least one "identifier" attribute that is used for identification, e.g. GenBank (AC000061), UniProtKB (P13569) or UniGene (Hs.489786) accession numbers. The Life Sciences Identifiers (LSIDs) specification [27, 28] fills the gap for a standardized, universal schema and system for assigning and recognizing identifiers in this domain. More specifically, it addresses the needs for a standardized naming schema for biological entities, for a service assigning unique identifiers complying with such naming schema, and for a resolving service that specifies how to retrieve the entities identified by such naming schema from repositories. These issues are particularly important for the analysis and processing of data from high-throughput techniques, including microarrays and mass spectrometry.

LSIDs are not intended to be semantically transparent or expressive, but opaque and meaningless, in that they should not be used to describe the characteristics or attributes of the resources they are referring to. LSIDs are then expressed as URN namespaces and their declarations consist of the following parts, separated by double colon: a fixed reference label ("URN:LSID"), an authority identification, a namespace identification, the object identification, and a revision identification, that is optional.

An LSID example is the following:

URN:LSID:ebi.ac.uk:SWISS-PROT.accession:P34355:3

Here, "ebi.ac.uk" specifies the authority, that is the organism or institution that define and guarantee the accuracy of the identifier, in this case the European Bioinformatics Institute (EBI). Instead, "SWISS-PROT.accession" is the namespace that specify the context, among all contexts maintained by the authority, where the identifier is defined. Finally, "P34355" is the object identifier, while "3" is the version identifier.

Together with the LSIDs format, specifications were given for enabling the implementation of services that can support a proper definition of and access to entities defined by identifiers. In this context, the LSID Resolution service provides access to entities identified by LSIDs and the LSID Assigning service supports the creation of LSIDs for given data entities. For example, this can be a function of a database system, that can assign LSIDs to each record or field in the database[15].

Recently, LSIDs have been criticized because they violate good practice of reusing existing URI schemes. This criticism has also arisen since it is more and more evident that URIs can perform similar tasks. Anyway, there are good reasons for using LSIDs. They are non-URL paths and related entities can be moved without changing them, as it would be needed for URI identifiers. Also, they start with a specific prefix, 'urn:', instead of the prefix 'http:' that is used for real web contents and services and this can reduce misunderstandings and misuses, since nobody can interpret them as standard URLs. Moreover, LSIDs foresee a specification for revisions. In this way, they can explicitly make reference to a specific version of a data. This is especially important because biological databases are continually updated, while repeatability of data analysis requires a proper definition of original data sources.

It also is noteworthy that there already are some LSID users, like the well known and used Taverna Workbench workflow management system and the BioMOBY Web Services registry.

4   Adoption of Semantic Web Tools and Techniques

With such a heterogeneous and fragmented domain, the need for semantic integration is of the outmost cruciality. This impacts both the definition of shared conceptualizations, or ontologies, and the development of tools. In this chapter, we discuss reasons for adopting Semantic Web tools, introduce briefly the current status of their use (this will be expanded in next chapters) and present shortly workflow management tools as a way for building flexible tools that can support automation of data retrieval, integration and analysis processes.

---

[15] See the entry point for the development of new LSID software and documentation at the following address: http://lsids.sourceforge.net/.

4.1   Reasons for the Adoption of the Semantic Web in the Life Sciences

As a result of the diffused and uncoordinated development of databases and information processing resources that was already introduced in previous chapters, biological data is now spread over hundreds of Internet sites where it is stored using heterogeneous Database Management Systems and, especially, data structures. There are no common information sets and the semantics of data, i.e. the actual meaning associated to each piece of data, is left to developers, buried in the software, and can be different, even when using same or similar names, thus leading to potential extremely dangerous confusions. User interfaces and query methods are also different and searching, retrieving and integrating information becomes very difficult. Data is often manually retrieved by researchers making access to several servers through their web browsers, with the "cut and paste" technique being widely used to transfer data from one web resource to another for further analysis.

The main benefits of biological data integration are the achievement of a wider view of information, the automatic carrying out of analysis involving more databases and software and the execution of large scale analysis. But some reasons make the benefits of data integration in Life Sciences even more outreaching. The availability of high-throughput data is making possible new ways for biological investigation. Traditional biology has been an hypothesis-driven science, where experiments were made to confirm (or disprove) single hypothesis, usually related to one or a few genes. Biology is now turning into a data-intensive science: measurements such as microarrays generate observations on the behavior of all genes in one or more organisms under some conditions. Analysis of these data may lead to conclusions that were not previously foreseen. Even more important, this data, and the collection of high-throughput data generated with possibly uncorrelated motivations, may reveal unknown relations among biological entities and pose the basis for reverse engineering of biological systems. Only a tight integration of all information can support an effective and real data mining.

In particular, information specific to biology, regarding molecular mechanisms active in biological systems, are of course correlated to information relative to their outcomes in other domains, such as clinical records, although in an unknown and still unpredictable way. It is not hard to imagine the benefits that proper data mining tools could provide for the discovery of new drugs: this is the basis of what is called translational medicine. The connection of molecular-level measurement of individuals to medical know-how also allows the development of personalized medicine where treatments are selected not only on the basis of the diagnosis and disease, but also on the individual genomic characterization of patients. In this context, measurement technologies are increasing in performance following a law similar to Moore's law for semiconductor transistors density.

Measurements of several organisms in several conditions are taken by many research groups, and often stored in public repositories. Private and public research and health institutes take similar measurements, and archive similar records of patients data. What is outmost missing is the integration with further available data.

Data integration is very sensible to the stability in time both of information and of desired analysis processes. It is made easier by a sound and thorough knowledge of the domain and by well defined information and data. Under these conditions, formats for data exchange and information integration can be developed. This way of acting relies on the assumption that there is a shared, well understood semantics that can lead the interpretation of these data.

This is not the case, as we have seen, in areas where knowledge is developing fast, or where different disciplines are converging. In biology, the complexity of information makes it difficult to design data models which are valid for different application domains and over time. The same hold for analysis processes since the goals and the needs of researchers evolve very quickly, according to new theories and discoveries that lead to new data types, goals, and processes.

There is hence the need for a framework for the integration of information that can cope with heterogeneous data and systems, uncertain domain knowledge, highly specialized and quickly evolving information, lack of predefined, clear goals and originality of procedures and processes.

The majority of current integration tools are based on syntactical integration: links are provided without any associated explicit meaning. Links can be explicit cross-references, implicit links (e.g., shared names) or they can be based on common contents (terms from shared vocabularies and lexicons). Their processing requires manual curation of data, which is a slow and expensive task, prone to errors.

Examples of current integration tools are those that manage local copies of the information sources (like SRS, the Sequence Retrieval System[29]). Due to this requirement, they pose many problems that mainly derive from the size of the sources, the need for continuous updates, and the need for coping with frequently modified data structures and new databases. Data warehouses have similar problems and a considerable effort is therefore required to define them and to set them up.

The Semantic Web helps addressing these issues. It supports integration of heterogeneous information systems since it operates as a de-normalized meta-database over heterogeneous information sources. It intrinsically supports a distributed environment, hence reducing problems related to the need of maintaining local copies of databases, or the need of coping with the evolution of data. It also supports evolving domain knowledge since it relies on ontologies for the definition of the semantics of information (as opposed to having a shared implicit semantics, or semantics rigidly encoded in database structures and software tools). It also supports semantic based integration methods.

4.2   Use of Semantics Technologies for Data Integration in Life Sciences

Up to now, little has been made for supporting semantics-based integration of biological data.

What is mostly needed are shared definitions of knowledge domains, i.e. ontologies. As it is shown in the following chapters, many efforts are now made towards this direction. The association of ontological terms and concepts to existing data is still in its infancy and it only refers to a few recognized and well known ontologies, like the Gene Ontology. The definition of new ontologies and their application to software and database tools is as a necessary step in order to organize information, overcoming heterogeneity of data structures and terminologies, but the problem of associating the information sources and the huge amount of data with concepts defined in these ontologies really is a big one. The addition of semantic contents in current databases would give an essential contribution to the integration of distributed biological information.

Metadata information, describing information sources, is still lacking or even missing. Some initial attempts to define the requirements and to develop some demonstration systems and prototypes started very recently, e.g. see the Resourceome presentation later.

Biological data archives or databases based on Semantic Web standards, like RDF or OWL, are also starting to appear as demonstration systems or prototypes, while a huge amount of data is still available in unstructured or partially structured formats, mainly accessible only through web user-oriented interfaces. This is mainly due to the essential requirement of keeping production systems running and accessible by means of current data analysis tools. Most recent database implementations include releases that are based on XML languages: this supports the idea that systems that can automatically convert data from such languages to RDF could be extremely useful and could constitute a crucial key for the exploitation of Semantic Web tools in this domain.

Text mining is of a fundamental importance since literature still is the most relevant information source in biomedical research[16]. Moreover, it is the most clear example of an unstructured information source whose content should be integrated with structured data in order to be fully exploited.

Search tools able to make the best use of ontologies, information sources metadata and RDF stores could also be implemented. Once RDF or OWL stores are set up, since search tools based on currently defined query standards (SPARQL, RDF Query Language) and reasoners are in place, the problem should mainly consist in the definition of proper interfaces.

Finally, it can be pointed out the increasing role that social networks techniques, such as tagging, can play in the development of integration tools for biological data. Recently, the use of Wiki systems supporting community-based genomic and proteomic annotation and revision has been proposed [30, 31]. The system proposed by Mons et al, in particular, is based on Knowlets, basic knowledge units about biological entities and their relations, that can be exported in RDF or OWL forming an archive that can then be queried by means of SPARQL. Although this prototype is too recent to demonstrate the actual usefulness of its approach, it certainly is worth further research and analysis.

4.3 The Possible Role of Workflow Management Systems

The variability of data models, software, analysis procedures and objectives fosters the adoption of workflows that can benefit from a semantic approach and / or from semantic integration tools. Pre-computed analysis of data is in fact rare in this domain, as well as rigid analysis procedures.

User-friendly graphical interfaces do not solve these issues, since they still require knowledge of services, data formats and programming skills.

Integrating biological information in a distributed, heterogeneous environment requires flexible, expandable and adaptable technologies and tools that, while able to cope with the heterogeneity of data sources and to select and manage properly the right

---

[16] The use of ontologies in text mining is two-fold. One one hand, text mining techniques can be used to populate ontologies. On the other hand, ontologies may be used to support text-mining. The latter is an ongoing area of research. Some references on this can be found at http://bootstrep.eu.

information, would allow to move towards an automation of data analysis through systems that automatically access remote sites, retrieve information from the databases of interest and/or use the appropriate software to achieve the desired analysis.

These technologies should include features like metadata management, association of concepts to systems and databases, format conversions, automatic iteration management and visualization of multiple formats.

Integration methods based on semantics, such as those that can be implemented by using reference ontologies for associating metadata descriptions to data sources seem promising and are increasingly used.

The best interface would allow researchers to build workflows by describing the required processing in natural language. This of course is a long term objective, but the adoption of Semantic Web technologies effectively supports this goal.

For instance, shared data definitions and ontologies of data types allow Web Services with homogeneous data types to be set up so that workflow systems could automatically (and transparently) introduce in the workflow transformation processors between linked services having different, but compatible, data types.

Only a few data sources currently have a semantic characterization of data: this, however, is not a strong limitation in the context of developing semantic enabled workflows, since semantics should be conveyed to Web Services, especially in terms of a shared reference ontology of bioinformatics data types and tasks. This would avoid the need for associating detailed semantic information to each and all database structural information, such as tables and attributes, that, anyway, would not be retrieved by software accessing the database remotely. In other words, semantics can be associated to the information that actually is exchanged, instead to every single piece of information.

5 Biomedical Ontologies

We outline in this chapter an overview of ontologies in use in the Life Sciences. Instead of providing a list of resources, we have chosen to introduce a few examples representative of the role of ontologies in this domain, and we trace their evolution and role in this context.

We focus on ontologies derived from large terminologies (GO), on ontologies related to data structures for complex systems (BioPAX), on ontologies that support annotation of experiment's data (OBI), and on ontologies for bioinformatics data types and tasks. We finally conclude by discussing limitations of biomedical ontologies.

5.1 GO, OBO, BFO and RO

One of the most successful ontologies in biology and bioinformatics is the Gene Ontology (GO) [32, 33]. This ontology organizes three terminologies that respectively characterize molecular functions, cellular components and biological processes along "*is-a*" and "*part-of*" relations. The resulting structure of the ontology is a directed acyclic graph (DAG). Each of the three branches contains approximately 20 to 30,000 terms[17]. An example of a fragment from this ontology can be seen in fig. 5.

---

[17] We use the word "term" here for what corresponds to the OWL notion of "Class" in OBO ontologies. We intend in this way to refer to the information resource itself, rather that what it represents.

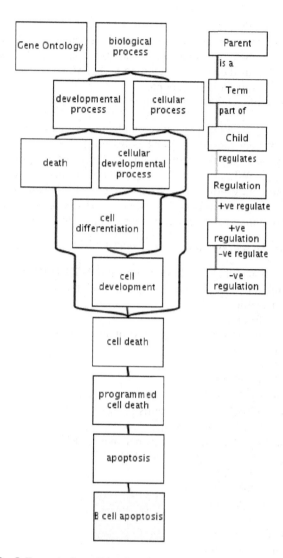

Fig. 5. Example from Gene Ontology (source: quickGO at EBI)

The Gene Ontology is expressed in the OBO language [34].

A fragment from the description in OBO of GO.

[Term]
id: GO:0001781
name: neutrophil apoptosis
namespace: biological_process
    def: "The process of apoptosis in neutrophils." [GOC:add, PMID:12752675, PMID:12960266]

synonym: "apoptosis of neutrophils" EXACT []
synonym: "neutrophil programmed cell death by apoptosis" EXACT []
synonym: "programmed cell death of neutrophils by apoptosis" EXACT []
synonym: "programmed cell death, neutrophils" EXACT []
is_a: GO:0033028 ! myeloid cell apoptosis
relationship: part_of GO:0001780 ! neutrophil homeostasis

Specific tools exist to edit and visualize ontologies expressed in OBO (a list can be found at http://www.geneontology.org/GO.tools.shtml).

Gene Ontology, and in general all ontologies that can be expressed in OBO, can also be expressed in OWL, and edited and queried by means of any standard compliant tool, like Protégé (see http://protege.stanford.edu/)[18]. When expressed in OWL, "terms" correspond to classes, the *is-a* relation to owl:subclassOf and the *part-of* relation to a property (more details on this mapping can be found in [36]).

An extract from the representation of GO in OWL

```
<owl:Class rdf:about="http://purl.org/obo/owl/GO#GO_0001781">
  <rdfs:label xml:lang="en">neutrophil apoptosis</rdfs:label>
  <oboInOwl:hasDefinition>
   <oboInOwl:Definition>
    <rdfs:label xml:lang="en">The process of apoptosis in neutrophils.
    </rdfs:label>
    ...
    <oboInOwl:hasDbXref>
     <oboInOwl:DbXref>
      <rdfs:label>PMID:12752675</rdfs:label>
      <oboInOwl:hasURI rdf:datatype=
      "http://www.w3.org/2001/XMLSchema#anyURI">
       http://purl.org/obo/owl/PMID#PMID_12752675
      </oboInOwl:hasURI>
     </oboInOwl:DbXref>
    </oboInOwl:hasDbXref>
    ...
   </oboInOwl:Definition>
  </oboInOwl:hasDefinition>
  <oboInOwl:hasExactSynonym>
   <oboInOwl:Synonym>
    <rdfs:label xml:lang="en">apoptosis of neutrophils</rdfs:label>
   </oboInOwl:Synonym>
  </oboInOwl:hasExactSynonym>
  ...
  <oboInOwl:hasOBONamespace>
   biological_process
  </oboInOwl:hasOBONamespace>
  <rdfs:subClassOf rdf:resource=
```

---

[18] A Protégé plugin allows to directly import ontologies in their OBO representation [35].

```
"http://purl.org/obo/owl/GO#GO_0033028"/>
<rdfs:subClassOf>
 <owl:Restriction>
  <owl:onProperty>
   <owl:ObjectProperty rdf:about="http://purl.org/obo/owl/obo#part_of"/>
  </owl:onProperty>
  <owl:someValuesFrom rdf:resource=
  "http://purl.org/obo/owl/GO#GO_0001780"/>
 </owl:Restriction>
</rdfs:subClassOf>
</owl:Class>
```

The Gene Ontology is extensively used to annotate the functions, processes and cellular localizations of genes and their products (proteins) in a consistent way across organisms[19] and databases (an example of which is provided in fig. 1). Its success can be explained by the fact that it provides an extensive and shared language for the annotation of biological systems. This explains its limited ontological commitment[20]: in the trade-off between depth of annotation and extensiveness, the latter is of primary importance in the post genomic era, especially when detailed information on biological systems is relatively sparse.

It is interesting to note that the Gene Ontology is used as a source of know-how on the domain for computational characterization of functions of biological systems in relation to high-throughput measurements. For instance, in a transcriptomics experiment, tenths of thousands of genes can be characterized as being over-expressed or under-expressed in accordance to a given condition. It is a standard practice, via the annotations of genes to GO terms, to derive which GO terms are more specifically associated to this condition[21], and hence which functions or processes characterize, in a first approximation, the observed data. An extensive review on these methods can be found in [37]. As it is pointed out, an improved evaluation function can be developed when more information from ontologies is taken into account.

This is only one of the possible examples of how GO (and other ontologies) can be used as a "knowledge source" to evaluate experimental evidence. Other examples include its use to evaluate microarray clustering functions and to infer the function of non characterized proteins[22] (guilt by association approach). Also, computations based on GO have been proposed as, for instance, the computation of "semantic distances" between genes (these can be derived by navigating the ontology from terms associated with one gene to terms associated with the other) [38].

---

[19] GO provides the terms used to annotate genes and proteins. The annotations are not part of GO and they are provided by several consortia (see http://geneontology.org/GO.current. annotations.shtml).

[20] These ontologies are relatively poor in the characterization of their entities and adopt a few relations. Some of them are close to taxonomies.

[21] In particular, terms are ranked according to how unlikely they can be associated to expressed genes, as opposed to a random subset of genes.

[22] Characterization of the functions or other properties of entities is of paramount importance in the post-genomic era. There is in fact a gap between the easiness with which entities can be individuated and measured, and the expensiveness of their experimental characterization.

Table 1. Example of relations from the Relation Ontology (RO) (the full list of relations can be found at http://obofoundry.org/ro/)

Name	Properties	inverse of	Definition
is_a	transitive reflexive anti-symmetric		For continuants: C is_a C' if and only if: given any c that instantiates C at a time t, c instantiates C' at t. For processes: P is_a P' if and only if: that given any p that instantiates P, then p instantiates P'.
part_of	transitive reflexive anti-symmetric	has_part	For continuants: C part_of C' if and only if: given any c that instantiates C at a time t, there is some c' such that c' instantiates C' at time t, and c *part_of* c' at t. For processes: P part_of P' if and only if: given any p that instantiates P at a time t, there is some p' such that p' instantiates P' at time t, and p *part_of* p' at t. (Here *part_of* is the instance-level part-relation.)
integral_part_of	transitive reflexive anti-symmetric		C integral_part_of C' if and only if: C part_of C' AND C' has_part C
proper_part_of	transitive	has_proper_part	As for part_of, with the additional constraint that subject and object are distinct
located_in	transitive reflexive	location_of	C located_in C' if and only if: given any c that instantiates C at a time t, there is some c' such that: c' instantiates C' at time t and c *located_in* c'. (Here *located_in* is the instance-level location relation.)

It is clear that ontologies can give an extremely important contribution in the interpretation of high-throughput data.

Beyond Gene Ontology, a wide set of ontologies is expressed by using the OBO language and is made publicly available. The acronym "OBO" stands for Open Biomedical Ontologies. A number of ontologies is collected and distributed by organizations like the NCBO[23] and are accessible through resources like BioPortal[24] or the Ontology Lookup Service at EBI [39][25]. Currently BioPortal lists over 100 ontologies. These ontologies can be generally accessed, browsed and queried through the cited websites[26].

The development of a subset of these ontologies is carried out in the context of the OBO Foundry (see http://www.obofundry.org/). This is a collaborative initiative to develop and maintain a set of orthogonal reference ontologies in the Life Science domain [40]. OBO ontologies vary in size and complexity, but they mainly consist of large terminologies structured by "*is-a*" and "*part-of*" relations.

While these ontologies are, at least in principle, independent, many relations between the entities they represent can be traced. As an example, terms in a processes ontology can have relations to terms referring to entities such as chemicals[27]. Tracing relations between entities in ontologies is an important step in order to assess their completeness and consistency and it is an active area of research [41, 42, 34]. Support for relations will be present in the next release of the BioPortal.

Tab. 1 lists some relations that can be asserted among elements within or across OBO ontologies. These relations are defined in the Relation Ontology (RO) [43] (definitions are provided in human language and fragments of first order logic). While human curation of ontologies is indispensable for their evolution, and at the current stage there is limited support for logic validation (also as a consequence of the poor axiomatic definition of these ontologies), there is a general trend to making their development more systematic and logically sound.

Within OBO, an upper ontology is being proposed to harmonize the semantics of all OBO ontologies. This is BFO (Basic Fundamental Ontology), which is a realistic, prescriptive upper ontology. It should be noted that while BFO is a reference for OBO, it doesn't encompass all of the Life Sciences.

5.2 SBML, BioPAX and PathwayCommons

Some areas of biology are amenable for a more complex formalization, given the current state of knowledge. This is the case of pathways. Pathways are aggregates of processes usually characterized by the overall effect they produce[28]. For some of them, a detailed knowledge of involved molecular events is available. Some examples of representations of pathways are provided in fig. 3, fig. 6 and fig. 7.

It is out of the scope of this paper to explain the biology behind these representations. Here, we can consider them as descriptions of processes, where different kind of elements interact in different ways with each other, with specific constraints. Such

---

[23] National Center for Biomedical Ontologies, USA, see http://www.bioontology.org/

[24] See http://www.bioontology.org/ncbo/faces/index.xhtml

[25] See http://www.ebi.ac.uk/ontology-lookup/

[26] Queries are limited to sub-string matching in Ids, terms, and descriptions.

[27] Also equivalence relations among terms from different ontologies can be stated.

[28] This is not a definitive definition of a pathway. In an organism, a network of reactions can take place, as elements (for instance proteins or chemicals) interact with each others. Pathways are sub-networks of this network of interactions, that have been defined and named as they have been recognized to implement a specific function, or simply for historical reasons. To some extent, thus, the definition of a pathway is arbitrary and related to a consensus among observers.

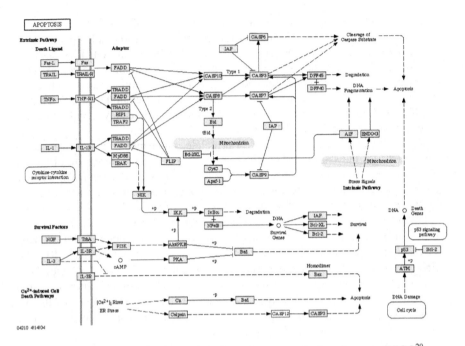

Fig. 6. Example of the representation of a pathway: apoptosis pathway in KEGG[29]

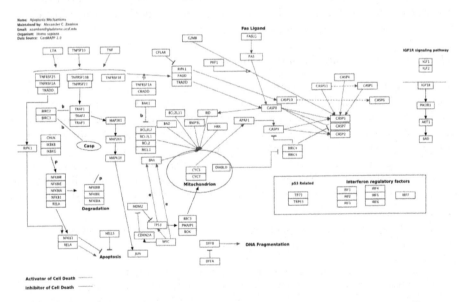

Fig. 7. Example of the representation of a pathway: apoptosis in WikiPathways[30]

---

[29] See http://www.genome.jp/kegg/
[30] See http://www.wikipathways.org/index.php/WikiPathways

information is amenable for a more complex level of formalization than the one presented in the previous section.

As a consequence, the description of pathways can be formalized in different ways that relate to, or constitute, ontologies.

A detailed representation of pathways can be expressed in the Systems Biology Markup Language (SBML) [25]. SBML is an XML language that is used to represent biochemical (dynamic) models. It is mostly designed as a standard for the exchange of models between editing and simulation tools and it is the format in which biological models are stored in the BioModels repository at EBI (see http://www.ebi.ac.uk/biomodels/).

Fragment from the SBML specification of a reaction

```
<reaction metaid="_584655" id="J1" name="MAPKKK inactivation"
reversible="false">
  <annotation>
    <rdf:RDF xmlns:rdf="http://www.w3.org/1999/02/22-rdf-syntax-ns#"
    xmlns:bqbiol="http://biomodels.net/biology-qualifiers/"
    xmlns:bqmodel="http://biomodels.net/model-qualifiers/" >
      <rdf:Description rdf:about="#_584655">
        <bqbiol:isVersionOf>
          <rdf:Bag>
            <rdf:li rdf:resource="urn:miriam:ec-code:3.1.3.16"/>
            <rdf:li rdf:resource="urn:miriam:obo.go:GO%3A0006470"/>
            <rdf:li rdf:resource="urn:miriam:obo.go:GO%3A0051390"/>
          </rdf:Bag>
        </bqbiol:isVersionOf>
      </rdf:Description>
    </rdf:RDF>
  </annotation>
  <listOfReactants>
    <speciesReference species="MKKK_P"/>
  </listOfReactants>
  <listOfProducts>
    <speciesReference species="MKKK"/>
  </listOfProducts>
  <kineticLaw>
    <math xmlns="http://www.w3.org/1998/Math/MathML">
      <apply>
      <divide/>
      <apply>
       <times/>
       <ci> uVol </ci>
       <ci> V2 </ci>
       <ci> MKKK_P </ci>
      </apply>
      <apply>
```

```
        <plus/>
        <ci> KK2 </ci>
        <ci> MKKK_P </ci>
      </apply>
    </apply>
  </math>
  <listOfParameters>
    <parameter id="V2" value="0.25"/>
    <parameter id="KK2" value="8"/>
  </listOfParameters>
  </kineticLaw>
</reaction>
```

SBML specifies the format in which information is represented and relies on a shared know-how on the domain for its interpretation. To support this, terms contributing to the description of SBML models are defined in an ontology (SBO, Systems Biology Ontology) that is part of the OBO family.

A language of particular interest for the specification of biological pathways is BioPAX[31]. BioPAX is an ontology for the representation of different kind of pathways, that has been intended to be a vehicle for the exchange of various pathway information between tools and databases. It is represented in OWL-DL.

Unlike SBML, BioPAX aims at representing and integrating metabolic pathways, signaling pathways, protein-protein interaction networks, gene regulation networks, and genetic interaction networks. It provides an encompassing framework for the description of biomolecular processes, not necessarily known with the same level of detail. As a consequence, it specifically encodes the semantics of the entities and relations it represents.

An excerpt from BioPAX (level 2[32]) that shows part of its class structure is reported in fig. 8. In this figure it can be seen, for instance, as a biochemical reaction from a metabolic pathway database and a protein-protein interaction would respectively be mapped to the classes BiochemicalReaction and MolecularReaction, both of which are subclasses of an interaction class. This is the interpretation of the commonalities among the two reactions encoded in the ontology.

As SBML, and unlike the Biological Process branch of GO , BioPAX is an ontology whose objects are the elements and relations that constitute pathways, rather than pathways themselves[33]. The class structure of BioPAX is fixed: in its standard

---

[31] See http://www.biopax.org/

[32] Development of BioPAX proceeds in levels, level-1 being able to represent metabolic pathways, level-2 including features to represent protein-protein interactions, and so on. The same development process is adopted by SBML.

[33] GO describes the relations between generic and specific pathways, and between pathways and their sub-pathways or parts. Very abstract pathways as "metabolism" can be easily represented in GO, but don't find an easy representation in a pathway ontology. On the other hand, while through annotations GO can "express" the association between genes and pathways, ontologies as BioPAX allow the description of the components of pathways, and the relations among them at a level of detail that is not captured in GO.

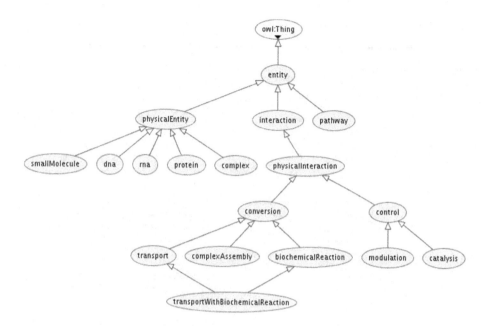

Fig. 8. Extract from the BioPAX ontology, class hierarchy

implementation, the content of pathway databases is to be expressed as instances of BioPAX classes[34].

In it original view, this ontology also serves as an exchange language. For this reason, it needs some interpretations of its constructs that are outside OWL semantics, like for instance for validation purposes. It relies for this on a purposely developed library, PaxTools[35]. As the class structure of BioPAX is fixed, it doesn't allow to leverage on DL features to support integration. The overall support for inference is limited[36]. Experiences to extend BioPAX to support reasoning can be found in [44, 45, 46].

It also has to be pointed out that the class structure of BioPAX, despite being close to an upper ontology for biology, is not derived from an upper ontology, such as BFO.

Despite these limitations, BioPAX provides the largest collection of pathways available over the Semantic Web[37]: the PathwayCommons initiative[38] makes publicly

---

[34] Pathways in BioPAX (and pathways in databases in general) are represented as a collection of individuals and relations among individuals. However this is not logically sound as most if not all of the element we can refer to in pathways are classes. In fact each of the elements represented in fig. 6 and fig. 7 represent a collection of elements existing in the world, whose abstraction is referred to in the map. A proper representation of these element is challenging, at they are classes defined on a variety of properties, including their structure and their functions.

[35] See http://www.biopax.org/paxtools/

[36] For instance, biopax lacks a simple transitive notion of containment.

[37] While the definition of BioPAX is in part outside OWL semantics, a pathway represented in compliance with the BioPAX ontology is expressed in a valid RDF.

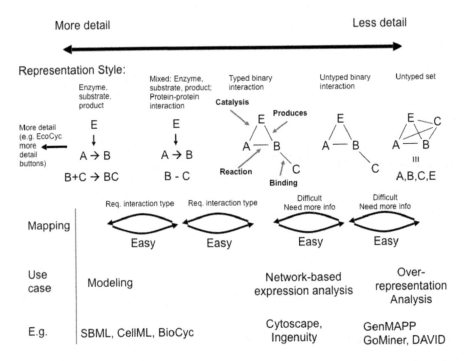

Fig. 9. Relations among pathway representations, languages, tools and detail of the information represented (courtesy of the BioPAX workgroup)

available on the web a collection of pathways available in this format. This collection currently includes Reactome, HumanCyc, Mint [47] and others, for an amount of more than 1,000 pathways, about 50,000 elements and 250,000 interactions. Limits and perspectives of pathway ontologies are discussed in the last section of this chapter. We conclude this presentation illustrating the relations among languages to represent pathways, and the detail of information that they capture, with the self-explicative fig. 9.

5.3 MIAME, MAGE, FUGO, OBI

Microarrays measurements have greatly influenced the adoption of ontologies in the Life Sciences. Since each microarray experiment is capable of measuring the expression of all the genes of an organism in a given condition, the idea of having a repository of such information, to be later mined to verify or derive hypothesis, is extremely appealing.

Given the variety of platforms, techniques, organisms, conditions, it has been clear from the early time that the design of such a repository should have included not only data, but enough meta-data to make their interpretation possible.

A recommendation for a minimum set of information to describe a microarray experiment (MIAME [48]) was then first defined. At the same time, an object model to express this information was defined with a corresponding XML language for data

---

[38] http://pathwaycommons.org

storing and exchange (MAGE-OM [49] and MAGE-ML, where MAGE stands for Microarray Gene Expression). These activities were carried out under the umbrella of a community effort driven by the Microarray and Gene Expression Data (MGED) Society[39]). The terms used in this object model were derived from an ad-hoc developed dictionary called MGED Ontology (MO). It is clear that, despite this name, the real ontology was constituted by the object model, although this was at times misunderstood [50].

It was with the MIAME initiative that some major scientific journals started to require submission to public repositories of supporting data with MIAME compliant annotations as a prerequisite for publication. This meant, e.g. in the case of the ArrayExpress database, that experiments where annotated in a machine readable, ontology based, way. Despite the limitations of this approach, MIAME, MAGE and ArrayExpress had the merit to affirm the attention for proper definition of information in a relevant area of Biology. The same approach was then followed by other areas in the Life Sciences (an example can be found in [51]).

With the advent of other high-throughput technologies, the initial goal of formally describing experimental conditions was extended to the development of FuGO (Functional Genomics Ontology) [52], that later was absorbed into the OBI project (Ontology for Biological Investigation). OBI is developed in line with OBO principles, most notably with the adoption of BFO and RO.

5.4 Ontologies for Bioinformatics Data Types and Tasks

In the context of the automation of biological data analysis processes, ontologies referring to bioinformatics data types and tasks are of the highest relevance. They can be used to characterize Web Services by annotating their inputs and outputs, data sources and computation type (e.g. alignment, homology searches, and data retrieval). Such characterization can support both search and discovery of services and interoperation between them.

The BioMOBY ontology [53] consists of three interdependent hierarchies related to data types, services and namespaces. The data types hierarchy specifies possible MOBY objects, i.e. data that can be transferred between a client and a service. The services hierarchy specifies the possible analyses, like alignments, data retrieval and computation of phylogenetic distance. The namespaces hierarchy includes contexts where services and data types can be applied.

The MyGrid ontology [54] has been designed to support semantic discovery of bioinformatics services. It includes two components: the service ontology and the domain ontology. The latter includes descriptions of data types relevant to bioinformatics and their relationships, while the former describes characteristics of Web Services. By combining the two ontologies, Web Services can then be characterized on the basis of their computation, data sources and I/O data types. A similar ontology was developed to support search and selection of workflows in the biowep workflow enactment portal [55].

The System for the Integration of Bioinformatics Services (SIBIOS) ontology [56] is used to support the discovery of Web Services within the SIBIOS workflow system.

---

[39] See http://www.mged.org/

This ontology is structured as three connected components referring to biological and bioinformatics concepts and software tools.

Finally, a proposal has recently been published for the setting up of a registry of all bioinformatics resources, the Resourceome, where the resources are annotated on the basis of a domain ontology including definitions of bioinformatics data types and tasks. This will be presented later.

It is important to point out that Web Services constitute the only interface to the systems they expose. In an automated analysis process, all data exchange is carried out through them. So, it is essential that a shared reference ontology of bioinformatics data types and tasks be used by these services. At the same time, association of semantic metadata to databases' components (such as tables and attributes) may become useless since these are not directly accessed by users. This could be an important technical improvement since this task would be difficult and very demanding, if at all possible.

5.5 Current Limitations in Biomedical Ontologies

There currently are several limitations in the definition and adoption of ontologies in the biomedical domain.

The first limitation is intrinsic to the limited knowledge we have, and indeed can have, of biological systems. This is by far incomplete and, moreover, information amenable for a rich formal representation is rare. Furthermore, biological knowledge evolves quickly and continuously, and an accurate description of systems needs to follow this evolution.

Another important limitation derives from the fact that the ontology construction process is by large a manual curation work. This has several drawbacks: it is expensive in terms of resources, hence limited in its output, and it is error-prone. There is very little logic associated to ontologies that can be used to check their consistency, or the relation with other ontologies. Often, term labels are complex expression with an inherent semantics that should be externalized and the separation of domains across ontologies is not always respected.

Development of ontologies proceeds mostly by manually collecting large dictionaries of terms, which are related to a few basic properties. In most cases, only is-a and part-of relations among terms are used, although there are exceptions to this. This is changing, since the definition of ontologies is now incorporating more logic. Also, upper level ontologies (BFO) are proposed to provide organizational principles and institutions such as NCBO and the OBO Foundry are providing a framework to support a coordinated development of ontologies along common principles. This poses the problem of versioning of ontologies. While current ontologies keep track with specific relations of obsolete terms, often even basic versioning policies are not in place[40].

Further limitations are posed by the expressivity of the language that is used to define ontologies. Most of the OBO ontologies rely on the OBO language, that can be represented in OWL. OWL is the most common language for representing ontologies.

---

[40] In some cases, ontologies may change contents without updating version number or URI, with the consequence of modifying and influencing correctness of other ontologies that include them, without ways to detect this.

However, even for ontologies having only a few relations, neither OWL nor OBO (at least in its current implementation) can easily express the semantics associated with properties such as ro:partOf, that includes the notion of time.

Pathways representation through ontologies should allow for computation on pathways. For this, languages such as OWL can only provide a limited support[41].

A relevant limitation is in the representation of quantitative aspects such as time. While time can be introduced to some extent in ontologies (and a topological view of time is already present in ontologies like BioPAX), deductions such as the one that can be derived through numeric simulations of models seems out of context for reasoning possibilities that a language for the definition of ontologies should support.

On the other hand, the expressivity of OWL-DL is promising for the integration of resources: when merging to distinct pathway ontologies, it may be possible, in theory, to identify equivalence or subsumption relations among pathways and their components. Research in this direction is still at its earlier stages [58].

It should also be noted that, in the current implementation of Semantic Web based pathway resources, even the association of stable URIs to entities is not always implemented.

For OWL ontologies of the complexity of BioPAX, a limit imposed by the language is the inability to encode information that directs the drawing of pathway diagrams, such as those previously represented. The layout and the graphical notation in pathways are used to convey meaning and readability to their representation. These should be encoded in the language. However, in the Semantic Web context, it's not possible to know a priori the extension of information to be visualized, hence such graphical information should be encoded as generic directives over pathway constructs (an approach similar to the one found in [59]).

More imitations can be found in the overall Semantic Web framework, when applied to the Life Science domain. Most notably, its complexity. Among bioinformaticians, there is a limited knowledge of OWL, that is often interpreted as an object oriented language. In this condition, many errors and omissions are generated when information present in databases is exposed over the Semantic Web [60].

Even if increasing, the role of ontologies in the overall research process is still of a limited impact. Most often, the availability of simple but extensive resources and of reliable and user friendly tools associated is more effective than resources more sophisticated, but narrower in scope and usage.

6 Biomedical Applications Semantically Aware and Based on Semantic Web Technology

As already mentioned, applications based on Semantic Web technologies are still limited in the biomedical domain, although their usefulness is more and more clear and there is a clear consensus on it. In the following paragraphs, we present some exemplar, but preliminary, prototype applications that are not widely used, but present

---

[41] The interested reader is invited to read [57] for a list of typical pathway queries. Several of these queries or deductions cannot be expressed in OWL. One example is the set of all proteins interacting with a given protein along a transitive interaction chain of N steps.

nonetheless some special interests. These applications relate to an overall registry of information resources with semantic support, two semantic browser for different applications and a system with network visualization capabilities that can extend its capabilities by adding ontological information. We conclude the chapter by trying to summarize the reasons that, in our opinion, limit the applicability of Semantic Web technologies in the the field.

6.1 Resourceome

In 2005, a proposal for setting up of a global, machine understandable registry of all bioinformatics resources, the Resourceome, was published [61]. A proposal for a general purpose resource ontology and the prototype of a web accessible semantic browser for Resourceomes were also recently proposed by the same group [62].

The starting assumption of these initiatives is that bioinformatics tools are becoming so numerous that it already is impossible for an average researcher to know of their existence, goals, and possible uses. From here, the main aim of the Resourceome should be the building of a unique repository including an explicit characterization and a hierarchical organization of the full set of bioinformatics resources and of their relationships. Many issues arise from this concept, including individuating interdependence among resources, automatic reasoning, verifying resources availability and quality, proper resources' annotation, automatic discovery and classification.

The building of the Resourceome is meant to be carried out by means of a distributed development approach, implying classification and annotation of resources done by experts of focused knowledge domains. For this to be successful, a classification schema for resources, including literature, is needed, and Semantic Web technologies can support it.

Authors proposed to set up two interconnected orthogonal ontology layers: one for the domain knowledge, and one for information on resources. It is noteworthy that resources, in this context, are not limited to software tools, databases and web services, but also include actors (people and institutions), events, courses, projects, methods and literature. Within layers, navigation can be achieved by using internal semantic relationships, mainly of the "is-a" kind. A "concerns relation" allows to connect a resource to the domain layer and it therefore permits to switch among layers.

The prototype of a semantic browser for bioinformatics Resourceomes was made available, allowing to explore main areas of bioinformatics research. The browser includes two frames: the left one allows to navigate on the resource ontology, while in the main one the domain ontology is visualized as a Direct Acyclic Graph (DAG). In the graph, resources and related topics are connected by an arc. Different icons represent different kinds of resources.

More recently, iTools, a framework for classification of resources in computational biology, was presented [63]. The proposed system is meant to be a decentralized, extensible, lightweight, scalable and portable framework to enable resource location, management, evaluation and mediation. The system also aims at facilitating communication between tool developers, users and the general community and the interoperability of resources. The system includes a schema for classifying, categorizing and integrating different computational biology resources at different space-and-time scales, coping with various computational infrastructures, and facing heterogeneous biomedical problems. An ontology of computational biology resources (NCBC Biomedical Resource Ontology, http://Bioportal.Bioontology.org/) was developed and implemented. The ontology can be used by developers as a reference for terms to describe their software tools and by researchers for seeking them.

6.2 SeaLife Browser

The objective of the SeaLife project[42] is the realization of a Semantic Web browser for Life Sciences linking the emerging eScience infrastructure with existing Web sites [64, 65]. The browser allows users to link many Web servers and services to the Web site they are visiting. This is accomplished using eScience's growing number of Web Services.

The browser automatically identifies in the page being browsed by the user those terms which are included in its background knowledge, that is held in ontologies. These terms are then linked to remote services by using links which can be defined as Semantic Hyperlinks. The SeaLife Browser therefore offers a new way for context-based data integration. When the user moves the mouse over a Semantic Hyperlink, both the definition of the term and the relevant services are shown. The user can then add the term to a list. This list is finally made available to the user when he finishes to browse the web, together with the type of identified terms and pages they were collected from.

The SeaLife Browser is also able to offer specific services that can be applied to combinations of collected terms, depending on their data type (e.g., proteins can be compared to create multiple alignments because the system knows that proteins are sequences of aminoacids: they can therefore be compared and matched to find if they are similar and which differences, e.g., substitutions, insertions, deletions, exist between them).

The main components of the browser are background ontologies, text mining and concept mapping, and service composition. Ontologies are the basis for the knowledge of the browser and can of course be varied, determining specialization of browsers. Text mining is based on natural language processing technologies that help supporting a proper, context-dependent identification of terms. Service composition supports linking ontology terms to applicable services, thus allowing the creation of mappings for complex services.

The SeaLife Browser is meant to make web servers and services available to bench scientists by using simple concepts and implementing them in a user-friendly framework. Semantic Hyperlinks are generated on the fly and allow to link biological knowledge to relevant services in a quick and effective way.

The browser's components are based on some existing systems, such as the ontology editors provided by the Gene Ontology Next Generation Project (GONG)[43], the ontology-based literature search engine GoPubMed[44], and the grid system myGrid[45].

---

[42] Sealife web site: http://www.biotec.tu-dresden.de/sealife/
[43] GONG web site: http://www.gong.manchester.ac.uk/
[44] GoPubMed web site: http://www.gopubmed.org/
[45] myGrid web site: http://www.mygrid.org.uk/

6.3 BioDash

Based on the semantic browser Haystack, Biodash [66] attempts to aggregate hetero-geneous yet related facts and statements concerning drug development into an intui-tive, visually descriptive and interactive display using an RDF-based model.

The system is applied to a scenario in which knowledge of different types (ge-nomic, pathways, diseases, chemicals, mutation data) and from different sources are brought together to support the discovery process for the drug target Glycogen Syn-thase Kinase 3 beta (GSK3b).

The browser includes a component, called "Semantic Lens", that makes it possible to filter and visualize information to isolate specific meaning within an arbitrary chunk of information, so that users are not overwhelmed by all available data. Bio-Dash uses Semantic Lens for creating Topic Views, Pathway Views, and SNP Views.

Original information, stored in XML, is converted to RDF triples by XSLT trans-formation rules.

The browser itself is an extremely user-friendly interface, specialized for the do-main, although this, of course, reduces the flexibility of the interface and it therefore limits the possibilities offered to the researcher, it makes it possible to optimize the performances of the browser.

This poses two main issues that are discussed later in the final chapter: current technologies are not yet sufficiently friendly for a large adoption by researchers and performances can only be achieved by using rigid analysis tools, but these are not the best solution in biology. The latter point is also discussed in the previous chapter, when workflow management systems are shortly introduced.

6.4 RDFScape

RDFScape is a Cytoscape[46] plugin that adds Semantic Web functionalities to this popular network analysis software [46]. It is common practice in the bioinformatics world to treat ontologies as plain annotations, sometimes making use of their inheri-tance structure to compute semantic distances or generalizations. RDFScape introduces the possibility to derive consequences from known facts represented in ontologies, standard entailments and custom inference rules defined by the user to interpret its domain. This is implemented in a highly graphical interactive environment where mul-tiple query functionalities and specific ontology rendering functions are provided. In RDFScape, the user can thus use ontologies effectively as a knowledge base, as op-posed to a set of labels representing biological entities. Furthermore, RDFScape allows to relate a-priori information represented in ontologies with observed experimental data, and to derive interpretations for the latter.

6.5 Limitations of Semantic Web Tools in Biology

Limitations exist most of all in the technical infrastructure that is needed to build Se-mantic Web applications. In particular, reasoners pose problems due to their scalability

---

[46] Cytoscape is an open source bioinformatics software platform for visualizing molecular in-teraction networks and integrating these interactions with gene expression profiles and other information. See http://www.cytoscape.org/ .

and predictability. In the ontology design phase, it is not clear how modeling choices would impact performance of reasoners, both in terms of space and time. And similar problems are present for query processors.

The result is that neither the performance of systems can be estimated a priori, nor their scalability in the extension of data they can cope with. This is, in general, a serious constraint for the diffusion and application of Semantic Web technologies that leverage on reasoning in production environments in the area of bioinformatics. A more detailed discussion on the possibility that the Semantic Web be exploited in biology is presented in the final chapter.

7 The Activity of the W3C Interest Group on Semantic Web for Health Care and Life Science

The implementation of an Interest Group for Health Care and Life Sciences (HCLSIG)[47] in the context of the Semantic Web activities of the World-Wide Web Consortium (W3C) was first discussed in October 2004 and the group was announced in November 2005. In 2008, the group was confirmed and restarted with an updated charter and new chairs.

7.1 Mission and Activities

As stated in its current charter [67], its mission is "to develop, advocate for, and support the use of Semantic Web technologies for health care and life science, with focus on biological science and translational medicine". As already stated in previous chapters, these domains depend on the interoperability of information from many knowledge areas and many analysis processes: they can therefore take profit from Semantic Web technologies.

Currently, the HCLSIG mainly provides an open forum for collecting application and implementation experiences and addresses valuable use cases. It also promotes implementations based on Semantic Web tools and technologies in conferences and workshops by giving oral communications, tutorials and courses.

Three main application domains are currently considered: biological sciences, translational medicine and health care.

HCLSIG activities in the biological sciences are meant to be concentrated on main data repositories towards their semantic integration. HCLSIG intends to assist researchers, tools and systems creators and publishers in their effort to make information accessible using Semantic Web technologies. The group intends to make large use of ontologies for data integration. Moreover, it plans to show how biological data structured by using Semantic Web standards can be used by common analysis tools.

Translational and personalized medicine are recent concepts that relates to the possibility of delivering a personalized treatment to each patient based on his/her molecular (genomic, proteomic, metabolomic, ...) characterization. Such treatment would include not only the right dose and time but also, and especially, the right drug. It

---

[47] The HCLSIG web site is available at http://www.w3.org/2001/sw/hcls/

is now clear that the same disease (phenotype) can be better fought by knowing the individual characteristics (genotype) of the patients. This implies linking genomic information of individuals from the biological laboratory with the clinic data ("bench to bedside"). Biological and medical data, however, have seldom been linked and so they do not share nomenclatures at all.

HCLSIG activities should therefore focus on connecting pre-clinical and clinical trial data with clinical decision support knowledge. One of the most interesting examples of potential applications is the creation of dashboards for enabling integration of so heterogeneous and disparate data in support to treatment and therapy selection.

HCLSIG goals in the health care domain aim both at improving care quality and at supporting clinical research. Integration of medical records and clinical research systems, such as clinical trials, is meant to be one of the first applications. This will imply efforts for standardizing and harmonizing medical data. Also, the development of ontologies for clinical medicine and investigations and of mappings between terminologies will be carried out.

Five task forces have been defined within the HCLSIG in order to address key areas where implementation of Semantic Web technologies may best be exploited. These includes: BIORDF (Structured Data to RDF), Scientific Publishing, Ontologies, Adaptive Healthcare Protocols and Pathways, Drug Safety and Efficacy. Their activity did not yet started, but for the BIORDF group, that already was active in the previous years. The main goal of the BIORDF group is the exploration of the effectiveness of cur-rent tools for making biomedical data available as RDF. For this, a specific use case was defined, referring to the creation of an integrated neuroscience data environment based on RDF and OWL.

One of the most interesting products to the realization of which the HCLSIG is actively collaborating is the GRDDL. Gleaning Resource Descriptions from Dialects of Languages (GRDDL) is a known technique for extracting RDF data from XML structured documents[48]. Of course, special transformation rules are needed for each XML schema, depending also on application objectives. Rules can either be specified in the head of the document, by using XSLT, or in an external file, where they can be defined through a metadata profile or a namespace document. In the latter case, needed transformations are retrieved from the Internet by using appropriate methods, as described in the GRDDL specification.

GRDDL can be particularly relevant for biomedical information because this is often expressed in XHTML, as a result of a progressive evolution of documents which were first designed for access through web browsers and therefore made available by using plain HTML. Also, extraction of biomedical data from XML sources may be useful, since more and more biological databases are now being stored by using XML languages.

By means of GRDDL, researchers have the possibility of transforming data in a coherent RDF archive and, then, of applying all Semantic Web tools, like reasoners and query languages, while at the same time integrating data from diverse sources by using reference ontologies.

---

[48] GRDDL Working Group site: http://www.w3.org/2001/sw/grddl-wg/. See also the GRDDL Health Care Use Case at http://www.w3.org/TR/2007/NOTE-grddl-scenarios-20070406/#health_care_use_case

7.2 The Banff Demonstration

A demonstration of current and perspective possibilities offered by Semantic Web technologies was given at WWW2007 in Banff. Related information can be found in the ESW Wiki site at http://esw.w3.org/topic/HCLS/Banff2007Demo. A detailed description of the demonstration and of related technical choices and implementation specifications is impossible to be reported here. In this paper we only summarize essential information. The complete and up-to-date description can be found in [68]. In [69] goals, methods and some results are also presented.

At the basis of the demonstration is a biomedical knowledge base that integrates 15 distinct data sources using Semantic Web technologies. The system was constructed using open source technologies for storing data and it was queried by using the SPARQL language for answering complex queries allowing to identify genes involved in Alzheimer's Disease.

The knowledge base assembles several resources with the aim of integrating related knowledge and providing insight into the mechanisms of the disease. In the demo, information about signal transduction pathways, CA1 Pyramidal Neurons (CA1PN), their genes, and gene products, were integrated and a query was generated with the aim of identifying drug target candidates.

Information sources included, among the others, ontologies (GO, Galen, all OBO ontologies), literature and nomenclature (Medline, MeSH), genomic sources (HomoloGene, GOA) and Alzheimer specific sources (Semantic Web Applications in Neuromedicine, SWAN). Incorporated data created a total of approximately 350M triples occupying approximately 20GB when stored in RDF.

The scientific question was summarized as "What genes are involved in signal transduction that are related to pyramidal neurons?". A complex query was created by using SPARQL. This task was certainly not at the level of an average biologist and implied a hard work. The query searched for gene names and processes from four data sources within the knowledge base, namely MeSH was used to retrieve papers related to pyramidal neurons, these were retrieved from Medline (through PubMed) for information on involved genes whose data was retrieved from Entrez Gene and, with support from Gene Ontology, checked for signal transduction function.

Results showed that many genes were indeed linked to Alzheimer disease through the activity of the gamma secretase (presenilin) protein.

8 Conclusions: Short- and Mid-Term Perspectives of a Semantic Biomedical Web

The promises of the Semantic Web can really be of a paramount importance for Life Sciences and, in particular, for bioinformatics.

In the BioDash paper[66], authors defined six areas where Semantic Web technologies can indeed offer a critical support: i) database conversions and wrappers; ii) unique identifiers, supported by the Semantic Web URI model; iii) coordination and management of terminologies and ontologies; iv) tools and viewers conversant in RDF-OWL; v) knowledge encoding: theories, hypotheses, models; vi) semantics accounts and channels: store and share annotations based on the Semantic Web.

Benefits have been already discussed by many researchers, including, e.g., participants of the HCLSIG. In the introduction to the demonstration presented at WWW08, Susie Stephens proposed many possible advantages. Fusion of data across many scientific disciplines is especially relevant for Life Sciences recent developments, including translational medicine and systems biology. Easier recombination of data can be supported by the use of ontologies and by unique identifiers. Querying of data at different levels of granularity can be easily implemented by the use of proper selections of data subsets, e.g. above cited BioDash semantic lens.

Further benefits can derive from the automation of data retrieval and analysis, i.e. from the machine processable approach that is specially adequate to Semantic Web technologies. Such benefits include the achievement of inferences across data sets, that is made possible by the nature of RDF triples and the proper use of query languages and reasoning tools, and the assessment of data for inconsistencies, that can also be implemented by querying and reasoning on data sets.

The HCLSIG demonstration showed that some of these advantages can already be achieved in some domains, where data structures and supporting ontologies are adequate. Unfortunately, this is possible only in selected cases.

Undoubtedly, there is still a lot to do before these optimistic hypothesis can be applied to routine activity of researchers. Indeed, the current phase can still be considered as a pioneering one, in which scientists are getting familiar and becoming aware of the possibilities and possible scenarios that are offered by this framework, and data providers are developing new tools and improving existing ones, so that they can really support semantics-based applications. At the same time, related technologies and tools still need to be improved and adapted or tuned.

Moreover, the benefits of using the Semantic Web approach need to be proved, in order for developers and maintainers of services to be willing to switch or improve current implementations, since the related paradigm shift for tools development and maintenance would involve a huge effort. The HCLSIG has provided an important contribution to this aim too, most notably with the demonstrations and tutorials proposed in many workshops.

As to current viability of Semantic Web tools for the biomedical domain, in general RDF related technologies, like triple stores or SPARQL, are well established, given their research status. Most of ontologies are available in RDF or OWL format. The adoption of OWL semantics is on the other hand lagging behind.

Controlled vocabularies and ontological frameworks already acquired a wide diffusion in biomedical sciences. Now, one of the main issues consists in bridging them. Centers like the National Center for Biomedical Ontology (NCBO, http://www.bioontology.org/) offers a repository and tools for ontologies' curation and integration.

Scientists should be urged to expose their data and should be instructed on how to present these to the world, and on how to identify and represent them. In this, the experience with MAGE, that was reported above in this paper, and the consequent role of some main scientific journals set a reference. They require deposit of well annotated data in public repositories as a condition for publication of results. Similar statements should be proposed, supported and defined for the routine use of ontologies and shared data models and languages.

Also data sharing in the community is a major necessity. In a first approximation, data can also be kept as they are, i.e. in their current structures, systems and formats, while semantic layers and links can be built upon them by the community itself. In some cases, some initiatives can take a catalytic role in this, as are the cases of the already cited OBO foundry and Pathway Commons.

It should be noted again that not all information in the Life Sciences domain shares the same degrees of openness. Microarrays are at one extreme, where public repositories, exchange formats and ontologies to annotate data exist. Instead, proteomics for instance is relatively poor in public available data, and this limits the development of effective solutions to integrate this kind of information. Other areas, like clinical data, pose even more sensitive privacy problems.

In general, important concerns of life scientists about the data are trust and provenance and transparency. Actually, moving from the current scenario, where every single information is double checked as to its origin, to the Semantic Web scenario, where the system is able to extract information and, indeed, mine new data, can only be pursued in a transparent environment where origin of data and relations between information can be effectively shown to the researcher.

As for the Semantic Web technology, it is generally considered complicated. End users would like to have friendly tools and to find everything "on their desktop". Developers in the bioinformatics area are often Object Modeling and XML oriented: semantics is usually embedded in the software that manages and analyzes the data. In order to facilitate the advent of the Semantic Web, this knowledge should be removed from the code and presented along the data as an interpretation layer, thus realizing a shift from "intelligence in the software" to "intelligence in the data".

Acknowledgments. This work has partially been carried out with the contribution of the Italian Ministry for Education, University and scientific and technical Research (MIUR) Strategic Projects "Oncology over Internet" and "Laboratory of Interdisciplinary Technologies for Bioinformatics", and partially carried out in the context of the EC's 6th fp project BOOTStrep (Bootstrapping Of Ontologies and Terminologies STrategic REsearch Project).

References

[1] Spear, A.D.: Ontology for the Twenty First Century: An Introduction with Recommendations, Saarbruecken, Germany (2006), http://www.ifomis.uni-saarland.de/bfo/manual/manual.pdf

[2] Lodish, H., Berk, A., Kaiser, C.A., Krieger, M., Scott, M.P., Bretscher, A., Ploegh, H., Matsudaira, P.: Molecular Cell Biology, 6th edn. W.H.Freeman, New York (2000)

[3] Rebholz-Schuhmann, D., Arregui, M., Gaudan, S., Kirsh, H., Jimeno, A.: Text processing through Web services: calling Whatizit. Bioinformatics 24(2), 296–298 (2008)

[4] Fink, J.L., Kushch, S., Williams, P.R., Bourne, P.E.: BioLit: integrating biological literature with databases. Nucleic Acids Res. (May 31, 2008)

[5] Bourne, P.: Will a biological database be different from a biological journal? PloS Comp. Biol. 1(3), 34 (2005)

[6] Bons, M.: Which gene did you mean? BMC Bioinformatics 6, 142 (2005)

[7] Bourne, P.E., Fink, J.L., Gerstein, M.: Open Access: Taking Full Advantage of the Content. PloS Comput. Biol. 4(3), 1000037 (2008)

[8] Ball, A.C., Sherlock, G., Parkinson, H., Rocca-Serra, P., Brooksbank, C., Causton, H.C., Cavaliaeri, D., Gaasterland, T., Hingamp, P., Holstege, F., Ringwald, M., Spellman, P., Stoeckert, C.J., Stewart, J.E., Taylor, R., Brazma, A., Quackenbush, J.: An open letter to the scientific journals. Bioinformatics 18(1), 1409 (2002)

[9] Internationl Human Genome Sequencing Consortium, Initial sequencing and analysis of the human genome. Nature 409, 860–921 (2001)

[10] Lin, S., Lopez, Q., Lorenc, R., McWilliam, D., Mukherjee, H., Nardone, G., Plaister, F., Robinson, S., Sobhany, S., Vaughan, S., Wu, R., Zhu, D.: Priorities for nucleotide trace, sequence and annotation data capture at the Ensembl Trace Archive and the EMBL Nucleotide Sequence Database. Nucleic Acid Res. 36(Database issue), D5–D12 (2008)

[11] Parkinson, H., Kapushesky, M., Shojatalab, M., Abeygunawardena, N., Coulson, R., Farne, A., Holloway, E., Kolesnykov, N., Lilja, P., Mani, R., Rayner, T., Sharma, A., William, E., Sarkans, U., Brazma, A.: ArrayExpress – a pcublic database of microarray experiments and gene expression profiles. Nucleic Acids Res. 35(DB issue), D747–D750 (2007)

[12] Galperin, M.Y.: The Molecular Biology Database Collection: 2007 update. Nucleic Acids Res. 35, D3–D4 (2007)

[13] Benson, D.A., Karsch-Mizrachi, I., Lipman, D.J., Ostell, J., Wheeler, D.L.: GenBank. Nucleic Acids Res. 36 (January 2008) (Database issue)

[14] Sugawara, H., Ogasawara, O., Okubo, K., Gojobori, T., Tateno, Y.: DDBJ with new system and face. Nucleic Acids Res. 36 (January 2008) (Database issue)

[15] Olivier, M., Eeles, R., Hollstein, M., Khan, M.A., Harris, C.C., Hainaut, P.: The IARC TP53 database: new online mutation analysis and recommendation to users. Hum. Mutat. 19(6), 607–614 (2002)

[16] Hamroun, D., Kato, S., Ishioka, C., Claustres, M., Béroud, C., Soussi, T.: The UMD TP53 database and website: update and revisions. Hum. Mutat. 27(1), 14–20 (2006)

[17] Forbes, S.A., Bharma, G., Bamford, S., Dawson, E., Kok, C., Clements, J., Menzies, A., Teague, J.W., Futreal, P.A., Stratton, M.R.: The Catalogue of Somatic Mutations in Cancer (COSMIC). Curr Protoc Hum Genet. 2008, ch. 10: Unit 10.11 (April 2008)

[18] The UniProt Consortium: The Universal Protein Resource (UniProt). Nucleic Acids Res. 36, D190–D195 (2008)

[19] Peters, B., Sidney, J., Bourne, P., Bui, H.H., Buus, S., Doh, G., Fieri, W., Kronenberg, M., Kubo, R., Lund, O., Nemazee, D., Ponomarenko, J.V., Sathiamurthy, M.S., Choenberger, S., Stewart, S., Surko, P., Way, S., Wilson, S., Sette, A.: The immune epitope database and analysis resource: from vision to blueprint. PloS Biol. 3(3), 91 (2005)

[20] Karp, P.D., Christos, A., Ouzounis, A., Moore-Kochlacs, C., Goldovsky, L., Kaipa, P., Ahrén, D., Tsoka, S., Darzentas, N., Kunin, V., Lopez-Bigas, N.: Expansion of the Bio-Cyc collection of pathway/genome databases to 160 genomes. Nucleic Acids Res. 33(19), 6083–6089 (2005)

[21] Paley, S.M., Karp, P.D.: The Pathway Tools cellular overview diagram and Omics Viewer. Nucleic Acids Res. 34(13), 3771–3778 (2006)

[22] Krummenacker, M., Paley, S., Mueller, L., Yan, T., Karp, P.D.: Querying and computing with BioCyc databases. Bioinformatics 21(16), 3454–3455 (2005)

[23] Romero, P., Wagg, J., Green, M.L., Kaiser, D., Krummenacker, M., Karp, P.D.: Computational prediction of human metabolic pathways from the complete human genome. Genome Biology 6, R2 (2004)

[24] Vastrik, I., D'Eustachio, P., Schmidt, E., Joshi-Tope, G., Gopinath, G., Croft, D., de Bono, B., Gillespie, M., Jassal, B., Lewis, S., Matthews, L., Wu, G., Birney, E., Stein, L.: Reactome: a knowledge base of biologic pathways and processes. Genome Biology 8, R39 (2007)

[25] Hucka, M., Finney, A., Sauro, H., Bolouri, H., Doyle, J., Kitano, H., Arkin, A., Bornstein, B., Bray, D., Cornish-Bowden, A., Cuellar, A.A., Dronov, S., Gilles, E.D., Ginkel, M., Gor, V., Goryanin, I.I., Hedley, W.J., Hodgman, T.C., Hofmeyr, J.H., Hunter, P.J., Juty, N.S., Kasberger, J.L., Kremling, A., Kummer, U., Le Novère, N., Loew, L.M., Lucio, D., Mendes, P., Minch, E., Mjolsness, E.D., Nakayama, Y., Nelson, M.R., Nielsen, P.F., Sakurada, T., Schaff, J.C., Shapiro, B.E., Shimizu, T.S., Spence, H.D., Stelling, J., Takahashi, K., Tomita, M., Wagner, J., Wang, J.: SBML Forum: The systems biology markup language (SBML): a medium for representation and exchange of biochemical network models. Bioinformatics 19(4), 524–531 (2003)

[26] Le Novère, N., Borsntein, B., Broicher, A., Courtout, M., Donizelli, M., Dharuri, H., Li, L., Sauro, H., Schilstra, M., Shapiro, J.L., Hucka, M.: BioModels Database: a free, centralized database of curated, published, quantitative kinetic models of biochemical and cellular systems. Nucleic Acids Res. 34, D689–D691 (2006)

[27] LSR: Life Sciences Identifiers RFP Response,
http://www.omg.org/docs/lifesci/03-12-02.pdf

[28] Clark, T., Martin, S., Liefeld, T.: Globally distributed object identification for biological knowledgebases. Briefings in Bioinformatics 5, 59–70 (2004)

[29] Etzold, T., Ulyanov, A., Argos, P.: SRS: information retrieval system for molecular biology data banks. Meth. Enzymol. 266, 114–128 (1996)

[30] Mons, B., Ashburner, M., Chichester, C., van Mulligen, E., Weeber, M., den Dunnen, J., van Ommen, G.-J., Musen, M., Cockerill, M., Hermjakob, H., Mons, A., Packer, A., Pacheco, R., Lewis, S., Berkeley, A., Melton, W., Barris, N., Wales, J., Meijssen, G., Moeller, E., Roes, P.J., Borner, K., Bairoch, A.: Calling on a million minds for community annotation in WikiProteins. Genome Biology 9, R89 (2008)

[31] Salzberg, S.L.: Genome re-annotation: a wiki solution? Genome Biology 8, 102 (2007)

[32] Ashburner, M., Ball, C.A., Blake, J.A., Botstein, D., Butler, H., Cherry, J.M., Davis, A.P., Dolinski, K., Dwight, S.S., Eppig, J.T., Harris, M.A., Hill, D.P., Issel-Tarver, L., Kasarskis, A., Lewis, S., Matese, J.C., Richardson, J.E., Ringwald, M., Rubin, G.M., Sherlock, G.: Gene ontology: tool for the unification of biology. The Gene Ontology Consortium. Nat. Genet. 25(1), 25–29 (2000)

[33] Gene Ontology Consortium. The Gene Ontology project in 2008. Nucleic Acids Res. 36(Database issue), D440–444 (January 2008)

[34] Mungall, C.J.: Obol: integrating language and meaning in bio-ontologies. Comp. Funct. Genomics 5, 509–520 (2004)

[35] Moreira, D.A., Musen, M.A.: OBO to OWL: a protege OWL tab to read/save OBO ontologies. Bioinformatics 23(14), 1868–1870 (2007)

[36] Aranguren, M.E., Bechhofer, S., Lord, P., Sattler, U., Stevens, R.: Understanding and using the meaning of statements in a bio-ontology: recasting the Gene Ontology in OWL. BMC Bioinformatics 8, 57 (2007)

[37] Khatri, P., Drăghici, S.: Ontological analysis of gene expression data: current tools, limitations, and open problems. Bioinformatics 21(18), 3587–3595 (2005)

[38] Lord, P.W., Stevens, R.D., Brass, A., Goble, C.A.: Investigating semantic similarity measures across the Gene Ontology: the relationship between sequence and annotation. Bioinformatics 19(10), 1275–1283 (2003)

[39] Côté, R.G., Jones, P., Apweiler, R., Hermjakob, H.: The Ontology Lookup Service, a lightweight cross-platform tool for controlled vocabulary queries. BMC Bioinformatics 7, 97 (2006)

[40] Smith, B., Ashburner, M., Rosse, C., Bard, J., Bug, J., Ceusters, W., Goldberg, J.L., Eilbeck, K., Ireland, A., Mungall, C.J., Leontis, N., Rocca-Serra, P., Ruttenberg, A., Sansone, S.A., Scheuermann, R.H., Shah, N., Whetzel, P.L., Lewis, S.: The OBO Foundry: coordinated evolution of ontologies to support biomedical data integration. Nature Biotechnology 25, 1251–1255 (2007)

[41] Bada, M., Hunter, L.: Enrichment of OBO ontologies. J. Biomed. Inform. 40(3), 300–315 (2007)

[42] Myhre, S., Tveit, H., Mollestad, T., Laegreid, A.: Additional gene ontology structure for improved biological reasoning. Bioinformatics 22(16), 2020–2027 (2006)

[43] Smith, B., Ceusters, W., Klagges, B., Köhler, J., Kumar, A., Lomax, J., Mungall, C., Neuhaus, F., Rector, A.L., Rosse, C.: Relations in biomedical ontologies. Genome Biol. 6(5), R46 (2005)

[44] Cheung, K.-H., Qi, P., Tuck, D., Krauthammer, M.: A semantic web approach to biological pathway data reasoning and integration. Web Semantics: Science, Services and Agents on the World Wide Web (Journal of Web Semantics) 4, 207–215 (2006)

[45] Chen, H., Doherty, D., Forsberg, K., Gao, Y., Kashyap, V., Kinoshita, J., Luciano, J., Marshall, M.S., Ogbuji, C., Rees, J., Stephens, S., Wong, G.T., Wu, E., Zaccagnini, D., Hongsermeier, T., Neumann, E., Herman, I., Cheung, K.-H.: Advancing translational research with the Semantic Web. BMC Bioinformatics 8(suppl. 3), S2 (2007)

[46] Splendiani, A.: RDFScape: Semantic Web meets Systems Biology. BMC Bioinformatics 9(suppl. 4), S6 (2008)

[47] Chatraryamontri, A., Ceol, A., Palazzi, L.M., Nardelli, G., Schneider, M.V., Castagnoli, L., Cesareni, G.: MINT: the Molecular INTeraction database. Nucleic Acids Res. 35, D572–D574 (2007)

[48] Brazma, A., Hingamp, P., Quackenbush, J., Sherlock, G., Spellman, P., Stoeckert, C., Aach, J., Ansorge, W., Ball, C.A., Causton, H.C., Gaasterland, T., Glenisson, P., Holstege, F.C., Kim, I.F., Markowitz, V., Matese, J.C., Parkinson, H., Robinson, A., Sarkans, U., Schulze-Kremer, S., Stewart, J., Taylor, R., Vilo, J., Vingron, M.: Minimum information about a microarray experiment (MIAME)-toward standards for microarray data. Nat. Genet. 29(4), 365–371 (2001)

[49] Ball, C.A., Brazma, A.: MGED standards: work in progress. OMICS 10(2), 138–144 (2006)

[50] Soldatova, L.N., King, R.D.: Are the current ontologies in biology good ontologies? Nat. Biotechnol. 23(9), 1095–1098 (2005)

[51] Le Novère, N., Finney, A., Hucka, M., Bhalla, U.S., Campagne, F., Collado-Vides, J., Crampin, E.J., Halstead, M., Klipp, E., Mendes, P., Nielsen, P., Sauro, H., Shapiro, B., Snoep, J.L., Spence, H.D., Wanner, B.L.: Minimum information requested in the annotation of biochemical models (MIRIAM). Nat. Biotechnol. 23(12), 1509–1515 (2005)

[52] Whetzel, P.L., Brinkman, R.R., Causton, H.C., Fan, L., Field, D., Fostel, J., Fragoso, G., Gray, T., Heiskanen, M., Hernandez-Boussard, T., Morrison, N., Parkinson, H., Rocca-Serra, P., Sansone, S.A., Schober, D., Smith, B., Stevens, R., Stoeckert, C.J.: FuGO Working Group.: Development of FuGO: an ontology for functional genomics investigations. OMICS 10(2), 199–204 (2006) (review)

[53] Wilkinson, M.D., Links, M.: BioMOBY: an open-source biological web services proposal. Briefings in Bioinformatics 3, 331–341 (2002)

[54] Wroe, C., Stevens, R., Goble, C., Roberts, A., Greenwod, M.: A suite of DAML+OIL ontologies to describe bioinformatics web services and data. International Journal of Cooperative Information Systems – Special issue on Bioinformatics 12, 197–224 (2003)

[55] Romano, P.: Automation of in-silico data analysis processes through workflow management systems. Briefings in Bioinformatics 9(1), 57–68 (2008)

[56] Mahoui, M., Ben-Miled, Z., Srinivasan, S., Dippold, M., Yang, B., Li, N.: SIBIOS Ontology: a robust package for the integration and pipelining of bioinformatics services. In: Leser, U., Naumann, F., Eckman, B. (eds.) DILS 2006. LNCS (LNBI), vol. 4075. Springer, Heidelberg (2006)

[57] Leser, U.: A query language for biological networks. Bioinformatics 21(suppl. 2), 33–39 (2005)

[58] Ruttenberg, A., Rees, J., Zucker, J.: What BioPAX communicates and how to extend OWL to help it. In: Proceeding of OWLed (2006), http://ftp.informatik. rwth-aachen.de/Publications/CEUR-WS/Vol-216/

[59] Karp, P.D., Paley, S.: Automated drawing of metabolic pathways. In: Lim, H., Cantor, C., Robbins, R. (eds.) Proceedings of the Third International Conference on Bioinformatics and Genome Research. Florida State Conference Center, pp. 225–238. Tallahassee, Florida (1994)

[60] Good, B.M., Wilkinson, M.D.: The Life Sciences Semantic Web is full of creeps. Brief Bioinform. 7(3), 275–286 (2006)

[61] Cannata, N., Merelli, E., Altman, R.B.: Time to Organize the Bioinformatics Resourceome. PLoS Computational Biology 1(7), 76 (2007)

[62] Cannata, N., Corradini, F., Gabrielli, S., Leoni, L., Merelli, E., Piersigilli, F., Vito, L.: Intuitive and machine understandable representation of the bioinformatics domain and of related resources with Resourceomes. In: Felicioli, C., Romano, P., Marangoni, R. (eds.) Proc. of the 7th International Workshop NETTAB 2007 on A Semantic Web for Bioinformatics: Goals, Tools, Systems, Applications, Pisa, June 12-15, 2007, pp. 35–46 (2007)

[63] Dinov, I.D., Rubin, D., Lorensen, W., Dugan, J., Ma, J., Murphy, S., Kirschner, B., Bug, W., Sherman, M., Floratos, A., Kennedy, D., Jagadish, H.V., Schmidt, J., Athey, B., Califano, A., Musen, A., Altman, R., Kikinis, R., Kohane, I., Delp, S., Parker, D.S., Toga, A.W.: iTools: A Framework for Classification, Categorization and Integration of Computational Biology Resources. PLoS ONE 3(5), 2265 (2008)

[64] Schröder, M., Burger, A., Kostkova, P., Stevens, R., Habermann, B., Dieng-Kuntz, R.: From a Services-based eScience Infrastructure to a Semantic Web for the Life Sciences: The Sealife Project. In: NETTAB 2006, Santa Margherita di Pula, CA, July 10-13 (2006)

[65] Alexopoulou, D., Wachter, T., Pickersgill, L., Eyre, C., Schroeder, M.: Terminologies for text-mining; an experiment in the lipoprotein metabolism domain. BMC Bioinformatics 9(Suppl. 4), S2 (2008)

[66] Neumann, E.K., Quan, D.: BioDash: a Semantic Web dashboard for drug development. In: Proc. Pacific Symposium Biocomputing (PSB 2006), pp. 176–187 (2006)

[67] HCLS Charter, http://www.w3.org/2008/05/HCLSIGCharter

[68] A Prototype Knowledge Base for the Life Sciences, W3C Interest Group Note (June 4, 2008), http://www.w3.org/TR/hcls-kb/

[69] Lam, H.Y.K., Marenco, L., Clark, T., Gao, Y., Kinoshita, J., Shepherd, G., Miller, P., Wu, E., Wong, G.T., Liu, N., Crasto, C., Morse, T., Stephens, S., Cheung, K.-H.: AlzPharm: integration of neurodegeneration data using RDF. BMC Bioinformatics 8(suppl. 3), S4 (2007)

Web Services Discovery Utilizing Semantically Annotated WSDL

Jorge Cardoso[1], John A. Miller[2], and Savitha Emani[2]

[1] SAP Research CEC Dresden
Chemnitzer Strasse 48
01187 Dresden, Germany
jorge.cardoso@sap.com
[2] LSDIS Lab, Department of Computer Science
University of Georgia
Athens, GA 30602 – USA
jam@cs.uga.edu, emani@cs.uga.edu

Abstract. To make semantic Web services accessible to users, providers use registries to publish them. Unfortunately, the current registries use discovery mechanisms which are inefficient, as they do not support discovery based on the semantics of the services and thus lead to a considerable number of irrelevant matches. Semantic discovery and matching of services is a promising approach to address this challenge. This paper presents an algorithm to match a semantic Web service request described with SAWSDL against semantic Web service advertisements. The algorithm is novel in three fundamental aspects. First, the similarity among semantic Web service properties, such as inputs and outputs, is evaluated using Tversky's model which is based on concepts (classes), their semantic relationships, and their common and distinguishing features (properties). Second, the algorithm, not only takes into account services' inputs and outputs, but it also considers the functionality of services. Finally, the algorithm is able to match a semantic Web service request against advertisements that are annotated with concepts that are with or without a common ontological commitment. In other words, it can evaluate the similarity of concepts defined in the context of different ontologies.

Keywords: We Semantic Web, Web services, Ontologies.

1 Introduction

Semantic Web services are the new paradigm for distributed computing. They have much to offer towards the integration of heterogeneous, autonomous and large scale distributed systems. Several standards such as WSDL [1, 2], UDDI [3], and SOAP [4] have been developed to support the use of Web services. Significant progress has been made towards making Web services a pragmatic solution for distributed computing on the scale of the World Wide Web. With the proliferation of Web services and the evolution towards the semantic Web comes the opportunity to automate various Internet related tasks. Applications should be able to automatically or semi-automatically

C. Baroglio et al. (Eds.): Reasoning Web 2008, LNCS 5224, pp. 240–268, 2008.

discover, invoke, compose, and monitor Web services offering particular services and having particular properties [5].

Given the dynamic environment in e-businesses, the power of being able to discover Web services on the fly, to dynamically create business processes is highly desirable. The discovery of Web services has specific requirements and challenges compared to previous work on information retrieval systems and information integration systems. Several issues need to be considered. The discovery has to be based, not only on syntactical information, but also on data, as well as functional and QoS semantics [6].

Discovery is the procedure of finding a set of appropriate Web services that meets user requirements [7]. The discovery of Web services to model Web processes differs from the search for tasks/activities to model traditional processes, such as workflows. One of the main differences is in terms of the number of Web services available to the composition process. On the Web, potentially thousands of Web services are available which make discovery a difficult procedure. One cannot expect a designer to manually browse through all the Web services available and select the most suitable one. Therefore, one of the problems that needs to be overcome is how to efficiently discover Web services [6].

Currently, the industry standards available for registering and discovering Web services are based on UDDI specifications [3]. An important challenge is that of finding the most appropriate Web service within a registry [7]. This challenge arises due to the discovery mechanism supported by UDDI. In an attempt to disassociate itself from any particular Web service description format, UDDI specification does not support registering the information from the service descriptions in the registry. Hence the effectiveness of UDDI is limited, even though it provides a very powerful interface for keyword and taxonomy based searching. Suggestions [8] have been made to register WSDL descriptions, which are the current industry's accepted standard, in UDDI. However, since WSDL descriptions are syntactic, registering them would only provide syntactical information about the Web services. The problem with syntactic information is that the semantics implied by the information provider are not explicit, leading to possible misinterpretation by others. Therefore, discovering Web services using UDDI is relatively inefficient since the discovery mechanism only takes into account the syntactic aspect of Web services by providing an interface for keyword and taxonomy based searching.

The key to enhance the discovery of Web services is to describe Web services semantically [9] and use semantic matching algorithms (e.g. [6, 10-12]) to find appropriate services. Semantic discovery allows the construction of queries using concepts defined in a specific ontological domain. By having both the advertisement description and request query explicitly declare their semantics, the results of discovery are more accurate and relevant than keyword or attribute-based matching. Adding semantics to Web service descriptions can be achieved by using ontologies that support shared vocabularies and domain models for use in the service description [7]. Using domain specific ontologies, the semantics implied by structures in service descriptions, which are known only to the writer of the description, can be made explicit. While searching for Web services, relevant domain specific ontologies can be referred to, thus enabling semantic matching of services.

In this paper, we will review the state-of-the-art in the discovery of Web services. We then present a new algorithm for Web service discovery that is novel in three fundamental aspects. First, the similarity among semantic Web service properties, such as inputs and outputs, are determined based on a feature-based model, Tversky's model. Using Tversky's model, we consider that similarity is a judgment process that requires two services to be decomposed into aspects in which they are the same and aspects in which they are different. Evaluating the similarity is based on concepts (classes), their semantic relations, and their common and distinguishing features (properties). Second, the algorithm, not only takes into account services' inputs and outputs, but it also considers the functionality of services. This allows for increasing the precision of search. Providers can express in a better way the objective of their services and customers can give a better characterization of the services they are looking for. Finally, the algorithm is able to match a semantic Web service request against advertisements that are annotated with concepts that are with or without a common ontology commitment. In other words, it can evaluate the similarity of concepts defined in the context of different ontologies. This last characteristic is important since in some situations it is perfectly acceptable to find similar services (or even equivalent services) annotated with semantic concepts that exist in the context of different ontologies.

The remainder of this paper is structured as follows. Section 2 provides an overview on how Web services can be semantically annotated or described so that they can be considered semantic Web services. We present an approach to add semantics to WSDL. The tool Radiant is used to exemplify the essential functionalities needed for an annotation tool. In section 3, we present our semantic Web service matching function (called SM-T) to discover services. It also describes a ranking algorithm that uses the matching function previously presented and that can be used by discovery mechanisms. Section 4 explains how the SM-T function can be integrated in the METEOR-S Web Services discovery infrastructure. This system supplies an infrastructure of registries for semantic publication and discovery of Web services. Section 5 discusses the related work in this area and the last section presents our conclusions.

2 Semantic Web Service

Many believe that a new Web will emerge in the next few years, based on the large-scale research and development ongoing on the semantic Web and Web services. The intersection of these two, semantic Web services, may prove to be even more significant. Academia has mainly approached this area from the semantic Web side, while industry is beginning to consider its importance from the Web services side [13]. Three main approaches have been developed to bring semantics to Web services:

- The first approach uses OWL-S, a Web Service description language that semantically describes the Web using OWL ontologies. OWL-S services are then mapped to WSDL operations and inputs and outputs of OWL-S are mapped to WSDL messages.
- The second approach, WSMO, is a meta-model for semantic Web services devised to facilitate the automation of discovering, combining and invoking electronic services over the Web. WSMO elements include: Ontologies, Web services, Goals and Mediators.

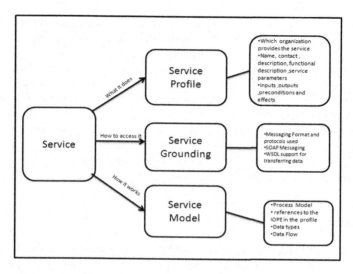

Fig. 1. OWL-S: Service ontology overview

- The third approach to creating semantic Web services is by mapping concepts in a Web service description (WSDL specification) to ontological concepts. The WSDL elements that can be marked up with metadata are operations, messages, preconditions and effects, since all the elements are explicitly declared in a WSDL description.

The approaches will be discussed in the following subsections.

2.1 OWL-S

OWL-S [14] (formerly DAML-S) is a standard ontology or language which gives providers a computer-interpretable description of a Web service. It supplies a set of classes and properties which describes capabilities of a Web service in an unambiguous, computer form. This ontology uses OWL as the web compatible representational language. As OWL-S gives a markup to the Web services it helps in automated discovery, composition and interoperation of services. OWL-S employs an upper level ontology to describe Web services. It consists of three parts expressed in accordance with OWL ontologies: the service profile (What does the service provide for prospective clients?), the service model (How is it used?), and the service grounding (How does one interact with it?), each of these perspectives provide essential information about the service (Figure 1).

The Service Profile used to discover a Web service gives complete information on whether a particular service meets the requirement of a user or not. This information involves what the service capabilities are, its limitations and the quality of service. It gives detailed information about the name, contact, description of the service, specification of parameters (properties) according to the process ontology, Inputs, Outputs, Preconditions and Effects (IOPE). The Service Model gives a layout of how a consumer should pass requests and how the service accomplishes the task. When services are composed the consumer can use the description in different ways: to analyze whether the service meets the requirements in detail, to compose multiple services for a specific task, to synchronize and coordinate different participants and to monitor the execution of the services. The services are modeled as processes; the IOPEs declared in the service profile are referenced here. If the processes are connected with each other then the dataflow between these processes is specified. The Service Grounding specifies the communication protocol, message formats and other details used to access the web service. Concrete messages are specified in grounding i.e., how the inputs and outputs are of a process are realized as messages in some transmittable format. WSDL is used to support initial grounding mechanism as a set of endpoints for messages along with SOAP binding where HTTP is the communication protocol that is used.

2.2 WSMO

The Web Service Modeling Ontology (WSMO [15]) comprises an ontology of core elements for semantic Web services, described in WSML (Web Services Modeling Language), a formal description language, and also an execution environment called WSMX (Web Service Execution Environment). In WSMO, ontologies provide the terminology used by other WSMO elements to describe the relevant aspects of the domains of discourse. Goals symbolize user desires which can be satisfied by executing a Web service and Mediators express elements that surmount interoperability problems between distinct WSMO elements. WSMO and OWL-S, both accept the same view towards having service ontologies to construct semantic Web services. WSMO has it own family of languages, WSML, which is based on Description Logics and Logic Programming.

As WSMO provides ontological specifications for the elements of Web services it is designed on the basis of few principles: it identifies the resources with the help of URIs, it is based on an ontology model and supports ontology languages designed for the semantic Web, each resource is defined independently, it handles heterogeneity, it separates between client and the available services, it provides and differentiates between description and implementation, it describes Web services that provide access to a service (actual value obtained after a Web service is invoked).

WSMO uses different approaches to discover Web services which require different annotation and description of goals and services. Web service discovery is done by matching goal descriptions with semantic annotations of Web services. This type of discovery happens in an ontological level. Two main processes are required for this discovery: the user input will be generalized to more abstract descriptions and services and their descriptions should be abstracted to classes of services.

2.3 Adding Semantics to WSDL

It has been recognized [5] that due to the heterogeneity, autonomy and distribution of Web services and the Web itself, new approaches should be developed to describe and advertise Web services. The most notable approaches rely on the use of semantics to describe Web services. This new breed of Web services, termed semantic Web services, will enable the automatic annotation, advertisement, discovery, selection, composition, and execution of inter-organization business logic, making the Internet become a common global platform where organizations and individuals communicate with each other to carry out various commercial activities and to provide value-added services. The academia has mainly approached this area from the semantic Web side, while industry is beginning to consider its importance from the point of view of Web services [13]. As we have already seen, three main approaches have been developed to bring semantics to Web services: SAWSDL (formally WSDL-S), OWL-S [14], and WSMO [15]. Since our work has been carried out with the research group that has defined SAWSDL, we will focus our study on this specification.

2.3.1 WSDL

WSDL [2] is primarily an interface description language for Web services, just as IDL was for CORBA. As an interface, it describes capabilities that Web services implementing the interface should provide. The main thing to describe about an interface is the set of operations. In WSDL, the meaning of an operation is given by the operation name, the input parameter names and types, the output parameter names and types as well as the possible faults that can be thrown. In addition, further information can be obtained from the interface itself and in WSDL 2.0 one interface can extend another (interface inheritance).

A WSDL document describes a Web service as a collection of ports. Messages specify data being exchanged between the services and port types are collection of operations. As such a WSDL document has certain elements to define data types, messages, operations, port types, binding, ports and services. Figure 2 shows a complete example of how a WSDL looks like.

```
<?xml version="1.0" encoding="UTF-8" ?>
<!-- Published by JAX-WS RI at http://jax-ws.dev.java.net.
RI's version is JAX-WS RI 2.1.2-hudson-182-RC1.-->
<!-- Generated by JAX-WS RI at http://jax-ws.dev.java.net.
RI's version is JAX-WS RI 2.1.2-hudson-182-RC1. -->

<definitions xmlns:wsu="http://docs.oasis-
open.org/wss/2004/01/oasis-200401-wss-wssecurity-utility-
1.0.xsd"
    xmlns:wsp="http://schemas.xmlsoap.org/ws/2004/09/policy"
    xmlns:soap="http://schemas.xmlsoap.org/wsdl/soap/"
    xmlns:tns="http://stock/"
    xmlns:xsd="http://www.w3.org/2001/XMLSchema"
    xmlns=http://schemas.xmlsoap.org/wsdl/
    targetNamespace="http://stock/" name="estockincService">

<types>
    <xsd:import namespace=http://stock/ "
schemaLocation="http://localhost:8080/WebService/estockincServi
ce?xsd=1" />
</types>

<message name="stockquoterequest">
```

Fig. 2. An example WSDL Document

```
        <part name="parameters" element="tns:stockquoterequest" />
    </message>
    <message name="stockquoterequestResponse">
        <part name="parameters" ele-
ment="tns:stockquoterequestResponse" />
    </message>

    <portType name="estockinc">
        <operation name="stockquoterequest">
            <input message="tns:stockquoterequest"/>
            <output message="tns:stockquoterequestResponse"/>
        </operation>
    </portType>

    <binding name="estockincPortBinding" type="tns:estockinc">
        <soap:binding trans-
port="http://schemas.xmlsoap.org/soap/http" style="document" />
        <operation name="stockquoterequest">
            <soap:operation soapAction="" />
                <input>
                  <soap:body use="literal" />
                </input>
                <output>
                  <soap:body use="literal" />
                </output>
        </operation>
    </binding>

    <service name="estockincService">
        <port name="estockincPort"  bind-
ing="tns:estockincPortBinding">
          <soap:address
location="http://localhost:8080/WebService/estockincService" />
        </port>
    </service>
    </definitions>
```

Fig. 2. (*continued*)

Although the intent of WSDL is to give the syntax of a Web service interface, some level of semantics or meaning is necessary for the interface and its operations to be usable. The real issue is not whether WSDL descriptions themselves have any semantics, but rather how complete and precise are the semantics, and whether the semantics can be effectively and automatically processed.

2.3.2 SAWDL
WSDL as it stands is most useful if standards (naming conventions and even standard predefined interfaces) are used. Then automation is possible if exact matching is used and you are sure everyone has fully followed the standard. Automation tools for discovery and composition may blindly find and connect components. Unfortunately, this brittle solution has only worked in the past in narrow domains or with controlled organizations and is unlikely to scale to the Web.

Table 1. Allowable SAWSDL annotations

	Model Reference	Lifting SchemaMapping	Lowering SchemaMapping
`<interface>`	Yes	No	No
`<operation>`	Yes	No	No
`<complexType>`	Yes	Yes	Yes
`<simpleType>`	Yes	Yes	Yes
`<element>`	Yes	Yes	Yes
`<attribute>`	Yes	No	No
`<fault>`	Yes	No	No

One could jump to an approach that provides a much richer and more formalized description of Web services (e.g., OWL-S [14]), but maybe a simple augmentation of WSDL may suffice (or at least provide substantial improvement). This is the idea behind WSDL-S [16] and the even simpler Semantic Annotations for WSDL (SAWSDL). As of August 2007, SAWSDL has been accepted as a W3C recommendation or standard for augmenting WSDL and associated XML Schema documents with semantic annotations. Although SAWSDL was designed for WSDL 2.0, which itself was accepted as a W3C recommendation in July 2007, SAWSDL also works with WSDL 1.1 as it is the one currently in predominate use. SAWSDL focuses on the Interface portion of WSDL 2.0 (or PortType in WSDL 1.1) and its sub-elements. Semantics is attached to the principal elements within an interface description, simply by annotating them with concepts from a semantic model (e.g., classes within an OWL ontology). These annotations are innocuous in that they can be easily filtered out, leaving the original WSDL.

There are three types of annotations provided by SAWSDL: model references, lifting schema mappings and lowering schema mappings. The model references tell what an element means in the ontological world, while the mappings allow data to be transformed up (lifted) to the ontological world and returned back down (lowered). Note that these mappings are really descriptions as well, since they need not be applied directly at run time. For example, when one service may need to invoke another, a semantic discovery and composition tool could use these mappings to determine what services can talk to each other. In composition, the mappings could be composed providing transformations from one XSD to another and never actually going up to the ontological world. In Table 1, the SAWSDL annotations are cross referenced with the elements they annotate.

Let us now consider how this information can be used to discover Web services. Note that this information is also useful in the composition of Web services, but that is not the focus of this paper (see [17] for its use in composition). One may reasonably discover Web services by either looking for operations or interfaces. The other elements annotated by SAWSDL are too low level, but of course come into play when looking for operations or interfaces. Let us begin by considering the discovery of operations. The following is a fragment of SAWSDL from the Rosetta Ontology [18].

```
<wsdl:operation name="order"
pattern="http://www.w3.org/2006/01/wsdl/in-out"
sawsdl:modelReference="http://www.w3.org/2002/ws/sawsdl/s
pec/ontology/purchaseorder#RequestPurchaseOrder">
```

```
    <wsdl:input element="OrderRequest" />
    <wsdl:output element="OrderResponse" />
</wsdl:operation>
```

The annotation of the operation named `order` is a model reference to the `Request-PurchaseOrder` class in the `purchaseorder` ontology. This ontology is loosely based on the RosettaNet standard for e-commerce, which includes well-defined operations and sub-operation in their Partner Interface Process (PIP) specifications. In other words, essential functionality is prescribed. One could view this as a high-level description of functionality or in some cases simply as a categorization of functionality. Other aspects of an operation include the inputs and outputs and even preconditions and effects (preconditions and effects are part of WSDL-S, but are initially left out of SAWSDL for simplicity). Next we look at annotations related to the order operation's input.

```
<xs:element name="OrderRequest"
sawsdl:modelReference="http://www.w3.org/2002/ws/sawsdl/s
pec/ontology/purchaseorder#OrderRequest"
sawsdl:loweringSchemaMapping="http://www.w3.org/2002/ws/s
awsdl/spec/mapping/RDFOnt2Request.xml">
    <xs:complexType>
      <xs:sequence>
        <xs:element name="customerNo" type="xs:integer" />
        <xs:element name="orderItem" type="item"
                    minOccurs="1" maxOccurs="unbounded" />
      </xs:sequence>
    </xs:complexType>
</xs:element>
```

Here the `OrderRequest` element is annotated with `OrderRequest` from the ontology. This reference opens up the richer typing structures of a language like OWL versus XSD (e.g., classes, subclasses, named references and restrictions) as well as inferencing capabilities (e.g., subsumption). Finally, we examine annotations related to the order operation's output.

```
<xs:element name="OrderResponse" type="confirmation" />
  <xs:simpleType name="confirmation"
  sawsdl:modelReference="http://www.w3.org/2002/ws/sawsdl
/spec/ontology/purchaseorder#OrderConfirmation">
    <xs:restriction base="xs:string">
      <xs:enumeration value="Confirmed" />
      <xs:enumeration value="Pending" />
      <xs:enumeration value="Rejected" />
    </xs:restriction>
  </xs:simpleType>
```

Here the `OrderResponse` element is annotated with `OrderConfirmation` from the ontology. Similar annotations can be provided for faults, while this is likely to be more important for composition than discovery.

Although operation discovery is fundamental, practically speaking one often wishes to invoke multiple operations from a Web service, so in this sense interface discovery is also important. In this paper, we mainly leave this aspect for future work, but of course some of the obvious issues are the following: discovery of a set of operations, temporal dependencies between the operations and statefulness. From a two party point of view these issues are of concern to a conversation protocol, if generalized to multiple parties they are of concern to a choreographer (e.g., following the emerging WS-CDL standard). From the point of view of one of the parties, they can orchestrate their interactions with the other parties (or partners) via a process specification (e.g., following the WS-BPEL standard).

2.3.3 Using Radiant to Add Semantics to WSDL

Radiant [19] is a tool that can be used for marking up Web service descriptions with ontologies. Radiant is a part of an ongoing project, METEOR-S, in an effort to create semantic Web processes, at the LSDIS lab – University of Georgia. This tool provides support for WSDL-S, a joint UGA-IBM specification and SAWSDL. WSDL-S and SAWSDL allow users to easily add semantics to Web services by using the extensibility elements of WSDL. Radiant provides an intuitive UI for annotation of WSDL files using ontologies. All the annotations described in the WSDL-S/SAWSDL specifications are supported by this tool. The framework includes algorithms to match and annotate WSDL files with relevant ontologies using domain ontologies to categorize Web services into domains. A key enabling capability is to achieve annotation with as much automation as possible without losing quality (see [19] to understand how automation is achieved). Figure 3 shows a screenshot of the interface used for annotation. In this figure, the interface provides the user with capabilities of a specifying WSDL file (on the left side) and an ontology (on the right side) used for mapping. The user may then simply drag an element (a class or property) from the ontology on drop it an element in the WSDL file.

While many other efforts have talked about adding semantics to Web services, practical implications of actually annotating Web services with the use of real world applications and ontologies have not been discussed in great detail. Manifestly, there is a lack of real world systems and solutions. The following steps can be followed to annotate Web services using Radiant

1. Start the Eclipse Workbench[1].
2. Open the "Help" menu.
3. Open the "Software Updates" submenu
4. Select "Find and Install"
5. Select the "Search for new features to install" radio button and click next
6. Click "New Remote Site"
7. Enter "http://lsdis.cs.uga.edu/Radiant/UpdateSite" without the quotes in the URL box.
8. Enter "Radiant" without quotes for the name field.

---

[1] http://www.eclipse.org/

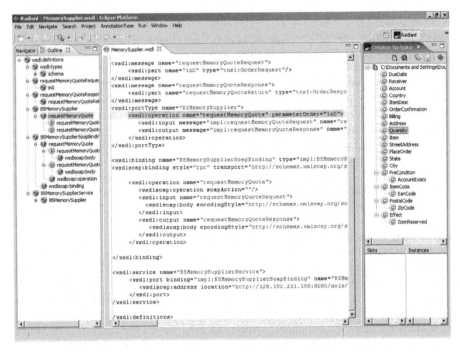

Fig. 3. Radiant tool to annotated WSDL-S and SAWSDL documents

9. Make sure there is a check in the box next to Radiant and click next.
10. Click Finish.
11. When the new dialog box opens, put a check next to Radiant and click next.
12. Select the "I accept terms in the license agreement" radio button and click next.
13. Then follow any onscreen dialogs and the plug-in will be installed.
14. Click on window drop down menu select open perspective and select Radiant.

The Eclipse screen is divided into three parts one is the navigator/outline part, the uddi, wsdl viewer and editor, ontology navigator.

1. Create a new project and open an existing WSDL document.
2. On the ontology navigator load the ontology by clicking on 🖹 or 🔷 icon.
3. From the Annotation type drop down menu select the annotation type.
4. Click on outline to get the tree view of the WSDL document and select the concept for annotation. Drag the element to the appropriate section of the WSDL tree. The annotations are added to the document automatically.

3 Matching Algorithm for Semantic Web Services

This section presents an algorithm for matching semantic Web services, called SM-T (Semantic Matching Web services using Tversky's model). The algorithm presented computes the degree of match between two output concepts, two input concepts, and two functionality concepts of a service request and advertisement, represented by an ontology. Given a service request and several advertisements for available Web services, this algorithm can be used to find the more suitable Web services. Web services can be annotated using Radiant [20], as explained previously, and MWSDI [7] and Lumina [21] can use the SM-T algorithm as part of its discovery infrastructure to discover Web services.

We exploit the fact that the input, output, and functionality concepts which are matched may have (in addition to their name) properties (e.g., in the form of attributes) associated with them, and we also take into account the level of generality (or specificity) of each concept within the ontology as well as their relationships with other concepts. Notice that in contrast to semantic-based matching, syntactic-based matching cannot use this information.

Matching input, output, and functionality concepts differs slightly from calculating their semantic similarity. One difference is that the functions to compute the semantic similarity of ontological concepts are usually symmetric, while matching functions are asymmetric [6]. For example, let us assume that SUMO Finance Ontology[2] in Figure 4 is used to semantically annotate or describe a set of Web services (only an extract of the ontology is shown). The METEOR-S SUMO Finance Ontology was created by converting SUMO financial ontology from KIF to OWL.

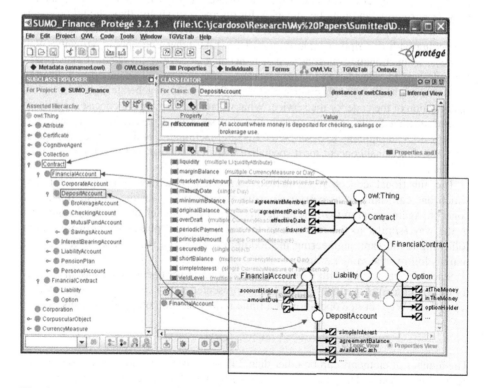

Fig. 4. Example of the SUMO Finance ontology used to semantically annotate a set of Web services

<hr/>

[2] http://lsdis.cs.uga.edu/projects/meteor-s/wsdl-s/ontologies/SUMO_Finance.owl

Let us assume that we have a semantic Web service request R with the input concept *FinanceAccount* (c_1) and an advertisement A with the input concept *Contract* (c_2). In this scenario, request R matches advertisement A (i.e., *match*(c_1, c_2)=*true*), since *FinanceAccount* is a subclass of *Contract*. Our rationale is that if A is able to deal with the input *Contract* it must also be able to deal with the input *FinanceAccount*. We can think that when the Web service is invoked there will be some kind of cast (as in C programming) from *FinanceAccount* to *Contract*. This idea and concept have been first introduced in [22].

Now, let us assume that we have a semantic Web service request R with the input concept *Contract* (c_2) and an advertisement A with the input concept *FinanceAccount* (c_1). In this scenario, it is possible that the semantic Web service A cannot be invoked with the input *Contract* since A may need properties that only exist in the class *FinanceAccount*. Therefore, *match*(c_2, c_1)=*false*. As we can see from these two scenarios, the function *match* is asymmetric, since *match*(c_1, c_2) $\neq$ *match* (c_2, c_1).

3.1   Formal Definition of a Semantic Web Service

One way to handle functionality of a Web service operation is through preconditions, postconditions and effects. These specifications are usually detailed and precise enough to work at runtime and may be unwieldy for discovery. Usually, they should be specified in a rule language like SWRL or RIF. For discovery, however, there are advantages to sticking with description logic (e.g., OWL). Like other concepts in semantic Web services, a functionality concept is given meaning according to where it stands in a hierarchy and by considering its sub-functions. Of course, a fully detailed specification of sub-functions along with control and data flow could degenerate into a complete specification of the code for the service. What we are looking for is a concise, high-level description that facilitates comparison between services. Consequently, we assign a concept from an ontology to describe the overall functionality of the Web service operation. This functional concept must specialize its parent concept and generalize all of its child concepts.

The functional concept can include component functional concepts (children) which one can think of as carrying out the steps required for the overall functional concept. Again, programmatic level details should not be included, as they would get in the way (similar to the situation in the early and mid phases of software design following a software engineering methodology). The need for annotating inputs and outputs follows the same rational.

Since we are dealing with input parameters, output parameters, and the functionality of semantic Web services operations (represented with c_i, c_o and c_f, respectively), we define a Web service operation as a finite sequence of ontological concepts as:

$$sws(c_i, c_o, c_f)$$

The number of elements can be other than 3 if we consider more or fewer concepts to be used in a match. The functionality and QoS of Web services [6] can also be considered when matching requests with advertisements. The functions and algorithm that we present can be easily extended to include the notion of functionality, since functionality can be treated in a similar way as inputs or outputs. What the reader needs to keep in mind is that we always use the Tversky's model [23] to match requests with advertisements, independently of the elements (e.g. inputs, outputs, functionality, QoS, etc) being considered.

3.2 Comparing Semantic Web Services Based on a Single Common Ontology

In this scenario, Web service input, output, and functionality concepts are related to one global and unique ontology providing a common vocabulary for the specification of semantics. Comparing a concept with the ontology is translated into searching for the same or similar concepts within the ontology.

There are several functions that can be adapted and used to compute the degree of match between two input, output, or functionality concepts belonging to the same ontology. The following four main techniques have been identified [24]:

1. **Ontology based approaches.** These approaches [25-27] use an ontology and evaluate the semantic relations among concepts. The most basic metric simply computes the distance between two concepts in an ontology. This corresponds to calculating the distance of nodes in a graph.
2. **Corpus based approaches.** These approaches [28-30] use a corpus to establish the statistical co-occurrence of words. The rationale is that if two words constantly appear together we may conclude that some relation exists between them.
3. **Information theoretic approaches.** These approaches [23, 31-33] consider both a corpora and an ontology, and use the notion of information content from the field of information theory. By statistically analyzing corpora, probabilities are associated to concepts based on word occurrences. The information content for each concept is computed in such a way that infrequent words are more informative than frequent ones. By knowing the information content of concepts it is possible to calculate the semantic similarity between two given concepts.
4. **Dictionary based approaches.** These approaches [34, 35] use a machine readable dictionary to discover relations between concepts. For example, one approach determines the sense of a word in a given text by counting the overlaps between dictionary definitions of the various senses.

Most of these approaches are not suitable to compute the degree of matching between input and output concepts of the semantic Web services. All these metrics are symmetric (except [23]). This means that $f(c_1, c_2) = f(c_2, c_1)$. As explained previously, when matching inputs, outputs and functionality, the matching function needs to be asymmetric.

Furthermore, ontology-based approaches are rather limited since only the taxonomy of the ontology is used to find similarities between concepts. Corpus and dictionary-based approaches require associating a probability with each concept and finding a specific meaning of a word according to the context in which it is found in a dictionary, respectively. These approaches are not simple to implement for Web services. Questions raised include which corpus and dictionaries to use and how to deal with the heterogeneity of Web service discourse domains.

In our opinion, Tversky's model [23] needs to be considered when matching semantic Web services, since it has been considered one of the most powerful similarity models to date [36]. It is also known as a feature-counting metric or feature-contrast model. This model is based on the idea that common features tend to increase the perceived similarity of two concepts, while feature differences tend to diminish perceived similarity. The model takes into account the features that are common to two concepts and also the differentiating features specific to each. More specifically, the similarity of concept c_1 to concept c_2 is a function of the features common to c_1 and c_2, those in c_1 but not in c_2 and those in c_2 but not in c_1. For instance, a truck (Sport Utility Vehicle) and a sedan are similar by virtue of their common features, such as wheels, engine, steering wheel, and gears, and are dissimilar by virtue of their differences, namely the number of seats and the loading capacity.

Based on Tversky's model, we introduce the matching functions $S_i^=(c_R, c_A)$,

$S_o^=(c_R, c_A)$ and $S_f^=(c_R, c_A)$ which analyze the number of properties (which may be inherited) shared among two input, output or functionality concepts c_R and c_A (R stands for a Web service request, A stands for a Web service advertisement, i stands for input, o stands for output, and f stands for functionality) conceptualized within the same ontology. In our functions $S^=$, function $p(c)$ retrieves all the properties associated with concept c and function $|s|$ calculates the number of elements in set s. The equal symbol between two concepts (e.g, $c_R = c_A$) indicates that the concepts are the same. The symbol '>' between two concepts (e.g. $c_R > c_A$) indicates that concept c_R is a specialization of concept c_A. Finally, the symbol '<' between two concepts (e.g. $c_R < c_A$) indicates that c_R is a generalization of concept c_A ($c_R < c_A$).

$$S_i^=(c_R, c_A) = \begin{cases} 1, & c_R = c_A \\ 1, & c_R > c_A \\ \dfrac{|p(c_R)|}{|p(c_A)|}, & c_R < c_A \\ \dfrac{|p(c_R) \cap p(c_A)|}{|p(c_A)|}, & c_R \neq c_A \end{cases}$$

$$S_o^=(c_R, c_A) = S_f^=(c_R, c_A) = \begin{cases} 1, & c_R = c_A \\ \dfrac{|p(c_A)|}{|p(c_R)|}, & c_R > c_A \\ 1, & c_R < c_A \\ \dfrac{|p(c_R) \cap p(c_A)|}{|p(c_R)|}, & c_R \neq c_A \end{cases}$$

Since functions $S_i^=(c_R, c_A)$, $S_o^=(c_R, c_A)$ and $S_f^=(c_R, c_A)$ are very similar we will only describe function $S_i^=$. Four distinct cases can occur:

Case 1: In the first case, since the two input concepts are equal ($c_R = c_A$) their similarity is maximal and therefore the degree of match is one.

Case 2: In the second case, concept c_R is a specialization of concept c_A ($c_R > c_A$). As a result, a Web service with input concept c_A is able to process concept c_R. For example, let us consider the ontology from Figure 4. If a Web service request specifies concept *FinanceAccount* as input and an advertisement specifies concept *Contract* as input then the advertised service is able to process the input concept *FinanceAccount*. This is because the concept c_R is a subclass of concept c_A and it has at least the same set of properties as c_A. In this case, the similarity is also one.

Case 3: In the third case, if the request concept c_R is a generalization of advertisement concept c_A ($c_R < c_A$), then c_A has probably some properties that do not exist in c_R. Therefore, it is possible that a Web service advertisement with input c_A is not able to process the input concept c_R due possibly to missing properties. For example, if a Web service request R specifies concept *Record* as input and an advertisement A specifies concept *FinanceAccount* as input then Web service A may not be able to process the input concept *Contract*. This is because A may need the property *Degree* and *Competencies* of the input concept to work properly.

Case 4: In the last case, concepts c_R and c_A are not equal and do not subsume each other in any way ($c_R \neq c_A$). In this scenario, we evaluate the matching by analyzing how many common properties exist between the two concepts and how many properties are different. Also, we analyze the percentage of input advertisement properties that were satisfied.

As an example, let us illustrate the use of function $S_i^{=}(c_R, c_A)$ for the four cases – 1), 2), 3) and 4) – that can occur when matching a request c_R with an advertisement c_A. In our example, the Web services' input is annotated with concepts from the ontology illustrated in Figure 4. The four cases that may occur are listed in Table 2 and are evaluated as follows:

- In case 1), both c_R and c_A are associated with the same concept (*FinanceAccount*). Since the request matches the advertisement perfectly. The result is 1.
- In case 2), the request c_R is associated with the concept *FinanceAccount* and the advertisement c_A is associated with the concept *Contract*. Since the concept *Contract* is a generalization of concept *FinanceAccount*, the properties of the concept *FinanceAccount* (the set {*agreementMember, agreementPeriod, effectiveDate, insured, accountHolder, amountDue*}) is a superset of the properties of the concept *Contract* (the set {*agreementMember, agreementPeriod, effectiveDate, insured*}). All the properties of c_A exist in c_R. As a result, the similarity is evaluated to 1.
- In case 3), the request c_R is associated with the concept *FinanceAccount* and the advertisement c_A is associated with the concept *DepositAccount*. Since the concept *FinanceAccount* is a superclass of concept *DepositAccount*, the properties of the concept *FinanceAccount* (the set {*agreementMember, agreementPeriod, effectiveDate, insured, accountHolder, amountDue*}) is a subset of the properties of the concept *DepositAccount* (the set {*agreementMember, agreementPeriod, effectiveDate, insured, accountHolder, amountDue, simpleInterest, agreementBalance, availableCash*}). In this case, when the request c_R matches the advertisement c_A some properties of c_A are left unfulfilled (the properties *simpleInterest, agreementBalance,* and *availableCash*). To indicate this mismatch the matching is set to the

ratio of the number of properties of c_R and the number of properties of c_A, which in this case is $|p(c_R)|/|p(c_A)| = 6/9 = 0.67$.

■ In the last case (4), the request c_R is associated with the concept *FinanceAccount* and the advertisement c_A is associated with the concept *Option*. The concept *FinanceAccount* has the set of properties {*agreementMember, agreementPeriod, effectiveDate, insured, accountHolder, amountDue*} and the concept *Option* has the set of properties {*agreementMember, agreementPeriod, effectiveDate, insured, atTheMoney, inTheMoney, optionHolder*}. Since the concepts do not have a parent/children relationship, we compute the percentage by the advertisement's properties that are fulfilled with a property from c_R. The similarity is evaluated as follows:

$$S_i^=(c_R,c_A) = \frac{|p(c_R) \cap p(c_A)|}{|p(c_A)|} = \frac{4}{7}$$

The result of evaluating the function indicates a low degree of matching between the concepts *FinanceAccount* and *Option*. Only one of the three advertisement's properties are satisfied by request properties. The following table shows the results for the four cases presented.

Table 2. An example of matching inputs with a common ontology commitment

Request c_R	Advertisement c_A	$S_i^=(c_R,c_A)$
FinancialAccount	*FinancialAccount*	1
FinancialAccount	*Contract*	1
FinancialAccount	*DepositAccount*	0.67
FinancialAccount	*Option*	0.57

As we can see, the concept *DepositAccount* is closer to the concept *FinanceAccount* than the concept *Option*. This result corroborates our perception and visual analysis of the ontology and its concepts.

3.3   Comparing Semantic Web Services Based on Multiple Ontologies

In this scenario, different Web services are described by different ontologies. Since there is no common ontology commitment, there is no common vocabulary which makes the comparison of different concepts a more complicated task.

Web service parameters (such as inputs, outputs, and functionality) are identified by words (classes) and there are two major linguistic concepts that need to be considered: synonymy and polysemy. Polysemy arises when a word has more than one meaning (i.e., multiple senses). Synonymy corresponds to the case when two different words have the same meaning. To tackle with the existence of these linguistic concepts we will use a feature-based similarity measure that compares concepts based on their common and distinguishing features (properties).

The problem of determining the similarity of concepts defined in different ontologies is related to the work on multi-ontology information system integration. Most of the similarity measures previously presented [25-35] cannot be directly used to match

Web services since they are symmetric, and more importantly, they can only be used when the concepts to be compared are defined in the same ontology.

Nonetheless, the Tversky's feature-based similarity model [23] is interesting since it takes into account the features or properties of concepts and not the taxonomy that defines the hierarchy of concepts. When matching inputs and outputs, the features of concepts need to be considered, especially when we compare concepts from different ontologies we cannot rely on their taxonomy. One can argue that, in scenarios with different ontologies, we need to take into account the context of ontologies when comparing concepts. In our approach, the context of a concept is transparently represented by its inherited properties.

Based on Tversky's model, we introduce matching functions $S_i^{\neq}(c_R, c_A)$, $S_o^{\neq}(c_R, c_A)$ and $S_f^{\neq}(c_R, c_A)$ for semantic Web services with no common ontology commitment based on the number of properties shared among two input or output concepts c_R and c_A conceptualized within the same ontology. The function computes the geometric distance between the similarity of the domains of concept c_R and concept c_A and the ratio of matched input properties from the concept c_A. Our similarity functions are defined as follows:

$$S_i^{\neq}(c_R, c_A) = \sqrt{ \frac{\Pi(p(c_R), p(c_A))}{|\, p(c_R) \cup p(c_A)\,| - \Pi(p(c_R), p(c_A))} * \frac{\Pi(p(c_R), p(c_A))}{|\, p(c_A)\,|} }$$

$$S_o^{\neq}(c_R, c_A) = S_f^{\neq}(c_R, c_A) = \sqrt{ \frac{\Pi(p(c_R), p(c_A))}{|\, p(c_R) \cup p(c_A)\,| - \Pi(p(c_R), p(c_A))} * \frac{\Pi(p(c_R), p(c_A))}{|\, p(c_R)\,|} }$$

Function Π establishes a mapping between the properties of two concept classes. Figure 5 illustrates two ontologies involved in a mapping.

For example, when matching the class concepts *DepositAccount* and *Deposit* we need to establish a mapping between the properties of the two classes. The mapping is

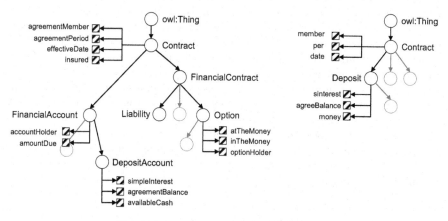

Fig. 5. Two ontologies involved in a mapping

258 J. Cardoso, J.A. Miller, and S. Emani

computed with the function $\Pi(p(DepositAccount), p(Deposit))$, which is equivalent to $\Pi(\{agreementMember, agreementPeriod, effectiveDate, insured, accountHolder, amountDue, simpleInterest, agreementBalance, availableCash\}, \{member, per, date, sinterest, agreedBalance, money\})$. Possible mappings that can be established are the following:

$$\Pi_{i,1}: (simpleInterest , sinterest)$$
$$\Pi_{i,2}: (agreementBalance , agreeBalance)$$
$$\Pi_{i,3}: (availableCash, money)$$

Function Π establishes the best mapping between two sets of properties, pl_1 and pl_2, and it is defined as follows:

$$\Pi(pl_1, pl_2) =$$
$$\begin{cases} Max(\Pi(pl_1 - p_1, pl_2 - p_2) + ss(p_1, p_2)), & ss(p_1, p_2) = 1 \text{ and } pl_1 \neq \emptyset \wedge pl_2 \neq \emptyset \\\\ \Pi(pl_1 - p_1, pl_2 - p_2), & ss(p_1, p_2) = 0 \text{ and } pl_1 \neq \emptyset \wedge pl_2 \neq \emptyset \\\\ 0, & pl_1 = \emptyset \vee pl_2 = \emptyset \end{cases}$$

Function $ss(p_1, p_2)$ determines if two properties are considered to be equal using function g. If two properties match syntactically then function ss returns 1, otherwise it returns 0. Properties match syntactically only if function g determines that the syntactic similarly is greater that a constant β.

$$ss(p_1, p_2) = \begin{cases} 1, & g(p_1, p_2) \geq \beta \\ 0, & g(p_1, p_2) < \beta \end{cases}$$

Function $g(p_1, p_2)$ is a function that computes the syntactic similarity of two words. In our approach, we use "string-matching" as a way to calculate similarity. Function g can be implemented using several existing methods such as equality of name, canonical name representations after stemming and other preprocessing, q-grams, synonyms, similarity based on common sub-strings, pronunciation, soundex, abbreviation expansion, stemming, tokenization, etc. Other techniques borrowed from the information retrieval area may also be considered. A very good source of information on retrieval techniques can be found in [37]. Constant β determines the sensibility of the matching. As β gets closer to 1, the matching function returns less false positives. As β gets closer to 0, it returns more false positives.

For example, let us consider the request query with c_R = "DepositAccount" and an advertisement with c_A ="Deposit". When computing $\Pi(p("DepositAccount"), p("Deposit"))$ of these inputs, we obtain value 2. This number represents the two valid mappings obtained:

$$\Pi_{i,1}: (simpleInterest , sinterest)$$
$$\Pi_{i,2}: (agreementBalance , agreeBalance)$$

Mapping $\Pi_{i,1}$ is found since the results of $ss("simpleInterest", "sinterest")$ and ss $(agreementBalance , agreeBalance)$, using the q-grams methodology [38] as an implementation of g with $\beta = 0.5$, is greater than 0.58 (e.g., $g($"agreementBalance", "agreeBalance"$)=0.58$). Please refer to [38] to understand this result from applying q-grams. As a result, in both cases ss is evaluated to 1.

All the other mappings are not part of Π. For example, if we compute $ss($"agreementBalance", "money"$)$ we obtain a result of 0 (function g has a value of 0), which means that we do not consider the properties to be syntactically equal.

The result of computing $S_i^{*}(c_R, c_A)$ is done in the following way. The concept *DepositAccount* has 9 properties (i.e., *agreementMember, agreementPeriod, effectiveDate, insured, accountHolder, amountDue, simpleInterest, agreementBalance, availableCash*) and concept *Deposit* has 6 properties (i.e., *member, per, date, interest, balance, cash*). Furthermore, $\Pi(p($"DepositAccount"$), p($"Deposit"$))=2$. Applying function $S_i^{*}(c_R, c_A)$ we obtain:

$$S_i^{*}(c_R, c_A) = \sqrt{\frac{2}{(9+6)-2} * \frac{2}{6}} = \sqrt{\frac{2}{13} * \frac{1}{3}} = \sqrt{\frac{2}{39}} = 0.2265$$

This result corroborates our intuition since only two of the six properties of the concept *Deposit* are satisfied by the properties of concept *DepositAccount*. Furthermore, the concepts *DepositAccount* and *Deposit* are rather distinct since only two properties are shared between the two.

3.4 Ranking Algorithm

In this section we present the actual algorithm for ranking Web service advertisements, following the functions presented previously.

```
REQ(c_i, c_o, c_f) = Web service request
ADV_j (c_ji, c_jo, c_jf) = List of advertisement

For all j get ADV_j(c_ji, c_jo, c_jf)
If same_ontology(c_i , c_ji) i = S_i^=(c_i,c_ji)
else i = S_i^*(c_i,c_ji)


If same_ontology(c_o ,c_jo) o = S_o^=(c_o,c_jo)
else o = S_o^*(c_o,c_jo)


If same_ontology(c_f ,c_jf) f = S_f^=(c_f,c_jf)
else f = S_f^*(c_f,c_jf)


match[j] = (i+o+f)/3;

Forall
Sort match[j]
```

The algorithm uses the function *same_ontology* that determines if two concepts are defined in the same ontology. Once the matching degree of the input, output, and functionality between a Web service request and a Web service advertisement is calculated, we define the overall degree of the match as the arithmetic mean of the input match degree, output match degree, and functionality match degree. Of course, a weighted function can be implemented if one of the dimensions (inputs, outputs, and functionality) is more important than the others to a service provider or consumer.

4   Using SM-T with METEOR–S WSDI and Lumina

The SM-T algorithm can be integrated in the implementation of METEOR-S Web Services Discovery Infrastructure (MWSDI) [7] and Lumina [21]. One of the authors of this paper was one of the architects of MWSDI and Lumina. Both projects utilize the METEOR-S Discovery API that matches a semantic Template with closely matching Web services that, for example, could be plugged into an abstract process with little or no human intervention. The METEOR-S Discovery API is built on of jUDDI discovery engine and maps semantic information to the business, service and tModel components of UDDI. It thus provides a semantically enhanced UDDI.

4.1   UDDI

UDDI [39], sponsored by OASIS, is an XML-based registry for business and Web services world-wide to list services in the internet. The focus of UDDI is it dynamically allows businesses or enterprises to publish and discover Web services. That is UDDI provides a foundation for both publicly available Web services as well as those which present internally in an organization. UDDI model has persistent data structures called entities expressed in XML and stored in UDDI nodes. The information model is made of the following entity types:

- businessEntity: represents an business
- businessService: the set of Web services that are provided by a business
- bindingTemplate: provides information on how to use a Web service
- tModel: gives a technical model categorizing Web service type
- publisherAssertion: provides the relationship between business entities
- subscription: reports changes in the business entities

The programming interface of UDDI has two parts: inquiry and publishing. To inquire for a Web service through the UDDI several methods are available. The combinations of these search methods can be used through the registry to get optimized results. The methods can be used according to the business of interest by keyword search which gives a set of summarized results for further or deeper search, look for services based on a particular category a business offers and tModel search which returns a set of tModels from different services according to the search criteria. As we go deeper, we can search for the operations a business service offers.

4.2 Approaches to Discovery

Service registries need to provide suitable discovery mechanisms to consumers. We can categorize matchmaking approaches according to various criteria. One possible classification is to take into account what elements are used to match a service advertisement and a service request. We present four approaches: IO matching, multilevel matching, graph-based approaches, and syntactic matching.

IO matching. One of the first works in the field of service discovery (semantic Web service discovery) is described in [40] and [6, 41]. Paolucci [40] follow the idea that "an advertisement matches a request when all the outputs of the request are matched by the outputs of the advertisement, and all the inputs of the advertisement are matched by the inputs of the request". Cardoso also takes into account the semantic and syntactic similarity of concepts using Tversky model. Thus, these methods takes into account only the inputs and outputs of services during matchmaking. Cardoso and Sheth [6] go a step further and include the QoS of services during the matching process.

Multilevel Matching. Using this matching strategy, presented by Jaeger [42], the matchmaking process is performed at many levels, that is, between inputs/outputs, service categories and other custom service parameters (e.g., related to QoS issues). Such approach reflects the intuition that ideal service discovery should exploit as much of the available functional and non-functional service information as possible.

A Graph-Based Approach. Trastour [43] proposes a semantic graph matching approach. A service description (request or advertisement) is represented as a directed graph (RDF-graph), whose nodes are instances of concepts (i.e., individuals) and arcs are properties (i.e., concept roles) relating such instances. The root node of each graph is the individual representing the service advertisement/request itself. The other nodes refer to concepts borrowed from domain ontologies (capabilities, constraints, etc.). The matchmaking between two graphs, one representing a service request and another representing a service advertisement, is performed with a recursive algorithm.

Syntactic matching. While the IO matching, multilevel matching, and graph-based matching rely on exploiting the subsumption relations in various ontologies in order to assess the similarity of services, service capabilities, this is not sufficient to enable an effective discovery. One extension that can be made is to use similarity measures and information retrieval (IR) techniques. The objective is to use implicit semantics of services, besides the explicit semantics that are described by the domain ontologies. The core idea in this approach is that IR similarity measures could be applied when logic-based (subsumption) matching fails. For example, TFIDF (Term Frequency/Inverse Document Frequency) term weighting schemes [44] can be used to evaluate the semantic distance/closeness between concepts, words or documents.

4.3 Lumina

The focus of Lumina works closely with MWSDI [7] to provide a user friendly GUI for specifying semantic templates and discovering matching services. MWSDI is an infrastructure that addresses the challenge of integrating a large number of registries from diverse domains. MWSDI supplies an infrastructure of registries for semantic publication and discovery of Web services. The primary motivation was the expected growth in the number of registries and the lack of semantics in Web service representation. The system provides a scalable architecture to access such registries. In addition, it provides semantic publication and discovery capabilities by using a domain specific ontology for each registry. Two algorithms are made available for semantic publication and discovery using WSDL descriptions. Both these algorithms map inputs and outputs of Web services to ontological concepts. Subsequently, searching can be carried out using constructed templates using the ontological concepts.

MWSDI was implemented with an underlying peer-to-peer network which gives the scalability and flexibility required for creating an infrastructure for diverse Web service registries.

Lumina may be viewed as Radiant's companion. While Radiant annotates and publishes semantic Web services, Lumina is used for discovering these published services. It allows to search for services, individual operations or interfaces (i.e., combinations of operations). In order to create a semantic template, the GUI provides input text boxes and selections that can be filled in by data entry, mouse clicking or dragging a class or property from an ontology. Figure 6 illustrates how to fill in a semantic template using Lumina.

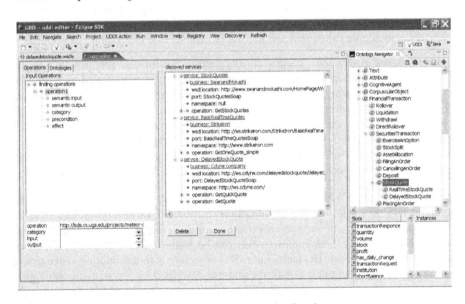

Fig. 6. Semantic template using Lumina

Lumina was designed to support WSDL-S and this provides a means for specifying inputs, outputs, functionality/category, preconditions and effects. Later a simplified SAWSDL mode was added that does not support preconditions and effects.

SM-T, MWSDI and Lumina basically follow the same approach concerning their vision of Web services. They all treat a Web service as an abstract interface (black box) consisting of multiple operations which each having its own set of inputs and set of outputs as well as functionality. Annotating the inputs, outputs and functionality of Web service operations gives a significant improvement in discovery and is better than the approach used by current UDDI registries. This is because current UDDI implementations are only based on the syntactic matching of properties. Semantic approaches have already shown in several domains to improve search precision. Section 3.2 and section 3.3 show that the SM-T algorithm is able to compare concepts beyond a simple syntactic match. Let us assume that a user issues a request to a UDDI registry for a service with an input *FinanceAccount* (see Section 3).

Let us also assume that the registry has only an advertisement with the input *Contract*. In such a case, the registry informs the user that no Web service matching the search criteria was found. This search was based solely on a syntactic analysis. Now, let us assume that Web services descriptions are annotated with ontological concepts. The two Web services' inputs, *FinanceAccount* and *Contract*, are annotated with concepts with the same name in the ontology shown in Figure 4 (the names are the same for simplicity reasons, they could be different). Using this ontology, a semantically enhanced UDDI registry can use the ontological information to improve the search.

In such a situation, the results of the match would return a Web service since the concept *Contract* is a generalization of concept *FinanceAccount*. That is, the properties of the concept *FinanceAccount*,

{*agreementMember, agreementPeriod, effectiveDate, insured, accountHolder, amountDue*}

are a superset of the properties of the concept *Contract*,

{*agreementMember, agreementPeriod, effectiveDate, insured*}.

Since all the properties of *Contract* exist in *FinanceAccount*, there is a match and a reference to the Web service is returned to the user. This example shows that different concepts from the same ontology can be matched by our algorithm even when their properties do not match semantically. The example shown in section 3.3 also illustrates that two concepts from two different ontologies can be matched by our algorithm even if their properties do not match syntactically.

From the business perspective SM-T, MWSDI, and Lumina are all about grouping services and distributing them in different registries based on domain knowledge, for locating the right services easily. On the other hand, from the technical perspective, SM-T, MWSDI, and Lumina can provide a scalable infrastructure for accessing multiple registries and semantic enhancements to current service discovery mechanisms. We believe that to develop processes in the current network economy [45], architectures and algorithms like SM-T, MWSDI, and Lumina will drive the evolution of businesses' interactions using Web services. This infrastructure will also help Web services by changing the focus from a static to a more dynamic business settings. To discover Web services using Lumina the following steps can be followed:

- Download Lumina and install it as the eclipse plug in. Radiant has to be installed before installing Lumina.
- The screen is divided into six parts: Navigator/Outline, UDDI editor WSDL editor, Information list, Discovered results and Ontology navigator.

- Follow the same steps as for Radiant to load the ontology, create a new project and WSDL.
- Click on the Registry drop down menu and select registry. A window pops up. Add a new registry and connect.
- Click on the Publish menu and publish a business followed by the WSDL.
- In the UDDI editor select the operation, input, and output according to what you want to discover the web service and drag and drop the concept on them from the ontology navigator.
- At the information list the selected operations or IOPEs will be displayed select on them and click on discover.
- The web services discovered will be displayed on the discovered results pane.

5   Related Work

The discovery of services "boils down" to determining the similarity of services' properties which are typically annotated with ontological concepts. In the literature we can find four distinct approaches to calculate the semantic relations among concepts. In [25-27], ontology based approaches are presented. The most basic metric simply computes the distance between two concepts in an ontology. Corpus based approaches are described in [28-30]. These approaches use a corpus to establish the statistical co-occurrence of words. Information theoretic approaches [23, 31-33] consider both a corpora and an ontology, and use the notion of information content from the field of information theory. By statistically analyzing corpora, probabilities are associated to concepts based on word occurrences. Dictionary based approaches [34, 35] use a machine readable dictionary to discover relations between concepts. For example, one approach determines the sense of a word in a given text by counting the overlaps between dictionary definitions of the various senses.

Some of the above approaches, to calculate the semantic relations among concepts, have been used to deploy discover algorithm for semantic Web services. The OWL-S/UDDI Matchmaker [46] introduces semantic search into the UDDI directory by embedding an OWL-S Profile in a UDDI data structure, and augmenting the UDDI registry with an OWL-S matchmaking component. The matching algorithm recognizes four degrees of match between two concepts defined in the same ontology: (1) *exact*, (2) *plug in*, (3) *subsume*, and (4) *fail*. The function used by the algorithm is asymmetric and is based on the existence of relationships between concepts. When no direct relationship exists among two concepts the algorithm simply returns *fail*. Unlike the algorithm presented in this paper, the OWL-S/UDDI Matchmaker searches for services based on inputs and outputs within the IOPEs (Input, Output, Precondition, and Effect) of the profile which must belong to the same ontology. Our approach allows evaluating the similarities of IOPE that are annotated with concepts from distinct ontologies.

The METEOR-S [20] Web Service Annotation Framework (WSAF) allows semi-automatically matching WSDL concepts (such as inputs and outputs) to DAML and RDF ontologies using text-based information retrieval techniques (for example, synonyms, n-grams and abbreviation). The strength of matches (SM) is calculated using a scoring formula which involves element (ElemMatch) and structure level schema (SchemaMatch) matching. The ElemMatch function performs the element level matching based on the linguistic similarity of the names of the two concepts. The SchemaMatch function examines the structural similarity between two concepts. A concept in an ontology is usually defined by its properties, superclasses and subclasses. Since concept labels are somewhat arbitrary, examining the structure of a concept description can provide more insight into its semantics. In WSAF, the XML representation of WSDL is matched against the concepts of a given ontology. The best match between WSDL and ontological concepts are returned to users as a suggestion of potential mappings. It should be noticed that the work presented in [20] cannot be easily adapted to our problem. There are several reasons for this. First, the weight values for calculating the MS function were set without empirical testing and validation. Also, the weights are not defined for a set of ElemMatch and SchemaMatch values. For example, if 0.5<ElemMatch<0.65 then no weights are suggested. Furthermore, the function that computes the ElemMatch of a WSDL concept and an ontological concept is not defined when the MatchScore is other than zero, but is less than one, using the NGram or Synonym matching algorithms.

In [47], the authors present a hybrid approach to Semantic Web service matching. The hybrid matchmaker, called OWLS-MX, is to be used to find service requests specified in OWL-S. OWLS-MX can be seen as an extension of the OWL-S/UDDI Matchmaker presented in [46]. Their approach is somewhat similar to our in that they "complement logic based reasoning with approximate matching based on syntactic information retrieval (IR) based similarity computations". The IR based methods used include: the extended Jacquard similarity coefficient, the cosine similarity value, and the Jensen-Shannon information divergence based similarity value. Our approach differs in the sense that we have used *q-grams* for syntactic matching. But this is only a minor difference since, as we have explained previously in section 4.3, in our approach other syntactic matching functions can be used such as: soundex, abbreviation expansion, stemming, tokenization and other techniques borrowed from the information retrieval (see [37].), including the matching function used by OWLS-MX. The major difference in our work lies on the use of the Tversky's model. While OWLS-MX mainly compares concepts syntactically when the logic-based comparison fails, in our approach we compare syntactically, not the concepts themselves, but the properties of the concepts. For example, if the concepts 'car' and 'automobile' are compared using OWLS-MX and the concepts are not related with a parent -child relationship (i.e., an *exact*, *plug-in*, or *subsumes* relationship is not found), the algorithm will answer fail, meaning that there is no match. Using SM-T, the algorithm will try to syntactically match the properties of the concepts. Therefore, if the concept 'car' has the properties: 'engine', 'body' and 'wheels' and the concept 'automobile' has the properties; 'bigengine', 'car_body' and 'fourwheels', the SM-T algorithm will indicate that there is a partial match (this will be expressed with a normalized value).

6 Conclusions

In this paper we have described a semantic matching algorithm to be used by UDDI registries enhanced with semantics. Our algorithm can work with Web services described with WSMO and OWL-S, or annotated with SAWSDL (previously WSDL-S). Compared to previous work [46], we do not limit the classification of the accuracy of matching a request with an advertisement using a four value schema (i.e. *exact, plug in*, *subsume*, and *fail*). The accuracy of matching is assessed with a continue function with the range [0..1]. Furthermore, and compared to [46], we allow the matching of semantic Web services both with and without a common ontology commitment. This aspect is important since it is not realistic to assume that Web services will always be defined by the same ontology. In some cases, similar services may be defined by different ontologies. Furthermore, we take into account functionality.

Our algorithm relies on Tversky's feature-based similarity model to match requests with advertisement. This model takes into account the features or properties of ontological concepts and not the taxonomy that defines the hierarchy of concepts. We believe that when matching inputs, outputs and functionality, the analysis of features of concepts is fundamental when matching concepts from different ontologies, since they typically have distinct taxonomies. The matching process can be easily extended to include non-functional capabilities of services.

References

1. Chinnici, R., et al.: Web Services Description Language (WSDL) Version 1.2, W3C Working Draft 24 (2003)
2. Chinnici, R., et al.: Web Services Description Language (WSDL) Version 2.0 Part 1: Core Language (2006), http://www.w3.org/TR/wsdl20/
3. UDDI. Universal Description, Discovery, and Integration (UDDI v3.0) (2005), http://www.uddi.org/
4. SOAP. Simple Object Access Protocol 1.2 (2003), http://www.w3.org/TR/soap12-part1/
5. Cardoso, J., Sheth, A.P.: Introduction to Semantic Web Services and Web Process Composition. In: Cardoso, J., Sheth, A.P. (eds.) Semantic Web Process: powering next generation of processes with Semantics and Web services, pp. 1–13. Springer, Heidelberg (2005)
6. Cardoso, J., Sheth, A.: Semantic e-Workflow Composition. Journal of Intelligent Information Systems (JIIS) 21(3), 191–225 (2003)
7. Verma, K., et al.: METEOR-S WSDI: A Scalable P2P Infrastructure of Registries for Semantic Publication and Discovery of Web Services. Journal of Information Technology and Management (ITM), Special Issue on Universal Global Integration 6(1), 17–39 (2005)
8. Curbera, F., Ehnebuske, D., Rogers, D.: Using WSDL in a UDDI Registry, Version 1.07, UDDI Best Practice, May 21 (2002), http://www.uddi.org/pubs/wsdlbestpractices-V1.07-Open-20020521.pdf (Retrieved October 12, 2006)
9. Sheth, A., Meersman, R.: Amicalola Report: Database and Information Systems Research Challenges and Opportunities in Semantic Web and Enterprises. SIGMOD Record 31(4), 98–106 (2002)
10. Smeaton, A., Quigley, I.: Experiment on Using Semantic Distance Between Words in Image Caption Retrieval. In: 19th International Conference on Research and Development in Information Retrifval SIGIR 1996, Zurich, Switzerland (1996)
11. Rodríguez, A., Egenhofer, M.: Determining Semantic Similarity Among Entity Classes from Different Ontologies. IEEE Transactions on Knowledge and Data Engineering 15(2), 442–456 (2002) (in press)
12. Klein, M., Bernstein, A.: Searching for Services on the Semantic Web Using Process Ontologies. In: International Semantic Web Working Symposium (SWWS), Stanford University, California, USA (2001)

13. Cardoso, J., et al.: Academic and Industrial Research: Do their Approaches Differ in Adding Semantics to Web Services. In: Cardoso, J., Sheth, A. (eds.) Semantic Web Process: powering next generation of processes with Semantics and Web services, pp. 14–21. Springer, Heidelberg (2005)
14. Martin, D., et al.: Bringing Semantics to Web Services: The OWL-S Approach. In: Cardoso, J., Sheth, A.P. (eds.) SWSWPC 2004. LNCS, vol. 3387. Springer, Heidelberg (2005)
15. Roman, D., et al.: WWW: WSMO, WSML, and WSMX in a nutshell. In: Mizoguchi, R., Shi, Z.-Z., Giunchiglia, F. (eds.) ASWC 2006. LNCS, vol. 4185. Springer, Heidelberg (2006)
16. Akkiraju, R., et al.: Web Service Semantics - WSDL-S (2006), http://www.w3.org/Submission/WSDL-S (Retrieved October 10, 2006)
17. Sivashanmugam, K., et al.: Framework for Semantic Web Process Composition. International Journal of Electronic Commerce (IJEC), Special Issue on Semantic Web Services and Their Role in Enterprise Application Integration and E-Commerce 9(2), 71–106 (2004-2005)
18. Farrell, J., Lausen, H.: Semantic Annotations for WSDL (2006), http://www.w3.org/2002/ws/sawsdl/spec/SAWSDL.html
19. Gomadam, K., et al.: Radiant: A tool for semantic annotation of Web Services. In: 4th International Semantic Web Conference ISWC 2005, Galway, Ireland (2005)
20. Patil, A., et al.: MWSAF - METEOR-S Web Service Annotation Framework. In: 13th Conference on World Wide Web, New York City, USA (2004)
21. Cardoso, J., Sheth, A.: Semantic Web Services, Processes and Applications. In: Jain, R., Sheth, A. (eds.) Semantic Web and Beyond: Computing for Human Experience. Springer, Heidelberg (2006)
22. Paolucci, M., et al.: Semantic Matching of Web Services Capabilities. In: Horrocks, I., Hendler, J. (eds.) ISWC 2002. LNCS, vol. 2342. Springer, Heidelberg (2002)
23. Tversky, A.: Features of Similarity. Psychological Review 84(4), 327–352 (1977)
24. Zavaracky, A.: Glossary-Based Semantic Similarity in the WordNet Ontology, in Department of Computer Science, University College Dublin, Dublin (2003)
25. Wu, Z., Palmer, M.: Verb Semantics and Lexical Selection. In: 32nd Annual Meeting of the Associations for Computational Linguistics (ACL 1994), Las Cruces, New Mexico (1994)
26. Rada, R., et al.: Development and Application of a Metric on Semantic Nets. IEEE Transactions on Systems, Man, and Cybernetics 19(1), 17–30 (1989)
27. Leacock, C., Chodorow, M.: Combining local context and WordNet similarity for word sense identification. In: Fellbaum, C. (ed.) WordNet: An Electronic Lexical Database, pp. 265–283. MIT Press, Cambridge (1998)
28. Turney, P.D.: Mining the Web for Synonyms: PMI-IR versus LSA on TOEFL. In: 12th European Conference on Machine Learning. Springer, Heidelberg (2001)
29. Keller, F., Lapata, M.: Using the Web to Obtain Frequencies for Unseen Bigrams. Computational Linguistics (2003)
30. Church, K.W., Hanks, P.: Word association norms, mutual information, and Lexicography. In: Vancouver, B.C. (ed.) 27th Annual Meeting of the Association for Computational Linguistics. Association for Computational Linguistics, Vancouver (1989)
31. Lin, D.: An information-theoretic definition of similarity. In: 15th International Conf. on Machine Learning. Morgan Kaufmann, San Francisco (1989)
32. Resnik, P.: Using Information Content to Evaluate Semantic Similarity in a Taxonomy. In: 14th International Joint Conference on Artificial Intelligence (1995)

33. Jiang, J., Conrath, D.: Semantic Similarity Based on Corpus Statistics and Lexical Taxonomy. In: International Conference on Computational Linguistics (ROCLINGX), Taiwan (1997)
34. Lesk, M.: Automatic sense disambiguation using machine readable dictionaries: how to tell a pine cone from an ice cream cone. In: 5th annual international conference on Systems documentation. ACM Press, New York (1986)
35. Banerjee, S., Pedersen, T.: Gloss Overlaps as a Measure of Semantic Relatedness. In: Eighteenth International Joint Conference on Artificial Intelligence, Acapulco, Mexico (2003)
36. Richardson, R., Smeaton, A.: Using WordNet in a Knowledge-Based Approach to Information Retrieval. Dublin City University/School of Computer Applications, Dublin, Ireland (1995)
37. Belew, R.K.: Finding Out About: A Cognitive Perspective on Search Engine Technology and the WWW, p. 356. Cambridge University Press, Cambridge (2000)
38. Salton, G.: Automatic Text Processing: The Transformation, Analysis and Retrieval of Information by Computer. Addison-Wesley, Massachusetts (1988)
39. UDDI. UDDI Spec. Technical Committee, UDDI Version 3.0.2, (2004),
    http://uddi.org/pubs/uddi_v3.htm
40. Paolucci, M., et al.: Semantic matching of Web services capabilities. In: First International Semantic Web Conference on the Semantic Web, Sardinia, Italy. LNCS. Springer, Heidelberg (2002)
41. Cardoso, J.: Quality of Service and Semantic Composition of Workflows, in Department of Computer Science, p. 215. University of Georgia, Athens (2002)
42. Jaeger, M.C., Tang, S.: Ranked matching for service descriptions using DAML-S. In: Persson, A., Stirna, J. (eds.) CAiSE 2004. LNCS, vol. 3084. Springer, Heidelberg (2004)
43. Trastour, D., Bartolini, C., Gonzalez-Castillo, J.: A Semantic Web approach to service description for matchmaking of services. In: The first Semantic Web Working Symposium, California, USA (2001)
44. Cohen, W., Ravikumar, P., Fienberg, S.: A comparison of string distance metrics for name-matching tasks. In: Kurumatani, K., Chen, S.-H., Ohuchi, A. (eds.) IJCAI-WS 2003 and MAMUS 2003. Springer, Heidelberg (2003)
45. Sheth, A.P., v.d Aalst, W., Arpinar, I.B.: Processes Driving the Networked Economy. IEEE Concurrency 7(3), 18–31 (1999)
46. Srinivasan, N., Paolucci, M., Sycara, K.: An efficient algorithm for OWL-S based semantic search in UDDI. In: Cardoso, J., Sheth, A. (eds.) Lecture Notes in Computer Science. Springer, Heidelberg (2005)
47. Klusch, M., Fries, B., Sycara, K.: Automated Semantic Web Service Discovery with OWLS-MX. In: Alonso, E., Kudenko, D., Kazakov, D. (eds.) AAMAS 2000 and AAMAS 2002. ACM Press, New York (2006)

Author Index

Lecture Notes in Computer Science

Sublibrary 3: Information Systems and Application, incl. Internet/Web and HCI

For information about Vols. 1– 4803
please contact your bookseller or Springer

Vol. 5005: V. Christophides, M. Collard, C. Gutierrez (Eds.), Semantic Web, Ontologies and Databases. VII, 153 pages. 2008.

Vol. 4997: B. Monien, U.-P. Schroeder (Eds.), Algorithmic Game Theory. XI, 363 pages. 2008.

Vol. 4993: H. Li, T. Liu, W.-Y. Ma, T. Sakai, K.-F. Wong, G. Zhou (Eds.), Information Retrieval Technology. XIII, 685 pages. 2008.

Vol. 4976: Y. Zhang, G. Yu, E. Bertino, G. Xu (Eds.), Progress in WWW Research and Development. XVIII, 699 pages. 2008.

Vol. 4969: R. Kronland-Martinet, S. Ystad, K. Jensen (Eds.), Computer Music Modeling and Retrieval. XII, 508 pages. 2008.

Vol. 4956: C. Macdonald, I. Ounis, V. Plachouras, I. Ruthven, R.W. White (Eds.), Advances in Information Retrieval. XXI, 719 pages. 2008.

Vol. 4952: C. Floerkemeier, M. Langheinrich, E. Fleisch, F. Mattern, S.E. Sarma (Eds.), The Internet of Things. XIII, 378 pages. 2008.

Vol. 4950: A. Kerren, J.T. Stasko, J.-D. Fekete, C. North (Eds.), Information Visualization. IX, 177 pages. 2008.

Vol. 4947: J.R. Haritsa, R. Kotagiri, V. Pudi (Eds.), Database Systems for Advanced Applications. XXII, 713 pages. 2008.

Vol. 4936: W. Aiello, A. Broder, J. Janssen, E.E. Milios (Eds.), Algorithms and Models for the Web-Graph. X, 167 pages. 2008.

Vol. 4932: S. Hartmann, G. Kern-Isberner (Eds.), Foundations of Information and Knowledge Systems. XII, 397 pages. 2008.

Vol. 4928: A.H.M. ter Hofstede, B. Benatallah, H.-Y. Paik (Eds.), Business Process Management Workshops. XIII, 518 pages. 2008.

Vol. 4918: N. Boujemaa, M. Detyniecki, A. Nürnberger (Eds.), Adaptive Multimedia Retrieval: Retrieval, User, and Semantics. XI, 265 pages. 2008.

Vol. 4903: S. Satoh, F. Nack, M. Etoh (Eds.), Advances in Multimedia Modeling. XIX, 510 pages. 2008.

Vol. 4900: S. Spaccapietra (Ed.), Journal on Data Semantics X. XIII, 265 pages. 2008.

Vol. 4892: A. Popescu-Belis, S. Renals, H. Bourlard (Eds.), Machine Learning for Multimodal Interaction. XI, 308 pages. 2008.

Vol. 4882: T. Janowski, H. Mohanty (Eds.), Distributed Computing and Internet Technology. XIII, 346 pages. 2007.

Vol. 4881: H. Yin, P. Tino, E. Corchado, W. Byrne, X. Yao (Eds.), Intelligent Data Engineering and Automated Learning - IDEAL 2007. XX, 1174 pages. 2007.

Vol. 4877: C. Thanos, F. Borri, L. Candela (Eds.), Digital Libraries: Research and Development. XII, 350 pages. 2007.

Vol. 4872: D. Mery, L. Rueda (Eds.), Advances in Image and Video Technology. XXI, 961 pages. 2007.

Vol. 4871: M. Cavazza, S. Donikian (Eds.), Virtual Storytelling. XIII, 219 pages. 2007.

Vol. 4868: C. Peter, R. Beale (Eds.), Affect and Emotion in Human-Computer Interaction. X, 241 pages. 2008.

Vol. 4858: X. Deng, F.C. Graham (Eds.), Internet and Network Economics. XVI, 598 pages. 2007.

Vol. 4857: J.M. Ware, G.E. Taylor (Eds.), Web and Wireless Geographical Information Systems. XI, 293 pages. 2007.

Vol. 4853: F. Fonseca, M.A. Rodríguez, S. Levashkin (Eds.), GeoSpatial Semantics. X, 289 pages. 2007.

Vol. 4836: H. Ichikawa, W.-D. Cho, I. Satoh, H.Y. Youn (Eds.), Ubiquitous Computing Systems. XIII, 307 pages. 2007.

Vol. 4832: M. Weske, M.-S. Hacid, C. Godart (Eds.), Web Information Systems Engineering – WISE 2007 Workshops. XV, 518 pages. 2007.

Vol. 4831: B. Benatallah, F. Casati, D. Georgakopoulos, C. Bartolini, W. Sadiq, C. Godart (Eds.), Web Information Systems Engineering – WISE 2007. XVI, 675 pages. 2007.

Vol. 4825: K. Aberer, K.-S. Choi, N. Noy, D. Allemang, K.-I. Lee, L. Nixon, J. Golbeck, P. Mika, D. Maynard, R. Mizoguchi, G. Schreiber, P. Cudré-Mauroux (Eds.), The Semantic Web. XXVII, 973 pages. 2007.

Vol. 4823: H. Leung, F. Li, R. Lau, Q. Li (Eds.), Advances in Web Based Learning – ICWL 2007. XIV, 654 pages. 2008.

Vol. 4822: D.H.-L. Goh, T.H. Cao, I.T. Sølvberg, E. Rasmussen (Eds.), Asian Digital Libraries. XVII, 519 pages. 2007.

Vol. 4820: T.G. Wyeld, S. Kenderdine, M. Docherty (Eds.), Virtual Systems and Multimedia. XII, 215 pages. 2008.

Vol. 4816: B. Falcidieno, M. Spagnuolo, Y. Avrithis, I. Kompatsiaris, P. Buitelaar (Eds.), Semantic Multimedia. XII, 306 pages. 2007.

Vol. 4813: I. Oakley, S.A. Brewster (Eds.), Haptic and Audio Interaction Design. XIV, 145 pages. 2007.

Vol. 4810: H.H.-S. Ip, O.C. Au, H. Leung, M.-T. Sun, W.-Y. Ma, S.-M. Hu (Eds.), Advances in Multimedia Information Processing – PCM 2007. XXI, 834 pages. 2007.

Vol. 4809: M.K. Denko, C.-s. Shih, K.-C. Li, S.-L. Tsao, Q.-A. Zeng, S.H. Park, Y.-B. Ko, S.-H. Hung, J.-H. Park (Eds.), Emerging Directions in Embedded and Ubiquitous Computing. XXXV, 823 pages. 2007.

Vol. 4808: T.-W. Kuo, E. Sha, M. Guo, L.T. Yang, Z. Shao (Eds.), Embedded and Ubiquitous Computing. XXI, 769 pages. 2007.

Vol. 4806: R. Meersman, Z. Tari, P. Herrero (Eds.), On the Move to Meaningful Internet Systems 2007: OTM 2007 Workshops, Part II. XXXIV, 611 pages. 2007.

Vol. 4805: R. Meersman, Z. Tari, P. Herrero (Eds.), On the Move to Meaningful Internet Systems 2007: OTM 2007 Workshops, Part I. XXXIV, 757 pages. 2007.

Vol. 4804: R. Meersman, Z. Tari (Eds.), On the Move to Meaningful Internet Systems 2007: CoopIS, DOA, ODBASE, GADA, and IS, Part II. XXIX, 683 pages. 2007.